Schiller's Literary Prose Works

Studies in German Literature, Linguistics, and Culture

Schiller's Literary Prose Works

New Translations and Critical Essays

Edited by
Jeffrey L. High

CAMDEN HOUSE
Rochester, New York

First published 2008 by Camden House
Reprinted in paperback and transferred to digital printing 2011

Camden House is an imprint of Boydell & Brewer Inc.
668 Mt. Hope Avenue, Rochester, NY 14620, USA
www.camden-house.com
and of Boydell & Brewer Limited
PO Box 9, Woodbridge, Suffolk IP12 3DF, UK
www.boydellandbrewer.com

Paperback ISBN-13: 978-1-57113-496-7
Paperback ISBN-10: 1-57113-496-4
Hardback ISBN-13: 978-1-57113-384-7
Hardback ISBN-10: 1-57113-384-4

Library of Congress Cataloging-in-Publication Data

Schiller, Friedrich, 1759–1805.
[Prose Works. English. Selections]
Schiller's literary prose works : new translations and critical essays / edited by Jeffrey L. High.
p. cm. — (Studies in German literature, linguistics, and culture)
Includes bibliographical references and index.
ISBN-13: 978-1-57113-384-7 (hardcover : alk. paper)
ISBN-10: 1-57113-384-4 (hardcover : alk. paper)
I. High, Jeffrey L. II. Title. III. Series.

PT2473.A5H54
838'.608—dc22

2008031263

A catalogue record for this title is available from the British Library.

This publication is printed on acid-free paper.
Printed in the United States of America.

For Liz

Contents

Foreword ix
Lesley Sharpe

Preface xvii
Jeffrey L. High

Acknowledgments xxi

Notes on the Translations xxiii

Introduction: Schiller and the German Novella 1
Jeffrey L. High

The Translations

1: A Magnanimous Act from Most Recent History (1782) 9
Translated by Ian Codding

2: A Remarkable Example of Female Revenge (Taken from a Manuscript by the late Denis Diderot) (1785) 12
Translated by Robert Ellis Dye

3: The Criminal of Lost Honor. A True Story (1786) 39
Translated by Jeffrey L. High

4: The Duke of Alba's Breakfast at Rudolstadt Castle in the Year 1547 (1788) 56
Translated by Ian Codding

5: Game of Fate. A Fragment of a True Story (1789) 59
Translated by Edward T. Larkin

6: *The Spiritualist. From the Memoirs of Count von O*** (1789) 67
Translated by Francis Lamport

7: The Philosophical Dialog from *The Spiritualist* (1789) 150
Translated by Helen Kilgallen

8: Haoh-Kiöh-Tschuen (The Tale of a Perfect Match) (1800–1801) 169
Translated by Carrie Collenberg

The Critical Essays

9: (A fragment of) A True Story (from most recent history): The *Truth* in Schiller's Literary Prose Works 173
Jeffrey L. High

10: Playing with the Rules: Schiller's Experiments in Short Prose Fiction, 1782–1789 188
Nicholas Martin

11: Diderot and Schiller's "Revenge": From Parisian Parody to German Moral Education 202
Otto W. Johnston

12: True Crime and Criminal Truth: Schiller's "The Criminal of Lost Honor" 222
Gail K. Hart

13: *Der Geisterseher*: A Princely Experiment or, the Creation of a "Spiritualist" 234
Dennis F. Mahoney

Chronological List of Schiller's Literary Prose Works in English Translation 251
Compiled by Tanya Doss

Works Cited 253

Notes on the Contributors 261

Index 263

Foreword

Lesley Sharpe

THIS IS THE FIRST VOLUME that makes Schiller's prose fiction available to English-speaking readers in new and fluent translations and combines these with up-to-the-minute critical comment and interpretation. For present-day readers in the German- and English-speaking world, Friedrich Schiller — dramatist, poet, philosopher, aesthetic theorist, historian — is not immediately associated with prose fiction. Yet in its day the unfinished novel *Der Geisterseher. Aus den Memoires des Grafen von O*** (The Spiritualist. From the Memoirs of Count von O**) was the writer's most popular and widely read work; readers hung on every installment and were hugely disappointed when he brought it to an abrupt and provisional conclusion. While it would be perverse to overstate the originality of these stories or their significance within their author's oeuvre, it is equally unjust to dismiss them, as Schiller scholars regularly did up to the middle of the last century, as unimportant potboilers, spin-offs from Schiller's various journalistic ventures. As the following translations and essays demonstrate, even when exploiting popular and fashionable themes such as the criminal story or the secret society, Schiller brings to his writing his characteristic intellectual energy and psychological subtlety. The increased critical attention given in the last forty or so years to popular fiction generally (a category into which almost all German novels and stories from the eighteenth century fall) has helped to highlight his ingenious blending of popular motifs with more profound and enduring moral and philosophical concerns. The stories complement his better known works of the 1780s, in particular his plays, by offering new perspectives on some of his favorite themes: political conspiracy, the mysteries of human motivation, the ambiguities of the pursuit of reason, the abuse of power, the basis of moral action. Whereas in the nineteenth century, by virtue of his emphasis on their truth or their foundation in fact, his stories were sometimes seen as variations on his historiography and both were dismissed as inferior, the "linguistic turn" in historical studies has provided impetus to examine the sophistication of Schiller's understanding of the relationship between historical and fictional narratives.[1]

Born in 1759 in the small town of Marbach in the state of Württemberg, Schiller was the son of a low-ranking army officer. His early ambition to become a Protestant clergyman was thwarted when, against his parents' and his own wishes, he was obliged to become a pupil at the military academy set up by Württemberg's autocratic ruler, Duke Karl Eugen. There he studied law and then medicine, finally graduating in 1780 as an army surgeon. His first play, *Die Räuber* (The Robbers, 1781), which was premiered on 13 January 1782 at the Mannheim National Theatre in the neighboring Palatinate, brought him into conflict with Karl Eugen, who forbade him to write any more literary works. Schiller therefore took the desperate step of fleeing from the dukedom in the hope of finding refuge and support at the Mannheim theatre. This support was, however, slow to come and the young writer was not engaged as resident playwright until a year later and then only for one year. *Die Verschwörung des Fiesko zu Genua* (The Conspiracy of Fiesco at Genoa, 1783) and *Kabale und Liebe* (Intrigue and Love, 1784) were premiered at the theatre in 1784, but when his contract ran out, in September 1784, he was again thrown back on freelance writing to make a living. Deeply in debt, he was rescued by the generosity of four young admirers, who invited him to enjoy their hospitality in Leipzig and then Dresden, where he completed his fourth play, *Don Karlos* (Don Carlos), in 1787.

The same year Schiller, anxious to achieve independence, set off for Weimar, home of Johann Wolfgang von Goethe, already Germany's most celebrated literary figure, and of numerous other leading writers, scholars, and publishers such as Christoph Martin Wieland and Johann Gottfried Herder. His first major historiographical work, *Geschichte des Abfalls der vereinigten Niederlande von der spanischen Regierung* (History of the Revolt of the United Netherlands from Spanish Rule, 1788) gained him a professorship at the University of Jena, and though it was an unsalaried post it gave Schiller for the first time a respectable place in the social hierarchy. By the early 1790s he was turning his energies to the pressing aesthetic problems he saw as blocking his development as a tragedian, while continuing his historiographical writing with a second major work, his *Geschichte des Dreißigjährigen Kriegs* (History of the Thirty Years' War, 1792). Then disaster struck. He became seriously ill in 1792 with a chest infection from which he never fully recovered and which left him a semi-invalid for the rest of his life. Despite this disability he went on to write his great aesthetic treatises, major reflective poems, and his ballads. Financial pressure eased and in his final decade, from the mid-1790s onwards, he was able to devote his limited strength substantially to the creative task he considered the most important, that of writing tragedies; beginning with *Wallenstein* (1799), a series of dramatic masterpieces flowed from his pen until his death, aged forty-five.

Schiller's prose fiction, apart from the 1800 fragment "Haoh-Kiöh-Tschuen," arose in the 1780s, when, in almost constantly straitened circumstances, he was testing the possibilities of making a living as a writer and thus trying his hand at different genres. Living by one's pen without some other source of income was a bold, indeed arguably a foolhardy, venture at that time. While the rise in literacy in the course of the eighteenth century, the developing taste for prose fiction, the eagerness for news of new works, and the emergence of the female reader were all factors boosting the literary market, there were as yet no copyright laws, the reading public was still quite small by modern standards, and books were comparatively expensive and so bought by only a small part of the potential readership. Literary journals were therefore the means by which readers gained cheaper access to the latest writing and, although titles came and went with astonishing rapidity, many surviving for only a few numbers, these journals provided a useful outlet for writers of prose fiction. They depended on the right variety of contributions and on swift response to the trends popular with readers: for example, the moral tale, the developing taste for the Gothic, or the criminal story.[2] Schiller's stories show he recognized the trends and the market and tried to capitalize on them. "Eine großmütige Handlung aus der neusten Geschichte" (A Magnanimous Act from Most Recent History) first appeared in 1782 in the *Wirtembergisches Repertorium der Litteratur* (Württemberg Literary Repertorium), the journal he, as a poorly paid army surgeon, co-founded with Stuttgart friends before his flight. The *Rheinische Thalia* (Rhineland Thalia), later the *Thalia,* in which "Merkwürdiges Beispiel einer weiblichen Rache" (A Remarkable Example of Female Revenge), "Der Verbrecher aus verlorener Ehre" (The Criminal of Lost Honor), and *Der Geisterseher* first appeared, was the journal he founded in 1784 when his contract with the Mannheim National Theatre ended. The manuscript copy of unpublished works by Diderot, from which Schiller translated and adapted "Merkwürdiges Beispiel," was lent to him by the director of the Mannheim theatre, Wolfgang Heribert von Dalberg, with whom Schiller had a difficult relationship. He gave Schiller his first great opportunity in 1782 by staging *Die Räuber* with great success, but his ambivalent attitude to the young playwright he had first encouraged was one of the many reasons why Schiller grew to hate Mannheim. The title *Thalia* points to the journal's original conception as primarily a theatre journal, but from the start Schiller recognized the need for varied appeal and hence for prose fiction. To publish a story in installments, as in the case of *Der Geisterseher,* was already a familiar ploy to secure loyal readers. "Herzog von Alba bey einem Frühstück auf dem Schlosse zu Rudolstadt. Im Jahr 1547" (The Duke of Alba's Breakfast at Rudolstadt Castle in the Year 1547) and "Spiel des Schicksals. Ein Bruchstück einer wahren Geschichte" (Game of Fate. A Fragment of a True Story) were published in one of the most famous and lasting journals of the day, *Der Teutsche Merkur* (German Mercury), founded and edited in Weimar by Wieland, a useful connection for Schiller on his arrival there. Wieland also published his "Briefe über Don Karlos" (Letters on Don Carlos, 1788), his reviews of Goethe's *Egmont* and *Iphigenie auf Tauris* (Iphigenia on Tauris, verse version 1788) and his poem "Die Götter Griechenlandes" (The Gods of Greece) in its original, 1788 version. Historical writing was also a sought-after component; Schiller's *Geschichte des Dreißigjährigen Kriegs* first appeared in installments in the *Historischer Calender für Damen* (Historical Calendar for Ladies), an indication that it was always meant to straddle the realms of the scholarly and the popular.

Though never abandoning his honesty as a writer in favor of the sentimental and didactic prevalent in popular fiction, Schiller showed in his various experiments with prose narrative that he could combine complexity of perspective with narrative energy. These qualities are particularly in evidence in his two most substantial pieces, "Der Verbrecher aus verlorener Ehre" and *Der Geisterseher*. The former demonstrates how ably Schiller could draw on popular contemporary trends and subject matter while producing something altogether more challenging and thought provoking. The criminal story — an account of the misdeeds, trial, and final execution of a real-life or fictive criminal — was one such long-established trend. Such accounts catered to the taste for the sensational under the thin guise of moral improvement of the reader by means of warning examples. Gruesome details of crimes, torture, and punishment were often combined with an evocation of the improving spectacle of the malefactor's repentance. Instruction in and respect for the law were also held to make up the value of such narratives. Schiller deliberately thwarts the reader's expectations, delivering almost no details of the trial and execution and halting the narrative where Wolf hands himself over to justice. His aim is not to thrill or to shock but to dissect motive and circumstance (he uses the term *Leichenöffnung* [autopsy]), not to set his criminal apart from common humanity as a spectacle for the crowd but rather to enable the reader to understand how circumstances interact with natural propensities to produce criminal behavior. And far from calling for respect for the legal system, the story can be seen as a contribution to the reform debates of the period, for it is those who administer justice who by their lack of human sympathy and discrimination set the minor criminal on the road to depravity.[3] Schiller strikingly anticipates more modern debates about the function of punishment in the legal system, not only appealing for the importance of individual psychology and circumstances in forming legal judgments but also suggesting that it is excessive punishment and the brutality of prison itself that turn people into criminals and rob them of hope. In the end it is not any respect he might have for the law as represented by the judiciary and those in authority but Wolf's own moral compass that directs him toward expiation. In that regard he is similar to Schiller's more famous robber and murderer, Karl Moor, who also gives himself up to justice after he has judged himself morally, even though in other respects Karl, the fallen angel, has little in common with the ill-favored Wolf.

Like several of Schiller's prose narratives, *Der Geisterseher* draws on and transforms factual material — in this case, the fear that a Protestant prince might be manipulated into converting to Catholicism and thus laying his territory open to Catholic influence. Such fears were aroused in Protestant Württemberg in 1786 by Duke Karl Eugen's nephew, Friedrich Heinrich Eugen, who was third in line to the throne and published an essay concerning the conjuration of spirits and evincing sympathy for the Catholic faith. Schiller combines this fear with the prevalent taste for conspiracy stories, the suspicion of secret societies, and the notoriety of the Sicilian adventurer and confidence trickster Count Cagliostro (Guiseppe Balsamo). Schiller's skill is in debunking the vividly evoked supernatural happenings in the narrative, while at the same time arousing dread at more sinister, if human rather than supernatural, machinations behind the events in the Prince's life; the marvelously atmospheric conjuration is subsequently fully explained to the characters and to the reader, but the ubiquity and powers of self-transformation of the mysterious Armenian are not. These machinations, we are led to feel, are more to be feared because they aim at influencing the Prince's state of mind and from there his moral and religious outlook, effecting lasting changes with immense political implications. This is a tale that has to be read against the background both of absolutist government and of more than two centuries of religious strife in the German states.

A sign that Schiller's interests were moving away from his narrative to some of the underlying issues is shown by "Das philosophische Gespräch" (The Philosophical Dialog), a lengthy exchange in which the Prince, having abandoned the modest habits he has maintained up to that point, also questions the assumptions that have sustained him about the value of moral action and expounds his views on the delusions human beings entertain about a divine order and purpose to their existence. He thus paints a fascinating portrait of his new moral and intellectual rootlessness, a condition that is the prelude to his embracing Catholicism. Schiller recognized the difficulty of integrating such a protracted discussion into the narrative and published it as a discrete item. Though he incorporated it into the first book edition of 1789, he reduced it progressively for later editions. Fascinating though "Das philosophische Gespräch" is, it indicates that he had grown impatient with the constraints of the work. By 1789, when the last installment appeared, he was mentally turning toward the aesthetic questions that would dominate the next half-decade: the moral and aesthetic foundations of tragedy and the philosophical basis of aesthetic responses.

Tragedy was for Schiller the greatest creative challenge and the highest form of literature. Prose fiction was in his eyes frankly inferior. Yet his last play of the 1780s, *Don Karlos,* had caused him immense compositional problems and the end product left him dissatisfied and convinced that in order to mature as a writer he must understand art forms as well as his calling as a writer. This conviction made him impatient with those who did not share his ambition or earnestness. One such seemed to him the popular poet Gottfried August Bürger. In 1790, the year after bringing *Der Geisterseher* to a close, Schiller published a review, "Über Bürgers Gedichte" (On Bürger's Poems), of Bürger's latest collection. Bürger was an established poet, whose earlier Gothic ballad "Lenore" (1773) had an international impact. In the review Schiller is uncompromising in distinguishing between high art and works written for popular taste. In an ideal world, he suggests, it might be possible to produce writing that both satisfied the highest aesthetic criteria and also enjoyed universal admiration and popularity. But the writer who aspires only to popularity has betrayed his calling.

The review's purist stance and haughtiness do not really do Schiller credit. While they indicate his frustration at the diversion of his own energies to projects he thought unworthy, they also obscure the fact that he himself was unable to exist independently of the literary market or of princely patronage. Taken together, the Bürger review and *Der Geisterseher* reveal the tension in Schiller between a vision of high art and the more pragmatic approach he had to take to his activities in order to survive and provide for his family. While devoting himself primarily to aesthetic issues in the early 1790s, he still needed to earn money from projects that would sell, primarily at this time his *Geschichte des Dreißigjährigen Krieges.* A project to reconcile this basic tension was his new journal *Die Horen* (Horae), conceived in 1794 as a response to the polarizing conflicts engendered among Germans by the French Revolution. It was to combine philosophy, aesthetics, and poetry and bring together a community of intellectually demanding writers and readers. But it failed to buck the market and after two years ceased publication. By contrast, Schiller's *Musenalmanach* (Muses' Almanac, 1796–1800), an annual poetry anthology he compiled from his own and others' poems, struck a more popular note and brought him in substantial funds. To the end of his life he was floating ideas with publishers for new projects that would bring them and him money, among them a new German edition of the Chinese novel, *Haoh-Kiöh-Tschuen,* the existing fragment of which is included in this volume and which was to appear with the Berlin publisher Unger.

In 1794 Schiller began his friendship and literary alliance with Goethe. Their aim was to raise standards and aspirations among writers and readers. Goethe agreed to contribute to *Die Horen*. When the journal failed, the two writers' unsympathetic attitude to many respected and popular authors of their day, whom they took to task in the jointly composed satirical distiches, the *Xenien* (Xenia), left a legacy of critical prejudice against those authors and against popular writing in general that consigned much writing of their day to subsequent oblivion. Ironically, however, since the 1960s, when serious challenges began to be mounted to the dominance of Goethe's and Schiller's aesthetic values, a wide range of popular writing being enjoyed by the reading public of their day has come again to light. Among that writing is Schiller's prose fiction, which has come into its own again and can be read anew in its contemporary context. This volume reveals its strengths and subtleties.

University of Exeter

Notes

[1] See, for example, the recent collection of essays, *Schiller und die Geschichte,* ed. Michael Hofmann, Jörn Rüsen, and Mirjam Springer (Munich: Wilhelm Fink, 2006).

[2] On *Der Geisterseher*'s place in the development of German Gothic fiction, see Daniel Hall, *French and German Gothic Fiction in the Late Eighteenth Century* Oxford, Berne, Frankfurt am Main: Peter Lang, 2004).

[3] See, for example, Klaus Oettinger, "Schillers Erzählung 'Der Verbrecher aus Infamie.' Ein Beitrag zur Rechtsaufklärung der Zeit," *Jahrbuch der Deutschen Schillergesellschaft* 16 (1972): 266–76 and Thomas Nutz, "Vergeltung oder Versöhnung?: Strafvollzug und Ehre in Schillers 'Verbrecher aus Infamie,'" *Jahrbuch der Deutschen Schillergesellschaft* 42 (1998): 146–64.

Preface

Jeffrey L. High

IT IS DIFFICULT TO DRAW THE LINE between Schiller's original literary prose works, his short historical works and anecdotes, his adaptations and translations, and his shorter philosophical prose in the form of fictional letters and dialogs. The following is a brief justification for the selection of the works included in this collection and the exclusion of those short prose works not included.

Aside from his four original short prose works, Schiller wrote numerous short prose works that do not necessarily fit into a collection of "literary" prose works — as opposed to critical, philosophical, or historical short prose works — for a variety of reasons. Schiller's "Brief eines reisenden Dänen" (1785, Letter from a Traveling Dane) is foremost an essay on aesthetics expressed largely in the idiom of Johann Joachim Winckelmann's theories of classical art, which analyzes the classical statues of the Mannheim collection from the perspective of a Danish traveler. The philosophical dialog, "Der Spaziergang unter den Linden" (1782, The Walk under the Lindens), in which the melancholy Wollmar and the optimist Edwin debate the meaning of happiness, and "Philosophische Briefe" (1786, Philosophical Letters), an exchange of letters between the fictional Julius and Raphael, are philosophical discussions, without story or event. They are not included here.

The historical anecdote, "Herzog von Alba bey einem Frühstück auf dem Schlosse zu Rudolstadt im Jahr 1547" (The Duke of Alba's Breakfast at Rudolstadt Castle in the Year 1547), demonstrates most of the characteristics of literary prose. The focus is on moral character and event over actual history, close to the tradition of the eighteenth-century morality tale, revolving around the "unfailing courage" of the heroine, Countess Katharina von Schwarzburg, in morally upstaging the terrible Duke of Alba and the Spanish army. "Das philosophische Gespräch aus dem Geisterseher" (The Philosophical Dialog from The Spiritualist, 1789), though it would appear to resemble the philosophical dialogs mentioned above, was first published as part of the unfinished serial novel *Der Geisterseher,* and readers seeking the text might expect to find it here along with the translation of *Der Geisterseher,* which they will. Two of Schiller's adaptations of existing prose works, his adaptation of a segment of Diderot's novel *Jacques le Fataliste et son*

Maitre, "Ein merkwürdiges Beispiel einer weiblichen Rache" (1785, A Remarkable Example of Female Revenge), and "Haoh-Kiöh-Tschuen," a fragment based on a Chinese novel, are indeed short works of fiction, play no minor role in the reception history of both works, and are adapted so freely by Schiller as to deserve inclusion among his literary prose works. These texts are translated here with Schiller's four original literary prose works.

In summary, this volume includes translations of Schiller's four original prose works — "Eine großmüthige Handlung aus der neusten Geschichte," "Der Verbrecher aus verlorener Ehre," "Spiel des Schicksals. Ein Bruchstück aus einer wahren Geschichte," *Der Geisterseher* and "Das philosophische Gespräch aus dem Geisterseher" — as well as the historical anecdote "Herzog von Alba bey einem Frühstück auf dem Schlosse zu Rudolstadt" and two adaptations: "Ein merkwürdiges Beispiel einer weiblichen Rache" from Diderot and "Haoh-Kiöh-Tschuen," a fragment based on a Chinese novel by an unnamed Ming Dynasty author,[1] possibly Mingjiao zhongren. All translations are of the texts in their final versions as published by Schiller[2] and as they appear in German in the Schiller *Nationalausgabe.*[3]

California State University Long Beach

Notes

[1] The novel was originally translated into German by Christoph Gottlieb von Murr: Christoph Gottlieb von Murr, trans., *Haoh Kjöh Tschwen, das ist die angenehme Geschichte des Haoh Kjöh.* Ein chinesischer Roman in vier Büchern (Leipzig: Johann Friedrich Junius, 1766).

[2] The texts appear in the *Nationalausgabe* as follows: "Eine großmütige Handlung" appeared in *Wirtembergisches Repertorium der Literatur, Eine Vierteljahr-Schrift, Zweites Stück.* Auf Kosten der Herausgeber, 1782; "Herzog von Alba" appeared in *Der Teutsche Merkur vom Jahre 1788. Ihr Römisch-Kayserlichen Majetsät zugeeignet. Mit Königl. Preuss. Und Churfürstl. Brandenburg gnädigstem Privilegio. Viertes Vierteljahr,* Weimar, Oktober 1788, 79–84; *Der Geisterseher* is taken from *Der Geisterseher. Aus den Memoires des Grafen von O**.* Herausgegeben von Schiller. Erster Theil. Dritte verbesserte Ausgabe. Leipzig, bey Georg Joachim Göschen, 1798; "Das philosophische Gespräch aus dem Geisterseher" appeared in *Thalia.* Herausgegeben von Schiller. Erster Band, welcher das I. bis IV. Heft enthält, Leipzig, bei Georg Joachim Göschen, 1787, hier Viertes Heft, 1787, *Der Geisterseher. Aus den Papieren des Grafen von O,* 68–94; "Ein merkwürdiges Beispiel" appeared in *Thalia.* Herausgegeben von Schiller. Erster Band, welcher das I. bis IV. Heft enthält, Leipzig, bei Georg Joachim Göschen, 1787. Here Viertes Heft, 1785, 27–94; "Hao-Kiöh-Tschuen" is taken from Schiller's handwritten manuscript; and "Der Verbrecher aus verlorener Ehre" and "Spiel des Schicksals" are taken from *Kleinere Prosaische Schriften von Schiller. Aus Mehrern Zeitschriften vom Verfasser selbst gesammelt und ver-*

bessert. Erster Theil, Leipzig, 1792, bey Siegfried Lebrecht Crusius: "Spiel des Schicksals" 263–90, "Verbrecher" 291–345.

[3] Friedrich Schiller, *Schillers Werke. Nationalausgabe,* ed. Julius Petersen et al. (Weimar: Herrman Böhlaus Nachfolger, 1943ff.). Here volume 16, *Erzählungen,* ed. Hans Heinrich Borcherdt (1954).

Acknowledgments

I OWE A DEBT OF GRATITUDE to Friederike von Schwerin-High (Pomona College), Jennifer M. Hoyer (University of Arkansas), Carrie Collenberg (University of Minnesota, Twin Cities), George Peters (Michigan State University), Frederick Burwick (University of California, Los Angeles), and Steve Fleck and Clorinda Donato (California State University Long Beach) for their close reading of parts of the manuscript and advice, as well as my research assistants, Sophia Clark, Lisa Beesley, and Ryan Sweeney (California State University Long Beach) for their dedication to the pursuit of sources. Many thanks to the participants in my Fall 2007 "Novella" class at California State University Long Beach, who sacrificed two weeks of discussing short prose works and books about them while helping to edit this one: Michele Amato, Christina Bacht, Annie Chou, Adan Gallardo, Meike Gilmer, Stephanie Gilmore, Paul Knight, Erik Knoedler, Gregory Lindsey, Andreas Mihaly, Nicholas Mihaly, Elinor Parks, Melissa Scholz, Henrik Sponsel, and Christine Lucht. Harald Becker, Glenn Trujillo, Patrick Hughes (St. Edward's University), and Melissa Etzler (University of California, Berkeley) provided consultation and editorial assistance. Tim Xie (California State University Long Beach), Allan Barr (Pomona College), and Eileen Cheng (Pomona College) delivered thorough responses to queries regarding Schiller's adaptation of *Haoh-Kiöh-Tschuen*. I would like to thank Peter Lang publishers in Oxford for their kind permission to reprint parts of my earlier article, "Schiller, the Author of Literary Prose," and Paul Kerry for his excellent editorial work on the volume in which it appeared, *Friedrich Schiller. Playwright, Poet, Philosopher, Historian* (Oxford: Peter Lang, 2007). Joseph C. High is a remarkably patient and insightful critic, and for this and so much more, I thank him. I thank Jim Walker of Camden House for his patient and thorough work as editor.

I have had the pleasure of working with a rare group of contributors who went well beyond the call of duty in their willingness to exchange ideas and read each other's work. Along with my own contributions, the book comprises original translations by Ian Codding (California State University Long Beach), Carrie Collenberg (University of Minnesota, Twin Cities), Ellis Dye (Macalester College), Francis Lamport (Worcester College, Oxford, UK), and Edward T. Larkin (University of New Hampshire), and critical essays by Gail K. Hart (University of California, Irvine), Otto W. Johnston (University of Florida, Gainesville), Dennis F. Mahoney (University of Vermont), Nicholas Martin (University of Birmingham, UK), a bibliography of Schiller's literary prose works in translation by Tanya Doss (California State University Long Beach), and a foreword by Lesley Sharpe (University of Exeter, UK). I applaud them all for their enthusiasm, hard work, and patience, and equally for their common interest in re-introducing Schiller and his works to an English-speaking audience.

California State University Long Beach

Notes on the Translations

IN THE PROCESS OF PREPARING the translations, the very knowledgeable translators and I have given a great deal of attention to the unity of Schillerian conventions common to all of the prose works. Throughout the prose works, Schiller follows a model of either short introductory or summary sentences, in stark contrast to the body of a paragraph characterized by often extraordinarily long sentences, and we have tried to mimic this. Schiller's staccato use of commas, semicolons, and hyphens have been retained wherever possible for scholarly orientation and to mimic Schiller's characteristic breathlessness, which, though many may recognize it as peculiar to the German novella, is much more extreme in Schiller's case than in most German — and certainly most English — prose works. The same attention has been given to uniformity regarding Schiller's favorite adjectives and philosophical terms. I hope that this approach has led to an approximation of the original tension between objectivity and emotion in all of the translations, including my own translation of *Der Verbrecher aus verlorener Ehre*. All of the translations in the volume are directly from Schiller's texts as printed in *Schillers Werke. Nationalausgabe,* vol. 16 (Weimar: Böhlau, 1954). In the case of Francis Lamport's translation of *Der Geisterseher,* British spelling and idioms have been retained out of respect for the integrity of the translation.

Jeffrey L. High, California State University Long Beach

"A Magnanimous Act from Most Recent History" and "The Duke of Alba's Breakfast at Rudolstadt Castle in the Year 1547"

Based on the experience of Christiane von Werthern, which Schiller learned of either through Henriette von Wolzogen or her children, "Eine großmüthige Handlung, aus der neusten Geschichte" appeared anonymously in March 1782 in the *Wirtembergisches Repertorium der Litteratur.* "Herzog von Alba bey einem Frühstück auf dem Schlosse zu Rudolstadt" first appeared in October 1788 in Wieland's *Der Teutsche Merkur.* With a fluent literal translation of the texts as they appear in the *Nationalausgabe* in mind, I have attempted to preserve the depth and suspenseful movement of these works by maintaining the original sequence of phrases through which information is revealed as well as the word connotations responsible for intricately woven, recurring themes and subtle shifts from one character description to another. In accomplishing this, the insightful suggestions of Dr. Jeffrey L. High at California State University Long Beach proved indispensable.

Ian Codding, California State University Long Beach

"A Remarkable Example of Female Revenge" (Taken from a Manuscript by the late Denis Diderot)

"A Remarkable Example," extracted and translated by Schiller from Diderot's *Jacques le Fataliste et son Maître*, was published in the first issue of Schiller's *Thalia*, 1785. The present translator has worked directly from Schiller's text, as printed in *Schillers Werke. Nationalausgabe* (Weimar: Böhlau, 1954), 16:187–224, occasionally consulting Diderot, in the edition by Marie-Thérèse Ligot (Pocket Classiques, 1989), as well as J. Robert Loy's translation: *Jacques the Fatalist and His Master* (New York University Press, 1959 — with introduction and notes). My hearty thanks to Jeffrey L. High for his confidence in assigning to me what has proven to be an instructive, invigorating, and very pleasant task. His knowledge of Schiller, his sharp editorial eye, and his fine sensitivity to style and idiom have benefited my translation in many ways.

Robert Ellis Dye, Macalester College

"Game of Fate. A Fragment of a True Story"

This translation, which is based on the version of "Spiel des Schicksals" contained in the *Nationalausgabe* vol. 16 (Weimar: Böhlau, 1954), pp. 33–44, is, like other translations, not the result of a single individual's efforts. I am grateful to the many people, who will have to remain anonymous here, whom I have called on for various levels of assistance. All inaccuracies, however, are the result of my own efforts. I have sought both to transmit the tenacity of Schiller's language and to make the text accessible to the modern reader, who may rightly puzzle over the use of the historical present tense and over some lengthy syntactical constructions. I have likewise not attempted to ease the many abrupt textual transitions, particularly in the opening paragraph, as these may be intentional to reflect the alleged fragmentary nature of the tale or to convey the flavor of the oral sources of this story, which first appeared in 1789 in Wieland's *Der Teutsche Merkur* and which is based on but diverges from other historical documentation of General Philipp Friedrich Rieger.

Edward T. Larkin, University of New Hampshire

*The Spiritualist. From the Memoirs of Count von O***

Der Geisterseher was first published in installments in Schiller's periodical *Thalia* in 1787–89. In 1789 a revised book edition also appeared, and Schiller made further revisions for the book editions of 1792 and 1798. The text translated is that of 1798, as it will be found in almost all modern collected editions, apart from the Frankfurt (Deutscher Klassiker Verlag) edition, which prints the original *Thalia* version. The translation of 1849 by Henry Bohn (reprinted by Camden House in 1992) combines elements of the 1789 and 1798 versions: See the introduction to that edition by Jeffery L. Sammons.

Sammons comments that "its Victorian stateliness somewhat stiffens and formalizes Schiller's unpretentious middle style"; I have tried to remain relatively informal. After some hesitation, I have kept the occasional switches between past and historical present tense by which Count von O** and his correspondent Baron von F*** seek to add immediacy to their narration at various particularly vivid or exciting points. The only other real problem of translation is the title. The transliteration *The Ghost-seer* seems to me unidiomatic, and Bohn's subtitle *The Apparitionist* (copied from the first English translation of 1795) no better (the word is not in the OED, nor in Johnson). I hope my choice will be thought appropriate. I have added notes to some allusions that may be obscure. Readers unfamiliar with the topography of Venice may care to consult some of the many maps and guides that are available.

Francis Lamport, Oxford University

"The Philosophical Dialog from *The Spiritualist*"

In the wake of its popularity in *Thalia*, several separate editions of *Der Geisterseher* were published. After the first edition, Schiller chose to substantially reduce the body of the philosophical dialog — Norbert Oellers suggests this may have been because of concern that the philosophical dialog interfered with the suspense of the story as a whole. This translation presents the entire philosophical dialog as originally published in *Der Geisterseher* in the journal *Thalia* in 1789. Schiller's distinctive punctuation has been preserved in this translation, to the extent that such faithfulness would not interfere with the meaning of the text. Two of Schiller's key philosophical terms — *Zweck* and *Kraft* — have several possible translations in English. Depending on the context, *Zweck* has been translated as both "purpose" and "end," *Kraft* as "energy" when referring to characteristics of human beings, and as "force" when referring to physical nature. To differentiate between Schiller's use of the terms *Handlung* and *Bewegung*, the former has been translated as "act" or "action" while the latter has been translated as ""motion" or "movement." I am deeply grateful to Jeffrey L. High and Dennis F. Mahoney for their invaluable criticisms and suggestions. I owe a particular debt to Francis Lamport, who not only made vital improvements to my draft, but also generously allowed me to draw on his translation — *The Spiritualist* — for guidance.

Helen Kilgallen, University of California, Irvine

"Haoh-Kiöh-Tschuen"

In a letter to Unger in 1800, Schiller included "Haoh-Kiöh-Tschuen," the first installment of an unfinished project to edit and abridge Christoph Gottlieb von Murr's German translation (1766) — from an English translation — of the Chinese novel *Haoqiu zhuan* (c. 1683). The original Chinese text is attributed to author Mingjiao zhongren and has been considered to be the first Chinese novel to be translated into a European language (1761). Because Schiller's fragment is generally unknown in the translation history of the Chinese text, I include here the standard Pinyin title of the work Schiller is referencing, *Haoqiu zhuan,* in order to facilitate an orthographic intersection where scholarship on Schiller and Sinology can meet. The original Chinese title translates roughly as "The Tale of a Perfect Match," and can be found elsewhere as *The Fortunate Union*. I have not altered the names of protagonists or places from Schiller's text but will include the Pinyin here: Tiehtschongu (Tie Zhong-yu); Tieh-ying (Tie Ying); Pikang (Bi Gan); Siautan (Xiao Dan); and Wey-tsioün (Wei Village). Otherwise, I have tried to translate as closely as possible to Schiller's text without forgoing English idiomatic expression. I would like to thank Tim Xie (California State University Long Beach), Allan Barr (Pomona College), and Eileen Cheng (Pomona College) for their indispensable suggestions.

Carrie Collenberg, University of Minnesota

Introduction: Schiller and the German Novella

Jeffrey L. High

THE LITERARY PROSE WORKS of Friedrich Schiller (1759–1805), some among the most resonant works in his time, remain today a largely overlooked area of his oeuvre and an unrecognized link in the evolution of German short prose. Until the 1780s, the moral tale, the historical anecdote, and the nascent German Boccaccio-Cervantes-novella of Christoph Martin Wieland ("Werkchen")[1] were the dominant German forms of short prose in number and in theoretical prominence.[2] Written almost entirely in his first decade as a published author, Schiller's prose works, which experiment with the same dark anthropological curiosity and moral confusion that made his first drama *Die Räuber* (1781, The Robbers) a sensation, mark a departure from the uncomplicated moral praise or condemnation of the moral tale, the singularly characteristic anecdote, and the frivolity of the Boccaccio-Cervantes novella, to the moral ambivalence, anthropological universality, and the grim verisimilitude of what was to become the German novella.[3] In so doing, Schiller provided his own prose fiction with an original artistry and profile, and provided subsequent German short-prose authors with a model that makes his literary prose works significant for the literary-historical consideration of scholars and students over 200 years after his death in 1805 and on the eve of his 250th birthday in 2009. In this volume, seven of Schiller's literary prose works appear in new translations, together with five scholarly essays, in the only English collection currently in print. These include one each on the two more prominent original prose works and the Diderot adaptation, as well as one essay on the more historical-anecdotal moral tales.

Given his relatively limited production, the importance of Schiller's prose works for the history of the German novella is remarkable, and his influence singular, even if his works remain a largely unrecognized link in the academic reception of the evolution of German short prose. That both August Wilhelm and Friedrich Schlegel named Boccaccio, Cervantes, Goethe, and even Shakespeare as the models for the (German) novella without mentioning Schiller is not surprising when one considers the resentment toward Schiller after he dismissed A. W. Schlegel from his position as contributor to

Schiller's journal *Die Horen* (The Horae) in May of 1797.[4] Of course, the Schlegels could also not yet know in the late 1790s that it would not be the grand panoramic frame-novella[5] cycle of amusing human foibles (Boccaccio, Cervantes, Wieland) that would inform the German novella from the beginning of the nineteenth century until the twenty-first, but rather, and on the contrary, its isolated, impatient, laser-focused, and not at all playful offspring — Schiller's inevitable narrative chain of the unexpected collision (chance) of exemplary susceptible character (human nature) plausible, extreme situation, and reaction, with the gravest of consequences (fate).[6]

One of the important histories of the German novella, Johannes Klein's *Geschichte der deutschen Novelle von Goethe bis zur Gegenwart* (History of the German Novella from Goethe to the Present),[7] inadvertently points out the relative critical silence toward Schiller's prose, and the lack of sufficient and accepted academic terminology appears to play an important role. Faced with a scholarly tradition that agreed that there is a clear dividing line between pre-Goethean short prose and the tradition of the German Boccaccio novella that began with Wieland, Schiller's novella "Der Verbrecher aus verlorener Ehre" (The Criminal of Lost Honor), though indeed discussed, appears at the beginning of "Part One: Goethe," under the subtitle "Prologue Schiller: *Der Verbrecher aus verlorener Ehre* . . ." (Klein ix). The implication is clear: There were by definition no serious German novellas prior to the age-of-novella theory that dawned in the mid-1790s with August Wilhelm and Friedrich Schlegel's theoretical essays and Goethe's works and contributions to the definition.[8] In "Part Two: Heinrich von Kleist," Klein repositioned Schiller's "Verbrecher" as heralding the "breakthrough of the [German] novella."[9] Gerhard Kaiser later called "Verbrecher" the "bridge between morality tale and novella."[10] Finally, in 1982, Gerhard Neumann articulated Schiller's place at "the beginning of the German novella."[11] By 1999, Hugo Aust situated his unit titled "Schiller" — the first unit to bear the name of a German author — in the chapter "Geschichte der deutschen Novelle" (History of the German Novella), between units on "Aufklärung" (Enlightenment) and "Das Aufkommen der Novellenbezeichnung" (The Rise of the Category Novella) (Aust 55–65). Most recently, Katherine Astbury further corroborated Schiller's role in the evolution from the moral tale to the German novella.[12]

Causing such a literary-historical problem is one of Schiller's most interesting distinctions. Too morally and politically complicated, unwilling — if not incapable — of complying with the prevailing German prose conventions of the Boccaccio novella, the morality tale, or the exemplary anecdote, Schiller's short prose works transformed the specifically German novella through the device of "truth" — socio-historical and psychological plausibility — resulting in riveting tales driven by biographical study, environmental psychology, and psychological profiling that examine rather than portray fate.[13] In his literary prose works more evidently than elsewhere, Schiller, who received his medical doctorate in 1780 at the age of twenty-one, demonstrates his fascination with the psychological-causal mechanisms of humankind in the scientific analysis of credible and almost exclusively actual occurrences — "realism and truth"[14] — which become a common feature of all of his original literary prose works, as well as the two prose adaptations.

The number of characteristics that later informed the canonized definition of the German novella present in Schiller's works is large, and the fact that many of them are defined explicitly in his theoretical introductions only makes their influence more evident. The transformation of the German novella — most often attributed to Goethe — from the "attraction of novelty" and the mere "playfulness of Boccaccio," "who immorally enjoys the life" of moral stupidity he observes (Klein 34), is self-evident in Schiller's serious short prose. Schiller analyzes, exposes, and criticizes individuals and society in moral crisis. The refinement of the "character and fate novella" (Klein 34), most often associated with Goethe, is the rule in Schiller's short prose works, all of which predate those by Goethe. The portrayal of the "confusion of feelings" often identified with Goethe's later prose works and with Kleist,[15] and Kleist's repetition and variation of events and motifs, are already genre-defining characteristics of Schiller's prose. The combination of the analytical empiricism of the narrators, the "unheard-of event," and the "amazing" (Klein 34) — later associated with Goethe and the post-Schillerian German Romantics — is characteristic of all of Schiller's earlier prose works.

Tellingly, Schiller's influence on the characteristic form and content of the German novella is evident in the works of subsequent German authors of short prose works. There can be no doubt that the canonized novellas of Kleist, the later novellas of Ludwig Tieck, Achim von Arnim, and Clemens Brentano, which were often inspired by remarkable newspaper stories[16] are closer first to the roots of Schiller's short prose, and then to Goethe's early novellas, than to Goethe's romantic-mythological *Novelle,* the work, ironically, most frequently cited as genre-defining.[17] Kleist for his part was indifferent to the term novella when he organized his collection of them in 1810 and proposed the title "Moralische Erzählungen von Heinrich von Kleist" (Moral Tales by Heinrich von Kleist).[18] However, Kleist's novellas mirror Schiller's not only in content and style, but foremost, in stark contrast to the German moral tale tradition, in the absence of any secure hope of reward for virtuous behavior.[19] Indeed, just when redemption seems near, it simply fails to show up and life — individual and situation — either indifferently goes on or, most often, ends. Schiller's prose prefigures the most prominent post-Goethean novella conventions: Tieck's "turning point," A. W. Schlegel's "turning points," Paul Heyses contributions of the "silhouette," Boccaccio's "falcon," and investigation of the "deepest moral questions," Theodor Storm's "sister of the drama" and "unity of form," Benno von Wiese's "pictorial and symbolic" portrayal and the "role of chance," and Frank Ryder's "non-linear narration."[20] The same can be argued for a large number of other novella conventions that contribute to the "family resemblance" of the genre,[21] from the common rhythm and summary nature of the titles and subtitles (subject-preposition-object, as in "Der Verbrecher aus verlorener Ehre") to the practice of artificially reinforcing the historical urgency of the tale by disguising names and places through omission. No doubt, there are older isolated examples of each of these authorial strategies, particularly in Wieland's earlier, mostly humorous, short prose works; however, there are no prominent German prose works prior to Schiller's that demonstrate the formal and thematic consistency in so many of the aforementioned novella conventions.

From Schiller's Marquis von A*** in "Ein merkwürdiges Beispiel" and Prinz von *** and Count von O** in his *Der Geisterseher* to Kleist's "Marquise von O" (1808); from Schiller's *Spiritualist* to E. T. A. Hoffmann's in "Der Sandmann" (The Sandman, 1816);[22] from the Venice of Schiller's Prince von *** and Count von O** to Gustav von Aschenbach's Venice in Thomas Mann's *Der Tod in Venedig* (1912, Death in Venice);[23] from eighteenth-century writers to Heinrich von Kleist, E. T. A. Hoffmann, Robert Musil, Thomas Mann, and Alfred Döblin,[24] Schiller's short prose works fairly hum in the background of two centuries of the most celebrated German short prose works. Indeed, the number of prominent writers of novellas he inspired might in part explain why Schiller's fascination with moral ambiguity, crime, and conspiracy, his dramatic changes of narrative perspective, and his tales appear so modern after over two hundred years.

California State University Long Beach

Notes

[1] Citing Boccaccio and Cervantes, Wieland's description of the novella as a "little work" (Werkchen) in 1772 is indicative of the light tone characteristic of his own novellas and of the novella tradition prior to Schiller. Introduction to *Don Sylvio von Rosalva,* in Christoph Martin Wieland, *Wielands Werke,* XIV. Theil (Berlin: Gustav Hempel, 1879), 167–68.

[2] Wieland's *Don Sylvio von Rosalva* (1764) comprises a series of novellas in the tradition of Boccaccio and Cervantes that delight in the parodistic exposure of moral stupidity. Although Wieland's first and subsequent collections of novellas are treated extensively in secondary literature on the German novella, they have little to do with the serious German novella from Schiller on, and have much more in common with the German fairy tale. Similarly, Goethe's *Unterhaltungen deutscher Ausgewanderten*

is often considered the beginning of the German novella, but was published in 1795 and thus years after Schiller's short prose works.

[3] Walter Silz, "Geschichte, Theorie und Kunst der Deutschen Novelle," in *Der Deutschunterricht* 11, 5 (1959): 82–100, here 86. For a review of the history and characteristics of the specifically German novella, see Frank Ryder, *Die Novelle* (New York: Holt, Rinehart and Winston, 1971), xviii–xxvi. Subsequent citations as "Ryder" with page number.

[4] See Schiller's letter to August Wilhelm Schlegel of 31 May 1797. *Schillers Werke. Nationalausgabe,* ed. Julius Petersen et al. (Weimar: Herrman Böhlaus Nachfolger, 1943ff.), 29:80. Subsequent citations as "NA" with volume and page number.

[5] Hugo Aust, *Novelle* (Stuttgart: Metzler, 1999), 15. Subsequent citations as "Aust" with page number.

[6] In 1804, August Wilhelm Schlegel does recognize that the novella commonly describes "Erfahrung von wirklich geschehenen Dingen" (things that actually happened); however, this statement is rarely true of canonical novellas prior to Schiller's short prose works and appears after Schiller's short prose career is over. August Wilhelm Schlegel, *Vorlesungen über schöne Literatur und Kunst. III Teil: Geschichte der romantischen Literatur.* Cited as in Bernhard Seuffert, *Deutsche Literaturdenkmale des 18. und 19. Jahrhunderts,* volume 19 (Heilbronn: Henninger, 1884), 242–43.

[7] Johannes Klein, *Geschichte der deutschen Novelle von Goethe bis zur Gegenwart* (Wiesbaden: Franz Steiner Verlag, 1956). Subsequent citations as "Klein" with page number.

[8] For a summary of the Schlegels' contributions to the theory of the novella, see Karl Konrad Polheim, ed., *Theorie und Kritik der deutschen Novelle von Wieland bis Musil* (Tübingen: Max Niemeyer Verlag, 1970), 3–20.

[9] "Durchbruch der Novelle," Klein 51.

[10] Gerhard Kaiser, *Von Arkadien nach Elysium. Schiller-Studien* (Göttingen: Vandenhoek and Ruprecht, 1978), 45–58, here 58. See Helmut Koopmann, ed., *Schiller Handbuch* (Stuttgart: Kröner Verlag, 1998), 704.

[11] Gerhard Neumann, "Die Anfänge deutscher Novellistik. 'Schillers Verbrecher aus verlorener Ehre' — Goethes 'Unterhaltungen deutscher Ausgewanderten,'" in: *Unser Commercium. Goethes und Schillers Literaturpolitik* (Stuttgart: Cotta, 1984), 433–60.

[12] Katherine Astbury, *The Moral Tale in France and Germany 1750–1789* (Oxford: Voltaire Foundation, 2002), 170–73.

[13] Helmut Koopmann, *Friedrich Schiller I: 1759–1794* (Stuttgart: Metzler, 1966), 66.

[14] *Der Verbrecher aus verlorener Ehre und andere Erzählungen,* mit einem Nachwort von Bernhard Zeller (Stuttgart: Reclam, 1964), 51.

[15] "Verwirrung des Gefühls," Klein 34.

[16] Fritz Strich, *Deutsche Klassik und Romantik* (Bern: Francke, 1962), 152–53.

[17] Note that in Goethe's "Die wunderlichen Nachbarskinder" (The Strange Neighbor Children) in *Wahlverwandschaften* (1808, Elective Affinities), and "Der Mann von funfzig Jahren" (The Man of Fifty Years) in *Wilhelm Meisters Wanderjahre* (1807–8,

Wilhelm Meister's Travels), the tone is closer to Schiller's psychological realism; however, Schiller's original prose works predate these.

[18] Letter from Kleist to Georg Andreas Reimer of May 1810. Heinrich von Kleist, *Sämtliche Werke und Briefe,* ed. Helmut Sembdner (Munich: Deutscher Taschenbuch Verlag, 1987), 2:835.

[19] Gert Vonhoff, "'Die Macht der Verhältnisse': Schillers Erzählungen," in *Friedrich Schiller,* ed, Heinz Ludwig Arnold and Mirjam Springer (Munich: Edition Text + Kritik, 2005), 82–95, here 89–90.

[20] Ryder xviii–xxvi.

[21] Ryder xv.

[22] E. T. A. Hoffmann, "Der Sandmann," in *Werke* (Frankfurt am Main: Insel, 1967), 2:7.

[23] Jeffrey L. High, "Goethe, Schiller, Kleist und Aschenbach: Thomas Manns Selbsterklärung zum Novellen-Klassiker in *Der Tod in Venedig,*" in *Memoria. Thomas Mann 1875–1955,* ed. Walter Delabar and Bodo Plachta (Berlin: Weidler, 2005), 89–105.

[24] In 1959 Fritz Martini drew a somewhat different line in the history of German prose from Schiller to Hugo von Hofmannsthal to Döblin. Fritz Martini, "Der Erzähler Friedrich Schiller," in *Schiller. Reden im Gedenkjahr 1959* (Stuttgart: Klett, 1961), 124–58, here 130.

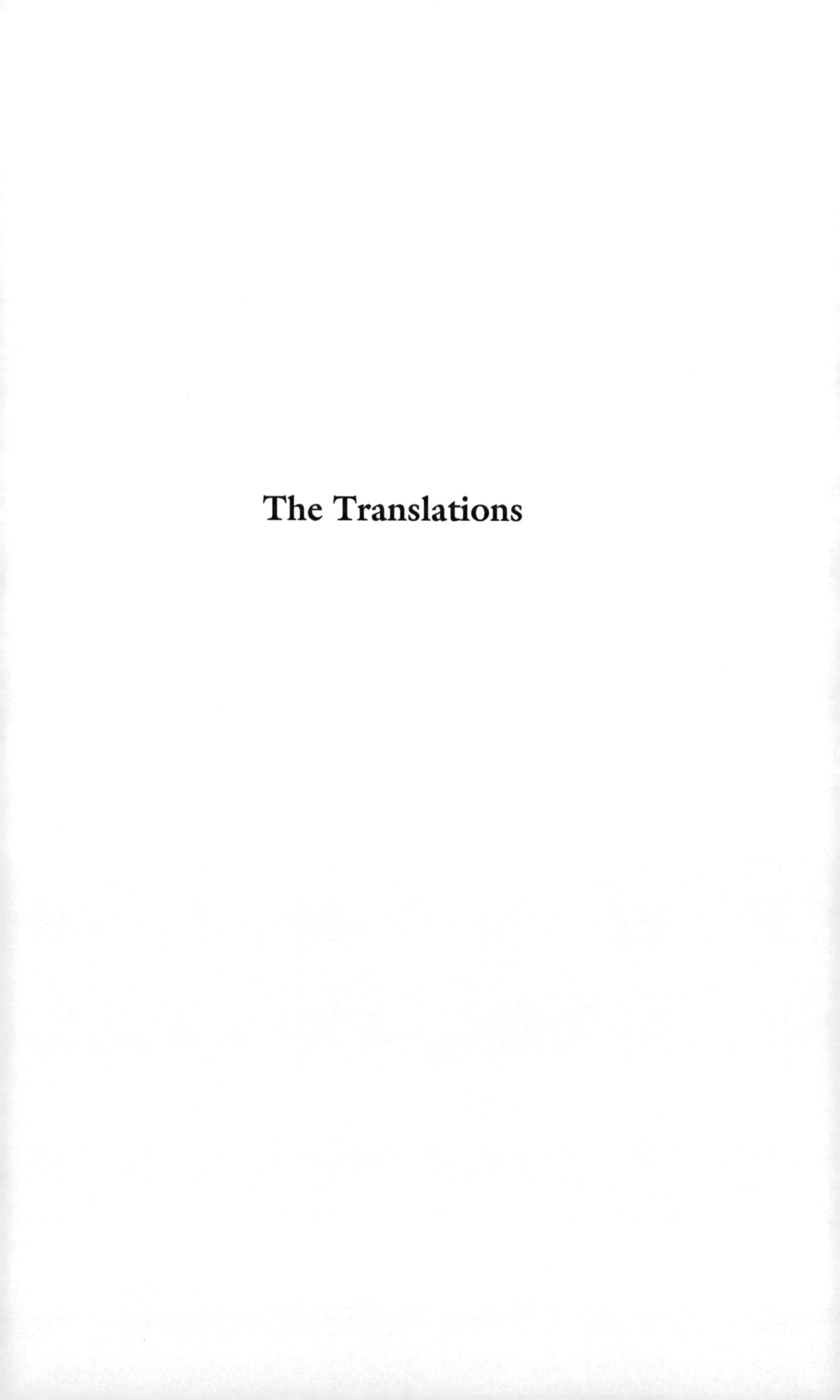

The Translations

1: A Magnanimous Act from Most Recent History

Friedrich Schiller (1782)
Translated by Ian Codding

PLAYS AND NOVELS REVEAL TO US the brightest attributes of the human heart; our imagination is ignited, our heart remains cold; at the very most, the fire, to which the heart is moved through these means, is merely fleeting, and soon grows too cold to be of any consequence in real life. At that same moment, just when the unadorned kindheartedness of a sincere novel character like Puff[1] nearly stirs us to tears, we can still impulsively shout down the knock of a needy beggar at the door. Who can say whether this same artificial existence in an idealistic world might not undermine our existence in the real one? We hover here, as it were, around the two poles of morality, angel and devil, and we leave the middle — humanity — lying in the breach.

The present anecdote of two Germans — which I am both proud and happy to write — has an indisputable merit: It is *true*. I hope that it will leave my readers warmer than all of Richardson's novels about Grandison and Pamela.[2]

Two brothers, the Barons of Wrmb., had both fallen in love with the young, in-every-way-exemplary Lady of Wrthr., without the one knowing about the other's passion. For both, love was strong and vulnerable, because it was their first. The young woman was beautiful and destined to sensitivity and sensibility. Both allowed their attraction to develop into a consuming passion, because neither one could recognize the peril in store, the worst a heart can suffer: to have his brother as a romantic rival. Both spared the girl an early confession of love, and so they unwittingly deceived each other, until an unexpected collision of their feelings exposed the whole secret.

Already, love in both had risen beyond the highest peak — the unhappiest emotion, which, in the human race, has brought about devastations nearly as cruel as its detestable opposite. This love had already filled the entire expanse of their hearts, so that, from either side, a sacrifice was hardly possible. The young woman, with the deepest compassion for the sad situation of both unfortunate rivals, dared not choose exclusively one or the other, and subjugated her feelings to the discretion of their brotherly love.

The older brother, the victor in this dubious struggle between duty and feeling — which is all too readily decided by our philosophers, yet approached so slowly by the practical person — said to the younger, "I know that you love my girl just as passionately as I do. I won't ask for whom the established right decides. You remain here; I will seek the whole wide world and will strive to forget her. If I can do that — brother, then she is yours, and may the heavens bless your love! If I cannot — then, so you must also leave and attempt the same!"

He left Germany abruptly and hurried off to Holland — but the image of his girl hurried after him. Far from the place of his love, banished from a region that held the entire bliss of his heart, and the only place he was able to live, the unfortunate brother became ill, like the withering plant that the violent European kidnaps from motherly Asia and forces far from the milder climate's sun into harsher beds. In desperation, he arrived in Amsterdam, where a high fever threw him into a dangerous state. The image of his one love dominated his mad dreams; his recovery hung on having her. The physicians feared for his life; only the promise of return to his beloved could tear him from death's embrace. He arrived in his hometown half dead, a wandering skeleton, the most frightening image of consuming sorrow. Dizzily, he stumbled over the steps of his beloved, and also of his brother's home. "Brother, I am home. *God* in heaven only knows what I expected of my heart. I can do no more." Unconscious, he sank in the arms of the young woman.

The younger brother was no less determined. In a few weeks, he stood there ready to depart: "Brother, you bore your pain all the way to Holland. I mean to try to bear it farther. Do not lead her to the altar until I write back to you! Brotherly love asks *only this one* condition. If I can be happier than you — in God's name, she is yours, and the heavens bless your love! If I cannot — well then, let the heavens pass judgment over us. Farewell! Keep this sealed package. Do not open it until I have gone! — I am going to Batavia!" — With this, he leapt into the carriage.

Nearly lifeless, the two left behind stared after him. He had surpassed his brother in gallantry. The love and, at the same time, the pain over the loss of the noblest man assailed the brother he left behind. The sound of the fleeing carriage thundered through his heart. They feared for his life. The young woman — but no! The end will reveal her fate.

The package was opened. It was a legal distribution of all his German possessions, which the brother was to inherit if the exile in Batavia succeeded.

Having mastered his true feelings, he traveled under the sails of a Dutch merchant ship and arrived safely in Batavia. A few weeks later, he sent his brother the following lines: "Here, where I thank God Almighty, here in a new land, I think of *you* and our love with all the joy of a martyr. The new places and fates have expanded my soul; God has given me strength to make the highest sacrifice for friendship. *Yours* — God! At this, a tear fell — the last. I have overcome. — The girl is *yours.* Brother, I was not meant to have her, which means that she would not have been happy with me. And if ever the thought occurred to her that she would have been happy with me — Brother! Brother! Painfully, I turn her over to your soul. Do not forget at what cost she came to be yours! — Always treat this angel as your young love teaches you now! — Treat her as a dear legacy of your brother, whom your arms will never again embrace! Farewell! Do not write to me when you celebrate your wedding night! My wound still bleeds. Write to me how happy you are! — My *deed* is my surety that God will not abandon me in this unknown world."

The marriage was consummated. The most blissful of marriages lasted *one year.* — Then, the woman died. Dying, she confessed to her confidant the unhappiest secret of her heart: She had loved the one who fled more.

Both brothers are still alive today. The older one lives on his estates in Germany, newly married. The younger one remained in Batavia and prospered into a happy man of fortune. He made a vow to never marry, and has kept it.

Translator's Notes

[1] Puff: a character from Johann Timotheus Hermes's novel *Sophiens Reise von Memel nach Sachsen* (1770–72).

[2] *Grandison* (1753), *Pamela* (1740): novels by Samuel Richardson.

2: A Remarkable Example of Female Revenge (Taken from a Manuscript by the late Denis Diderot)

Friedrich Schiller (1785)
Translated by Robert Ellis Dye

THE MARQUIS VON A*** WAS A YOUNG MAN who lived for pleasure. He was pleasant and likeable, but, all in all, had a lax opinion of female virtue.[1] It came to pass, nonetheless, that a lady upset his equanimity. She was called Madame von P***, a rich upper-class widow, distinguished by intelligence, refinement, and gentility. She was proud and exalted in feeling and thought.

The Marquis broke off all of his prior connections, determined to live for this lady alone. He courted her with the greatest diligence, made every imaginable sacrifice in order to convince her of the violence of his affection, and offered her his hand in marriage. The Marquise, however, had not yet forgotten the unhappiness of her first marriage, and preferred any of life's hardships to entering into a second.

This woman lived in secluded retirement. The Marquis had been an acquaintance of her late husband. She had always allowed him to come calling, and her door remained open to him after the death of her husband.

Gallant language toward women, deftly wielded by a man of the world, could not fail to please. The persistence of this man's courtship, reinforced by his personal qualities, his stature, his youth, signs of the most intimate and truest love, and then, on her side, the woman's loneliness, a temperament made for tender feelings, in a word, everything that could conspire to seduce a female heart, succeeded in this case as in others. After the most stubborn struggle with herself and a futile resistance lasting months, Madame von P*** finally surrendered. With all the proper formalities of a solemn oath, the Marquis became a lucky man — and would have continued in this blessed state if his heart had remained true to the tender sentiments it had promised and with which it had been so tenderly rewarded in turn.

Several years had passed when the Marquis began to find the lady's lifestyle somewhat monotonous. He suggested to her that they should go out into society (she consented), receive visitors (she complied with this, too), and give dinner parties (to this she agreed as well). By and by a day passed, or rather several days, without A*** putting in an appearance. He was absent at lunch and again at supper. When he did call, business soon drew him away again. He found it necessary to shorten his visit "this time." Often he would arrive, mumble one or two words, stretch out on the sofa, take this or that magazine in hand, toss it away again, play with the dog, and sometimes even fall asleep. Evening came, and his delicate health prompted him to take his leave at an early hour. This was explicitly insisted on by Tronchin[2] "Truly and beyond doubt, Tronchin is an incomparable man," A*** would say — and so saying, take his hat and cane and vanish, even forgetting to embrace Madame on his departure. Madame von P*** perceived that she was no longer loved, but she wanted to be sure, and this was accomplished as follows:

Once when they had just finished dinner, she began:

"Why so lost in thought, Marquis?"

"And why you, dear Lady?"

"Yes, me too, and melancholy thoughts besides."

"Why so?"

"Nothing."

"That's not true, Madame! Speak up!" — and, he added with a yawn — "Tell me what's bothering you? That will cheer up both of us."

"Are you so very much in need of that when you're with me?"

"No, of course not — but you know — there are times when a man —"

"When a man can't avoid being out of sorts."

"No, Madame, no, no — you're wrong, on my honor, you're wrong. It's nothing. Absolutely nothing. It's just that there are moments — I myself don't know how to put it."

"Dear Friend, there's something on my mind that I've wanted to say to you for some time, but I've been afraid of offending you."

"Offending me? You?"

"Maybe — but God may attest to my innocence. What I feel obliged to admit came about without my wishing it and without my knowledge. There must be a divine curse on the entire human race, since even I — I myself am no exception."

"Oh, Madame — perhaps you're worried that — hm — well, what is it then?"

"What it is? — Oh, I'm unhappy — and I will make you unhappy too. — No, Marquis, it's better that I remain silent."

"Speak up, my Dearest. Would you keep secrets from me? Could you have forgotten that the first stipulation of our liaison was that we would keep nothing from each other?"

"That's just what makes me worry. What you now reproach me with, is all that had been lacking to push my guilt to the limit. Don't you see that my former gaiety has vanished? I have no appetite, no need for sleep. Our intimacy has begun to repel me. I often ask myself at midnight: Is he no longer lovable? And I answer: But he is as he was; what cause do you have for complaint to him? — None in the least. Is it possible that he visits houses of ill repute? No reason to think so. Or do you perhaps find him less affectionate than before? — By no means. But if your friend is still the same, then it must be you who has changed? Yes, it's me. Oh I must confess that it's me. I no longer feel a spark of the longing with which I used to await you — no longer a trace of that sweet anxiety when you didn't come, no shadow of the sweeter delight when you arrived after all, when I heard the sound of your footsteps, when you were announced, when you came through the door — Oh, that's all past — gone, I have become indifferent to you."

"But, Madame?"

Here the lady pressed both hands to her face, let her head drop and was silent for a while. Finally she spoke again, and said:

"I know how you will answer. I'm prepared for your astonishment at hearing me say such bitter things — but be gentle, Marquis — no, don't, don't be gentle. Say everything. I deserve it. I'll have to swallow your reproaches. Yes, dear Marquis, that's how it is — it's true — but isn't it terrible enough that things had to come to this point — must I sink even further to the shame of having misled you? You are still as you were, but I am no longer the same woman. I still do honor and respect you, as much and even more than before, but — the woman you know me to be, a woman aware of the most secret stirrings of her heart, determined never to deceive herself — this woman can no longer deny to herself that her love has flown. This confession — oh, I feel it — it's horrid but nonetheless true — I, a fickle woman, a liar! — Rant and give vent to your feelings, dear Marquis. Curse and condemn me. Call me the vilest names. I've already done this to myself. I can stand to hear anything — everything that you might say except this one thing, that I misled you, that I have dissembled, for that I don't deserve.

Here Madame von P*** turned around on the sofa and began to weep out loud.

The Marquis threw himself at her feet.

"Excellent woman! Divine woman! Woman whose equal one will never find again! Your frankness, your integrity confounds me, moves me — I could die with shame. How grand you are compared to me at this moment, how small I feel in your presence! You have taken the first step in confessing — but it was I who was first at fault. Your sincerity transports me — I would have to be a monster if I hesitated a single moment in replying. Yes, Madame, I cannot deny it: The story of your heart is also the story of my own, word for word. Everything, everything you have said to yourself I too have said to myself. But I held out and kept silent — and would perhaps have kept silent for much longer — maybe I would never have found the courage to declare myself."

"Can that really be true, Marquis?"

"True, Madame — and thus we can both congratulate each other for simultaneously overcoming a passion that was as fleeting as ours proved to be."

"Indeed, Marquis, I would have to be much pitied if my love had outlasted yours."

"You may rely on it, Madame, it was my love that died first."

"Really, Sir! I sense that you may be right."

"Oh, my best Marquise! Never have I found you so charming, so lovely, so beautiful as in this moment. If experience had not made me cautious, who knows whether I would not love you now more passionately than ever before?"

As he said this, he took her two hands and kissed them passionately. Madame von P*** suppressed the deadly grief that tore at her heart and spoke:

"But whatever shall we do now, Marquis? Neither of us, it would seem, can accuse the other of deception. You still have the same claim on my respect as before — and I hope that I have not entirely lost my right to yours. Shall we continue seeing each other? Shall we try to transform our love into tender friendship? In the future this will spare us all those melancholy scenes, all of the petty perfidies, the childish reproaches, and the petulant moods that so often follow a short-lived passion. We will be the only example of our species. You — have your freedom back, now — give me mine back as well. Let us go together through the world in this fashion. You will make me your confidante with each new conquest. I will not hide mine from you, rest assured — if I should happen to experience any, for I am sorely afraid, dear Marquis, that on this point you have made me a little bit hesitant. But everything should go splendidly. You will give me the benefit of your advice from time to time, and I you the benefit of mine. And who knows in the end how things will turn out?"

"That we will, Madame, and it is virtually certain, that you will gain from every comparison — that day after day I will return to you with greater warmth and tenderness, that finally everything, everything will have shown the Marquise von P*** to be the only woman in the world who could possibly make me happy. And if I come back in this frame of mind it will be a holy certainty that I will be forever bound by my love for you."

"But what if, when you returned, you did not find me here? — For you do realize, Marquis, that people often behave oddly. I might some day be overcome by willfulness — caprice — passion for another, even someone perhaps who did not count for much in your eyes."

"That would grieve me, to be sure, Madame, but then I could not complain. I would have no recourse but to accept the fate that separated us, because that was its will, and that it would unite us again, if this were meant to be."

A boring sermon followed on this exchange about the fickleness of the human heart, the vanity of oaths, and about the constraints of marriages. After a cursory embrace the two separated.

As great as was the discipline that the lady had imposed on herself in the presence of her lover, quite as great was the outburst of terrible pain after he had gone. "So it is true," she exclaimed, "it is more than true. He no longer loves me!" — When the first waves of emotion had subsided and she had brooded in quiet rage over the insult she had suffered, she decided on a revenge without example, a revenge that would serve as an awful warning to all men who might take it into their heads to seduce and deceive a woman of honor. And she proceeded to carry out this revenge.

The Marquise had once been acquainted with a certain woman from the provinces who, because of a lawsuit, had moved to Paris with her daughter, a girl of great beauty and good upbringing. She had now learned that this woman had lost her entire fortune in the trial and had been reduced to running a bawdy house. People gathered there, gambled, ate supper, and usually one or two of the guests stayed overnight, to enjoy himself with mother or daughter, according to his preference.

The Marquise dispatched her servants to sleuth out the whereabouts of these women. They were located and invited to pay a visit to Madame von P***, a name that they could barely remember. The women, who went by the names of Madame and Mademoiselle Aisnon in Paris, accepted the invitation with pleasure. The very next morning the mother called on the Marquise, who after the customary initial compliments turned the conversation to the subject of the woman's current way of life.

"To speak frankly, dear Lady," she responded, "we live by a profession that unfortunately brings in very little, is awkward and dangerous, and is moreover one of the most disreputable. It revolts me to death, but necessity knows no law, as the proverb says. I had half a mind to try to place my daughter in the opera, but her voice suffices at best for chamber singing, and she is a mediocre dancer besides. During my litigation and afterward I introduced her to the persons of rank in this city, to government officials, to financiers and prelates, one after another, but — such is the way of the world — the gentlemen cooperated for a short time and in the end left her in the lurch. Dear Lady, it's not as if she were not as pretty as an angel — nor is she without understanding and good manners, but she's lacking in flair for the business[3] and in all the little tricks required to entertain men."

"Are you well known here?" asked the Marquise.

"Unfortunately, only too well known!" said the woman.

"And, as I see, neither of you seems to find much satisfaction or happiness in your profession?"

"Certainly not. My daughter least of all. She never stops begging me either to take her away from it all or take her life. What is more, she is afflicted with persistent bouts of melancholy, and at such times she is totally useless."

"Supposing, then, let us say that I should take it into my mind to effect a splendid improvement in your fate. You wouldn't object too much?"

"I should say not."

"But the question is, whether you will be able to promise to follow in strict obedience and in the smallest detail all orders that I might decide to give you."

"You can count on it, Madame. However hard they might be."

"And I could rely on you to obey whenever it may occur to me to command?"

"We will await your orders with impatience."

"Good. Go home now, Madame. You will soon hear of my further arrangements. In the meantime get rid of your furnishings and household effects; dispose of your clothes, too, especially those with bold or garish colors. These things would only frustrate my plan of attack."

The woman left. Madame von P*** threw herself into her carriage and asked to be driven into the suburbs that seemed to her to be farthest away from Madame Aisnon's apartment. Here, not far from the parish church, she rented a simple apartment in a worthy burgher's house and had it sparsely furnished. She summoned the two Aisnon women there, turned the place and its management over to them, and presented them with a list of the rules they were to follow. These were the following:

"You will not take walks in public, for everything depends on your not being discovered by anyone.

"You will receive no visitors, not even from the neighborhood, for it must appear as though you had completely renounced the world.

"Starting tomorrow, you must wear the attire of devout women.

"Only pious books are to be tolerated at your place, so that you run no risk of backsliding.

"You must attend worship services both on work days and Sundays, and with the most fervent zeal.

"You must endeavor to gain entry to the consulting rooms of some monastery. The monks' gossip may be of use to you.

"You must become well acquainted with the parish priest and the other ministers. We may need to solicit their testimony.

"You are to go to confession and communion at least twice a month.

"Resume your family name, for it is an honorable one, and inquiries may be made about your identity.

"Give alms from time to time, but I expressly forbid you to accept any charity.[4] You are to be seen as neither rich nor poor.

"At home, occupy yourself with sewing, knitting, spinning, and embroidery, and let your work be sold for the benefit of houses for the poor.

"Your way of life is to be one of extreme moderation. I can allow you no more than two small portions at a restaurant from time to time.

"The daughter is never to go out without her mother, the mother never without her daughter. In general, wherever you see a chance to do something edifying without expense, you should never miss the opportunity.

"But once and for all — neither priests nor monks nor friars are ever to be seen within your four walls.

"If you cross the street, walk with eyes modestly cast down to the earth. In church you are to see no one but God.

"I admit that these are hard constraints, but they won't last forever and your reward will be extraordinary. Now take counsel with yourselves. If you're afraid that these rules will exceed your powers, say so frankly now. It will neither offend nor alienate me. I forgot to say, by the way, that it would be good to practice using the vocabulary of mystics and to become so familiar with the idioms of Holy Scripture as to make them second nature. Express your hostility to the *philosophes*[5] at every opportunity and go around referring to Voltaire as the Antichrist. Farewell now. We will not see each other again in your house, for I am unworthy to socialize with such holy women. But don't be distressed about that. You may quietly come to my place, and there behind closed doors we will recoup what we may have missed.

"However, I expressly ask of you — take care that with all your pious acting you don't become pious on me in earnest. The expenditures for your household will be my concern. If our scheme works, the day will come when you will be in no need of my support. Should it fail through no fault of your own, I have resources enough to make your lives bearable and, indeed, infinitely more bearable than the life you're giving up as a favor to me. But remember, obedience. Blind, unconditional obedience to my commands or I guarantee nothing, neither for the present nor for the future."

While our two devout women went about edifying the world and spreading the sweet aroma of their holiness everywhere, Madame von P*** showed every sign of respect and a trusting friendship toward the Marquis. He was welcome whenever he came in sight, was received cordially and without any sulking or any change at all on her part, even when he had been absent for longer periods and proceeded to unpack all of his little adventures for her delectation. She listened with the most genuine amusement and offered him sympathy and advice in every predicament. Once in a while she let fall a word about marriage, but always in the spirit of the most disinterested friendship and without seeming to refer to herself in any way. If at tender moments the Marquis was moved to become gallant and say flattering things to her — things a man can hardly resist saying when talking with a woman he has known so well — she replied only with a smile or pretended not to have noticed. A friend such as he was, she said, assured her of complete happiness — her youth was behind her, her passions extinguished.

"But, Madame!" he answered in amazement. "And you have nothing new to confess to me?"

"Nothing at all."

"Not even about the little count who used to be such a fierce rival?"

"My door is closed to him. I will never see him again."

"But that is odd, Madame. Why, for heaven's sake?"

"Because he is repulsive to me."

"Admit it, Madame. Admit it. I see it in your eyes. You still love me, don't you?"

"That could well be."

"And are counting on my return?"

"Why should I be denied that comfort?"

"And if I should have the good fortune — or misfortune? — of falling in love with you again, would you not reap some compensatory satisfaction from your nobleness in drawing a veil over my past misconduct?"

"You have a high opinion of my generosity."

"Oh, Madame, after all that you have already done, there is no act of heroism that I would put past you."

"I am infinitely pleased by that."

"On my honor, Madame, you are truly a dangerous woman. That much is certain."

Thus matters stood when the third month had already passed and the lady finally concluded that the time had come to begin to play her cards. One beautiful summer day when the Marquis was expected for dinner she directed the two Aisnons to go for a walk in the royal garden. The Marquis appeared at table, dinner was served, a little earlier and more lavishly than usual, the conversation was at its liveliest. After they had dined the lady proposed a short stroll, if this would not interfere with more important commitments. It happened that neither a play nor an opera was being given, and the Marquis suggested that they take a look at the exhibition of prints in the Royal Cabinet.[6] Nothing could have been more welcome to the lady. She did not hesitate to agree. The horses are called for and hitched up. They climb aboard. They are soon in the royal garden and, in the bustle of the great world, gaping at everything and seeing nothing, as is usually the case.

After they had left the Royal Cabinet, they mingled among the others strolling in the garden. Their course led them along a path in the direction of the plant nursery, when Madame von P*** suddenly cried out in surprise: "Is it they? It *is* they! No, I am not mistaken! It is really they!" And with these words she ran ahead of the Marquis and flew toward our two pious sisters. The young Aisnon was enchanting, her modest dress permitting the observer to lose himself entirely in the contemplation of her person.

"Ah, is it you, Madame?"

"Yes, it's me. Yes, of course. And how are you now? How have you been in the eternity since we last saw each other?"

"You know of our bad luck, Madame. What was to be done? We have had to restrict our lifestyle, cut our coat according to our cloth, and say farewell to a world in which we could no longer appear with the former dignity."

"But to forsake me, me of all people — for I too no longer belong to the world and find it as distasteful as it in fact is! That was not right, my dear ones."

"Mistrust, dear Lady, has been the companion of misfortune from time immemorial. Victims of misfortune are quick to fear becoming a burden."

"A burden? You a burden on me? How could you not know that I would resent such thoughts for the rest of my life?"

"It is not my fault, dear Lady," said the daughter. "I have spoken to Mother of you a hundred times, but her answer was always: 'Madame von P***? Say no more, my child. Nobody thinks of us any more.'"

"How unjust you are! But let us sit down. Let us mend things right here on the spot. Here, my dear friends, meet the Marquis von A***, a good friend of mine who will not disturb us in the least. But my! How Mademoiselle has grown up. How beautiful she has become since we last saw each other!"

"This we owe to our poverty, Madame, which at least has the merit of improving our health. Look at her eyes, look at her arms. That's what regularity and moderation, what sleep, hard work, and a clear conscience can do. Not a small thing, dear Lady."

They sat down and chatted cordially. The older Dame Aisnon spoke well, the younger very little. Both maintained a demeanor of pious humility, but without putting on airs or exaggerating. Long before evening the two devout sisters took their leave. They were urged to stay, the sun was still high in the sky, but the mother whispered to the Marquise — audibly enough — that they were going to attend a devotional service, which they never missed. When they were some distance away, Madame von P*** realized that she had neglected to ask for their address. The Marquis immediately ran after them to rectify this oversight. But although the women gladly took down the noble lady's address, the Marquis' efforts to obtain theirs were in vain. He couldn't find the courage to offer them his carriage, an impulse that had been on the tip of his tongue, as he later admitted to Madame von P***.

The first thing he did was to inquire in greater detail who these women were. "Two creatures," was her answer, "who are at least happier than you and I. Did you not notice their exuberant health? The serenity on their faces? The innocence and propriety of their speech? You never see anything like that in our circles. We pity the devout, but the devout pity us in turn, and in the end who knows but that they may be in the right?"

"But pray, reassure me, Madame. You haven't taken it into your head to become a lady of prayer yourself?"

"And pray tell, why not?"

"I implore you, Madame. Heaven forbid that the rupture in our relations, if that's what it was, should drive you to insanity."

"So you would like it better if I again opened my door to the little count."

"A thousand times better."

"And you yourself would advise me to do so."

"Without hesitation."

Madame von P*** told the Marquis what she knew of the origins and fortunes of her two lady friends, mixing as many interesting details into the story as she could. Finally she added:

"What you have here are two female creatures such as you will rarely find, especially the daughter. In Paris a figure such as that girl's would insure its possessor against any need whatsoever if she were inclined to turn it to her advantage, as you well know. But these women have chosen an honorable indigence over a disgraceful affluence. So little remains of their fortune that I can't imagine how they get by. They work night and day. To bear poverty when one was born poor is a virtue of which thousands may be capable, but to trade the greatest wealth for the most extreme poverty and still be satisfied, even deem oneself happy, is a phenomenon that I will never be able to explain. Only religion can accomplish this. It's all very well for the high and mighty to show off their worldly wisdom, but religion is truly glorious."

"For the unfortunate, certainly."

"And who is not unfortunate, more or less — sooner or later?"

"I will be totally confounded, Marquise, if you are not one day declared a saint."

"As if this were such a terrible sentence! How little this life means to me when I weigh it against the future of eternity."

"You already talk like an apostle."

"I speak as someone with conviction. My dear Marquis, answer me this — honestly and without reservation — what if the joys and horrors of that future world were dangled more visibly before us? To what tiny dimensions would the riches of this one shrink in our eyes? Who but a madman would undertake to seduce a young girl or a loving wife at her husband's side if the thought occurred to him: I could die in her arms and be damned for all eternity?"

"And yet this happens every day."

"Because nobody believes in God any more — because everyone is out of his mind."

"Or rather, Madame, because our customs have nothing to do with our religion. But, my dear Marquise, what am I to make of you just now? You seem to be rushing head over heels to the confessional box."

"You suppose there's something more clever that I could do."[7]

"Go on! You're pulling my leg! You still have a good twenty years to fritter away however you like. First enjoy them and then regret them, or boast about them to your father confessor, for all I care. — But our conversation has taken such a melancholy turn. Your imagination, Madame, is becoming unbearably morose. And this comes from your abominable cloistered existence, I swear. Follow my example, Madame. Bring the little count back, and I'll wager soul and salvation that you'll stop dreading hell and the devil and become as lovable as before. Are you perhaps afraid that I will condemn you because of this in the event that our former relationship were eventually restored? — For it could turn out that we won't come together again, and then you would have deprived yourself of the sweetest time of your life for the sake of a stubborn chimera. And if I am to speak plainly, Madame, the triumph of proving yourself more virtuous than I is not worth such a sacrifice."

A few more strides up and down the path and they climbed back into their carriage. After several moments' pause Madame von P*** began again.

"Amazing, how old you can suddenly feel! The girl was not much taller than a head of cabbage when she came to Paris for the first time."

"You mean the young woman we just encountered with her mother?"

"Yes, her. You see, Marquis. She reminds me of a garden where fresh roses keep springing up to replace the wilted ones. Did you take a good look at her?"

"I did not fail to do so."

"Well, and what did you think of her?"

"The head of the Virgin Mary, as painted by Raphael, on the body of his Galatea. — Oh, and the inexpressibly lovely voice —."

"And the modesty in her eyes!"

"And the propriety and grace of her every gesture."

"And the maturity of her conversation, which is otherwise never found in a girl like her. You see what a good upbringing will do."

"Yes, given such an excellent native endowment."

The Marquis brought Madame von P*** home. She could hardly wait to inform her two friends of her satisfaction with the first act of the farce.

From this time on the Marquis began to double his visits to the Marquise. She pretended not to notice. Never did she steer the conversation to the subject of the two women, it was he who always had to mention them first, and he did so with impatience — but with a feigned indifference that invariably failed its intended effect.

"Have you seen your two friends?"

"No."

"Do you know that you're not the least bit nice, dear Lady? You enjoy a fortune, these two women suffer want, and you don't even offer them an occasional dinner?"

"But I would have thought that the Marquis von A*** might have been more familiar with my way of thinking. In earlier days love might have loaned me this or that virtue, but now I have only friendship, which gives me nothing but weakness. Nonetheless, I have invited them to dinner at least ten times, but they always decline. They have their reasons for avoiding my house, and if I go to see them, I'm obliged to leave my carriage at the end of the block and to remove all jewelry and make-up beforehand. Don't be surprised at this unusual precaution. Their benefactors could all too easily be put off by somebody's ambiguous interpretation of things. It is not easy to do good these days, Marquis."

"Especially for the devout."

"When one can escape an obligation on the slightest pretext. If it came to light that I was involved, people would soon say, Madame von P*** is their benefactress. They need no further subsidy — and the alms would stop."

"What, alms?"

"Yes, Milord, alms."

"These women are your friends and obliged to live on charity?"

"Just as I thought! Dear Marquis, I see clearly now that you have stopped loving me. I've lost not only your tender feelings but also your esteem at the same time. Whoever gave you the idea that it is my fault that these women live on money offerings?"

"My apologies, Madame. I spoke too soon. I beg a thousand times for your forgiveness. But what reason could they possibly have to refuse the support of a good friend?"

"Ah, my dear Marquis, we people of the world have little comprehension of the marvelous scruples of saints. They regard it as improper to indiscriminately accept benefits from strangers."

"But then they deny us the only means of once in a while making up for our senseless indulgences."

"I don't see it that way at all. Supposing the Marquis von A*** took the fate of these two persons to heart, could he not find a way of sending his gifts to them by worthier mediators?"

"Worthier but perhaps less reliable ones?"

"That may well be."

"What do you think, Madame, if for example I wanted to send them twenty louis, would they reject my gift?"

"There is nothing more certain. To you, though, my dear Marquis, such obstinacy on the part of the mother of such a beautiful child would seem senseless, without a doubt."

"So you imagine I was tempted to go visit them myself?"

"You are right, Marquis, right you are. Marquis, you'd best be on guard! The sympathy that is beginning to stir in your heart strikes me as very unexpected and more than suspicious."

"Maybe. But tell me, would they have received me?"

"No, you may rely on it, they would not have. The splendor of your carriage, the opulence of your clothes, the obsequiousness of your servants, the image of a handsome young man — no more would have been required to alarm the whole neighborhood and destroy the poor unfortunates."

"What you say hurts me, Madame, for, on my honor, that was not my intention. So I guess I must deny myself the pleasure of seeing them and doing them a kindness."

"So it seems."

"But if my gifts were relayed by you?"

"I would not like to lend my good offices to such a questionable benevolence."

"But that is downright perverse."

"Perverse! Yes, you may be right!"

"The things you imagine! I believe you are jesting with me, Madame. A girl that I've seen only once in my life!"

"Take care, I tell you. You are on the verge of making yourself unhappy. Better for me to be your guardian angel now than your comforter later. Do you really suppose that you are dealing here with creatures like others you know well enough? Make no mistake, good Marquis. Women such as these are not easily tempted, overcome, and conquered. They won't understand your signals. They won't fall into your trap."

An urgent obligation suddenly occurred to the Marquis. He arose abruptly and sullenly left the room.

Things went on in this way for many weeks. The Marquis let no day go by without seeing Madame von P***. He arrived, threw himself upon the sofa, and said nothing. Madame von P*** conversed, seemingly with herself. The Marquis stayed for a quarter hour and then disappeared again. At last he stayed away for a whole month, then he reappeared, full of melancholy and looking like a corpse. Madame von P*** was shocked at his appearance.

"How you look, Marquis? Where have you been? Were you bound in chains this last month?"

"In truth, by God! In desperation I threw myself into the most despicable fool's paradise."

"How so, desperation?"

"Exactly, Madame, desperation."

With these words he paced to and fro, hither and thither, went to the window, stared at the clouds, returned, stopped in front of her, went to the door, called one of his servants, sent him away again, came to a stop in front of the lady, wanted to speak — but couldn't. Madame von P*** sat quietly at her desk, without seeming to notice him. Finally she took pity on his plight and spoke:

"What's the matter with you, Marquis? You're out of sight for an entire month, and now you return looking like a man who has just thrown off his death shroud and carrying on like a soul in purgatory!"

"I can stand it no longer. I will — I must — You shall hear all. That girl, the daughter of your friend, has made a deep impression on my heart. I've tried every means of forgetting her, but in vain — the more I struggled against it, the deeper was the memory engraved on my mind. I am possessed by this angelic creature. You must come to my aid."

"Well?"

"There's no help for it. I must, must see her again, and it's only you who will be able to arrange this. I've arranged disguises for my servants and sent them to spy on the ladies. They go nowhere but to church and back, out the door and then back home. A dozen times have I gone on foot and put myself in their way. They haven't deigned to honor me with a glance. I've planted myself in vain beside their door. In an effort to forget them I turned into the most dissolute scoundrel, in an effort to please them, I became devout and holy as a martyr and went to mass fifteen days in a row. Oh, what a figure, my dear Friend! How charming! How inexpressibly beautiful!"

Madame von P***, who knew everything already, replied to the Marquis: "That is, you've done everything to make them shun you and left no stone unturned to make yourself appear the fool to them, and in this you have fully succeeded."

"Oh, and succeeded to an awful degree. Will you not take pity on me, Madame? Will you help me to the inestimable bliss of seeing this angel again?"

"The matter requires thought. I certainly will not consider it unless you make me the most solemn promise to leave this poor unfortunate girl in peace and stop persecuting her. And I won't conceal from you, Marquis, that the women have most grievously expressed to me their discomfort at your importunities. Take a look at this letter."

The letter she handed to the Marquis had been concocted by the three women together. It was designed to make it appear that the younger Aisnon had written it under the supervision of her mother, but they did not neglect to weave into it as many noble and tender sentiments, as much taste and intelligence, as was needed to turn the Marquis' head completely. He reacted to every thought expressed with a shout of joy, read every word twice, and tears of delight flowed from his eyes.

"You must agree, Madame, that nothing more divine has ever been written. Oh, Madame, I worship the woman who can feel and write like that."

"As you are obliged to do."

"I swear to you, I will keep my word, but I beg you, I entreat you, you must do the same."

"Truly, Marquis. I almost feel like the greater fool of the two of us. It must be so, you must have unlimited power over me. This terrifies me."

"So, when can I see her?"

"That, I cannot yet tell you. Above all, any meeting must be so well prepared that no suspicion is aroused. The women know of your obsession. You need to consider in what kind of light my friendship would appear if they should arrive at the remotest suspicion that I was helping you. But — honestly, dear Marquis — why should I become entangled in all this embarrassment? What concern is it of mine whether you're in love or not in love? Whether you're a fool or a clever fellow? Untie your own twisted knot. The role you want me to play is odd indeed."

"If you abandon me, my dear Friend, I am lost. I will avoid weighing my own interest in the balance. I know that this would only offend you. But I do exhort you to help me, for the sake of these dear, good, these heavenly creatures. You know how I am, Madame. Spare them the fits of madness of which you know me capable. I will go to them on my own. Yes, that I will — in God's name — I warn you. I'll break down their door — I'll use violence to gain entry. I will sit down, and say —. I will —. Oh, how can I know what I will say to them, what I will do? But I can be terrible when I'm in this state of mind."

His every word was like the thrust of a dagger in Madame von P***'s heart. She nearly suffocated with resentment and inner rage, but, stammering, she continued:

"I cannot entirely condemn your ardor. — But —— Yes! If someone had loved me with such passion, maybe —. But enough of this. It is not for your sake that I will act. I only hope that Milord the Marquis will give me some time."

"The shortest possible time."

"Oh, how this hurts!" she cried when he was gone. "My suffering is terrible, but I will not suffer alone. Most despicable of men, how long my torment will last is unclear, but yours shall be — eternal."

She was able to put off the Marquis' expectation of the promised meeting for a month. During this interval he languished, blunted his passion with drink, and found that his feelings were only intensified by conversations with Madame von P***. He asked about the women's origins, from which province they came, about their education, and could never learn enough, so he kept on asking and was informed and stimulated anew. The Marquise, for her part, was wicked enough to call attention to every increase in his fervor, and, under the pretext of cautioning him, prepared him for the desperate outcome of the adventure that she foresaw and held in store.

"Be careful," she said. "This could take you farther than you wish to go. The time could come when I could no longer defend our friendship, which you so mercilessly abuse — neither to myself nor to others. To be sure, hardly a day passes without some insane farce being played out somewhere, but I am afraid, Marquis, I'm afraid this woman will never be yours — or yours only on conditions that would hardly be to your liking."

After Madame von P*** had satisfied herself that the Marquis was ripe for the roasting, she arranged for the two Aisnons to have dinner with her, telling the Marquis that he should drop in on them, dressed in travel clothes. This plan was carried out.

They were in the midst of the second course when the Marquis had his presence announced. He, Madame von P*** and the two Aisnons affected the most authentic surprise.

"Madame," he said, "I have just arrived from my estates. It is too late that I should now return home, where they can hardly still expect me. I hope you will allow me to be your guest."

With these words he fetched a chair and took his place at the table, which was carefully set so that he was seated by the mother and across from the daughter, for which he thanked Madame von P*** with a subtle wink. The two women had recovered from their initial embarrassment. All chattered gaily and were even in high spirits. The Marquis treated the mother with the most fitting attentiveness and the daughter with the finest courtesy and tact. The women were greatly amused to observe how anxiously the Marquis avoided any hint of indelicacy. They let him chatter blissfully on for three whole hours, and finally Madame von P*** said to him:

"Your conversation, Marquis, does your parents the greatest honor. The first lessons of childhood are never lost. Truly, you have so fully researched the secrets of spiritual love that one would think you had spent your entire life in monasteries. Were you never tempted to become a Quietist?"

"Not that I recall, Madame."

We need hardly mention that our two devout women seasoned the conversation with every wit, finesse, and seductive grace. Only in passing did anyone touch on the topic of passion, and Mademoiselle Duquenoi — for that was her family name — proclaimed that of all the passions only one was dangerous. The Marquis whole-heartedly agreed. Between six and seven, mother and daughter arose to leave; every attempt to keep them longer was futile. Madame von P*** and Madame Duquenoi averred that pleasure must yield to duty, if they were not to end each day with a guilty conscience. So, to the Marquis' great disappointment, the women went home and left him and Madame von P*** to have a tête-à-tête by themselves.

"Now, Marquis? Am I not a complete fool? — Show me another woman in Paris who would have done as much."

"No, Madame, never! No one else would have done it!" — and here he threw himself at her feet. "There's no one else in the world like you. Your goodness shames me. You are the only true friend on earth."

"Are you sure, Marquis, that you will always judge my conduct in the same way as today?"

"I would be an ungrateful monster if I ever changed my mind."

"Well, then, on another matter, how do things now stand in your heart?"

"If I am to speak frankly, the girl must be mine or I am lost."

"Indeed, she must, but the question is — at what price?"

"We will see."

"Marquis, I know you. And I know these women. The scheme could go awry."

The Marquis stayed away for two months. In the meantime he was more active than ever. He approached the father confessor of the two Duquenoi women in order to add the power of religion to the force of his desire. This little cleric, who slyly and hypocritically adduced all of the difficulties that his faith would have placed in opposition to the Marquis' base intentions, sold his good offices as dearly as possible, and, duly remunerated, resigned himself to everything required of him.

The first piece of villainy to which the man of God resorted was to deny the two devout women the charity of the congregation and to make representations to the diocese implying that the protégées of Madame von P*** were illegally accepting contributions at the expense of needier members of the congregation. His intention was to add increased misery to the test of their virtue.

Further, he strove in the confessional box to incite discord between mother and daughter. If the mother criticized the daughter, he sought to magnify the latter's transgressions and to heighten the mother's displeasure. If the younger woman complained, he made it clear that there was a limit to parental power and that, if her mother's persecutions did not stop, the Church might find it necessary to free her from maternal tyranny. In the meantime, he urged her to multiply her confessions as penance.

On another occasion he brought up the subject of her handsome figure and said that beauty was the most dangerous gift that heaven could bestow upon a woman. He let fall a word in passing about an honest nobleman who had fallen for her, a man he didn't want to name but whom he described accurately enough nonetheless. He proceeded to praise God's mercy and heaven's indulgence of human needs that were the legacy of the flesh — certain desires that even the holiest of humans could not entirely avoid. He inquired whether certain urges were not beginning to stir in her heart, whether from time to time she didn't experience certain undulations of spirit — whether she didn't have certain dreams — whether the presence of men didn't inspire certain foolish thoughts. And he wondered whether it was better for a woman to resist a man's desire or to yield to it, whether one should risk letting a man die of passion, a man for whom the redeemer's blood had been shed as much for anybody else. He would not presume to answer this question himself. He ended with a deep and holy sigh, turned his eyes heavenward and prayed for the souls in purgatory. Mademoiselle Duquenoi left him to himself and faithfully reported everything to her mother and to Madame von P***, who suggested new secrets that she might betray to the holy confessor.

They now expected with great confidence that sooner or later the man of God would offer his services as a conveyor of love letters to his spiritual daughter, and this expectation was fulfilled. But how carefully he undertook this! The priest could not say whose hand had written the letter — no doubt, some sympathetic soul in his congregation, who, moved by their poverty, sought to be of assistance while remaining anonymous. He had often enough received such requests.

"One more thing, Mademoiselle," he continued, "do be careful. Your mother is a reasonable woman. Permit me to urge you to open this letter in her presence."

Mademoiselle pocketed the letter and then handed it over to her mother, who in turn sent it to Madame von P***. The Marquise, now in possession of a solid piece of evidence, summoned the priest, dressed him down severely, and threatened to reveal the entire affair to his superiors if she heard another word about him.

The letter overflowed with the Marquis' praise, praise both for himself and for the mademoiselle. It painted his passion in the strongest and most terrible colors, made incredible promises, spoke even of the possibility of abduction.

After Madame von P*** had duly read the text to the priest, she summoned the Marquis and declared how much she lamented such unbecoming behavior in a man of honor and how hurtful it had been that he had implicated her. She then showed him the letter and declared that the duties of the most tender friendship, which heretofore had obtained between them, would not stop her from contacting Madame Duquenoi, yes, even the authorities, if his persecutions should continue.

"Marquis, Marquis," she added, "love is making a wicked man of you. Perhaps you were born wicked, for what would inspire great deeds in someone else, seems only to bring out vile actions from you. Whatever did these two poor women do to you that you now conspire to make their poverty bitterer by compounding it with scandal? Because the girl is beautiful and determined to preserve her virtue, you decide to persecute her. Do you want to be the reason that she comes to curse heaven's best gift? And what have I done to deserve to become an accomplice of your scurrilous deeds, most ungrateful of men? No doubt you will soon kneel before me, beg me for forgiveness, and swear to leave my unhappy friends in peace." — The Marquis promised to take no further step without first informing Madame von P***, but he had to have the girl, whatever the price.

In no way did he keep his promise. For one thing, since the mother, Madame Duquenoi, knew of the whole affair, he felt no scruples about turning to her directly. He conceded the baseness of his intentions, offered her large sums of money, spoke of the brilliant hopes that would ripen in time, and attached to his letter a box of the most precious jewels.

The three women took counsel with each other. The mother and the daughter appeared much inclined to accept the bargain, but Madame von P*** did not see herself sufficiently compensated. She reminded them of the first article of their contract and even threatened to reveal the whole deception if they did not obey her. To the great distress of the two saints, the daughter in particular, who was as slow as possible to take off the new earrings that so enhanced her beauty, the jewels, accompanied by a letter expressing all the pride of offended virtue, had to migrate back to their owner.

Madame von P*** bitterly reproached the Marquis for his breach of word. He excused himself with the explanation that he would not have dared to demean her with a commission of this sort. "Dear Marquis," she said to him, "I warned you at the beginning and I now repeat that you are a long way from the goal you're striving for. But now the time to preach to you has passed — more words would be in vain. You are simply lost, once and for all." The Marquis answered that his hopes were still high and that he only wished to be granted permission to try a final stratagem.

This was to declare himself ready to offer the women a very considerable annuity, indeed to share his entire fortune with them in equal parts, and to give them ownership of one of his houses in Paris and another on his estates for as long as they should live. "Do as you please," said the Marquise, "I forbid only violence. — But uprightness and true honor, believe me, my friend, cannot be bought. Your latest offer will be no more acceptable than your earlier ones. I know these people and can vouch for their virtue."

The Marquis' latest proposals were aired in a plenary session of the three women. The madame and mademoiselle silently awaited the Marquise's final judgment. — She paced up and down the length of the room without speaking. ——— "No! No! No!" she finally shouted. "That is much too merciful. — No! Much too little for my wounded heart" and declared her refusal, irrevocably. Both mother and daughter threw themselves weeping at her feet, pled with her and said how unspeakably cruel it would be to deny them a fortune they could accept without any risk at all.

Madame von P*** coldly replied: "Do you imagine that everything we've done so far was done for your sake? Who are you to me? What debts do I owe you? What would stop me from sending you both, the mother as well as the daughter, back to your former profession? I will gladly believe that the Marquis' offers are too great for you to resist, but for me they are still much too little. Sit down, Madame — write exactly what I dictate to you, that the letter may be dispatched right here in my presence." —— More incredulous than unhappy, the women struck out for home.

The Marquis arrived at the Marquise's house soon thereafter. "Well," she said. "How did you make out with your latest gifts?"

"Offered and rejected. I despair. If I could just tear this passion from my heart, tear my heart out with it, I would be satisfied! — Tell me, Marquise, do you not discern little similarities in the girl's features with my own?"

"I never wanted to bring it up, but, yes, I do recognize some. Now, however, is not the time to talk of them. What have you decided?"

"How do I know? How can I know? Oh, Madame, I feel overcome with desire to throw myself into the first post chaise and to travel as far away as the globe is round. A moment later my strength is gone. I am as though lame. My head spins. My senses grow dull. I forget who I am, and what is to become of me."

"No, don't travel. What's the point of going to the Villejuif[8] if you're only going to turn around and come back home?"

The next morning a letter came from him to Madame von P*** in which he announced that he had gone to his country estate and would remain there for as long as his feelings permitted — and he most earnestly beseeched her to remember him to her two friends. His absence was brief. He came back to town and stopped at the house of the Marquise. She was away. On her return she found him rigidly stretched out on the sofa with his eyes closed.

"Ah! So you're back, Marquis? The country air seems not to have agreed with you."

"Oh, Madame, no place agrees with me. You see me here again, and see me ready to commit the most monstrous folly that a man of my position, rank, birth, and fortune could ever imagine. But better anything than submit forever to this torture. I'm going to marry."

"Marquis! Marquis! This is a big step and needs serious thought."

"Thought? I have only one thought, the most fundamental of all. It is that I could never become more miserable than I already am."

"You can't yet be sure about that."

"Well, Madame. This, I should think, is finally a mission that I can assign to you in good conscience. Go see them. Speak with the mother, look into the daughter's heart, and deliver my proposal of marriage."

"Easy, dear Marquis. To be sure, I have thought myself sufficiently well acquainted with these two women to dare to act on their behalf to the extent that I have. But now that it is a question of my good friend's happiness, he will surely allow me to consider the matter more closely. I'll inquire about them in their home province and trace their steps, one after another, through their entire stay in the city."

"A precaution, Madame, that strikes me as unnecessary. Women who in misfortune were so steadfastly honorable and who so stoutheartedly resisted my seduction must be the rarest of creatures. — I would have won a duchess with such presents. — Besides, did not you yourself say ——?"

"Yes, indeed, yes, yes. I said everything you wanted me to say. Nonetheless, you will be so gracious as to let me have my way."

"Why don't *you* get married too, my dear Marquise?"

"To whom? If I may ask."

"To whom? —— Your little count. He's bright — has money — and comes from a good family."

"And who would guarantee me that he would be faithful? — You perhaps?"

"Well, no, but with husbands no one takes that too seriously any more."

"Do you think? But if I were foolish enough to be offended anyway, what then? And I do have a *vengeful* streak, Marquis."

"Well, yes, but then you should go ahead and take your revenge. That goes without saying. You know what, Marquise? We four could live together, in a commune. We would make the nicest little club in the world."

"That all sounds wonderful, but I will never marry again. The only man I might yet have given my hand to ——."

"Not me, surely, Madame?"

"Now I can confess it without any risk."

"Now? Why only now? Why didn't you tell me this before?"

"I did well not to, as present circumstances persuade me. And all in all the one you are now planning to marry suits you better than I in every respect."

Madame von P*** carried out her research with the greatest precision and haste. She presented the Marquis with the most flattering testimony about his future bride, from both the province and the capital, but insisted nevertheless that he should take another fourteen days to consider the matter thoroughly. The two weeks seemed like an eternity to him, and Madame von P*** finally saw herself obliged to accede to his infatuated impatience. The next meeting took place at the home of the two Duquenoi women. The engagement was sealed, the marriage banns were published, the Marquis presented Madame von P*** with a precious diamond, and the wedding was celebrated.

The *wedding night* went as hoped for. The next morning Madame von P*** sent the Marquis a letter in which she summoned him briefly to her place for the sake of an urgent bit of business. He did not keep her waiting and was received by a woman whose countenance was a portrait of indignation and *Schadenfreude* combined, painted in the most vivid colors. His surprise was soon dispelled.

"Marquis," she said to him, "it is time you finally learned who I am. If others of my sex enjoyed enough self-esteem to emulate my revenge, *you* and *your* ilk would be less common. A noble lady gave herself to you without reservation. — You lacked the brains to keep her. *I* am that woman, but she has gotten even, traitor, and forever tied you to a woman who is worthy of you. Step across the street to the inn called the City of Hamburg. There they will be able to tell you all about the shameful trade that your wife and your mother-in-law plied for ten years under the name of Madame and Mademoiselle Aisnon.

No description could capture the horror with which the Marquis collapsed to the floor. He lost his senses, but his indecision lasted only as long as it took him to run from one end of the city to the other. He did not come home the whole day, he roamed the streets. His wife and his mother-in-law began to suspect what might have happened. At the first pounding on the door, the latter fled and bolted the door of her room. His wife awaited him alone in hers. His expression announced the rage in his heart as he entered. She threw herself at his feet, face down on the floor, and made no sound.

"Out, unworthy woman," he cried dreadfully, "get away from me!"

She tried to get up but fell unconscious on her face, her arms outstretched on the floor.

"Oh, merciful Sir," she said to him. "Kick me, trample me under your feet. — I deserve it. Do what you will with me, but mercy, have mercy on my mother."

"Get away," he yelled again. "Away, accursed wretch, out of my eyes. — Is it not enough that you blanket me with shame? Do you want to make me commit a crime as well?"

The poor creature stayed as she was, without moving or speaking. The Marquis fell into a chair, his head buried in his arms, his body half lying on the foot of his bed, and broke out in loud sobbing: "Get away from me, I say." — The silence of the unfortunate woman, who still lay on the floor as if dead, exhausted his patience. "Be gone from here!" he shouted louder and more violently, leaned down and was about to deliver a cruel blow — but he saw that she lay unconscious and almost lifeless. He seized her around the waist, laid her on the couch and watched her for a while, first with rage, then with pity in his eyes. Finally he rang the bell. His servants entered. Her women were called.

"Take care of your mistress," he said to them. "She is not well. Take her to your rooms and attend to her." — A little later he quietly sent someone to inquire about her condition. The news was that although she had regained consciousness after the first swoon, the frequency and duration of subsequent fainting fits made them fear for her life. An hour later, he sent a second secret inquiry and learned that she lay tortured by terrible attacks of anxiety and that a gouty choking had befallen her that could be heard down on the street. An inquiry the following morning brought the news that she had wept a great deal, but that the other symptoms had slowly abated.

He had the horses hitched to his carriage and disappeared for two weeks, during which period of time no one knew of his whereabouts. He had seen to it before leaving that both mother and daughter were provided with the necessities, and commanded his servants to obey the mother as they would himself.

While he was away the two women lived in misery together, hardly speaking. The young wife dissolved in sighs and tears or in sudden fits of screaming, wringing her hands and tearing at her hair in such wild despair that even her mother dared not approach and offer comfort. The older woman assumed a demeanor of callousness, the younger was the saddest picture of regret, pain, and despair.

A thousand times she called out: "Come, Mama, let us flee, let us find shelter against his vengeance!" A thousand times the mother resisted and replied, "No, my child, let us stay. Let us wait and see how far he will go. He can't murder us, after all." "Oh, if only he could," cried the daughter, "If only he had done it already!" — "Quiet," said the mother, "and stop talking like a fool."

The Marquis returned and secluded himself in his private room, where he wrote two letters, one to his wife, another to his mother-in-law. This woman departed that same day and traveled to a cloister, where she soon died. The daughter got dressed and staggered to her husband's room as he had asked. She knelt down on the threshold. He ordered her to get up. Instead, she crawled toward him on her knees. Her limbs trembled, her hair was undone and fell down over her shoulders,[9] her body hung heavy, but she held her head up, and her eyes, flowing with tears, met his.

"I see, oh, Milord," she said between sobs, "I see that your anger has softened, justified though it was. I presume to hope that I may yet experience your compassion. But, no — there's no rush. — So many virtuous girls have become ugly wives. Won't you let me see if I can become an example of the opposite? I am not yet worthy to be yours, but I beg you not to deny me all hope. Let me live apart from you, observe my conduct from afar and then judge me! — Happy, yes, unspeakably happy would I be if you deigned to call me to you once in a while. Pick any dark corner in your house that I could occupy, and I will confine myself there without complaint. — It was weakness, seduction, the authority and threats of others that brought me to this pass, but I have never been bad. If I were, how could I have risked showing you my face, how could I have ventured to behold you, to speak with you! — If you could see into my soul, you would convince yourself how far my former crimes lie from the desires of my heart, how abominable I find the customs of those whom I once viewed as my equals. Seduction stained my reputation, but it has not poisoned my heart. I know myself, oh, Milord. If I had been free to speak, it would have cost me only a word, and you would have known of the entire deception. Do with me as you please. Call your servants. Have these jewels and these clothes torn from my body. Have me thrown into the streets at midnight. I am willing to suffer anything, anything, to submit to any fate you may impose on me. Loneliness in the country, the stillness of a cloister can take me out of your sight forever. Only command and I will go. Your happiness is not irrevocably lost. You can still forget me."

"Get up," said the Marquis in a gentle voice, "I forgive you, please get up. Even in the midst of the horrible feeling of the shame I had suffered, I never failed to honor you as my wife. No word crossed my lips that could have demeaned you, and if any such thing had happened, I would be ready to beg your forgiveness. I give you my word that you will never hear such a thing from me again. Always remember that you cannot make your husband unhappy unless you yourself are unhappy. — Be noble and good. Be happy and take care that *I* too may be happy! Get up, I beg you. — You are not in your proper place, Marquise. Stand up! —— Stand up, Wife, and let me embrace you!"

While he was thus speaking, she still knelt before him, her face hidden in his hands, but hearing herself addressed as "Wife," she rose quickly, threw her arms around his neck and drew him in wild delight to her breast. Then she released him again, fell to the floor, and tried to kiss his feet.

"What are you doing?" he said full of emotion. "Have I not forgiven you for everything? Why don't you believe me?"

"Let it be, let it be" she said. "I can't believe it. I can't allow myself to believe it."

"By God!" cried the Marquis, "I am beginning to feel that I will have no regrets. This Madame von P*** thought to inflict misery and suffering on me, but I now see that she has brought me salvation instead. Come, my Wife, get dressed, while I make preparations for our departure. Let us remove to my estates where we can stay long enough for the trees of time to grow bark over the injuries of the past."

For three whole years they lived far from Paris, the happiest couple of their time.

Dear Reader, I see you rise up in indignation at the mention of Madame von P***. I hear you shout: "What a terrible woman! What a beast and hypocrite!" — No fits of temper, please. No prejudice. — Let the scales of justice decide!

Darker deeds than this are done every day, albeit with less determination and spirit. You may *hate* and *fear* the Marquise, but you can never *despise* her. Her vengeance was ghastly and unheard of, but not soiled by self-interest. If this lady had done this and more to obtain benefits for her legal husband — if she had sacrificed her virtue to a minister of state or even to a head clerk in order to procure her spouse a ribbon of honor or the leadership of a regiment — if she had sold herself to a dispenser of benefices in exchange for a handsome new assignment, you might find this quite natural, custom would speak for it. But when she takes her revenge on an unfaithful man, your feelings of indignation are ignited. It is not because your heart is too soft for you to imagine yourself emulating her — but because you cannot be bothered to feel empathy with her pain, because you are too proud to acknowledge female virtue, that you find her actions despicable. Have you weighed the sacrifices she made for her lover? I will ignore the fact that her purse was always open to him, that he dined at her place for years and went in and out as if her house were his. You might only scoff at this. But she had accommodated his mercurial moods, had slavishly indulged his tastes, and to please him she had completely destroyed the plan of her life. All of Paris had always revered her virtue — now, on his account, she had plummeted to the level of the common mob. Now, the voices of slander whispered to each other, "This grand P***, this wonder of the world, has become one of us." She had seen this scornful sneer with her own eyes, heard these calumnies with her own ears, and often enough, red-faced with shame, cast her eyes to the ground. She bore every insult that libel holds in store for a woman whose unspotted virtue makes nearby vice so much the more visible. — She had borne the loud laughter with which the wanton crowd takes its revenge on those who strike them as prudes and who proclaim their virtue like town-criers. — Proud and sensitive as she was, she would have preferred to sigh away her life in darkness than ever again step out onto the world's stage, where her forfeited honor could only meet with ridicule, her rejected love find only malicious sympathizers. She was approaching an age when a lost lover is not so easily replaced. A heart such as hers could only bleed away this fate in bitter loneliness.

When one man can strike down another because of a suggestive glance, why should we see it as a crime if a woman of honor casts her seducer — the destroyer of her honor and a traitor to her love — into the arms of a whore? Truly, dear reader, you are as fierce in your fault-finding as you are fickle with your praise. "But," you retort, "it is not revenge as such but only the manner of revenge chosen by this woman that I find so condemnable. My feelings rebel against such a tightly woven fabric of deliberate viciousness and such a chain of fabrications, lasting almost a year." — So, you are willing to forgive any first impulse, but, I ask you, what if the first impulse of a Madame von P*** or any lady of her character should last for an entire lifetime?

I see nothing here but a somewhat uncommon form of betrayal. And I would welcome a law that would present as his just reward a prostitute for a wife to every conscienceless scoundrel who brings down an honest woman and then leaves her — may a vulgar man be rewarded with vulgar women.

[Schiller adds this postscript to his translation:]

Even the eloquence of a Diderot can hardly rationalize the horror that this unnatural deed must arouse, but the bold novelty of the intrigue, the unmistakable truth of the narrative, the unadorned elegance of the description tempted me to venture a translation, which, I readily admit, cannot match the peculiarity of the original. It is taken from an essay (not yet known in Germany, so far as I am aware) by Messieur Diderot, called "Jacques and His Master, or the Fatalist." Baron von Dalberg in Mannheim possesses the original text, and I wish to thank him for his generosity in allowing me to make use of it for this issue of *Thalia.*

Translator's Notes

[1] Diderot: "très aimable, croyant peu à la vertu des femmes." Loy's translation: "and with little faith in the virtue of women" (J. Robert Loy: *Jacques the Fatalist and His Master.* New York University Press, 1959, 99). Note the echo on page 40: "because you are too proud to acknowledge female virtue."

[2] Identified by Loy as "Théodore Tronchin (1709–1781) . . . one of a famous family of Geneva Tronchins in the eighteenth century. He was a Geneva doctor with a wide reputation. To consult him, Mme d'Epinay planned a trip from her home in France when the great quarrel broke out between Jean-Jacques Rousseau and all his former friends because he refused to accompany his hostess, Mme d'Epinay, to Geneva" (277–78 n. 30).

[3] Diderot: "esprit de libertinage"; Schiller: "Pfiff für das Gewerbe," 193.

[4] An inconsistency in Diderot is preserved in Schiller's translation. In her proscriptions to the two women, Madame von P*** prohibits them from accepting charity, but their priest later puts the screws on them by taking away the congregation's charity (NA 16:195, see p. 28, below).

[5] Schiller translates Diderot's term as "die Weltweisen" (195), but it is clear from the example of Voltaire that Madame von P*** is referring not to philosophers in general but to the adversaries of the church known as "philosophes" in France.

[6] "Cabinet du Roi: Collection and exhibition of prints established by Louis XIV in 1667" (Loy 279 n. 36).

[7] Schiller's "Ich sollte freilich wohl etwas Klügeres tun" must be sarcastic. Diderot: "C'est bien ce que je pourrais faire de mieux" (181).

[8] Villejuif: "Judenmarkt," Jewish market.

[9] This is the topos of beauty in distress. Cf. Heinrich von Kleist, *Der Zweikampf*: "Aber wer beschreibt das Entsetzen der unglücklichen Littegarde, als sie sich, bei dem an der Tür entstehenden Geräusch, mit halb offener Brust und augelöstem Haar, von dem Stroh, das ihr untergeschüttet war, erhob und statt des Turmwächters, den sie erwartete, den Kämmerer, ihren edlen und vortrefflichen Freund, . . . sah" (But who could describe the dismay of the unhappy Littegarde when, hearing the noise at the door, she rose up from her bed of scattered straw with half exposed breast and hair undone, and saw not the tower guard, whom she expected, but the chamberlain, her excellent and noble friend) (Heinrich von Kleist, *Sämtliche Werke und Briefe* [Frankfurt am Main: Deutscher Klassiker Verlag, 1990], vol. 3, 337).

3: The Criminal of Lost Honor. A True Story

Friedrich Schiller (1786)
Translated by Jeffrey L. High

IN THE ENTIRE HISTORY OF HUMANKIND, there is no chapter more instructive for the heart and the mind than the annals of human aberrations. For every great crime committed, an equally great force was at work. If the mysterious play of desire is hidden in the faint light of normal emotion, how much more striking, colossal, and transparent it becomes in the state of overwhelming passion. The more sophisticated student of human nature, who knows just how predictable the mechanism of normal free will is, and to what extent it is possible to deduce through analogy, will transfer many an observation from this field into personal knowledge of psychology, and apply this insight in the realm of moral activity.

The human heart is something so simple, and yet so multifaceted. One and the same capacity or desire can play out in thousands of shapes and directions, can cause thousands of contradictory phenomena, can appear in different combinations in thousands of characters, and thousands of dissimilar characters and events can be spun from the one and the same impulse, even if the individual in question never recognizes the relationship of his actions to those of the rest. If a new Linnaeus were to appear and classify humankind into genus and species according to drives and inclinations, how astonished we would be to find those whose vice must now suffocate in a constricted bourgeois sphere and the narrow confines of the law, together in one and the same species with a monster like Cesare Borgia.

Considered with this in mind, there are a number of arguments to be made against the conventional treatment of this story, and convention, I suspect, is the problem that explains why the study of this topic has borne so little fruit in the everyday bourgeois sphere. An irreconcilable contrast prevails between the heated emotional state of an acting human being and the quiet mood of the reader to whom his story is presented; such a broad gap separates them that it is difficult, indeed impossible, for the latter to recognize any relationship to the former. A gulf separates the historical subject at hand and the reader that preempts any possibility of self-comparison or practical usefulness, and, instead of inspiring a therapeutic sense of terror, which could serve as a warning to an egotistical sense of normalcy, the story elicits only a distant, disapproving shake of the head. We see the unfortunate protagonist — who, even in the hour he committed his misdeed, as well as at that hour when he paid for his crimes, was a human being like we are — as a creature from a different genus, whose blood circulates differently than ours, whose will obeys other rules than do ours. His fate moves us very little since sympathy necessarily stems from a vague awareness of shared danger, and far be it from us to even dream of such a common relation. Lost with the relation is the lesson; and the story, instead of serving as an institution of learning, must make do with the meager accomplishment of satisfying our curiosity. If the story is to mean anything more to us, and achieve its noble end, then we must necessarily choose to adhere to one of the following two methods — either the reader must become as heated as the protagonist, or the protagonist must become as cold as the reader.

I know that many of the best storytellers of our own time and from antiquity have employed the former method and have appealed to the heart of the reader through a captivating rendering. But this approach is a usurpation on the part of the author and violates the republican freedom of the reading public, who have the right to judge for themselves. At the same time, this method is a transgression of genre boundaries, for it is the exclusive and characteristic domain of the rhetorician and the poet. The historian has no choice but the latter method.

The protagonist must become as cold as the reader, or, to that end, we must become familiar with the protagonist before he acts; we need to see him not only *perform* his deeds, we have to see him *want* to do so. His thoughts are endlessly more important to us than his deeds, and the inspirations of his thoughts even more so than the consequences of his deeds. The soil in the area of Mount Vesuvius has been examined in order to understand the cause of its eruptions; why pay less attention to a moral phenomenon than to a physical one? Why not pay the same attention to the properties and the constellation of things that surrounded such a person until deep inside him the accumulated tinder caught fire? The dreamer, who loves the fantastic, is drawn by the strangeness and the danger of such a phenomenon; the friend of truth seeks a mother to these lost children. He seeks her in the immutable structure of the human psyche and in the variable conditions that externally determined the state of the psyche, and in these two considerations he is certain to find her. He can now no longer be surprised to see the poisonous hemlock thriving in the same flower bed where otherwise only healing herbs blossom, to find wisdom and foolhardiness, vice and virtue, together in one cradle.

Even if I do not cite the many advantages to be drawn from such a psychological treatment of the story, psychology still remains the most advantageous approach, if only because it eradicates the cruel scorn and arrogant self-confidence with which virtue untested so often looks down on virtue failed, if only because it spreads the gentle spirit of tolerance without which no refugee can ever return, no offender can reconcile with the law, no member of society, once ignited, can ever be saved from total immolation.

Should not the criminal, about whom I will now speak, have also had a right to appeal to this same spirit of tolerance? Was he lost beyond any salvation for the state of law? — I will refrain from anticipating the judgment of the reader. Our gentle understanding is of no further help to him, for he died at the hand of the executioner, but the autopsy of his depravity will perhaps instruct humanity and — it is possible — also the justice system.

Christian Wolf was the son of an innkeeper in a ***ian provincial city (whose name must be concealed for reasons that will become clear in the following) and helped his mother take care of the inn on into his twentieth year, for his father was dead. Business at the inn was bad, and Wolf had idle hours. From his school days he was already well known as a wild boy. Older girls complained about his freshness, and the boys of the little city paid tribute to his inventive mind. Nature had neglected his body. A small unimpressive figure, frizzy hair of an unpleasant shade of black, a nose crushed flat and a swollen upper lip, which on top of this had been deformed from its original state by the kick of a horse, made his appearance so unattractive that it caused all women to shrink back from him and provided rich fodder for the wit of his companions.

Defiance drove him to take what had been denied him: Because he was pleasing to no one, he sought to please. He was sensual, and convinced himself that he was in love — or that he was capable of love. The girl that he chose mistreated him, and he had cause to believe that his rivals were having more luck; on the other hand, the girl was poor. A heart that remained locked to his pleading might well be open to his gifts, but he himself was burdened by poverty, and his idle attempts to improve his appearance swallowed up what little he was able to earn through the poor business at the inn. Too comfortable and too ignorant to improve his ruinous finances through investment, too proud and too weak to trade the role of the gentleman that he had played until now for that of the peasant and to sacrifice the freedom he worshipped, he saw only one way out left — a way traveled with better luck by thousands before him and thousands after him —, to *steal honorably*. His hometown bordered on a forest of the sovereign; he became a poacher, and the yield of his robbery flowed loyally into the hands of his beloved, Johanne.

Among Hanne's lovers was Robert, a huntsman for the forest warden. Robert quickly noticed the advantage that his rival, Wolf, had gained over him through his generosity, and with the eyes of envy he sought the source of this sudden change of fortune. To this end, he appeared more regularly in the "Sun" — the name on the sign of Wolf's tavern — his sly eye, sharpened by jealousy and envy, soon discovered the well that fed this flow of money. Not long before, a stricter enforcement of the regulation against poaching had been implemented, one that condemned the lawbreaker to the penitentiary. Robert was tireless in stalking the secret paths of his enemy, and finally he succeeded in catching the unwitting Wolf in the act. Wolf was brought in, and only with great difficulty was he able to avoid the statutory punishment by paying a fine, thus sacrificing his small fortune entirely.

Robert was triumphant. His rival had been swept from the field of battle and the beggar had lost any hope of Hanne's favor. Wolf had met his enemy, and this enemy was the happy owner of his Johanne. A crushing sense of inadequacy joined insulted pride; despair and jealousy simultaneously storm his sensibilities; while hunger drives him out into the wide world, revenge and rage bind him fast. A second time he turns to poaching, but a second time Robert's redoubled vigilance outwits him. This time he experiences the full severity of the law, for this time he has nothing left to give, and a few weeks later he is delivered to the penitentiary of the royal residence.

By the time the year's sentence was withstood, his rage had grown by the distance from his home, and his spite was magnified by the weight of his misfortune. He had barely regained his freedom when he hurried off to his place of birth to show himself to his Johanne. He appears, and everyone flees from him. His dire poverty has finally bent his pride and overwhelmed his weak constitution — he offers to serve the wealthy in the area as a day laborer. The farmer shrugs his shoulders at the delicate weakling; for this unfeeling patron, the rugged build of a sturdy competitor outdoes Wolf. He makes one final attempt. One position is still unfilled, the most extreme, forlorn outpost of honest reputation — he applies for the position of swineherd of the little city, but the farmer is unwilling to trust his swine to a miscreant. His every design denied, turned away at every door, he becomes a poacher for the third time, and for a third time he has the misfortune to fall into the hands of his vigilant enemy.

The double relapse had further compounded his guilt. The judges looked into the book of laws, but not one of them looked into the psychological constitution of the accused. The mandate against poaching demanded solemn and exemplary satisfaction, and Wolf was sentenced — the mark of the gallows branded on his back — to three years of hard labor at the dungeon.

This period also passed, and he left the dungeon — but quite different than when he had arrived. Here, a new era begins in his life; listen for yourself how he later confessed to his spiritual counsel and before the court. "I entered the dungeon," he said, "as a lost soul, and I left it as a criminal. I still had something in the world that was dear to me, and my pride was bowed by the disgrace. When I was brought to the dungeon, they locked me in with twenty-three prisoners, of whom two were murderers and the rest notorious thieves and vagabonds. I was ridiculed when I spoke of God and I was set upon and subjected to the most abominable blasphemy about the savior. They sang me songs about whores that even a slovenly scoundrel like me could not hear without disgust and horror, but the acts I saw them commit outraged my sense of decency even more. Not a day went by without the retelling of some disgraceful life story, or without plans forged for some wicked attack. At first, I fled this mob and crept away from their conversations the best I possibly could, but I needed another living creature, and the barbarous guards had slaughtered my dog. The work was hard and tyrannical, my body sickly; I needed someone to stand by me, and if I am to be entirely honest, I needed sympathy, and this I had to buy with the last remnant of my conscience. And so I finally became accustomed to the most repulsive behaviors, and in my final months there, I had even surpassed my teachers.

"From this point on I thirsted for the day of my freedom, just as I thirsted for revenge. All of humanity had offended me, for each of them was better and happier than me. I saw myself as the martyr of natural rights and as a sacrificial victim of the laws. Clenching my teeth, I chafed at my chains when the sun rose behind the hill of my dungeon; to be a prisoner with a wide view of the horizon is to suffer hell twice over. The free breeze that whistled through the air holes in my tower, and the swallow that landed on the iron rod that held my prison bars, seemed to mock me with their freedom and made my captivity even more horrible. At that time, I swore irreconcilable glowing hatred toward everything that even appeared human, and the oath I had sworn, I upheld with honor.

"My first thought, as soon as I was free, was my home town. Though it offered little hope for my future subsistence, it promised the greatest hope for my hunger for vengeance. My heart beat wilder as the church tower rose in the distance above the forest. It was no longer the warm sense of well-being that I had felt during my first pilgrimage. — The memory of all the public misfortune, all the persecutions, that I had once suffered there was suddenly awakened from a terrible deathly sleep, all the wounds bled again, all the scars burst open anew. I redoubled my stride, reinvigorated in anticipation that the sudden sight of me would terrify my enemies, and I now thirsted for humiliation just as much as I had once trembled for fear of it.

"The bells were ringing for vespers as I stood in the middle of the market place. The congregation teemed toward the church. I was recognized quickly, and everyone who ran into me stepped back timidly. I had always been very fond of little children, and even now I was spontaneously compelled to offer a penny to a little boy who was skipping past. The little boy stared at me for a moment and then flung the penny back in my face. If my blood had only run a little more peacefully, I would have remembered that the beard that I still had from the penitentiary lent my facial features a dreadful aspect — but my wicked heart had poisoned my sense of reason. Tears, like I had never cried them before, ran down my face.

"'The boy has no idea who I am, nor where I come from,' I said to myself half out loud, 'and yet he shuns me like some disgraceful animal. Am I marked somewhere on the forehead, or, because I feel that I can no longer love another human being, have I ceased to bear any resemblance to one?' — The contempt of this child pained me more bitterly than would a three-year sentence as a galley slave, for I had been kind to him and couldn't attribute his behavior to any personal hatred.

"I sat down at a framer's site across from the church. What I actually sought, I do not know, but I do still know that I stood up full of bitterness, when, of all of my acquaintances, not one deemed me worthy of a greeting, not even one. Indignant, I left my position to look for lodging; when I turned at the corner of an alley, I ran directly into my Johanne. 'Innkeeper!' she cried outloud and made a gesture to embrace me. 'You, here again, dear Innkeeper of the Sun! Thank God you've come back!' Her clothing told a tale of hunger and misery, and her face that of a shameful disease; her appearance described her descent to the most depraved of creatures. I quickly realized what had come to pass here; a group of royal dragoons, whom I had just encountered, led me to conclude that the garrison was now stationed in the little city. 'Soldiers' whore!' I shouted, laughing as I turned my back on her. It did me well to know that there was still one creature beneath me in the order of living things. I had never loved her.

"My mother was dead. My creditors had been paid with my little house. I no longer had anyone or anything. The entire world fled before me as if I were poisonous, but I had finally forgotten how to feel ashamed. Before, I had withdrawn from the sight of humanity, because their contempt was unbearable to me. Now I forced myself on them and took delight in scaring them away. It did me good, because I had nothing left to lose and nothing left to care about. I no longer needed even a single good trait, since no one expected any of me.

"The whole world stood open before me; in a foreign province I might have passed as an honest man, but I had lost the will to even pretend to be one. Desperation and disgrace had finally dictated my disposition. It was the final refuge left to me, to learn to live without honor, because I no could no longer lay claim to any. If my vanity and my pride had felt my humiliation, I would have committed suicide.

"What I had actually planned to do at this point was still not clear to me. I wanted to do evil, this much I still remembered vaguely. I wanted to earn my fate. The law, I thought, was a comfort to the world, and thus I resolved to violate the law. Previously, I had sinned out of necessity and recklessness, now I did so of my own free will and for my enjoyment.

"The first thing was to return to poaching. More and more, the hunt, for the sake of the hunt itself, had become my passion, and, of course, I had to survive. But it wasn't this alone; it thrilled me to mock the royal edict, and to undermine the ruler with all that was in my power. The thought of being arrested no longer worried me; this time I had a bullet ready for my arrestor, and, this much I knew, my shot would not miss its man. I killed every game animal I encountered, the very least of which I sold at the border. Most of it I let rot. I lived wretchedly, only to ensure my supply of lead and gun powder. My devastating exploits in the great hunt became infamous, but I myself was beyond any fear of suspicion. My appearance doused any danger of recognition. My name was forgotten.

"I pursued this way of life for several months. One morning, as was my habit, I had roamed through the woods in order to follow the tracks of a deer. For two hours I had worn myself out in vain, and I already began to give up my prey as lost, when all at once I came upon the deer within shooting distance. I prepare to take aim and pull the trigger — when suddenly I am startled by the sight of a hat laying on the ground just a few steps away from me. I look more carefully and recognize the forester, Robert, who, from behind the thick trunk of an oak tree, is taking aim at the very same deer I had intended to shoot. A fatal chill ran through my bones at this sight. Of all people, the one person I hated more intensely than any living thing in the world, and this person was suddenly subject to the mercy of my lead ball. In this moment, it seemed to me as if the whole world was at stake in my shot and that all the hatred of my entire life had rushed into the one fingertip with which I was to apply the deadly pressure. A terrible invisible hand hovered above me, the hour hand of my destiny pointed undeniably to this one black minute. My arm trembled as I left the dreadful decision to my musket — my teeth chattered as if in a fever chill, and my breath was frozen suffocating in my lungs. For an entire minute, the aim of my musket swayed undecided somewhere between the man and the deer — a minute — and another — and yet another. Vengeance and conscience wrestled unmercifully, uncertain, but vengeance won, and the forester lay dead on the ground.

"My weapon fell with the shot . . . 'Murderer' . . . I mumbled slowly — the forest was as still as a cemetery — I clearly heard that I said 'murderer.' As I crept closer, the man died. For a long time, I stood silent before the corpse; finally, bright laughter gave me my voice back. 'Now you are going to keep your mouth shut, my good friend,' I said, and stepped up to him, taunting, as I turned the murdered man's face up. His eyes stood wide open. I became serious and suddenly fell silent again. All of a sudden, I began to feel strange.

"Up until now, I had broken the law as compensation for my dishonor; now something had happened for which I had never done penance. An hour earlier, I think, no one in the world could have convinced me that there was anything worse than me under the heavens, now I began to feel that just an hour ago, I was in a position to be envied.

"God's judgments never even occurred to me — but one judgment that did, was the confused recollection of a trial, I know not whose, of noose and sword, and the execution of a woman who had murdered her child, which I had witnessed as a schoolboy. Something especially terrifying for me lay in the idea that, from this point on, my life had been forfeited. More than this I no longer recall. Right away I wished that he were still alive. I tortured myself to remember everything evil that the dead man had done to me in my life, but — how strange! — it was as if my memory had died. I could no longer recollect any of this that had brought me to such a rage a quarter of an hour ago. I could not comprehend how I had come to commit this murder.

"I was still standing before the corpse, even now. The crack of several whips and the rumbling of cargo wagons that drove through the woods brought me back to myself. It was barely a quarter mile off the main road, where the crime had occurred. I had to think of my safety.

"Instinctively, I lost myself deeper in the forest. On the way it occurred to me that the victim had been in possession of a pocket watch. I needed money in order to get to the border — but I lacked the courage to turn around to the spot where the dead man lay. Here I was suddenly stricken by the thought of the devil and the omnipresence of God. I summoned up all the courage I had, determined to take on all of hell, and I returned to the spot. I found what I was looking for, and, to this, in a green wallet, a little more than a thaler in coins. Just when I wanted to put both in my pocket, I suddenly stopped and reconsidered. It was not a sudden impulse of shame, neither was it the fear of doubling my crime by plundering. — Defiance, I believe it was, caused me to cast the watch aside and keep only half of the money. I wanted to be considered a personal enemy of the shooting victim, but not his mere robber.

"Now I fled into the forest. I knew that the wood stretched four German miles northward and there overlapped with the border. I ran breathless until high noon. The haste of my flight distracted me from my pangs of conscience, but they returned even more terrible as my strength subsided more and more. Thousands of horrible shapes swarmed over me and slashed at my chest like cutting knives. I was left with the terrible choice between a life full of unrelenting fear of death or a violent execution, and I had to choose. I did not have the heart to leave the world by suicide, and was appalled at the prospect of staying in it. I spent the sixth hour of my flight, an hour full of crushing torments, the likes of which no living person could possibly describe, crushed between the certain suffering of life and the uncertain horrors of eternity, equally incapable of living or dying.

"Deep in myself, and slowly, unknowingly having pulled my hat down low over my face, as if this could have hidden my identity from the indifferent eye of nature, I had followed a narrow path that led me through the darkest forest unobserved — when suddenly a raw, commanding voice ahead of me shouted 'Halt!' The voice was very close, my distraction and the low hat had hindered me from seeing. I opened my eyes wide and saw a savage man coming toward me, who was carrying a huge knotted club. His build approached that of a giant — at least my initial shock had made me believe this — and the color of his skin was of a yellow mulatto blackness, out of which the white of one crossed eye bulged hideously. In place of a belt he wore a thick rope wrapped twice around a green woolen shirt, into which he had stuck a wide butcher's knife next to a pistol. The command was repeated, and a powerful arm held me fast. The sound of a human being had filled me with terror, but the sight of a villain gave me heart. In the situation in which I found myself, I had every reason to tremble in the presence of an honest man, but none in the presence of a robber.

"'Who goes there?' said the apparition.

"'One of your own,' was my answer, 'if you really are who you appear to be.'

"'The path out of here does not go that way. What gives you the right to be here?'

"'What gives you the right to ask?' I replied defiantly.

"The man looked me over twice from my toes to the cowlick on my head. It seemed as if he wanted to compare my build to his own, and compare the tone of my answer to my figure. — Finally, he said, 'You speak as brutally as a beggar.'

"'That may well be. Just yesterday I still was one.'

"The man laughed. 'And I'd be willing to swear,' he said, 'even now you would not pass for much better.'

"'For something even worse, then,' — I wanted to move on.

"'Easy, friend! You act as if something were chasing you. What is so important about your time that you can't spare some?'

"I thought for a moment. Before I knew how, the answer was out of my mouth: 'Life is short,' I said slowly, 'and hell is eternal.'

"He looked at me blankly. 'I'll be damned,' he finally said, 'if you have not just come from a very close brush with a gallows somewhere.'

"'That may well still come. All right then, farewell, comrade!'

"'Cheers, comrade!' — he cried, as he produced a tin hipflask from his hunting bag, took a mighty gulp, and handed it to me. Flight and fear had exhausted all my might, and no drink had passed my lips this entire dreadful day. I had already feared that I would die of thirst in this forest, where I had no hope of refreshment for three miles. Judge for yourself how happily I reacted to this offer of a toast to my health. New strength flowed into my limbs with this refreshing drink and new courage into my heart, and hope, and love of life. This welcome drink made such an impact that I began to believe that I wasn't entirely wretched after all. Yes, indeed, I confess, my state of mind bordered on that of a happy man, for finally, after thousands of misplaced hopes, I had found a creature that seemed similar to me. In the state that I had sunk to, I would have drunk to camaraderie with the spirit of hell, just to have a friend.

"The man had stretched himself out on the grass; I did the same.

"'Your drink did me good!' I said. 'We must get to know each other better.'

"He struck a match to light his pipe.

"'Have you been at your handiwork for long?'

"He looked at me firmly. 'What do you mean by that?'

"'Has it been bloody often?' I pulled the knife from his belt.

"'Who are you?' he said in a terrible tone and set his pipe down out of the way.

"'A murderer like you — but only a beginner yet.'

"The man looked at me stiffly and picked up his pipe again.

"'You are not from here?' he said finally.

"'Three miles from here. The Innkeeper of the Sun in L***, in case you've heard of me.'

"The man leapt up as if he were possessed. 'The poacher Wolf?' he quickly blurted.

"'None other.'

"'Welcome, comrade! Welcome!' he cried, and shook my hands mightily. 'That is as it should be that I finally have you here, Inkeeper of the Sun. Year after year and day after day I have been plotting to get you here. I know you quite well. I know about everything. I have been expecting you for a long time.'

"'Expecting me? For what then?'

"'In the whole area you're all anyone talks about. You have enemies, a state official set you up, Wolf. They destroyed you, it's outrageous the way they treated you.'

"The man became heated — 'Because you shot a few boars that the Prince lets feed on our farms and fields, they dragged you around for years from the prison to the penitentiary, they stole your home and your business, they made you into a beggar. Has it come to this, brother, that a human being is not worth more than a hare? Are we not better than cattle in a field? — And a man like you could tolerate that?'

"'Could I have changed anything about it?'

"'We shall just see about that. But tell me something, where are you coming from right now, and what are you up to?'

"I told him my entire story. Without waiting until I had finished, the man jumped up with delighted impatience and dragged me along behind him. 'Come, brother Innkeeper,' he said, 'now you are ripe for the harvest, now I have you just where I need you. I will put in my word of honor for you. Follow me.'

"'Where do you want to take me?'

"'Don't ask so many questions. Follow me!' — He dragged me along by force.

"We had gone a short quarter mile. The forest became increasingly steep, rougher, and wilder, neither of us spoke a word until finally my guide's whistle startled me out of my contemplation. I opened my eyes, we stood at the abrupt brink of a chasm that fell away into a deep crevasse. A second whistle answered from the innermost belly of the chasm, and, as if of its own doing, a ladder slowly climbed up to us from the depths. My guide climbed down first, he told me to wait until he came back. 'First I need to have them put the dog on its chain,' and added, 'you are a stranger here, the beast would tear you apart.' With that he left.

"I now stood alone before the abyss, and I knew very well that I was alone. The carelessness of my guide had not escaped me. It would have cost me nothing more than a bold decision to pull up the ladder and I was free, and my flight was secured. I confess that this was clear to me. I looked down into the gullet that was about to swallow me; it reminded me darkly of the pit of hell, from which there is no deliverance. I began to shudder at the thought of the path I was about to embark upon; only a speedy flight could save me. I decide to flee — I already stretch my arm toward the ladder — but all of a sudden it thunders in my ears, it echoes around me like the scornful laughter of hell: 'What does a murderer have to lose?' — and my arm falls back as if paralyzed. My reckoning was complete, the time for regret was past, my murder, that I committed, stood behind me like a wall of stone and blocked my return forever. Just then, my guide reappeared and informed me that I was to come with him. Now there was no choice anymore. I climbed down.

"We had gone a few steps from the wall of the chasm when the floor space began to broaden, and several huts became visible. The center between them opened into a round lawn, on which some eighteen to twenty people were camped around a coal fire. 'Here, comrades,' said my guide and placed me in the middle of the circle. 'Our Innkeeper! Let him know he is welcome!'

"'Innkeeper!' every one cried at once, and all rose and gathered around me, men and women. Need I confess? The joy was sincere and heartfelt. Trust, even respect was evident on every face, this one shook my hand, another tugged in a friendly way on my shirt, the entire scene was like a reunion with an old acquaintance who is truly valued. My arrival had interrupted the feast that was just about to begin. They resumed right away and insisted that I have a welcome drink. The meal was game of all kinds, and the wine bottle traveled tirelessly from neighbor to neighbor. The good life and unity appeared to inspire the entire band, and everyone competed to demonstrate their unbridled happiness at having me there.

"I had been seated between two women, which was the place of honor at the table. I expected the absolute dregs of their sex, but how great was my astonishment when I discovered the most delightful female creatures I had ever set eyes upon among this disgraceful pack. Margarete, the older and the more beautiful of the two, was referred to as mademoiselle and could not have been twenty-five years old. Her speech was rather brazen and her gestures said even more. Marie, the younger of the two, was married, but escaped from a husband who had abused her. Her features were finer, but looked pale and frail and less eye-catching than her fiery neighbor. Both women competed with each other to ignite my desires; the beautiful Margarete appealed to my inebriation with lewd jokes, but everything about the woman was disgusting to me, and the shy Marie had captured my heart forever.

"'You see, brother Innkeeper,' the man who brought me here began, 'you see how we live together here, and every day is like today. Not so, comrades?'

"'Every day is like today!' the entire band repeated.

"'If you decide that you enjoy our way of life, then join us, and be our leader. Until now, I was the leader, but for you I will step aside. Don't you agree, comrades?'

"An enthusiastic 'Yes!' answered from every voice.

"My head was glowing, my brain was numbed; my blood simmered from wine and desire. The world had cast me out like a carrier of the plague — here I found fraternal acceptance, a life of luxury, and honor. However I wanted to choose, death awaited me in the end; here, however, I could at least sell my life for a more handsome price. Debauchery was my most fervent desire; until now the opposite sex had shown me nothing but contempt, but here the favor of women and unbridled pleasure awaited me. My decision cost me little. 'I will stay with you, comrades!' I cried outloud with conviction and stepped into the middle of the band, 'I will stay with you!' I cried again, 'if you will concede my beautiful neighbor here to be mine!' Everybody was in agreement to grant me my wish, and I was the undisputed owner of a wh*** and the head of a band of thieves."

The following part of the story I will pass over altogether; that which is merely repulsive contains nothing edifying for the reader. An unfortunate wretch who had sunk to this depth would in the end stop at no outrage to humanity, but he did not commit a second murder, as he himself testified under torture.

The reputation of this person quickly spread throughout the entire province. The country roads became unsafe, nightly burglaries spread unrest among the citizens, the name of the Innkeeper became the terror of the rural population, the justice system searched for him, and a price was put on his head. He was fortunate enough to foil every assault on his freedom, and sly enough to exploit the occult obsession of a superstitious peasantry for his own security. His henchmen were ordered to put out the word that he had made a pact with the devil and that he had the powers of witchcraft. The district where he played his part belonged then even less than today to the enlightened parts of Germany, the rumor was widely believed, and he was safe. No one displayed the least desire to tangle with the dangerous man who had the services of the devil at his disposal.

He had plied his sad handiwork for a year when it began to become unbearable to him. The pack that he had chosen to head failed to fulfill his dazzling expectations. In his wine-induced dizziness, a seductive exterior had blinded him; now to his horror he became aware of how hideously he had been deceived. Hunger and poverty replaced the abundance that had nurtured his false hopes; quite often he had to risk his life for a single meal that barely sufficed to stave off starvation. Every shadowy trace of that fraternal unity disappeared; envy, suspicion, and jealousy raged at the core of this depraved gang. The justice system had offered a reward to whomever could bring him in alive, and if it were an accomplice, guaranteed a solemn pardon — a tremendous temptation for the dregs of the world! The unfortunate wretch was aware of the risk he ran. The honest word of those who had turned on God and humanity was a poor guarantee of his life. From now on, sleep was a thing of the past, perpetual fear of death ate away at his peace; the dreadful apparition of suspicion rattled in the background regardless of where he sought refuge, tormented him when he was awake, lay down beside him when he went to bed, and terrified him in dreadful nightmares. His silenced conscience regained its voice, and the sleeping viper of remorse awoke in the all-consuming storm in his heart. He now felt all his hatred turn its terrible blade from humanity to himself. Now he forgave all of nature and found no one to condemn but himself alone.

Vice had completed its lessons on the unfortunate wretch, his natural, good sense of reason overcame the illusion. Now he felt how deep he had fallen, quiet melancholy took the place of grinding desperation. Through tears he yearned to relive the past, now he knew for certain that he would do so very differently. He began to hope that he might still be allowed to become upright because he felt within himself that he still could. At the highest peak of his deterioration, he was perhaps closer to goodness than he had been before his first false step.

It was at just this time that the Seven Years' War broke out, and the recruitment of soldiers was at its peak. The unfortunate wretch drew hope from this development and wrote a letter to his ruler, an excerpt of which I include here:

"If your Royal Indulgence is not too disgusted to lower yourself and hear me, if criminals of my kind are not beyond the Sovereign's mercy, then please grant me a hearing, Your Highness. I am a murderer and a thief, the law had condemned me to death, the courts are searching for me — and I herewith offer to turn myself in of my own free will. But at the same time I wish to make a rare request of your throne. I despise my life and do not fear death, but it is terrible for me to die without first having lived. I want to live in order to put right a part of the past; I want to live in order to reconcile myself with the state whose laws I have violated. My execution will be an example to the world, but no compensation for my deeds. I detest vice and long passionately for honesty and virtue. I have demonstrated my ability to be a terror to my fatherland, and I hope that I still have ability enough to be of service to my state.

"I know that what I ask is unprecedented. My life is lost, and it is not my place to engage the justice system in negotiation. But I do not appear before you in chains and irons — I am still free — and my fear plays the smallest part in my request.

"What I beg of you is an act of mercy. Even if I had any right to justice, I would no longer dare lay claim to it. — Yet, if I may remind my judge of one thing. The timeline of my crimes begins with the sentence that forever robbed me of my honor. If I had been treated with only slightly more compassion, then perhaps I would not be in need of mercy now. Let mercy go before for law, my Prince. If it is within your royal power to carry my plea to the authorities, then spare my life. I shall dedicate it to your service from this point forward. If you could, let me read your most merciful will through an announcement in the newspapers, and on your royal word, I will deliver myself to the capital. And if you decide my case otherwise, then let the law do what it must, and I will do what I must do."

This plea went unanswered, as did a second, and a third, in which the humble petitioner plead for a position as a cavalryman in the service of the Prince. His hope for a pardon was extinguished altogether, and thus he came to the decision to flee over the border of the state and to die as a brave soldier in the service of the King of Prussia.

He happily stole away from his band and embarked on this journey. The way led him through a small rural city where he wanted to spend the night. A short time before this, stricter mandates were imposed throughout the state regarding the compulsory search of travelers because the sovereign, an Imperial Prince, had taken a partisan position in the war. The guard at the city gate had received such an order and was sitting on a bench in front of the barrier as the Innkeeper came riding in. The appearance of this man had something ridiculous about it, but at the same time something terrible and wild. The gaunt nag he rode and the burlesque choice of his clothing, though most likely it was less his taste in clothes than the chronology of robberies that dictated his outfit, contrasted strangely enough with a face on which so many raging emotions lay bare, much like the disfigured corpses on display at the site of a pilgrimage. The guard was taken aback at the sight of this strange traveler. He had turned gray with age at the city gate, and forty years of executing his duties had sharpened an unerring eye for the physiognomy of all vagabonds. And this time, too, the eagle eye of the sleuth did not miss its man. He immediately closed the city gate and demanded to see the rider's passport, taking care to lead the horse by the reins. Wolf was prepared for situations like this and actually did carry a passport that he had recently stolen from a trader he had plundered. But this one document was not enough to outweigh forty years of experience and move this oracle at the gate to reconsider. The guard believed his eyes more than these papers, and Wolf was forced to follow him to the courthouse.

The chief judge of the city examined the passport and declared it valid. This man was a fanatical devotee of current events and he particularly loved to enjoy a bottle while discussing the newspaper. The passport told him that its owner had come directly from the enemy states, where the theater of the war was. He hoped to elicit some personal, first-hand news from the stranger, and sent a secretary back with the passport to invite him to a bottle of wine.

In the meantime, the Innkeeper waits in front of the courthouse; the ridiculous spectacle had gathered the slack-jawed gawkers of the little city around him in droves. They mumbled into each other's ears, pointed alternately at the horse and the rider; the courage of the mob finally rises to a loud tumult. Unfortunately, the horse that everyone now pointed to had been stolen; he suspected that it had been described in wanted posters and that it had been recognized. The surprising hospitality of the chief judge confirms his suspicion. Now he decides that it's over, that the swindle of his passport was exposed and the invitation merely the trap to capture him alive and without resistance. A bad conscience makes for a stupid decision; he gives his horse the spurs and rides off without giving an answer.

The sudden flight gives the signal for a riot.

"A criminal!" everyone shouts, and everyone bursts into pursuit of him. For the rider, it's a matter of life and death, he already has the head start, his pursuers gasp behind breathless, he is close to his escape — but a heavy hand invisibly pushes against him, the hourglass of his fate has run out, the unforgiving nemesis stops its debtor. The alley that he chose stops at a dead end, he has to turn back around toward his pursuers.

Meanwhile, the noise of this occurrence had brought the entire little city to a turmoil, crowds gather into mobs, all roads are blocked, an army of enemies marches against him. He shows them a pistol, the people retreat, he attempts to create a path through the crush by force. "This shot" he shouts,

"Is for the person foolhardy enough to try to stop me!" — Fear causes a sudden pause — finally an inspired journeyman locksmith seizes his arm from behind and grabs the finger with which the madman is just about to fire, and tears it out of its socket. The pistol falls, the defenseless man is ripped down from his horse and triumphantly dragged back to the courthouse.

"Who are you?" the judge asks in a rather brutal tone.

"A man who is determined not to answer a question until it is asked more respectfully."

"Who are you?"

"I am what I said I am. I have traveled throughout all of Germany and have never found disrespect to be so at home as it is here."

"Your sudden flight makes you look very suspicious. Why did you flee?"

"Because I was tired of being the laughing stock for your mob."

"You threatened to fire your weapon."

"My pistol was not loaded." They inspected the gun and it was not loaded.

"Why were you carrying a concealed weapon?"

"Because I am carrying items of value, and because I had been warned about a certain 'Innkeeper,' who is known to prowl these parts."

"Your answers say a lot about your audacity, but nothing for your own good cause. I'll give you some time until tomorrow, and we'll see then if you would like to reveal the truth to me."

"My testimony will remain the same."

"Take him to the tower."

"To the tower? — Your Honor, I hope there is still justice in this state. I will demand fair treatment."

"And I will give you fair treatment, as soon as you justify it."

The next morning the chief judge reconsidered, and decided that the stranger may well indeed be innocent, that the commanding tone would have no impact on his stubbornness, and it would perhaps prove better to approach him with decency and moderation. He gathered the city's jurors and had the prisoner brought before them.

"Excuse the initial outburst, Sir, if I treated you somewhat harshly yesterday."

"Gladly, when you speak to me like that."

"Our laws are strict, and your case caused commotion. I cannot simply let you go; to do so would be a dereliction of duty. All appearances speak against you. I wish you would say something to me that could prove the appearances false."

"And if I didn't have anything to tell?"

"Then I would have to report the occurrence to the government, and you would have to remain in prison."

"And then?"

"Then you would run the risk of being whipped across the border as a vagabond, or, if things go mercifully, you would fall into the hands of the military recruiters."

He was silent for several minutes and appeared to be in the midst of a terrible inner struggle; then he turned suddenly toward the judge.

"Can I have fifteen minutes alone with you?"

The jurors looked at each other doubtfully, but then left the room at the wave of their lord.

"Well, what is it you want?"

"Your behavior yesterday, Your Honor, would never have resulted in my confession, for I defy coercion. The modesty of your approach today has made me trust and respect you. I believe that you are a noble man."

"What is it you want to tell me?"

"I can see that you are a noble man. I have long wished to meet a man like you. Please, give me your right hand."

"What is the meaning of this?"

"This head is gray and honorable. — You have been in the world for a long time, have probably experienced many sorrows — haven't you? And you became more human."

"Sir — what is the meaning of this?"

"You stand just a short step before eternity; soon — soon, you will need mercy from God. You won't withhold mercy from others —— Didn't you suspect anything? With whom do you think you are talking?"

"What is the meaning of this? You are frightening me."

"You still have no idea? — Write to your prince how you found me, and that I betrayed myself of my own free will — and that God will have mercy on him some day, as he will on me now — plead for me, old man, and shed a tear on your report: I am the Innkeeper of the Sun."

4: The Duke of Alba's Breakfast at Rudolstadt Castle in the Year 1547

Friedrich Schiller (1788)
Translated by Ian Codding

As I LEAF THROUGH AN OLD CHRONICLE from the sixteenth century (*Res in Ecclesia et Politica Christiana gestae ab anno 1500 ad an. 1600*[1] by J. Soeffing, Doctor of Theology, Rudolstadt, 1676), I find the following anecdote, which for more than one reason deserves to be reclaimed from the annals of forgotten history. I find the story corroborated in a work entitled *Mausolea manibus Metzelii posita*[2] by Fr. Melch. Dedekindo, 1638. One can also look it up in Spangenberg's *Adelspiegel* part I. vol. 13, pg. 445.

There was a German lady from a house that had always shone with valor and had given the German Empire a Kaiser, who through her resolute behavior nearly brought the terrible Duke of Alba to his knees. After the battle at Mühlberg in the year 1547, when Emperor Charles V came through Thuringia on his way to Franconia and Swabia, the widowed Countess Katharina of Schwarzburg, born Princess of Henneberg, effected from him a letter of protection, so that her subjects should not have to suffer at the hands of the passing Spanish army. In return, she entered into an agreement to deliver bread, beer, and other provisions at an inexpensive price from Rudolstadt to the bridge over the Saale River, in order to supply the Spanish troops who would cross there. Before so doing, however, she took due precaution, quickly dismantled the bridge that was close to the town, and erected a new bridge across the water at a greater distance so that the all-too-convenient proximity of the town would not lead her plunder-hungry guests into temptation. At the same time, the inhabitants of all the villages through which the procession went were permitted to safekeep their best belongings in Rudolstadt Castle.

Meanwhile, the Spanish general, accompanied by Duke Heinrich of Braunschweig and his sons, approached the town and requested through a messenger, whom he sent ahead, that the Countess of Schwarzburg host his party for breakfast. Such a modest request made by the commanding officer of an army could not very well be refused. The Countess answered that they would serve the best that the house could provide; His Excellency may come and make do. At the same time, the point was made that the letter of protection was not to be forgotten, and the conscientious observation of the same was sincerely recommended to the Spanish general.

A friendly reception and a well-furnished table await the Duke in the castle. The Duke must concede that the Thuringian ladies run a very fine kitchen and dutifully uphold a guest's right to hospitality. Yet, they have hardly sat down when a messenger calls the Countess out of the dining hall. She is informed that the Spanish soldiers had subjected the peasants to violence in several villages on the way and had driven away their cattle. Katharina was a mother to her people; whatever befell the poorest of her subjects happened to Katharina herself. Enraged by the callous disregard for the agreement, yet maintaining her presence of mind, she orders her entire staff to arm themselves with all speed and discretion and to secure the castle gate. She herself proceeds again to the dining hall where the princes are still seated at the table. At this point, she complains to them in the most moving language about what was just revealed to her and about how poorly the Emperor's word has been upheld. Laughing in response, they assure her that these are the ways of war, and that on a soldiers' march, such regrettable mishaps are unavoidable. "We shall see about that," she answered indignantly. "The property of my poor subjects will be restored, or by God!" — raising her voice threateningly — "*the blood of princes for the blood of oxen!*" With this abrupt declaration, she left the room, which, in a few moments, was filled with armed men who planted themselves behind the princes' chairs, sword in hand yet with all due deference, and served the breakfast. Duke Alba's complexion changed with the entrance of this ready band; the assembled princes exchanged nervous glances, taken aback and dumbfounded. Cut off from the army and outnumbered by a stalwart host, what else could he do but summon all his patience and, whatever the conditions may be, reconcile with the indignant lady? Heinrich of Braunschweig composed himself first and burst into loud laughter. He seized the sensible way out, to turn the whole event into merriment, and showered the Countess with praise for her motherly care for her land and the resolute courage she had displayed. He asked her to remain calm and took it upon himself to gain permission from the Duke of Alba to do whatever was just. He also effectively convinced the Duke to issue an order to the army on the spot: The stolen cattle were to be returned to their owners immediately. As soon as the Countess of Schwarzburg was certain of their return, she thanked her guests most graciously, who very politely took their leave.

Without a doubt, it was this occurrence that earned Countess Katharina of Schwarzburg the name of Valorous. Her steadfast efforts in furthering the Reformation in her land, which her husband Count Heinrich XXXVII introduced there by abolishing monastic life and improving education, is still praised today. She granted protection and support to many Protestant ministers who had to endure persecution for the sake of religion. Among them was a certain Caspar Aquila, a minister in Saalfeld, who in his early years had accompanied the Emperor's army to the Netherlands as chaplain and, because he had refused to christen a cannonball, had been loaded into a fire mortar by rambunctious soldiers to be shot into the air — a fate that he fortunately escaped only because the powder wouldn't ignite. Now he was in deadly peril for the second time, and a price of 5000 guilder was offered for his head because the Emperor, whose edict he had condemned from the pulpit, was angry with him. At the request of the inhabitants of Saalfeld, Katharina had him secretly brought to her castle, where she kept him hidden for several months and looked after him with the noblest human kindness until he could show himself again without danger. She died universally honored and mourned in the fifty-eighth year of her life and the twenty-ninth year of her reign. The church in Rudolstadt houses her remains.

Translator's Notes

[1] Affairs in Christian Church and State Occurring from the Year 1500 to the Year 1600.

[2] Mausoleums Entombing the Metzel House.

5: Game of Fate. A Fragment of a True Story

Friedrich Schiller (1789)
Translated by Edward T. Larkin

ALOYSIUS VON G*** WAS THE ENNOBLED SON of a burgher in the service of the Prince of ***; early on, the seeds of his felicitous genius were encouraged by a liberal education. Young, but armed with a broad range of knowledge, he entered the military service of the Prince, who could not long remain unaware of the young man's great talents and even greater aspirations. G*** was in the full bloom of his youth, as was the Prince; G*** was quick and enterprising, and the similarly endowed Prince deeply admired such traits. With his prolific wit and comprehensive knowledge, G*** was able to inspire those around him; through his invariable good cheer he delighted the circles in which he moved; he brought zest and life to every situation that arose. The Prince had an eye for just these virtues, which he himself possessed to a great extent. Everything that G*** undertook, even his lighter pursuits, had a touch of grandeur; obstacles did not deter him, and failure could not shake his perseverance. The value of these virtues was heightened by a pleasing stature; the picture of his good health and his Herculean strength were ennobled by the expressive playfulness of his active mind. His countenance, his gait, and his being exuded an innate, natural majesty, which was tempered by a noble modesty. If the Prince was enchanted by his young companion's intellect, G***'s winning appearance appealed even more irresistibly to his sensual nature. Their closeness in age, harmonious inclinations and characters led quickly to a relationship that possessed all the power of friendship as well as all the fire and intensity of passionate love. G*** progressed rapidly from one post to the next, but these external signs could not nearly reflect what he truly meant to the Prince. His good fortune flourished with astounding swiftness because the creator of his happiness adored him and was his passionate friend. Not yet twenty years of age, G*** had reached heights that even the most fortunate appointees only attain at the end of their careers. But his active mind could not long rest in the lap of idle vanity, nor could it be content with the gleaming trappings of greatness; with a sense of his own power and daring he intended to put his advantages to use. While the Prince pursued the brass ring of pleasure, the young favorite buried himself in documents and books and dedicated himself with great diligence to the affairs of the state, executing them so skillfully and completely that soon every moderately important matter of the principality had to pass through his hands. From an indulgent companion G*** became a councilor, then minister, and finally master of his Prince. Soon there was no other way to the Prince than through G***. He appointed all officials, decided every rank, and bestowed all commendations and distinctions.

G*** had ascended to this preeminence at too early an age and at a pace too quick to enjoy it with appropriate moderation. The heights to which he had seen himself ascend left him dizzy with ambition. Modesty abandoned him as soon as his next goal was within reach. The humble submissiveness shown to such a young man by the highest-standing members of the principality — so far above him by virtue of their birth, renown, or property — intoxicated his pride, and the unlimited power that he now had at his disposal soon revealed in his character a certain hardness, a trait that had always been latent in his character and persisted through all the changes in his fortune. To his friends he was incapable of failure no matter how great or arduous the task, but his enemies trembled, for as much as he exaggerated his good will toward his friends, his lack of restraint with respect to revenge was every bit as extreme. He used his standing less to enrich himself than to make very many others happy, who had to then pay homage to him, the creator of their good fortune — but caprice, not a sense of justice, selected the objects of his attention. Through an arrogant, authoritarian manner, he alienated even those who had been most beholden to him, while he simultaneously made irreconcilable enemies out of his rivals and those who secretly envied him.

Among those who watched his every step with the eyes of jealousy and envy and who secretly arranged the instruments of his downfall was a count from Piedmont, Joseph Martinengo. Believing Martinengo to be trustworthy and devoted to him, G*** secured a position for him in the entourage of the Prince. In so doing, G*** had hoped that the Italian Count would replace him at the Prince's festivities, which began to bore him; he preferred to be involved with more important matters. G*** viewed the Count as a tool in his own hands, someone whom he could return to the obscurity whence he had come at his choosing; convinced of the Italian Count's fear and gratitude, G*** felt himself invulnerable. Thus he made the same error as had Cardinal Richelieu when he gave Louis XIII the young le Grand as a playmate. But, unlike the clever Richelieu, who corrected his error, G*** was unable to do so; he had in fact a more devious enemy to deal with than had the French minister. Martinengo did not show arrogance at his good fortune, nor did he let his benefactor feel that he no longer needed him. Rather, he took great pains to maintain the appearance of dependence and, through feigned submissiveness, to increasingly attach himself to the creator of his happiness. Moreover, he never missed the opportunity, the result of his new position, to be near the Prince and to make himself indispensable to him. In a short time he knew every aspect of the Prince's nature by heart; he ingratiated himself with him and quickly gained his trust. To achieve his goal, the Italian employed all of the devious arts that a noble pride and natural sublimity of soul had taught G*** to despise. But since Martinengo knew that man is nowhere in greater need of a leader and a guide than on the path of vice, and that nothing justifies intimacy more than the shared knowledge of secret weaknesses, he was able to evoke in the Prince feelings that had until now lay dormant. Then he thrust himself upon the Prince as confidant and accomplice. By drawing the Prince into debauchery such as no witness or intimate acquaintance would countenance, he was able to convince the unwitting Prince to reveal to him secrets that by their very nature need remain unknown to anyone else. Thus he at last succeeded in executing the scandalous plan for his own rising fortune through the moral decline of the Prince and since secrecy itself was the key, Martinengo was able to ensure that the Prince's heart was his alone before G*** could even imagine that he shared it with someone else.

One might wonder how such a significant change escaped G***'s notice, but he was too sure of his own importance to even imagine that a man like Martinengo could be his rival, and Martinengo was too self-aware, had too much presence of mind, to awaken his opponent from his arrogant sense of security through any indiscretion. What had caused thousands before him to make a false step on the slippery slope of a Prince's favor also preceded G***'s fall — too much self-assurance. The secretive intimacy between Martinengo and the Prince did not alarm him. He gladly granted the newcomer his newfound good fortune, one that he in his own heart disdained and that had never been the goal of his endeavors. Friendship with the Prince enticed him only because it paved the way to the highest power, and foolhardily he let the ladder fall behind him as soon as it had helped him climb to his desired height.

Martinengo was not a man to be satisfied with a subordinate role. With every stride he made into the Prince's heart, his desires became bolder, and his ambition immediately strove for ever-greater satisfaction. Up to this point, he had always been able to maintain a feigned submissiveness toward G***, his benefactor, but in time, the more his heightened standing with the Prince inspired his arrogance, the more oppressive his subservience to G*** became. G***'s attitude toward him had not progressed as well as had that of the Prince; G***, in fact, seemed all too visibly intent on limiting his inflated pride and position through a demeaning reminder that Martinengo served at his pleasure. In time, Martinengo's coercive and discordant relationship with G*** became so vexing that he developed a plan to destroy his rival once and for all. Because he was not yet in a position to engage his rival in public, he hatched his scheme behind the most impenetrable veil of harmlessness. Although the first flower of G***'s favored status at the court had indeed passed, his relationship with the Prince had begun much earlier and had taken root too deeply to be so quickly supplanted. The smallest turn of circumstances could return their relationship to its former strength; for this reason Martinengo understood that his coup had to be quick and lethal. What G*** might have lost of the Prince's *love,* he had won in his *respect.* The more the Prince had withdrawn from matters of governance, the less he could dispense with the man who, even at considerable expense to the principality, had looked after his affairs with the most conscientious devotion and loyalty — and as dear as he had been to him as a friend, he was now equally important to him as his minister.

How the Italian actually achieved his aim has remained a secret between those few who felt the blow and who delivered it. It is suspected that Martinengo presented the Prince with the actual letters of a secret and highly suspicious correspondence that G*** is rumored to have carried on with a neighboring court; opinions are divided whether the claim was legitimate or fabricated. Whatever the case might have actually been, Martinengo fulfilled his intention to a horrific extent. G*** appeared in the eyes of the Prince as the blackest and most ungrateful traitor, one whose crimes were so far beyond doubt that it was justified to proceed against him immediately and without further investigation. Every detail was prepared in deepest secrecy by Martinengo and the Prince, such that G*** did not even remotely sense the impending storm that gathered around him. He persisted in his false self-assurance until the terrible moment came when, instead of being the object of universal praise and envy, he would sink to the object of deepest pity.

When the critical day arrived, G*** attended the parade of the sentinels, as was his habit. He himself had advanced, within a short period of time, from the rank of officer cadet to that of colonel, and even this post was only a modest name for the ministerial office that he actually held and that placed him above the leading members of the principality. The parade of the sentinels was the usual place where he was paid homage, where for a brief hour he enjoyed the grandeur and adulation for having borne the administrative burdens through the long day. Here, the most distinguished members of society approached him with deferential caution, and those who were not sure whether they were in his good graces, with trepidation. The Prince himself, whenever he happened to be here, saw himself fairly ignored vis-à-vis his vizier, for it was far more dangerous to be disliked by the minister than it was advantageous to be a friend of the Prince. And just this place, where G*** had been revered as a God, was selected to be the terrible setting of his humiliation.

Without the least worry, G*** approached the familiar group of people, who, also unaware of what was to happen, welcomed him in their usual reverential manner and awaited his orders. After a short while Martinengo arrived, accompanied by several adjutant officers. No longer the compliant, subservient, smiling courtier, but rather impertinent and coarsely presumptuous — like a lackey turned master — Martinengo marches over to G*** with steady, defiant steps; he stands before him, with covered head, and demands his sword in the name of the Prince. It is handed to him with a look of silent outrage. Martinengo sticks the unsheathed blade into the ground and breaks it in two with his foot, the pieces falling at G***'s feet. At this prearranged signal two adjutant officers seize G***, the one cutting the medal from his chest while the other rips off the two aiguillettes, the lapels of his uniform, and the cordon and the plume from his hat. The entire terrible event unfolds in remarkable haste, and not a word is heard from the five hundred onlookers, who stand in a tight circle, not a single breath in the whole gathering. With pale faces, palpitating hearts, and in death-like stupor, the shocked crowd stands around him, in the freakish fragments of his costume — a unique sight of ridicule and horror — with that feeling only those can know who have stood on the gallows. The force of the initial shock would have caused thousands of others in this situation to faint dead away, but G***'s robust emotional condition and his strong spirit enabled him to experience and endure all the horror of the moment.

Hardly has he been seized when he is led through countless rows of spectators to the farthest end of the parade square where an enclosed coach awaits him. A silent nod commands him to climb into the coach; a company of Hussars escorts him. Meanwhile, rumors of what has happened quickly spread through the royal residence: the windows are flung open, and the streets fill with the curious, who shout at the departing coach; they chant his name, alternating between cries of scorn, malicious glee, and, even more humiliating, pity. He finally finds himself in the open space outside the palace, but here a new horror awaits him. Turning off the main street, the coach moves slowly along a deserted, seldom used road — at the explicit command of the Prince, G*** is taken down the route that leads to the gallows. Here, once he has been given time to suffer all the tortures of the fear of death, the coach turns into a populated street again. Tormented by the scorching heat, without nourishment, without words of comfort, he spends the next seven hours in the coach, and finally at sunset he arrives at the place of his destiny — the fortress. Bereft of consciousness, in that medial state somewhere between life and death (twelve hours without food and a burning thirst had finally overcome his powerful nature), he is dragged from the coach — and awakens in a dreadful subterranean shaft. The first sight that he encounters when he has opened his eyes is a ghastly prison wall, faintly illuminated by beams of moonlight that fall upon him through a few thin slits from a height of about thirty feet. — Nearby he finds a meager loaf of bread, a water jug, and a bundle of hay for his bed. He remains in this state until noon the next day, when a shutter in the middle of the tower opens and two hands can be seen lowering a hanging basket containing the same food he had found the previous day. Now for the first time since he had been subjected to this terrible change of fortune, his pain and longing compel him to ask some questions: How has he come to this? What crime has he committed? But there is no answer from above: The hands disappear, and the shutter is closed again. Without having seen a human face, without having heard a human voice, without having learned anything of his terrible fate, in equally dreadful despair about his future and his past, unrelieved by any ray of light or any healthy breeze to refresh him, beyond all help and untouched by human sympathy, he spends four hundred and ninety days in this place of damnation, counting the days with the same wretched bread that is lowered to him in dismal uniformity from one noon to the next. But one discovery, made in the first days of his sentence, completes the measure of his misery. He knows this prison — driven by base revenge, it was he who ordered it built a few months earlier in order to punish an officer of some merit, who had had the misfortune to attract his anger. With inventive cruelty, he himself had provided the means to make a stay in this prison even more gruesome. Not long ago, he had traveled here in person to inspect its construction and to hasten its completion. To increase his martyrdom to the most extreme, his jailer is the very same officer for whom the prison was built, an older, dignified colonel who has taken over for the recently deceased commandant of the fortress. No longer just another casualty of G***'s revenge, the colonel has become the master of his fate. Thus G*** could not even accuse fate of any injustice for his mistreatment, nor could he find some final pathetic consolation in self-pity. Moreover, in addition to the physical sensation of his misery, he felt a raging self-hatred and the painful awareness, the most bitter imaginable for the proud of heart, that he was dependent on the magnanimity of an enemy, to whom *he* had shown none.

But this upright man was too noble for common revenge. The severity with which his training dictated that he treat the prisoner took an enormous toll on his humane heart; still, as an old soldier accustomed to following orders with blind loyalty, he could do no more than pity his prisoner. The unfortunate G*** found a more active helper in the garrison chaplain, who was moved by his suffering and, once he had learned of G***'s fate (and this only through obscure and ambiguous rumors), immediately determined to do something to relieve his suffering. This admirable clergyman, whose name I unfortunately may not disclose, thought he could best fulfill his pastoral mission by placing himself in the service of this wretched prisoner, who had no hope of help in any other form.

Since the chaplain could not secure the assent of the commandant of the fortress to visit the prisoner, he took it upon himself to go to the capital where he submitted his petition directly to the Prince. He kneeled before the Prince and implored him to show mercy for the miserable wretch, who languished helplessly without the blessings of the church, which even the most heinous criminal should not be denied, and who was perhaps near complete despair. With all the intrepidness and dignity conferred by the consciousness of fulfilling one's duty, he demanded free access to the prisoner, a man who rightfully belonged to him as confessor and for whose soul he was answerable to heaven. The good cause for which he spoke made him eloquent, and time itself had weakened the reluctance of the Prince. He ultimately granted the request to allow the prisoner spiritual counsel.

The first human face that the wretched G*** saw after a period of sixteen months was that of his helper. The only friend that he had in the world he owed to his miserable condition; his prosperity had brought him no such friend. The chaplain's visit was like the appearance of an angel for him. I won't describe his emotions. But from this day forward G***'s tears flowed more gently, because he saw that one human being had wept for him.

Horror seized the clergyman upon entering the death pit. His eyes looked for a human being — but a horror-inspiring abomination crawled toward him from the corner of the pit, which itself resembled more the lair of a wild animal than the domicile of a human creature. There he found a pale, deathly-looking skeleton, whose coloring had disappeared from his face, a face that was lined with deep wrinkles of grief and despair. His beard and nails had grown monstrous from long neglect, and his clothing had decomposed from lengthy use; the air around him was fully befouled — this is how he found our darling of fortune, yet under it all, G***'s iron constitution had not capitulated! Beside himself at the sight, the chaplain hurried to the Governor to effect a second good deed for the unfortunate prisoner, without which the first would be of no avail.

But when the Governor again repeatedly refuses his request on the basis of the letter of the orders he received, the chaplain nobly decides to travel to the residence again to beseech the Prince for mercy. He explains that, as long as the prisoner is not allowed some semblance of humanity, he cannot take any clerical measures to minister to him without violating the sanctity of the sacrament. The Prince once again agrees, and only from this day on could one say that the prisoner G*** was again among the living.

G*** spent many more years in the fortress, but in much more tolerable circumstances once the brief summer of his rival Martinengo had faded and when others of a more humane heart, or at least others who harbored him no revenge, had assumed his post at the court. Finally, after a ten-year term in prison, the day of redemption arrived — however, without judicial investigation and without formal acquittal. G*** understood his release from prison as a merciful gift, a clear condition of which was that he leave the principality forever.

The information that I have been able to gather about G***'s fate, based solely on oral sources, ceases at this point; I have no choice but to skip over a period of twenty years, during which time G*** began a career in the military service of a foreign government, where the arc of his rise once again reached the heights from which he had been toppled in his homeland. In the end, Time, the friend to the hopeless, which slowly but surely exercises inevitable justice, took up his legal claim. The Prince's years of fervid passion had passed, and, as his hair lost its color, he had slowly come to understand humankind in a more favorable light. Nearing death, a longing awakened in him to see the darling of his youth. In order to compensate G***, as an old man, for the suffering that he had inflicted on him in his best years — if that be possible — he extended an invitation for his exiled companion to return to his fatherland, a silent desire that had likewise long since taken root in G***'s heart. The reunion was touching; the meeting was warm, and it was confusing, as if they had only parted yesterday. The Prince's eyes rested reflectively on the face that was both so familiar and at the same time so foreign to him; it was as if he counted the wrinkles that he himself had etched in the face. Scrutinizing the old man's features, the Prince looked in vain for the beloved traits of the youth, but what he sought, he no longer found. The two men forced themselves to a frosty intimacy. — The shame and fear in each of their hearts had parted them for now and for eternity. To behold the face that inspired him to recall his own fateful haste could not ease the Prince's pain, nor could G*** any longer love the author of his misfortune. Nevertheless, with solace and peace of mind, he could look back on his own past as one who is happy to have awakened from a deep, dark dream.

Not long thereafter, G*** could once again be seen restored to all his former glory, and the Prince overcame his inner aversion and offered him brilliant compensation for his past sufferings. But could he return to him the heart that is meant to enjoy life's pleasures, the heart that he had maimed forever? Could he give him back the years of hope, or even imagine a happiness for the old man that could hope to compensate for the robbery that he had committed against the young one?

For another nineteen years G*** enjoyed the cheerful twilight of his life. Neither fate, nor time had been able to extinguish the fire of his passion, nor had they clouded the geniality of his spirits. Even at seventy years of age, he hatched plans to acquire an estate that he had actually owned in his twenties. He finally died — as the commandant of the fortress ***, where prisoners of the state were incarcerated. One might imagine that he extended to these prisoners a degree of human kindness that he had had to learn to value from his own experience. But he treated them harshly and capriciously, and an explosion of anger toward one of them laid him in his coffin in his eightieth year.

6: *The Spiritualist. From the Memoirs of Count von O***

Friedrich Schiller (1789)
Translated by Francis Lamport

Book One

I AM GOING TO TELL YOU ABOUT a series of occurrences which many will find incredible, and which I largely witnessed with my own eyes. Those few who are familiar with a certain affair in the political world, if they should still be alive to read these papers, will find that they cast a welcome light on that matter; and even those others who lack this key to the story will perhaps find in it a significant contribution to the history of treachery and of the aberrations of the human spirit. They will be astonished at the *daring purposes* wickedness is capable of conceiving and pursuing; and they will be amazed at the extraordinary *means* which it contrives in order to achieve those aims. Truth pure and simple will guide my pen, for if these papers ever reach the public, I shall by then be no more and shall have nothing either to gain or to lose on account of what I have to report.

I was on my way back to Courland[1] in 17**, at about the carnival season, when I called on the Prince of ** in Venice. We had served together in the ** army, and were renewing an acquaintance which had been interrupted by the signing of peace. Since I in any case wanted to see the sights of the city, and as the Prince was only waiting for certain letters of credit before he could return to **, he easily persuaded me to postpone my departure so that I could keep him company until then. We agreed not to part from one another for as long as we remained in Venice, and the Prince graciously offered me accommodation in his own lodgings at the Moor's Head.

He was staying there under the strictest incognito, because he wanted to be left to himself, and also because his modest establishment would not have allowed him to display the full dignity of his rank. Two gentlemen, on whose discretion he could absolutely rely, made up together with a few loyal servants his whole entourage. He avoided extravagance, though as much from temperament as from financial necessity. He shunned the pleasures of the city; at the age of thirty-five he had managed to resist all its sensual temptations. The fair sex had up to this time had no attractions for him. A profound seriousness and a dreamy melancholy dominated his character. His inclinations were silent, but persistent to the point of obstinacy; his decisions slow and hesitant, his affections warm and lasting. In the midst of noisy crowds of people, he walked alone; rapt in the world of his own imagination, he was often a stranger in the real one. No one was more surely born to be dominated by others, though he was not weak. But once he had been won over, he was fearless and dependable, and was equally courageous whether in fighting one recognised prejudice or in facing death in the cause of another.

As the third in line of succession, he was unlikely ever to attain the throne. His ambition had never been awakened; his passions had taken another direction. Content to remain independent of the will of others, he felt no temptation to rule over them himself; the peace and freedom of private life and the enjoyment of cultivated company satisfied all his wishes. He read a good deal, but indiscriminately; a neglected education and early military service meant that his mind was still immature. All the knowledge he had subsequently acquired served only to increase the confusion of his ideas, because they lacked any solid foundation.

He was a Protestant, like the rest of his family — from birth, not as a result of serious enquiries, for he had never conducted any, although at one period of his life he had been something of a religious zealot. As far as I know he had never become a Freemason.

One evening when, by ourselves and heavily masked as usual, we were walking in St Mark's Square — it was getting late, and the crowds had dispersed — the Prince observed that a masked figure was following us everywhere. He was dressed like an Armenian priest, and appeared to be alone. We hastened our steps and tried to put him off our track by frequently changing direction, but it was useless — the masked figure remained close behind us. "You are not involved in some affair here, are you?" the Prince finally asked me; "Venetian husbands can be dangerous." "I have no relations with any Venetian lady," I replied. "Let us sit down here and speak German," he continued, "I think we may have been mistaken for someone else." We sat down on a stone bench, thinking that the masked figure would carry on past us. He came straight up to us and sat down close beside the Prince. The Prince took out his watch and said to me aloud in French, standing up as he did so, "Past nine o'clock. Come along, we are forgetting that they are expecting us in the Louvre."[2] He said this only to stop the masked figure from following us. "*Nine o'clock,*" repeated the masked man, slowly and emphatically, in the same language. "Congratulations, Prince" (and here he addressed the Prince by his proper name), "*he died at nine o'clock.*" And with that he stood up and left us.

We looked at each other in astonishment. — "Who has died?" said the Prince at last, after a long silence. — "Let us follow him," said I, "and ask him to explain himself." We explored every corner of St Mark's Square, but the masked man was not to be found. Dissatisfied, we returned to our hotel. On the way the Prince said not a word to me, but walked by himself to one side and seemed to be engaged in some intense inner struggle — as he afterwards confessed to me was indeed the case.

When we reached our lodgings, he spoke again for the first time. "It is ridiculous," he said, "that a madman can disturb a man's peace of mind with two words." We wished each other goodnight, and as soon as I reached my room I made a note of the day and of the time when this had happened. It was a Thursday.

The following evening, the Prince said to me, "Why don't we take a walk round St Mark's Square and see if we can't find our mysterious Armenian? I must admit I want to know the meaning of this masquerade." I agreed. We stayed in the square until eleven o'clock. The Armenian was nowhere to be seen. We did the same on the next four evenings, and with no better success.

When we left our hotel on the sixth evening, the idea came to me — whether by chance or by design, I do not know — of leaving a message with the servants to say where we could be found if anyone should ask for us. The Prince observed my precautions and approved them with a smile. There were crowds of people in St Mark's Square when we arrived there. We had hardly gone thirty paces when I saw the Armenian again. He was striding rapidly through the crowds and seemed to be looking out for someone. We were on the point of reaching him when Baron von F**, one of the Prince's retinue, approached us, out of breath, and handed the Prince a letter. "It's sealed in black," he added, "we thought it must be urgent." It struck me like a thunderbolt. The Prince went over to a streetlamp and began to read. "My cousin is dead," he cried. "*When?*" I interrupted hastily. He looked at the letter again. "Last Thursday. At nine o'clock in the evening."

Before we had had time to recover from our astonishment, the Armenian had joined us. "You have been recognised here, Your Highness," he said. "Hurry back to the Moor's Head. You will find a delegation from the Senate waiting for you there. Do not hesitate to accept the honour you will be offered. Baron von F** forgot to tell you that your letters of credit have arrived." With that, he was lost in the crowd.

We hurried back to our hotel. Everything was as the Armenian had told us it would be. Three Nobili of the Republic were standing ready to greet the Prince and to escort him with all due pomp to the Assembly, where the highest aristocracy of the city were awaiting him. He barely had time to indicate to me by a hasty gesture that I should wait up for him.

At about eleven at night he returned. Grave and thoughtful, he came into my room and took me by the hand, after he had dismissed the servants. "Count," he said to me in Hamlet's words, "there are more things in heaven and earth than are dreamt of in our philosophies."

"Your Highness," I replied, "you seem to have forgotten that you are going to bed much richer in hope than you were before." (The Prince who had died was the sole son and heir of the reigning ***, who was old and ailing and without further hope of a direct heir. An uncle of our Prince, also without heirs and with no hope of ever having any, was now the only one standing between him and the throne. I mention this circumstance because there will be occasion to speak of it later.)

"Don't remind me of it," said the Prince. "And even if I had gained a crown, I should have better things to do now than to speculate on such a trivial matter. — If this Armenian has not simply guessed —"

"How is it possible, Prince?" I interjected.

"— Then I will yield all my princely hopes to you for a monk's habit."

On the following evening we were at St Mark's Square earlier than usual. A sudden shower of rain drove us into a coffeehouse, where some men were seated at the gaming tables. The Prince placed himself behind a Spaniard's chair to watch the play. I had gone into a neighbouring room and was reading the newspapers. After a little while I heard a disturbance. Before the Prince arrived, the Spaniard had been losing all the time; now he was winning with every card. The whole game had taken a different turn, and the bank was in danger of being challenged by the lucky punter[3] who had been emboldened by this change of fortune. The Venetian who was keeping the bank addressed the Prince in an offensive tone of voice and told him to leave the table, because he was upsetting the run of the game. The Prince looked at him coldly and stayed where he was, remaining unruffled when the Venetian repeated his offensive remarks in French. Thinking that the Prince understood neither language, he turned to the others, laughing contemptuously: "Tell me, gentlemen, how can I make myself understood to this buffoon?" At the same moment, he stood up and tried to seize the Prince by the arm; the Prince lost his patience, laid a firm hand on the Venetian, and threw him roughly to the ground. The whole house was in commotion. Hearing the noise, I rushed in, and involuntarily called out to the Prince by name. "Take care, Prince," I added without thinking, "we are in Venice." The name of the Prince caused a general silence, which soon gave way to a murmuring which sounded dangerous to me. All the Italians present gathered together in groups and stood aside. One after another they left the room, until we were left alone with the Spaniard and a number of Frenchmen. "You are lost, Your Highness," they said, "unless you leave the city immediately. The Venetian that you mishandled is rich and highly regarded: it will only cost him fifty zecchini to have you disposed of." The

Spaniard offered to fetch the police to ensure the Prince's safety and to see us home himself. The Frenchmen would have done the same. We were still standing and considering what to do, when the door opened and a number of servants of the State Inquisition appeared. They produced a government warrant ordering us both to follow them immediately. We were marched off under a heavy escort to a canal. Here there was a gondola waiting, in which we were made to take our places. Before we disembarked, our eyes were blindfolded. We were led up a long stone staircase and then through a long, twisting passage with vaults beneath it, as I judged from the echoes which reverberated beneath our feet. Finally we came to another staircase, where twenty-six steps led us down into the depths. Here it opened into a large room, where our blindfolds were removed. We found ourselves encircled by a group of venerable old men, all dressed in black; the whole room was hung with black drapes and sparsely lit; there was a deathly silence in the whole assembly, which made a fearsome impression. One of these old men, presumably the chief State Inquisitor, approached the Prince and asked him ceremoniously, at the same time presenting the Venetian to him, "Do you recognise this man as the one who insulted you at the coffee house?"

"Yes," answered the Prince.

Upon this the Inquisitor turned to the prisoner: "Is this the person whom you this evening sought to have assassinated?"

The prisoner replied in the affirmative.

Immediately the men in the circle drew back, and we were horrified to see the Venetian's head severed from his body. "Are you content with this restitution?" asked the Inquisitor. — The Prince had fainted in the arms of his escort. — "Go now," continued the Inquisitor in a terrible voice, "and do not be so hasty to judge the justice of the Republic of Venice in future."

Who the unknown friend might be who had called upon the swift arm of the law to save us from certain death, we could not imagine. Rigid with terror, we reached our quarters after midnight. Chamberlain Z** was waiting impatiently on the steps.

"What a good thing that you had sent us your message!" he said to the Prince, as he lighted our way. "What Baron von F** told us when he returned from St Mark's Square shortly afterwards made us fear for your lives."

"What, I sent you a message? When was that? I know nothing about it."

"This evening just after eight. You told us that we were not to worry if you came home later than usual tonight."

At this the Prince turned to look at me. "Did you perhaps take this precaution without my knowledge?"

I knew nothing about it.

"But it must be so, Your Highness," said the chamberlain; "look, here is your repeater watch, that you sent us as a token." The Prince felt for his watch pocket. The watch was indeed missing, and he recognised that the one the chamberlain was holding was his. "Who brought it to you?" he asked in amazement.

"No one we knew, a masked man, dressed like an Armenian; he went away again immediately."

We stood staring at each other. — "What do you think of this?" said the Prince at last, after a long silence. "Someone is secretly watching over me here in Venice."

The fearful business of this night had given the Prince a fever, which confined him to his rooms for a week. During this time the hotel was swarming with both local people and strangers, drawn by the discovery of the Prince's rank. They vied with one another in offering their services, each one wanting to stake his claim in his own way. There was no further mention of the proceedings in the State Inquisition. Because the court at ** wanted the Prince to delay his departure further, some money changers in Venice had been instructed to pay him considerable sums. And so he found himself, against his will, in a position to prolong his stay in Italy, and at his request I too decided to postpone my departure further.

As soon as he was recovered enough to leave his room again, the doctor persuaded him to take an excursion on the Brenta for a change of air. The weather was fine, and so it was agreed. As we were about to board the gondola, the Prince found that he was missing the key to a small chest which contained some very important papers. We immediately turned back to look for it. He remembered quite clearly that he had locked the chest the very day before, and since that time he had not left the room. But all our searching was in vain, and we had to give up in order to lose no more time. The Prince, whose soul was innocent of all suspicion, said that it must simply be lost, and that we were not to mention it again.

The excursion was as pleasant as could be. A picturesque landscape, seeming to surpass itself in richness and beauty with every bend in the river; the clearest of skies, bringing a breath of May in the middle of February; charming gardens and tasteful villas without number adorning both banks of the Brenta; behind us Venice the magnificent, with a hundred masts and towers rising from the waters — all combined to give us the grandest spectacle in the world. We surrendered completely to the enchantment of this natural beauty; we were in the most cheerful of spirits, the Prince himself casting off his gravity and vying with us in jesting and merriment. As we disembarked a few miles from the city, we were greeted by the sounds of merry music. They came from a small village, where a fair was being held; here there was company of every kind. A troupe of youths and girls, all in costume, welcomed us with a pantomime dance. Everything was original, every movement inspired with lightness and grace. Before the dance had quite finished, the chief girl dancer, who played the part of a queen, was suddenly seized as if by an invisible arm. She stood lifeless, as did all about her. The music ceased. Not a breath was to be heard in the whole gathering, and she stood there as if paralysed, her gaze fixed upon the ground. Suddenly she started up furiously as if inspired, stared wildly about her — cried out "There is a king amongst us," tore the crown from her head and laid it — at the Prince's feet. Everyone present now turned their eyes upon him, uncertain for a long while whether there was any meaning in this performance, so convincing was the dancer's passionate seriousness. — Finally a general round of applause broke the silence. I looked towards the Prince. I observed that he was seriously affected and was trying hard to avoid the searching looks of the spectators. He threw some money to the children and hurried away to escape the crowd.

We had only gone a few paces when a venerable barefoot monk made his way through the assembled people and barred the Prince's way. "Sire," he said, "make a gift to the Madonna from your riches; you will have need of her prayers." We were taken aback by these words and by the tone in which he spoke them. Then he was swept away in the throng.

Meanwhile our company had grown in number. An English lord, whom the Prince had already met in Nice, some merchants from Livorno, a German canon, a French abbé accompanied by a number of ladies, and a Russian officer had joined us. There was something quite unusual about this man's physiognomy, which drew our attention to him. Never in my life have I seen so many *features* and so little *character,* such attractive benevolence and such frosty indifference combined in a single human face. All the passions seemed to have raged there and then left it again. Nothing remained but the silent, piercing look of an accomplished connoisseur of men, from whose gaze all those it met shrank back. This strange man followed us at a distance, but seemed to be taking only a casual interest in everything that was happening.

We found ourselves standing in front of a stall where a draw was taking place. The ladies paid their entries, and the rest of us followed their example; the Prince himself asked for a ticket. He won a snuffbox. When he opened it, I saw him start back and turn pale. — The key lay inside it.

"What is this?" said the Prince to me, when we were left alone for a moment. "Some higher power is pursuing me. I am surrounded by omniscience. Some invisible being, from which I cannot escape, is watching my every move. I must find the Armenian and get him to cast some light on all this."

The sun was beginning to set as we arrived at the hostelry where supper was being served. The Prince's name had caused our company to grow to sixteen people. In addition to those already mentioned, we had been joined by a virtuoso from Rome, a number of Swiss, and an adventurer from Palermo, who wore uniform and liked to be called Captain. We decided to spend the whole evening here and to return home by torchlight. There was animated conversation at the table, and the Prince could not resist telling the company about the occurrence with the key, which aroused general astonishment. It gave rise to a lively argument. Most of the company dismissed the matter out of hand by saying that all these occult arts were mere conjurer's tricks; the abbé, who was already well wined, threw down the gauntlet to the whole realm of spirits; the Englishman uttered blasphemies; the musician crossed himself for fear of the devil. A few, including the Prince, held that one should reserve judgement about these things; all this time, the Russian officer remained in conversation with the ladies and seemed not to be taking any notice of our discussion. In the heat of the argument no one had noticed that the Sicilian had gone out. After half an hour or so he returned, wrapped in a cloak, and positioned himself behind the Frenchman's chair. "You were bold enough just now to take on all the spirits — would you care to try your luck with just *one* of them?"

"Done!" said the Abbé — "if you will take it upon yourself to summon one up for me."

"I will," said the Sicilian, turning to us as he said this, "when these ladies and gentlemen have first left us."

"Why?" cried the Englishman. "A bold spirit won't be afraid of a merry company."

"I will not be responsible for what may happen," said the Sicilian.

"In heaven's name, no!" cried the ladies around the table and rose from their seats in terror.

"Let us see your spirit, then," said the abbé, defiantly; "but warn him beforehand that there are sharp blades here" — as he asked one of the other guests for his sword.

"Do as you please, when the time comes," said the Sicilian coldly, "if you find you still have a mind to." With this he turned to the Prince. "Your Highness," he said to him, "you maintain that your key has been in strange hands. Have you any idea in whose?"

"No."

"Can you not even guess?"

"It did cross my mind —"

"Would you recognise this person, if you saw him?"

"Certainly."

Here the Sicilian threw back his cloak and produced a mirror, which he held up to the Prince's face.

"Is this the man?"

The Prince started back in fright.

"What did you see?" I asked.

"The Armenian."

The Sicilian hid the mirror under his cloak again. "Was that the person you were thinking of?" everyone present asked the Prince.

"The very same."

Upon this everyone's expression changed, and all laughter ceased. All eyes were turned intently upon the Sicilian.

"Monsieur l'Abbé, this is looking serious," said the Englishman; "in your position I would consider beating a retreat."

"The fellow is possessed by the devil," cried the Frenchman, and ran out of the house; the ladies rushed screaming from the room, the virtuoso followed them, the German canon was snoring in an armchair; the Russian remained in his seat, indifferent as before.

"Did you just want to make a laughingstock of that boastful fellow," began the Prince again, when the others had left the room, "or might you have a fancy to keep your word for us?"

"It is true," said the Sicilian. "I didn't really mean it with the abbé, because I knew that the coward would not take me at my word. — But the matter is really too serious just to make a joke of."

"So you admit that it is within your power?"

The magician was silent for some time, and seemed to be scrutinising the Prince very carefully.

"Yes," he finally replied.

The Prince's curiosity had already reached fever pitch. To make contact with the spirit world had once been the fantasy dearest to his heart, and since that first encounter with the Armenian all those ideas which his maturer reason had meanwhile dismissed had once again risen to his mind. He took the Sicilian to one side, and I heard him negotiating with him very seriously.

"You have a man before you," he said, "who is burning with impatience to be convinced about this important matter. I would embrace any man as my benefactor, as my greatest friend, if he could disperse my doubts and draw the veil from my eyes. Would you be the man to deserve so much of me?"

"What is it that you want of me?" said the magician hesitantly.

"For now, merely a sample of your art. Let me see some manifestation."

"What is that to lead to?"

"That when you know me better, you may judge whether I am worthy of further instruction."

"Your gracious Highness, I have the greatest possible regard for you. A secret power in your countenance, of which you yourself are not yet aware, bound me to you as soon as I saw you. You are stronger than you yourself realise. All my powers are at your absolute command — but —"

"Then let me see some manifestation."

"But I must first be sure that you are not asking this of me out of mere curiosity. Even though the invisible powers are to some degree at my command, this is subject to the sacred condition that I do not profane the sacred mysteries, that I do not abuse my power."

"My intentions are the purest. I seek the truth."

Here they left their places and went to a window some way away, where I could no longer hear them. The Englishman, who had also been listening to their conversation, drew me aside.

"Your Prince is a fine man. I am sorry to see him getting involved with this charlatan."

"It will all depend," I said, "on how he manages to extricate himself."

"Shall I tell you something?" said the Englishman. "Now the wretched fellow is putting up his price. He isn't going to show off his tricks until he hears the money chinking. There are nine of us. Let's make a collection and tempt him with a big fee. That will show him up and open your Prince's eyes for him."

"Very well."

The Englishman tossed six guineas on to a plate and passed it round the company. Everyone put in a few louis; the Russian in particular seemed uncommonly interested in our proposal, and lay a banknote for a hundred zecchini on the plate — an extravagance at which the Englishman was astonished. We took our collection to the Prince. "Would you be so kind," said the Englishman, "to put in a word for us with this gentleman, and ask him if he would give us a demonstration of his art and accept this small token of our esteem." The Prince added a valuable ring to the collection and offered the plate to the Sicilian. The man hesitated for a few seconds. — "My lords, gentlemen and respected patrons," he then began, "your generosity shames me. It seems that you are mistaken in me — but I agree to your request. Your wishes shall be fulfilled." (At this he rang a bell.) "As far as this gold is concerned, which I have no right to, you will permit me to pass it to the nearest Benedictine monastery for some charitable purpose. The ring I will keep as a precious memento, to remind me of the worthiest of Princes."

Upon this the innkeeper appeared, to whom he immediately handed over the money.

"And he's a scoundrel, all the same," whispered the Englishman in my ear. "He's refusing the money because it's the Prince he is really after."

"Or the innkeeper knows his part," said another.

"Whom do you ask to see?" the magician now asked the Prince.

The Prince thought for a moment — "Let's see some great man," cried the English lord. "Ask for Pope Ganganelli.[4] That won't tax the gentleman much."

The Sicilian bit his lip. — "I may not summon anyone who has been admitted to holy orders."

"That's a pity," said the Englishman. "He might have been able to tell us what disease he died of."

"The Marquis de Lanoy," the Prince now put in, "was a brigadier on the French side in the previous war, and was my most trusted friend. He was fatally wounded at the battle of Hastenbeck;[5] they took him to my tent, and soon he died there in my arms. When he was already in his last agony, he called me to him. 'Prince,' he began, 'I shall never see my fatherland again, so let me tell you a secret to which no one but myself has the key. In a convent on the borders of Flanders there lives a —' With this he passed away. The hand of death severed the thread of his words; I should like to have him here and to hear the rest of them."

"By Jove, you are asking a lot," cried the Englishman. "If you can rise to this, I declare you are another Solomon."

We admired the Prince's ingenious choice and unanimously agreed in his request. Meanwhile the magician was pacing up and down and seemed to be struggling indecisively within himself.

"And that was everything the dying man entrusted to you?"

"Everything."

"Did you not make any further enquiries in his fatherland?"

"They were all fruitless."

"And was the Marquis de Lanoy's life beyond reproach? — I may not summon just anyone from the dead."

"He died repenting the extravagances of his youth."

"Do you happen to have any memento of him about you?"

"I do." (The Prince did indeed carry a snuffbox with a miniature portrait of the Marquis in enamel, and had had it lying beside him on the table.)

"I do not want to know about it. —— Leave me alone now. You shall see your late friend."

We were asked to wait in the other wing of the house until he should call us. At the same time he had all the furniture removed from the room, the sashes taken out and the shutters shut as tight as possible. He ordered the innkeeper, with whom he seemed already to be on close terms, to bring a brazier with hot coals and carefully extinguish all the other fires in the house with water. Before we left him, he made us all give our word of honour to remain silent for ever about anything we might see or hear. All the doors of our wing of the house were bolted behind us.

It was past eleven o'clock, and a profound silence reigned over the whole house. As we were leaving, the Russian asked me if we were carrying loaded pistols. "Why?" I asked. — "For all eventualities," he replied. "Wait a moment, and I will see if I can find some." He went away. Baron von F** and I opened a window which looked out towards the other wing, and we thought we heard two men whispering, and a noise as if a ladder was being put up. But it was only a suspicion on our part, and I cannot guarantee the truth of it. The Russian came back with a pair of pistols, after he had been away for half an hour. We watched as he loaded them. It was almost two o'clock when the magician reappeared and told us the time had come. Before we went in we were ordered to take off our shoes and to appear in shirtsleeves, underclothes, and stockinged feet. Behind us the doors were bolted as before.

When we returned to the previous room, we found that a circle had been drawn with charcoal, wide enough to hold the ten of us comfortably. All around the four walls of the room the floorboards had been removed, so that we were standing as if on an island. An altar, covered with a black cloth, had been set up in the middle of the circle, standing on a red silken carpet. A Chaldean bible lay open upon the altar, beside a death's head, and a silver crucifix had been set up on it. Instead of candles, spirits were burning in a silver container. A thick smoke of incense darkened the room, almost swallowing up the light. The celebrant had undressed, as had we, but was barefoot; at his bare throat hung an amulet on a chain of human hair, and about his waist he wore a white apron, adorned with secret signs and symbolical figures. He made us hold hands and observe a profound silence; in particular he urged us on no account to address any question to the apparition. He asked the Englishman and myself (we seemed to be the ones he trusted the least) to hold two unsheathed swords quite still and crossed just an inch above his head for as long as the proceedings should last. We stood round him in a half-moon; the Russian officer pushed in close to the Englishman and was standing next to the altar. The magician, his face turned towards the east, positioned himself on the carpet, sprinkled holy water to all four points of the compass and bowed three times towards the Bible. The conjuration, of which we understood not a word, lasted the best part of a quarter of an hour; when it was finished he signalled to those who were standing immediately behind him that they should now seize him tightly by the hair. Shuddering violently, he called upon the dead man three times by name, and the third time he stretched out his hand towards the crucifix —

All at once we all felt as if we had been struck by lightning, and our hands flew apart; a sudden thunderclap shook the building, all the locks resounded, all the doors rattled, the lid of the silver container fell to, extinguishing the light, and on the opposite wall, above the fireplace, appeared a human figure, in a bloodstained shirt, pale and with the features of a dying man.

"Who calls me?" spoke a hollow, barely audible voice.

"Your friend," replied the conjuror, "who honours your memory and prays for your soul," and at the same time he named the Prince by name.

Each answer followed after a long silent pause.

"What does he ask?" continued the voice.

"He wishes to hear you complete your confession, that you began in this world and did not finish."

"In a convent on the borders of Flanders there lives —"

At this the whole house shook again. The door sprang open of its own accord with a violent thunderclap, a flash of lightning illuminated the room, and a second, *corporeal* figure, pale and bloody like the first but more terrible, appeared on the threshold. The spirit-lamp caught light spontaneously, and the room was as bright as before.

"Who is in our midst?" cried the magician in terror, and cast a horrified glance over the whole company — "I did not summon you."

The figure strode with quiet, majestic steps towards the altar, took up a position on the carpet, facing us, and grasped the crucifix. The first figure was no longer visible.

"*Who calls me?*" said the second apparition.

The magician began to tremble violently. Terror and amazement had gripped us all. I seized a pistol, the magician snatched it from my hand and fired it at the apparition. The bullet rolled slowly over the altar, and the figure emerged unchanged from the smoke. Now the magician collapsed insensible.

"What is going on here?" cried the Englishman in amazement, and made to strike at the figure with his sword. The apparition touched his arm, and the blade fell to the ground. My forehead burst out in a cold sweat. Baron von F** confessed to me afterwards that he had uttered a prayer. But the Prince stood the whole time calm and fearless, his eyes fixed firmly upon the apparition.

"Yes, I recognise you," he cried at last, deeply moved, "you are Lanoy, you are my friend. —— Where have you come from?"

"Eternity is silent. Ask me about the life that is past."

"Who is it that lives in the convent you told me of?"

"My daughter."

"What? You were a father?"

"Alas for me, that I was not a better one."

"Are you not blessed, Lanoy?"

"God has judged."

"Can I do you no further service in this world?"

"Only by thinking of yourself."

"How am I to do that?"

"You will find out in Rome."

At this there was another thunderclap — a cloud of black smoke filled the room; when it had lifted, no figure was to be seen. I threw open one of the shutters. It was morning.

Now the magician recovered consciousness. "Where are we?" he cried, as he saw the light of day. The Russian officer was standing close behind him and looked over his shoulder. "Trickster," he said, fixing him with a terrible look, "*you will call up no more spirits.*"

The Sicilian spun round, looked more closely into his face, gave a loud cry and fell at his feet.

Now at once we all looked at the supposed Russian. The Prince recognised without difficulty the features of his Armenian, and the words which he was about to stammer died upon his lips. Terror and surprise had turned us all to stone. Silent and motionless we stared at this mysterious being, who penetrated us all with a gaze of silent power and grandeur. For a minute nothing stirred — and for another. Not a breath moved in the whole assembly.

Some violent blows on the door finally brought us to our senses again. The door fell splintering into the room, and some officers of the law entered with an armed guard. "Here they are, all together!" cried their leader, and turned to the men accompanying him. "In the name of the Government!" he cried to us, "I arrest you." We had little time to reflect; in a few moments we were surrounded. The Russian officer, whom I shall now once more call the Armenian, took the leader of the party on one side, and as far as I could make out in the confusion, he appeared to whisper a few words to him in secret and to show him a written document. The man immediately drew back with a silent and respectful bow, turned to us and took off his hat. "I beg your pardon, gentlemen," he said, "that I confused you with this charlatan. I will not ask who you are — but this gentleman assures me that you are honourable men that I see before me." At the same time he motioned to his men to molest us no further. The Sicilian he ordered to be tied up and closely guarded. "That fellow has had more than his due," he added. "We have been waiting for seven months now to catch him."

The wretched man was indeed a pitiable sight. The double fright of the second apparition and this unexpected raid had completely robbed him of his senses. He let himself be tied up like a child; his eyes stood wide open and staring in a deathlike face, and his lips were twitching silently, without producing a sound. We expected him to fall in convulsions at any moment. The Prince took pity on his condition and took it upon himself to ask the constable to release him, identifying himself as he did so.

"Your Highness," said the man, "do you realise who this man is that you are so generously pleading for? The trick he was planning to play on you is the least of his crimes. We have taken his accomplices. They have told us terrible things about him. He will be able to count himself lucky if he escapes with a spell in the galleys."

Meanwhile we also saw the innkeeper with his people being led across the courtyard, tied up with ropes. — "That man too?" cried the Prince. "What has he done then?" — "He was his accomplice and his receiver," answered the leader of the party, "he helped him in all his thievings and trickeries and shared the takings with him. You shall be convinced straight away, Your Highness" (and here he turned to his men). "Search the whole house and report to me immediately what you have found."

Now the Prince looked round for the Armenian — but he was no longer to be seen; in the general confusion which the raid had caused he had managed to escape without being noticed. The Prince was inconsolable; he would have sent all his people after him straight away; he wanted to hunt for him himself and drag me away with him. I hurried to the window; the whole house was surrounded by curious spectators who had been attracted by the rumour of these events. It was impossible to make one's way through the crowd. I put this to the Prince: "If this Armenian is determined to keep hidden from us, you can be sure he knows all the byways better than we do, and all our searching will be in vain. Let us rather stay here a while, Your Highness. Perhaps this servant of the law can tell us more about him, as if I am not mistaken, he made himself known to him."

Now we remembered that we were still undressed. We rushed to our rooms and hurried to throw our clothes on. When we returned, the search of the house had been completed.

After the altar had been removed and the remaining floorboards taken up, a spacious chamber was revealed, high enough for a man to sit upright in comfort, and with a door that led by a narrow staircase to the cellar. In this vault they had found an electric machine, a clock and a small silver bell, which like the electric machine was somehow connected with the altar and with the cross that was set up on it. One of the window shutters, immediately opposite the fireplace, had an opening in it, furnished with a sliding cover, in which, as we subsequently discovered, a magic lantern could be installed to throw the desired image on to the wall above the fireplace. The attics and the cellar yielded a variety of drums, with large leaden balls attached to them by strings, probably to produce the sounds of thunder which we had heard. When the Sicilian's clothes were searched, a case was found containing various powders, together with quicksilver in vials and boxes, phosphorus in a glass flask, a ring which we soon realised was magnetised, as it remained hanging on to a steel button with which it had happened to come into contact; in his coat pockets a rosary, a false Jewish beard, pistols and a dagger. "Let's see if they are loaded!" said one of the raiding party, taking one of the pistols and firing it off in the direction of the fireplace. "Mary and Jesus!" cried a hollow human voice, the very one which we had heard from the apparition — and in the same moment we saw a bloodied body fall down from the chimney. "Not at peace yet, poor spirit?" cried the Englishman, while the rest of us recoiled in terror. "Go back to your grave. You were not what you seemed then, but now for sure you will be."

"Mary and Jesus! I have been wounded," repeated the man in the fireplace. The bullet had shattered his right leg. Immediately they saw to it that the wound was bound up.

"But who are you then, and what evil demon had to bring you here?"

"A poor barefoot monk," answered the wounded man. "A strange gentleman here offered me a zecchine if I would —"

"Repeat some formula or other? And why didn't you make yourself scarce straight away?"

"He said he would give me a sign when it was time for me to go on, but the sign never came, and when I tried to climb out, the ladder had been taken away."

"And what was the formula that he made you learn?"

Here the man fainted away, so that nothing more could be got out of him. When we looked at him more closely, we recognised him as the one who had blocked the Prince's path on the previous evening and had addressed him so solemnly.

Meanwhile the Prince had turned to the leader of the raiding party.

"You have rescued us," he said, pressing some gold coins into his hand, "rescued us from the hands of a charlatan, and have done us justice without knowing who we were. Will you place us fully in your debt and tell us who the stranger was to whom it cost only a word to have us released?"

"Who do you mean?" asked the leader of the raiding party, with an expression which clearly indicated that the question was unnecessary.

"I mean the gentleman in Russian uniform, who took you aside just now, showed you a paper and whispered some words in your ear, upon which you immediately set us free."

"Do you not know that gentleman, then?" asked the man again. "Was he not in your party?"

"No," said the Prince, "and I have very important reasons for wanting to make his acquaintance more closely."

"Well," answered the man, "I don't know him closely either. I don't even know his name, and today is the first time in my life that I have ever seen him."

"What? And in such a short time, with a few words, he could persuade you that he and the rest of us were innocent?"

"Yes, indeed, with a single word."

"And what was that? I must confess I should like to know."

"That stranger, Your Highness" — and he weighed the zecchini in his hand — "Your Highness has been so generous to me that I cannot keep it secret any longer. That strange man was — an officer of the State Inquisition."

"The State Inquisition! — That man!"

"Indeed, your grace — and it was the paper he showed me that convinced me."

"That man, you say? It is impossible."

"I will tell you more, Your Highness. It was on his information that I was sent here to arrest the conjuror of spirits."

We all stared at each other in even greater amazement.

"That's the reason, then," cried the Englishman at last, "why that poor devil of a conjuror took such a fright when he got a closer look at his face. He recognised that he was a spy, and that's why he cried out and fell at his feet."

"Never," cried the Prince. "That man is whatever he wants to be, and whatever the moment calls for him to be. What he really is, no mortal has ever discovered. Did you see the Sicilian collapse when he cried in his ear, 'You will call up no more spirits!' There is more behind this. That a man can be so frightened by a mere mortal no one will ever persuade me."

"That is something the magician himself is best placed to explain," said the English lord, "if this gentleman (turning to the leader of the raiding party) will give us the opportunity of speaking to his prisoner."

The man gave us this undertaking, and we agreed with the Englishman that we would call for him the very next morning. We then returned to Venice.

Lord Seymour (this was the Englishman's name) met us early in the morning, and soon afterwards there appeared a familiar person who had been sent by the constable to take us to the prison. I have forgotten to mention that for some days the Prince had been missing one of his attendants, a native of Bremen, who had served him faithfully for many years and had enjoyed his full confidence. Whether he had had an accident, or been stolen from us, or indeed simply absconded, nobody could tell. That he had just run away seemed highly improbable, as he had always been a quiet and reputable man and no fault had ever been found with him. The only thing his colleagues could think of was that he had become very melancholy of late and whenever he could find a moment to spare had been frequenting a certain Franciscan establishment on the Giudecca, where he had been often associating with some of the brothers. This made us suspect that he had got into the hands of the monks and become a Catholic; and as the Prince was at this time quite indifferent to such things, after a few fruitless enquiries he let the matter drop. He nevertheless regretted the loss of this man, who had accompanied him on all his campaigns, had always shown him complete loyalty, and would not be so easy to replace in a foreign country. Now, this morning, just as we were ready to go, the Prince's banker was announced, who had been entrusted with the task of engaging a new servant. He brought with him a well-favoured and well-dressed middle-aged man, who had served one of the Procurators as a secretary for a considerable time, spoke French and also some German, and was moreover furnished with the best possible references. We liked the look of the man, and as he also said that he was content to be paid according to the Prince's satisfaction with his services, the Prince engaged him on the spot.

We found the Sicilian in a private prison, where as the constable told us he had been temporarily accommodated to suit the Prince's convenience, before he was taken up to the "leads," where he would no longer be accessible. These so-called leads are the most fearsome prison in Venice, under the roofs of the Doge's palace on St Mark's Square, where the wretched criminals are often driven mad by the baking heat of the sun accumulating on the lead surface. The Sicilian had recovered from yesterday's events, and stood up respectfully when he saw the Prince. One leg and one hand were chained, but apart from this he was free to move about the room. On our arrival the guard was taken off the door.

"I have come," said the Prince, after we had sat down, "to ask you to explain two things. The one you owe me, and it will not be to your disadvantage if you can satisfy me as to the other."

"My part is played out," said the Sicilian. "My fate is in your hands."

"Only if you are honest," rejoined the Prince, "will it be any easier for you."

"Ask me your questions, Your Highness. I am ready to answer, for I have nothing more to lose."

"You showed me the Armenian's face in your mirror. How did you do that?"

"What you saw was not a mirror. It was simply a pastel drawing of a man in Armenian dress, behind a glass, that deceived you. My sleight of hand, the dim light, your own astonishment helped the trick. You will find the picture among the other things that were confiscated at the inn."

"But how could you guess my thoughts so well and choose the Armenian of all people?"

"That was not difficult, Your Highness. No doubt you have often talked at table, in the presence of your servants, about the encounters you have had with the Armenian. One of my people happened to meet one of your attendants on the Giudecca, and was able to glean from him as much as I needed to know."

"Where is that attendant of mine?" asked the Prince. "I have been missing him, and I am sure you know what has happened to him."

"I swear I don't know the least thing about that, Your Highness. I have never seen him myself, and have never had any designs on him beyond what I have just told you."

"Go on," said the Prince.

"That was how I learnt in the first place about your presence and your affairs in Venice, and I decided immediately to take advantage of it. You see that I am telling you the truth, Your Highness. I knew about your proposed excursion on the Brenta; I had thought to make use of it, and a key which you happened to have dropped gave me the first opportunity of trying my arts on you."

"What? Then I was wrong? The business with the key was your handiwork, not the Armenian's? You say I had dropped the key?"

"When you took out your purse — and I took advantage of the moment, as no one was looking, to cover it swiftly with my foot. The woman running the lottery stall was in the business with me. She let you draw from an urn that had no blanks in it, and the key was in the snuff-box long before you won it."

"Now I understand. And the barefoot monk, who blocked my path and addressed me so solemnly?"

"Was the same one that they tell me was pulled wounded out of the chimney. He is one of my colleagues, who has done me many a useful service in that disguise."

"But what were you aiming at with all this?"

"To put thoughts into your mind — to put you into a frame of mind in which you would fall for the tricks I was going to play on you."

"But the pantomime dance which took such an unexpected turn — surely that was not part of your invention?"

"The girl who played the queen had been instructed by me, and her whole part was of my devising. I assumed that it would be no little surprise to Your Highness to find that you were known in those parts, and — forgive me, Prince — the business with the Armenian gave me hope that you would already be disposed to disregard any natural explanations and to look for higher causes of anything extraordinary."

"Really," cried the Prince, with an expression of both annoyance and admiration, with a significant glance at me in particular, "really, I was not expecting this."

"But," he continued, after a long pause, "how did you produce the figure that appeared on the wall above the fireplace?"

"With the magic lantern that was installed in the window shutter opposite — you will have seen the opening that was made for it."

"But how was it then that not one of us noticed it?" asked Lord Seymour.

"Your lordship will remember that when you came back the room was full of thick smoke. At the same time I had taken the precaution of having the floorboards that had been taken up stacked beside the window where the magic lantern was installed; so that you did not immediately notice that particular window shutter. Also, the lantern stayed concealed by a wooden slide until you had all taken your places and there was no longer any risk of your searching the room."

"It seemed to me," I broke in here, "that I had heard a ladder being set up in the neighbourhood of that room, when I looked out of the window in the other wing. Was that so?"

"Quite right. That was the ladder that my assistant had to climb up to the window with the magic lantern in order to work it."

"The figure," continued the Prince, "really did seem to bear a fleeting resemblance to my late friend; I noticed in particular that it had very blond hair. Was that just a coincidence, or how did you achieve it?"

"Your Highness will remember that you had a snuff-box lying beside you at table, with an enamel portrait of an officer in ** uniform. I asked you whether you did not have some memento of your friend about you? You answered yes, from which I deduced that it might be the snuff-box. I had taken a good look at it at table, and as I am very practised in drawing and can produce a very good likeness, it was easy for me to give the image the fleeting resemblance which you observed; all the more since the Marquis' features are very striking."

"But the figure seemed to be moving —"

"Yes, so it seemed, but it wasn't the figure, but the smoke which was lit up by it."

"And the man who fell out of the chimney — he answered on behalf of the apparition?"

"Exactly."

"But he could not hear the questions."

"Nor did he need to. Your Highness will recall that I forbade you all most strictly to put any questions to the phantom yourselves. What I was going to ask and what he should reply was agreed in advance; and so that nothing should go wrong, I told him to observe long pauses and to count them off with a watch."

"You ordered the innkeeper carefully to extinguish all the fires in the house with water; I suppose this was done —"

"So that my man in the chimney should be in no danger of choking, since the chimneys of the house all run into one another and I could not be sure what your servants might be doing."

"But how was it," asked Lord Seymour, "that your spirit appeared just when you wanted him, neither sooner nor later?"

"My spirit had been in the room for a good while before I summoned him; but as long as the spirit-lamp was burning, he was too faintly lit to be seen. When I had finished my conjuration formula, I dropped the lid on the container with the burning spirit, the room was as dark as night, and now at last you could see the figure on the wall, where it had already been projected for a long time."

"But just in the moment when the spirit appeared, we all felt an electric shock. How did you do that?"

"You saw the machine under the altar. You had also seen that I was standing on a silken carpet. I made you all stand in a half-circle around me and hold each other's hands; when the moment came, I signalled to one of you to catch me by the hair. The crucifix was a conductor, and you all felt the shock when I touched it with my hand."

"You told us, Count von O** and myself," said Lord Seymour, "to hold two naked swords crossed above your head for as long as the conjuration lasted. What was that for?"

"Only to keep you two, who were the ones I trusted the least, occupied throughout the whole proceedings. You will remember that I ordered you to keep them exactly an inch above me; and as you had to keep this distance constantly in your sight, you could not look in any direction I did not want. But at that time I had not yet caught sight of my most dangerous enemy."

"I must admit," cried Lord Seymour, "that you certainly took every precaution — but why did we have to undress?"

"Just to increase the solemnity of the occasion, and to heighten your imaginations by its unusualness."

"The second apparition stopped your spirit from speaking," said the Prince. "What exactly was it he was to have told us?"

"Very much what you did get to hear afterwards. I asked Your Highness on purpose whether you had told me everything the dying man had said to you, and whether you had not made any further enquiries about him in his fatherland; this was necessary so that I was aware of any facts that might contradict what my spirit had to say. Thinking of certain sins of youth, I asked whether the dead man had lived a blameless life; and on your answer I built my invention."

"I think," said the Prince after some moments of silence, "that you have satisfied me about these matters. But there is one most important thing remaining which I want you to throw some light on."

"If it is in my power, and if —"

"No conditions! The law, in whose hands you find yourself, might not ask so discreetly. Who was the stranger before whom we saw you fall down? What can you tell us about him? How do you come to know him? And what happened with that second apparition?"

"Your gracious Highness —"

"When you looked into his face, you cried out loud and collapsed in front of him. Why? What did it mean?"

"That stranger, Prince —" He paused, became visibly more agitated and looked at us all in turn with a look of embarrassment. "Yes, as God is my witness, Your Highness, that stranger is a terrible being."

"What do you know about him? What is your connection with him? — Don't think you can conceal the truth from us."

"I shall take care not to — for how can I be sure that he is not standing here with us at this very moment?"

"Where? Who?" we all cried out at once and looked around us in the room, half laughing, half startled. "That is impossible!"

"Oh! for that man — or who or what he may be — things are possible that are even less within our understanding."

"But who is he then? Where is he from? An Armenian or a Russian? What is the truth about him, whoever he pretends to be?"

"He is none of the things that he seems. There can scarcely be any character, nationality, or station in life that he has not used as a disguise. Who he is, where he comes from, where he is going, — no one can tell. Some say that he spent many years in Egypt, gathering his secret wisdom from one of the Pyramids — I will neither confirm nor deny it. We only know him as the *Unfathomable*. How old, for example, do you think he is?"

"To judge by his appearance, scarcely more than forty."

"And how old would you say I am?"

"Not far off fifty."

"Quite right — and if I now tell you that I was a lad of seventeen when my grandfather told me about this mysterious man that he had seen once in Famagusta looking about the age that he does now —"

"Ridiculous, incredible, exaggerated."

"Not a whit. If I were not chained up here, I could bring you witnesses whose reputable character would leave you in no doubt. There are reliable people who can recall having seen him in different parts of the world at the very same time. There is no sword that can pierce him, no poison that can affect him; no fire can burn him, no ship will sink with him on board. Time itself seems to have no power over him, the years do not wither him and age does not turn his hair white. No one ever saw him take nourishment, no woman was ever touched by him, no sleep closes his eyes; of all the hours of the day there is only one of which he is not master, in which he has never been seen, in which he has pursued no earthly affairs."

"Indeed?" said the Prince. "And what hour is that?"

"The twelfth hour of the night. As soon as the clock has struck its twelfth stroke, he is no longer among the living. Wherever he is, he must go, whatever business he is about, he must break it off. That terrible stroke of the clock tears him from the arms of friendship, tears him even from the altar, and would even summon him from the agony of death. No one knows where he goes then or what he does there. No one dares to ask him, still less to follow him; for his features suddenly take on, as soon as that terrible hour has struck, such a dark and terrifying earnestness, that no one has the courage to look him in the face or to speak to him. A deep and deathly silence puts a stop to the liveliest conversation, and all those who are in his company await his return with a shudder of reverence and awe, without daring as much as to rise from their places or to open the door through which he has passed."

"But," one of us asked, "is there nothing remarkable to be seen about him when he returns?"

"Only that he seems pale and exhausted, like a man who has undergone a painful operation, or received some terrible piece of news. Some claim to have seen flecks of blood on his shirt, but I'll not swear to that."

"And has no one ever as much as tried to hide the time of night from him, or to distract him so that he does not notice it?"

"Once and once only, they say, he let the hour pass. The company was numerous, people stayed till late into the night, all their watches were deliberately set wrong, and he was carried away by the heat of the conversation. But when the appointed hour came, he suddenly fell silent and rigid, all his limbs remained fixed in whatever angle chance had surprised them in, his eyes glazed over, his pulse stopped beating, and all attempts to rouse him again were fruitless; and this state of affairs lasted until the hour was past. Then he suddenly stirred again of his own accord, opened his eyes and went on speaking from the very syllable he had been interrupted in. The general amazement betrayed to him what had happened, and with fearful gravity he told them all that they could count themselves fortunate to have escaped with no more than a fright. But he left the town where this had happened the very same night, for ever. Most people believe that at that mysterious hour he converses with his guardian spirit. Some even claim that he is a dead man, who is allowed to go about among the living for twenty-three hours in the day, but in the twenty-fourth his soul has to return to the underworld to endure judgement. Many think he must be the famous Apollonius of Tyana,[6] others even that he is John the disciple, who is said to remain on earth until the Day of Judgement."

"Around such an extraordinary man," said the Prince, "there are bound to be all kinds of extravagant speculations. Everything you have said is all hearsay, but his behaviour to you, and yours to him, seem to me to suggest some closer acquaintance between you. Is there some particular story at the bottom of this, that you have been personally involved in yourself? Don't keep anything back."

The Sicilian looked at us with a doubtful expression and said nothing.

"If it is a matter that you do not want to be widely known," said the Prince, "then in the name of these two gentlemen I can promise you that not a word will be spoken of it outside this room. But tell us openly and honestly."

"If I can hope," began the man after a long silence, "that you will not let it be used in evidence against me, then very well, I will tell you about a remarkable occurrence involving this Armenian, one that I witnessed with my own eyes and that will leave you in no more doubt about the secret powers of this man. But," he added, "you must allow me not to name certain names."

"Can you not tell us without that condition?"

"No, Your Grace. There is a family involved whose interests I have reason to spare."

"Let us hear it, then," said the Prince.

"It must be about five years ago," began the Sicilian, "that I was in Naples, practising my arts with some success, when I got to know a certain Lorenzo del M**nte, Chevalier of the Order of St Stephen, a rich young gentleman from one of the leading houses of the kingdom, who plied me with favours and seemed to hold my secrets in high regard. He revealed to me that his father, the Marchese del M**nte, was a devotee of the Cabbala and would count himself fortunate to have an adept (as he was pleased to call me) under his roof. The old nobleman lived on one of his estates by the sea, about seven leagues from Naples, where he spent his time, in complete isolation from his fellow men, honouring the memory of a dear son who had been taken from him by a terrible fate. The chevalier hinted to me that he and his family might well have need of my assistance in a very serious matter, as my secret arts might be able to cast light on something regarding which all natural methods of enquiry had been exhausted. He in particular, he added very meaningfully, would perhaps one day have cause to regard me as the author of his peace of mind and of all his earthly happiness. I did not dare to question him more closely, and for the moment that was all I got to know. But this was the truth of the matter.

"This Lorenzo was the Marchese's younger son, and had accordingly been destined for holy orders; the family properties would go to his elder brother. Jeronimo, that was the elder brother's name, had been travelling for several years and returned to his fatherland about seven years before the events I am now recounting, in order to marry the only daughter of a neighbouring aristocratic family, the C***tti, as both families had agreed ever since the birth of these two children, in order that their considerable estates should be combined. Although this engagement had been merely devised for the convenience of the parents on both sides and the hearts of the two fiancés had never been consulted, the pair had nevertheless silently confirmed the wisdom of this choice. Jeronimo del M**nte and Antonia C***tti had been brought up together, and the freedom enjoyed by two children who were already regarded as an engaged couple had from early on led to a greater degree of affection between them; this was further strengthened by the harmony of their characters, and as they grew to maturity soon turned to love. Four years' separation had made their feelings for each other warmer rather than cooler, and Jeronimo returned to the arms of his fiancée just as fiery and true as if he had never been parted from her.

The joys of their reunion were scarcely over, and the preparations for the wedding were being vigorously pursued, when the bridegroom — disappeared. He would often spend whole evenings at a villa which had a view of the sea, and sometimes enjoy an excursion on the water. On one such evening it happened that he was away for an unusually long time. Messengers were sent for him, vessels searched for him at sea; no one had seen him. None of his servants was missing, so none of them could have gone with him. Night fell and he failed to appear. Morning came, afternoon and evening, and still no Jeronimo. Already people were beginning to entertain the most frightful suppositions, when the news was received that an Algerian pirate had landed on their shores on the previous day and that several of the local people had been taken away as prisoners. Immediately two galleys which were lying ready were manned; the old Marchese boarded the first one, determined to free his son even at the cost of his life. On the third morning they caught sight of the corsair, having the advantage of the wind over him; soon they had caught up with him, and came so close that Lorenzo, who was on board the first galley, thought that he could identify his brother on the deck of their adversary, when a sudden storm arose and drove them apart again. The ships were damaged and barely survived the storm, but their quarry was lost, and they were compelled to land on Malta. The family's grief knew no bounds; the old Marchese tore his hair in despair, and they feared for the life of the young Countess.

"Five years were spent in fruitless investigations. Enquiries were made all along the Barbary Coast; a huge ransom was offered for the young Marchese's liberty; but no one appeared to claim it. Finally it seemed the most probable explanation that the storm which had parted the two ships had sunk the pirate vessel, and that all on board her had perished in the waves.

"Plausible though this supposition was, it was still far from a certainty, and there was no cause to give up hope completely that the missing young man might after all show himself again one day. But assuming that he did not, the family would die out with him, or else the second brother would have to renounce holy orders and assume the rights of the firstborn. Bold though this step was, and in itself so unfair to exclude a brother who might still be living from the exercise of his natural rights, it was nevertheless not thought proper to risk the fate of an ancient and distinguished house, which but for this arrangement would disappear for ever. Grief and age were bringing the old Marchese ever nearer to his grave; with every new failure, his hopes of recovering his lost son sank further; he saw the impending downfall of his house, which could be prevented by a small breach of justice, namely by resolving to favour the younger brother at the expense of the elder. In order to fulfil his agreement with Count C***tti, he needed only to alter a single name; the aims of both families would be fulfilled in the same way, whether Countess Antonia were to call herself Lorenzo's wife or Jeronimo's. The remote *possibility* of Lorenzo's reappearance could not rank in importance with the immediate and evil *certainty* of the complete extinction of the family, and the old Marchese, who felt his death coming nearer every day, was impatient to die freed at least of this anxiety.

"The only person who delayed this step, and opposed it most obstinately, was the one who stood most to gain from it: Lorenzo. Unmoved by the delights of boundless wealth, indifferent even to the possession of the most charming creature who was to be delivered into his arms, he refused with the noblest professions of conscience to rob a brother who might still be alive and might return to claim his property. "Is my dear Jeronimo's fate," he said, "not already made terrible enough by this long imprisonment, that I should make it even more bitter by robbing him of all that was dearest to him? Could I have the heart to pray for his return, if his wife lay in my arms? Could I have the effrontery to run to welcome him, if one day a miracle should return him to us? And even if we admit that he is lost for ever, how can we better respect his memory than by leaving empty for ever the gap that his death has left in our circle, than by sacrificing all our hopes upon his grave and leaving what was his untouched like a holy of holies?"

"But all the reasons which fraternal delicacy could adduce were not sufficient to reconcile the old Marchese to the notion of seeing the extinction of a house which had bloomed for centuries. All that he would concede to Lorenzo was a grace of two years before he should lead his brother's bride to the altar. During this time investigations were pursued most vigorously. Lorenzo himself made several sea journeys, exposed himself to many dangers; no efforts and no expenses were spared to find the man who had disappeared. But these two years passed as fruitlessly as the ones that had gone before."

"And Countess Antonia?" asked the Prince. "You have said nothing about her condition. Can she really have submitted so calmly to her fate? I cannot believe it."

"Antonia's condition was a terrible struggle between duty and passion, revulsion and admiration. The unselfish magnanimity of fraternal love moved her; she felt herself swept away in reverence for the man whom she could never love; torn by conflicting feelings, her heart bled. But her repugnance towards the chevalier seemed to grow all the more as his claims on her respect increased. With profound sorrow he observed the silent grief that was consuming her youth. A tender pity imperceptibly took the place of the indifference with which he had previously regarded her; but this treacherous emotion deceived him, and a raging passion began to hinder him in the practice of a virtue which had till now been proof against all temptation. But still, even to the cost of his heart, he lent his ear to the promptings of his noble nature; he was the only one who protected the unhappy victim from the family's caprices. But all his efforts misfired; every victory that he gained over his passion showed him all the worthier of her, and the magnanimity with which he refused her served only to rob her resistance of every justification.

"And that was how things stood when the young chevalier persuaded me to visit him at his country estate. The warm recommendation of my patron assured me a welcome which exceeded all my desires. I must not forget to mention here that through certain curious proceedings I had succeeded in making my name well known among the local Masonic lodges, which may well have helped to increase the old Marchese's faith in me and to increase his expectations of me. How far I succeeded with him and what methods I employed there, you need not ask me; from what I have already confessed to you, you can guess everything else. As I made use of all the mystical books that I found in the Marchese's very respectable library, I was soon speaking to him in his own language and bringing my own system of the invisible world into harmony with his own opinions. In a very short time he was believing whatever I wanted him to, and would have sworn to the unions of the philosophers with sylphs and salamanders as readily as on an article of the canon. As he was in any case very religious and had developed his propensity to faith in that school to a high degree, it was all the easier for my fairy-tales to find a ready ear in him, and by the end I had him so entangled and entwined in mystifications that nothing normal and natural had any credit with him. In no time I was worshipped as the apostle of his house. The usual subject of my discourses was the exaltation of human nature and its commerce with higher beings, and my infallible authority the good Count Gabalis.[7] The young Countess, who since the loss of her lover had in any case lived more in the spirit world that in the real one and was drawn with passionate interest to matters of this kind by the fantastic flights of her imagination, took up my casual hints with a shudder of satisfaction; and even the servants found themselves things to do in the room when I was talking, so as to pick up a word or two of mine here and there, which oddments they then strung together after their own fashion.

"I must have spent about two months on the estate in this way, when one day the young chevalier came into my room. His face was marked by profound grief, his features were distorted, and he fell into a chair with every sign of desperation.

"'Captain,' he said, 'I am done for. I must get away. I can't bear it here any longer.'

"'What is it, your honour? What is the matter?'

"'Oh, this fearful passion!' (Here he sprang up from the chair and threw himself into my arms.) — 'I have fought it like a man. — Now I cannot go on.'

"'But my dear friend, whose fault is it then but your own? Is not everything in your own power? Your father, your family —'

"'Father! family! What do I care about that? — Do I want a forced hand or an affection freely given? — Do I not have a rival? — Ah! And what kind of rival? A rival perhaps among the dead? Oh, let me go, let me go! Even if it were to the ends of the earth — I must find my brother.'

"'What? After so many fruitless efforts, you can still hope —'

"'Hope! — In *my* heart it died long ago. But in *hers*? — What does it matter if *I* still hope? But can I be happy as long as a glimmer of hope remains in Antonia's heart? — Two words, my friend, could end my torments — but it is no use! My fate will be wretched until eternity breaks its long silence and graves bear witness for me.'

"'Is it *that* certainty then that can make you happy?'

"'Happy? Oh, I doubt whether I can ever be happy again! — But uncertainty is the torment of the damned!' (After a pause he calmed himself and continued in a melancholy tone.) 'If he could see how I suffer! — Can it make him happy, this faithfulness that is making his brother wretched? Is a living man to pine away on account of a corpse that can feel no pleasure? — If he knew my misery —' (here he began to weep copiously, and pressed his face to my breast) 'then perhaps — perhaps he would lead her into my arms himself.'

"'But is that wish quite so impossible?'

"'My friend! What are you saying?' — He looked at me with an expression of terror.

"'Much lesser occasions,' I said, 'have woven the departed into the fate of the living. And if all the worldly happiness of another human being — of a brother —'

"'All the worldly happiness! Oh, I feel it! How truly you have spoken! All my happiness!'

"'And is the peace of a mourning family not cause enough to invoke the aid of the invisible powers? Surely! if ever any earthly affair can justify disturbing the sleep of the blessed — making use of a power —'

"'In God's name, my friend, no more of this!' he interrupted me. 'Once upon a time, I admit, I did entertain such a thought — I think I told you about it — but I have long dismissed it as infamous and appalling.'

"You see now," continued the Sicilian, "where this was leading us. I did my best to dispel the young chevalier's doubts, in which I finally succeeded. It was resolved to summon up the dead man's ghost, upon which I asked for fourteen days' grace in order, as I said, to prepare myself appropriately. After this period had elapsed and my machinery had been properly set up, I chose one gloomy evening, when the family was gathered about me in the usual way, to persuade them to agree to this, or rather to bring them without their noticing to the point at which they made the request of their own accord. I had the greatest difficulty with the young Countess, whose presence was of course so essential; but here the fantastic flight of her passion came to my aid, and perhaps even more so, a faint glimmer of hope that the man we believed was dead was still alive and so would not answer our summons. Suspicion of the whole business, lack of faith in my arts, was the only obstacle I did *not* have to contend with.

"As soon as I had the family's agreement, the third day was fixed for the work. Prayers, which had to be prolonged into the middle of the night, fasting, vigils, solitude and mystical instruction, together with the use of a certain still unfamiliar musical instrument,[8] which I have found very effective in similar cases, made up the preparations for this solemn proceeding, and all went so exactly according to plan that the fanatical enthusiasm of my audience inflamed my own fantasy and helped in no small measure to increase the illusion which I had to strain to produce. At last came the hour all were awaiting —"

"I can guess," cried the Prince, "who it is you are going to produce for us now — But go on, go on —"

"No, your grace. The conjuration went exactly to plan."

"But how? And what about the Armenian?"

"Don't be afraid," answered the Sicilian, "the Armenian will appear all too soon.

"I shall not indulge in any description of my mystifications, which in any case would take too long. Suffice it to say that everything lived up to my expectations. The old Marchese, the young Countess together with her mother, the chevalier and some other relations were present. You can readily imagine that during the considerable time that I had spent in the house, I had had no lack of opportunity of making the most exhaustive enquiries about everything concerning the dead man. Several paintings of him which I found there enabled me to give the apparition the most convincing likeness, and as I only made the ghost speak through gestures his voice could not arouse suspicion. The dead man himself appeared in the dress of a Barbary slave, with a deep wound in his throat. You will notice," said the Sicilian, "that in this I departed from the general supposition that he had been drowned in the waves, because I had reason to hope that the very unexpected nature of this feature would increase the credibility of the vision in no small measure; just as contrariwise nothing seemed to me more dangerous than too close a correspondence with what was natural."

"I think that was very well judged," said the Prince, turning to us. "In a series of extraordinary phenomena, so it seems to me, it is precisely the *more probable* which falls out of line. The ease of comprehending the revelation received would only have compromised the means by which it had been made; the ease of devising it might well have cast suspicion on the proceedings, for why should one summon up a spirit just to learn something that could be discovered without him, simply by the exercise of everyday reasoning? But here the unexpected novelty and difficulty of the discovery is itself as it were a guarantee of the miraculous means by which it is made — for who will cast doubt upon the supernatural character of an operation when what it produces can *not* be produced by natural forces? — I interrupted you," said the Prince. "Finish your story."

"I put the question to the spirit," the man continued, "whether there was anything more in this world that he called his own and whether there was anything he had left behind that was dear to him? The spirit shook its head three times and raised one hand to heaven. Before he departed, he drew a ring from his finger, and after his disappearance it was found lying on the ground. When the Countess looked more closely at it, it was her engagement ring."

"Her engagement ring!" cried the Prince in amazement. "Her engagement ring! But how did you get hold of that?"

"I — It was not the real one, Your Highness — I had had it — It was only an imitation —"

"An imitation!" repeated the Prince. "But to make an imitation you would have needed the real one, and how did you manage that, since it would never have left the dead man's finger?"

"Yes, that's true," said the Sicilian, showing some signs of confusion — "but from a description which someone had given me of the real ring —"

"And *who* had given you that?"

"It was a long time ago," said the Sicilian — "It was a plain gold ring, I think, just with the young Countess's name — But you have quite confused me —"

"Well, what happened then?" asked the Prince, with a very dissatisfied and dubious expression.

"Now everyone was convinced that Jeronimo was no longer in the land of the living. From that day on the family publicly announced his death and formally went into mourning for him. The incident with the ring also left Antonia with no further doubts and lent force to the young chevalier's advances. But the violent impression that the apparition had made on her caused her to fall dangerously ill, which would soon have put an end to her lover's hopes for ever. When she had recovered, she insisted on taking the veil, from which she was only dissuaded by the most earnest representations on the part of her confessor, whom she trusted implicitly. Finally the combined efforts of this man and the family frightened her into agreeing. The last day of mourning was to be the happy day, which the old Marchese intended to make even more of a celebration by making over all his property to his rightful heir.

"The day arrived, and Lorenzo received his trembling bride at the altar. When the day drew to its close, a magnificent banquet awaited the merry guests in the brilliantly lit marriage-hall, and loud music accompanied the abandoned revels. The happy old man had wanted the whole world to share his joy; all the doors of the palace stood open, and everyone was welcome who would congratulate him on his good fortune. But then among the crowds —"

The Sicilian paused here, and a shudder of expectation made us hold our breath —

"Well then," he continued, "among the crowds my neighbour at table pointed out to me a *Franciscan monk,* who was standing there immobile as a statue, a tall lean figure with an ashen face, and a grave and gloomy look fixed upon the bridal pair. The pleasure on the laughing faces all around seemed to pass this one man by, his expression remained always the same, like a sculpted bust amidst living creatures. The extraordinary nature of this sight, which affected me all the more powerfully as it struck me in the middle of my enjoyment and contrasted so sharply with everything that surrounded me at that moment, made an indelible impression on my soul, so that this alone sufficed to make me recognise the monk's features in the physiognomy of our *Russian* (and you will have already understood that he and your *Armenian* are also one and the same person) — which otherwise would have been simply impossible. I tried again and again to turn my eyes away from this frightening figure, but they kept returning to him of their own accord, and every time found him quite unaltered. I nudged my neighbour, he nudged his likewise; the same curiosity, the same unease spread round the whole table; conversation dried up, suddenly there was complete silence, but the monk was unaffected. He stood there motionless and ever the same, his grave and gloomy look fixed upon the bridal pair. Everyone was horrified by this apparition; the young Countess alone found her own sorrow reflected in this stranger's face and hung with silent delight on the only object in the whole assembly which seemed to understand and to share her grief. Gradually the crowd dispersed, midnight was past, the music grew quieter and faded away, the candlelight grew dim as only a few were left burning, whispered conversations grew softer and softer — and bleaker and bleaker grew the scene in the half-light of the banqueting hall; the monk stood motionless and ever the same, a silent gloomy look fixed upon the bridal pair.

"We all rose from the table, the guests dispersed in various directions, the family drew together in a closer circle; in that closer circle the monk remained, uninvited. I do not know how it happened that no one would speak to him; no one spoke to him. The women amongst the bride's acquaintances were crowding around her, as she gazed imploringly at the venerable stranger, trembling and beseeching his aid; the stranger made no response.

"The men were similarly gathered around the bridegroom — a tense, expectant silence — 'Oh, that we are all so happy together,' began the old father, who alone of us seemed not to have noticed the unknown man or at any rate not to be surprised by his presence — 'That we are all so happy together, and that my son Jeronimo cannot be with us!'

"'Did you invite him then, and has he not come?' asked the monk. It was the first time that he had opened his lips. We gazed at him in terror.

"'Ah, he has gone to that place from where one can never come back,' replied the old man. 'Reverend Sir, you do me an injustice. My son Jeronimo is dead.'

"'Perhaps he is only afraid to show himself in such company,' continued the monk. '— Who knows how he may look now, your son Jeronimo! — Let him hear the voice that was the last voice he heard! — Ask your son Lorenzo to summon him.'

"'What is the meaning of this?' everyone was murmuring. Lorenzo turned pale. I won't deny that my hair was beginning to stand on end.

"Meanwhile the monk strode to the sideboard, where he seized a full wine-glass and raised it to his lips — 'To the memory of our dear Jeronimo!' he cried. 'Let all those who held him dear do as I do.'

"'Wherever you have come from, reverend Sir,' the old Marchese cried at last, 'you have named a name that is dear to us. Be welcome! — Come, my friends!' (as he turned to us and had the glasses passed around), 'do not let a stranger put us to shame! — To the memory of my son Jeronimo.'

"Never, I believe, was a health drunk with such ill grace."

"'One glass is still untouched. — Why is my son Lorenzo refusing to join in this friendly toast?'

"Lorenzo trembled as he took the glass from the Franciscan's hand — trembled as he raised it to his lips — 'To my dear brother Jeronimo!' he stammered, and shuddered as he set it down again.

"'That is the voice of my murderer,' cried a terrifying figure which was suddenly standing in our midst, its clothes drenched in blood, and disfigured by hideous wounds —

"But you must ask me no more," said the Sicilian, whose face bore every sign of horror. "My senses had left me from the moment when I cast my eyes upon that figure, and it was the same for everyone present. When we recovered our wits, Lorenzo was in the agony of death; the monk and the apparition had disappeared. The young chevalier was carried to bed in fearful convulsions; no one would attend the dying man but the priest and the grieving old father who followed him to the grave a few weeks later. His secrets are locked within the bosom of the priest who heard his last confession, and no living man knows what they may be.

"Not long after these occurrences it happened that it was necessary to clear out a well in the rear courtyard of the villa, which was overgrown with bushes and had been blocked with rubble for many years; and when the rubble was cleared away, a skeleton was found. The house where all this happened is no longer standing; the family of del M**nte has died out, and in a convent not far from Salerno they will show you Antonia's grave.

"So you see now," continued the Sicilian, as he saw that we were all standing in shocked silence, "you see now how it is that I came to know this Russian officer, or this Armenian, if you will. Judge now whether I did not have reason to tremble at the sight of a being who has now twice crossed my path in such a terrifying way."

"Answer me just one more question," said the Prince, standing up. "Have you been completely truthful in your story in everything concerning the young chevalier?"

"I have told you everything I know," replied the Sicilian.

"And so you really believed him to be an honest man?"

"In God's name, yes, I did," answered the man.

"Even then, when he gave you that ring?"

"What? — He never gave me a ring — I never said that *he* gave me the ring."

"Good," said the Prince, ringing the bell, and already on his way out. "— And the Marquis de Lanoy's ghost," he asked, turning back once more, "that this Russian caused to appear after the one you made, do you believe that was really and truly a ghost?"

"I can't think it was anything else," answered the man.

"Come," said the Prince to us. The gaoler came in. "We have finished," said the Prince to him. "You, sir," (turning to the Sicilian) "may expect to hear from me again."

"The last question, Your Highness, which you put to this trickster, I should like to put to you yourself," said I to the Prince, when we were alone again. "Do you believe that second ghost was a true and genuine one?"

"I? No, indeed, I no longer do so."

"No longer? Then you did before?"

"I will not deny that I did allow myself to be momentarily carried away, and to think it was more than a mere conjurer's trick."

"And I should like to see anyone," I cried, "who in those circumstances could have resisted such an impression. But what reasons have you now for changing your opinion? After what we have just heard about this Armenian, we should be more rather than less willing to believe in his miraculous powers."

"What we have just heard from this worthless fellow?" interposed the Prince with some force. "For I hope you can no longer doubt that that is what he is, this man that we have been dealing with?"

"No," I said. "But does that mean that his evidence —"

"The evidence of a good-for-nothing — even if I had no other grounds to doubt it — cannot stand up against truth and sound reason. Does a man who has tricked me more than once, who has made trickery his profession, does such a man deserve to be heard in a matter where even the purest devotion to truth must first establish its credentials before it can be believed? Does a man like that, who has probably never uttered a single truth for its own sake, deserve to be believed when his evidence runs counter to reason and the eternal laws of nature? It is as if I were to allow a branded villain to bring accusations against the most unspotted and irreproachable innocence."

"But what reasons could he have to give a man whom he has such good cause to hate, or at least to fear, such a glowing testimonial?"

"Even if I cannot see his reasons, does that mean he does not have them? Do I know *who* is paying him to trick me? I admit that I do not yet fully understand the workings of his deception, but he has served the cause for which he is fighting very ill in showing himself up as a charlatan — and perhaps as something worse."

"I confess I find the business with the ring rather suspicious."

"*It is more than that,*" said the Prince, "it is decisive. He got that ring (let me assume for the moment that the things he told us really occurred) from the murderer, and he must have known for certain at that very moment that it was the murderer. Who else but the murderer could have robbed the dead man of a ring which he never took from his finger? He tried to persuade us all through the story that he himself had been deceived by the chevalier, and that he had thought that *he* was deceiving *him*. Why these twists and turns, unless he realised himself how much he had to lose by admitting his complicity with the murderer? His whole tale is nothing but a series of fabrications designed to string together the few truths that he found it in his interest to reveal to us. And are you telling me, when I have caught a scoundrel out over ten lies, that I should have more scruple to accuse him of an eleventh, than to allow a fundamental breach of the order of nature, in which I have never yet found the least discord?"

"I have no answer to that," said I. "But the apparition we saw yesterday is still just as inexplicable to me."

"To me too," said the Prince, "though I am tempted to suggest a key to the mystery."

"What might that be?" said I.

"You surely remember that the second figure, as soon as it appeared, made for the altar, took hold of the crucifix and stood on the carpet?"

"Yes, so it seemed to me."

"And the crucifix, so the Sicilian told us, was electrified. So you see that the 'ghost' was quick to make an electric contact. So the blow that Lord Seymour struck at it with his sword could have no effect, because the shock paralysed his arm."

"Yes, that would account for the sword. But the bullet that the Sicilian fired at it, which we then heard rolling slowly over the altar?"

"Are you sure it was the same bullet that we heard rolling? — To say nothing of the fact that the marionette, or the person, if it was, that played the part of the ghost could have been so well armoured as to be sword- and bullet-proof. — But just consider *who* it was that had loaded the pistols."

"It's true," I said, and a sudden realisation struck me — "the Russian had loaded them. But it all happened in full view of us — how could any deception be possible?"

"And why could it not have been possible? Did you at the time have any suspicion regarding that man that would have made you think it necessary to keep a watch on him? Did you inspect the bullet before he loaded it? It could have been made of mercury, or even of painted clay. Were you quite sure that he really loaded it into the pistol, or that he didn't drop it into his hand? What makes you so certain — assuming that the pistols really were loaded — that it really was the loaded ones that he took with him into the other part of the building and that he did not substitute another pair, which would have been an easy matter, as it didn't occur to anybody to keep a watch on him, and as we were in any case busy undressing? And might not the 'ghost,' just as the pistol smoke concealed it from us, have dropped another bullet on the altar, which it had been provided with in case of just such an emergency? Which of these explanations is impossible?"

"You are right. But the striking resemblance between the ghost and your late friend — I have often seen him in your company, and I recognised the ghost as him on the spot."

"So did I — and I have to admit that the deception was carried out to perfection. But if that Sicilian could manage after a few stolen glances at my snuff-box to give *his* portrayal some degree of likeness, enough to deceive you and me, would it not have been so much easier for the Russian, who had the freedom to make use of my snuff-box throughout the whole meal, who had the advantage of never being watched at any time, and to whom I had also revealed in confidence who it was who was portrayed on the box? — Add to this — as the Sicilian also observed — that the Marquis' characteristic features are such as can readily be imitated in a rough kind of way — and what is there in this whole apparition that is inexplicable?"

"But the contents of his words? What he told us about your friend?"

"What? Didn't the Sicilian say that he had made up a similar story out of the few scraps he had gleaned from me? Doesn't that prove how natural it was to come up with this particular invention? And on top of that, the ghost's answers were so dark and oracular that he ran no risk of being caught out contradicting himself. If we allow that the trickster's accomplice, the one who played the ghost, was intelligent and self-possessed and knew even in some degree what it was all about — how much further might they not have taken this pantomime?"

"But imagine, Your Highness, what elaborate preparations the Armenian must have made for such a complicated deception! How much time he would have needed! How much time even to make one man's face resemble another as closely as was called for here? How much time to train this substitute ghost so well that nothing could go wrong? How much attention would have had to be paid to all the nameless little things that either contributed or, because they might upset things, had in some way to be anticipated! And now just consider that the Russian did not leave us for more than half an hour. Could everything, even the absolute essentials for such a performance, be set up in no more than half an hour? — Really, Your Highness, I don't think that even a playwright worried about his three Aristotelian unities would have crammed so much action into a single interval, or expected his audience to suspend their disbelief so completely."

"What? So you think it completely impossible that all these preparations could have been made in that mere half an hour?"

"Surely," I cried, "as good as impossible."

"I don't understand that phrase. Does it offend against all the laws of time, space, and physical causality that such a clever fellow as this Armenian undoubtedly is, with the help of his perhaps equally skilful accomplices, under cover of night, with no one to observe them, and equipped with all the means which a man of this profession will never be without — that such a man, in such favourable circumstances, could have accomplished so much in such a short time? Is it actually inconceivable and absurd to believe that with only a few words, commands, or signals he could have given his men complicated tasks, that he could have indicated lengthy and complicated operations with the minimum expenditure of words? — And can what is nothing but a manifest impossibility stand against the eternal laws of nature? Would you rather believe a miracle than admit an improbability? Rather overturn all the forces of nature than admit to an artificial and uncommon combination of those forces?"

"Even if the matter does not justify such a bold conclusion, you must allow me that it is far beyond our comprehension."

"I am almost tempted to argue that with you," said the Prince with a cheerful, roguish expression. "How would it be, my dear Count, if, for example, it were to turn out that not just during and after that half an hour, not just in haste and by the by, but the whole evening and the whole night everything was the work of this Armenian? Just consider that the Sicilian took almost three full hours for his preparations."

"The Sicilian, Your Highness!"

"And where is the proof, then, that the Sicilian did not have just as much to do with the second ghost as with the first?"

"What, Your Highness?"

"That he is not the Armenian's principal accomplice — in short — that the two of them are not hand in glove together?"

"That would be hard to prove," I cried in no small amazement.

"Not so hard as you think, my dear Count. Really? You think it is mere chance that these two men should be engaged in such a strange and complicated plot against the same person, at the same time and in the same place, that there should be such a remarkable harmony, such a thoroughly contrived agreement between their two operations, that the one should be as it were playing into the other's hands? Suppose that he made use of the cruder deception in order to set off the more subtle one. Suppose that he first employed the one in order to test the degree of credulity he could expect of me; to spy out the ways of worming himself into my confidence; to get acquainted with his target through this experiment, which could be allowed to fail without jeopardising the rest of his plan; in short, to tune his means to their end. Suppose that he deliberately challenged and alerted my attention on the one hand, precisely to lull it to sleep regarding another matter which was more important to him. Suppose that he needed to make certain enquiries which he wanted to be laid to the trickster's account, so as to put any suspicions on the wrong track."

"What do you mean?"

"Let us assume that he bribed one of my people in order to obtain certain secret information — certain documents, even — which would serve his purposes. My attendant has gone missing. What is there to stop me believing that the Armenian is involved in the disappearance of this man? But chance may bring it about that I discover these ruses; a letter might be intercepted, a servant might have gossiped. His whole reputation is ruined if I discover the sources of his omniscience. So he interposes this mountebank, who must have some design or other upon me. He takes good care to give me an early hint as to the existence and the intentions of this man. So whatever I discover, all my suspicions fall upon this trickster, and the Sicilian will lend his name to any discoveries which are to his, the Armenian's, advantage. The Sicilian was the decoy that he let me play with, while he himself, unseen and unsuspected, was spinning his invisible nets around me."

"Excellent! But how do you square it with these intentions that he helps to destroy the illusion himself and reveals the secrets of his art to profane eyes? Must he not fear that the exposure of a deception carried through with as high a degree of conviction as the Sicilian's in fact was, will weaken your faith altogether and so make the execution of his further plans all the more difficult?"

"What are the secrets he is giving away? None of those, you can be sure, that *he* has a fancy to try out on me. So by profaning them he has lost nothing. — But how much on the other hand has he gained, if my supposed triumph over deceit and trickery has given me a sense of security, if he has managed to divert my attention into a quite different direction, to fix my still vague and indeterminate suspicions on an object as far removed as possible from the real point of attack? — He could expect that sooner or later, from my own suspicions or prompted by someone else, I should look to find the explanation of his miracles in some sort of conjuring trick. — What could he do better than to put them side by side himself, to put as it were the yardstick to judge them by in my own hand, and by setting an artificial boundary to the one to give me a more elevated or at any rate more confused idea of the others? How many speculations has he cut off at once by this manoeuvre? How many explanations, that I might subsequently have fallen upon, disproved in advance?"

"Then at all events he has badly spoiled his own game by sharpening the eyes of those he was aiming to deceive and making them altogether less disposed to believe in miracles by allowing such a far-fetched deception to be exposed. You yourself, Your Highness, are the best refutation of his plan, if he ever had one."

"Perhaps he was mistaken in me — but his judgement was no less sharp for that. Could he have foreseen that I should happen to remember the very thing that gave us the key to the mystery? Was it part of his plan that the creature who served him should give himself away so badly? Do we know whether this Sicilian has not gone far beyond his brief? — Certainly about the ring — And yet it is especially this one thing that confirmed my suspicions of this man. How easily can a subtly conceived plan be frustrated by a crude instrument! It was surely not his intention that the mountebank should have trumpeted his fame so brazenly — that he should serve up tales that the slightest thought is enough to expose. So, for example — how can this trickster have the nerve to claim that his miracle worker has to break off all commerce with men at the stroke of midnight? Have we not seen him in our midst at that very hour?"

"That is true!" I cried. "He must have forgotten that."

"But it is in the character of people like that to exaggerate their stories, and by overstepping the mark to spoil everything that a more modest and restrained deception would have brilliantly achieved."

"All the same, Your Highness, I cannot bring myself to regard this whole business as nothing more than a deliberate contrivance. What? The Sicilian's terror, the convulsions, the fainting, the whole wretched state of the man that made us pity him ourselves — could all this be nothing but a part he had learnt? Granted that a theatrical illusion can be taken to such a pitch, surely the actor's art cannot command his whole physical being."

"As regards that, my friend — I have seen Garrick play Richard the Third[9] — And were we cold and detached enough at that moment to be totally unbiased observers? Could we have put this man's passions to the test, when we were so overwhelmed by our own? And apart from that, the critical moment, even in a game of deception, is such an important affair for the deceiver himself that *anticipation* can easily bring forth symptoms of such violence in *him* as the *surprise* does in his victim. And then add the unexpected arrival of the law —"

"But that very circumstance, your grace — it is good that you remind me of it — would he really have dared to expose such a dangerous plan to the eyes of the law? To put the loyalty of his creature to such a hazardous test? And for what purpose?"

"That is his business, but he will know his people. Do we know what secret crimes guarantee him this man's silence? — You heard what office he holds in Venice — And even if this claim is just another of his fairy-tales — how much will it cost him to help this fellow get off when he is the only witness against him?"

(And indeed the subsequent course of events only served to justify the Prince's suspicions. When we made enquiries about our prisoner a few days later, we were told that he had disappeared.)

"And for what purpose, you ask? How else but in this violent way could he cause such an improbable and disgraceful confession to be extracted from the Sicilian, when so much depended on it? Who but a desperate man with nothing more to lose would be capable of making such damaging admissions about himself? In what other circumstances would we have believed him?"

"I admit it all, Your Highness," said I at last. "May both the apparitions be mere conjuring tricks; may this Sicilian, for all I know, have spun us a tale that his master has had him coached in; may they both be working together in agreement to some common purpose, and may this agreement suffice to explain all the extraordinary coincidences that have amazed us in the course of this affair. That prophecy in St Mark's Square, the first of these miracles, that led to all the others, still remains unexplained; and what use is the key to all the others when we despair of explaining that one?"

"Look at it the other way, my dear Count," answered the Prince. "Ask yourself, what do all those miracles prove, if I can show that even one of them was no more than a conjuring trick? That prophecy — I freely admit it — is beyond my comprehension. If it stood by itself, if the Armenian had concluded his part with that as he had begun — then I confess I do not know how far he might have carried me along with him. But in this base company it begins to look a little suspicious."

"I agree, Your Highness! And yet it remains incomprehensible, and I defy all our philosophers to cast any light on it."

"Must it really be so inexplicable?" continued the Prince, after few moments' consideration. "I am far from claiming to be a philosopher, and yet I could be tempted to find a natural key to this miracle as well, or at any rate to rob it of every appearance of the extraordinary."

"If you can do *that*, Prince, then," said I with a sceptical smile, "then *you* shall be the only miracle I believe in."

"And to prove," he continued, "how little justification we have to have resort to supernatural powers, I will show you two different ways in which we can perhaps get to the bottom of this matter without violating the laws of nature."

"Two keys at once! Indeed, now you are making me most curious."

"You were with me when I read the detailed account of my late cousin's illness. He was suffering from a cold fever when he was killed by a stroke. The extraordinary manner of his death led me, I confess, to consult a number of doctors about it, and what I learnt from them puts me on the track of this magical business. The disease from which the dead man was suffering, a particularly rare and dangerous one, has this one peculiar symptom, that during a bout of shivering the patient is plunged into a deep coma from which he cannot be roused, and which causes him in the event of a second paroxysm to suffer a fatal apoplexy. As these paroxysms recur in strict sequence and at fixed intervals, the doctor is able, once his diagnosis of the patient's illness has been confirmed, also to predict the hour of death. Now it is known that the third paroxysm of a tertiary fever will occur on the fifth day of the illness — and this is just the time that it takes a letter from ***, where my cousin died, to reach Venice. Now let us assume that our Armenian has an attentive correspondent among the late man's retinue, that he has a keen interest in receiving news from that quarter, that he has some designs on me which would be advanced by a faith in miracles on my part and by the appearance of supernatural powers, — and you have a natural explanation of that prophecy which seems so incomprehensible to you. At all events you can see how it would be possible for a third party to bring me the news of a death which is taking place more than a hundred miles away at the very moment he is announcing it."

"Really, Prince, you are putting things together which taken one by one admittedly sound very natural, but in fact can only be connected in this way by something which is no better than magic."

"Indeed? Then you are less frightened by miracles than by what is merely surprising and unusual? As soon as we admit that the Armenian has an important plan, which is either aimed at me or needs me for its execution, — and are we not *obliged* to assume that, whatever else we may think about him personally? — then nothing is unnatural or forced which will lead him by the shortest route to his goal. But can there be a quicker way of getting a man into one's power than by gaining the reputation of a miracle worker? Who can resist a man whom the spirits obey? But I admit to you that my explanation is somewhat contrived; I confess that it does not really convince me. So I will not insist on it, as I do not think it worth invoking a contrived and fabricated solution, when mere chance is enough to explain everything."

"What?" I interrupted him, "you are saying that mere chance —"

"Hardly anything more," continued the Prince. "The Armenian knew that my cousin was in danger. He saw us in St Mark's Square. The opportunity tempted him to make a prophecy which, if it proved false, was no more than a word wasted — but if it should be fulfilled could have the most significant consequences. The outcome rewarded his venture — and it may well have been only then that he thought of basing a coherent plan on this present of good fortune. — Time will unravel this mystery, or perhaps it will not — but believe me, my friend" (and he laid his hand on mine and took on a very serious expression), "a man who can command higher powers will have no need of mere trickery, or he will disdain to use it."

And so ended a conversation which I have reported in full because it shows the difficulties which were to be overcome in the Prince's case, and because I hope it will clear his memory of the charge that he threw himself blindly and unthinkingly into the snares which an unheard-of devilry had laid for him. Not all of those — continues Count von O** — who as I write this are perhaps laughing his weakness to scorn and thinking themselves in the pride and self-regard of their unchallenged reason entitled to break the staff of condemnation over him, not all of these people, I am afraid, would have so doughtily withstood this first temptation. And if we are now to see him succumb despite this fortunate preparation, if we find the assault of evil, of whose furthest approach his good angel had warned him, nevertheless achieving its purpose with him, we shall be less inclined to mock his folly than to marvel at the magnitude of the wicked plot which overcame a mind so well defended. Worldly considerations can have no part in what I choose to reveal, for *he* whose gratitude I should earn is no more. His terrible fate has run its course; his soul has long since absolved itself before the throne of truth, before which my own will long have stood before the world reads these pages; but — and may I be forgiven the tear which against my will I shed for the memory of my dearest friend — but to guide the hand of justice I write this: He was a noble man, and he would surely have been an adornment of the throne which he was duped into trying to ascend by criminal means.

*

Book Two

Not long after these last occurrences — continues Count von O**'s narration — I began to notice a significant change in the Prince's disposition. Up till then the Prince had avoided examining his faith at all closely, and had been content merely to purify the crude and sensual notions of religion in which he had been brought up in the light of the better ideas which had subsequently presented themselves to him, without investigating the foundations of his belief. Religious matters in general, he confessed to me several times, had always seemed to him like an enchanted castle which was not to be entered without a feeling of terror, and he thought it better to pass by in respectful resignation, rather than running the risk of becoming lost in its twisting passages. And yet an opposite inclination drew him irresistibly to pursue investigations in that direction.

A bigoted and slavish upbringing was the origin of that fear; this had impressed images of horror on his tender mind, from which he never managed to free himself completely as long as he lived. Religious melancholy was a hereditary sickness in his family; the upbringing which he and his brothers had received was in accordance with this inclination, and the people to whom he was entrusted were chosen from that standpoint, that is, they were either religious zealots or hypocrites. The surest way for them to assure themselves of the total satisfaction of his princely parents was to stifle any sign of a lively spirit in the boy in gloomy spiritual repression.

This black nocturnal character dominated the whole of our Prince's youth; even from his games all joy was banished. All his notions of religion had something fearful about them, and it was this harshness and terror which first conquered his lively imagination and which also continued to dominate it. His God was a monster, an agent of retribution; his devotion a slavish trembling or a blind submission which stifled all vitality and courage. All the inclinations of his childhood and youth, made all the more explosive by blooming health and a robust constitution, were frustrated by religion; it was constantly at war with every impulse of a young man's heart; he never learnt to see it as a blessing, always as the scourge of his emotions. And so there grew a silent resentment against it in his heart, forming with reverent faith and blind fear the strangest mixture in his heart and mind — a resentment against a Lord for whom he felt in equal measure reverence and revulsion.

No wonder that he took the first opportunity of escaping from such an oppressive yoke; but he escaped as a slave might escape his harsh master, in his freedom still carrying the feeling of servitude with him. Just because he had not rejected the faith of his youth after reflection and choice, because he had not waited to be gradually weaned from it by maturer reason, because he was fleeing from it like an escaped serf still subject to the rights of his master — he had therefore always to return to it, even after the greatest distractions. He had escaped still bearing his chains, and for that reason he must always be easy prey for any charlatan who recognised them and knew how to exploit them. And that such a person was waiting, if the reader has not yet guessed it, the continuation of this story will show.

The Sicilian's confessions had left more significant traces in his mind than the whole affair was worth, and the small victory which his reason had won over this trivial deception had induced in him a greatly increased confidence in its powers. The ease with which he had succeeded in unmasking *this* trickery seemed to surprise even himself. Truth and falsehood had not yet separated themselves so clearly in his mind that he was never capable of confusing the evidence of the one with that of the other, and so it was that the blow that overturned his faith in miracles also caused the whole edifice of his religious faith to totter. He was like any inexperienced person who as a result of a mistaken choice has been deceived in friendship or in love, and now loses all faith in those emotions, because he mistakes mere accidentals for their essential qualities and characteristics. The revelation of a deception made him suspicious of the truth itself, because he had had the misfortune to uncover the truth by equally deceptive reasoning.

He took all the more pleasure in this supposed triumph because of the weight of the pressure from which it appeared to free him. From this moment on he developed a sceptical passion from which not even the most sacred matters were spared.

Many causes combined to keep and indeed to strengthen him in this frame of mind. The solitude in which he had been living had come to an end, and was replaced by a life full of distractions. His rank had been discovered. Attentions to which he had to respond, formalities which he owed his princely status, swept him willy-nilly into the maelstrom of the fashionable world. His rank as well as his personal qualities opened the most sophisticated circles in Venice to him; soon he found himself associating with the brightest luminaries of the Republic, both with scholars and with statesmen. This forced him to extend the narrow and unvarying circle in which his mind had hitherto been confined. He began to realise how limited his notions were and to feel the need for further intellectual nourishment. The old-fashioned cast of his mind, accompanied though it was by many advantages, appeared in a poor light beside the ideas current in this society, and his ignorance of so many commonly-known things often exposed him to ridicule; and he feared nothing so much as to appear ridiculous. The prejudice which was felt against the land of his birth he regarded as a challenge to be disproved in his own person. To all this was added the peculiarity of his character that made him resent any attentions which he believed to owe to his rank rather than to his personal worth. He felt this humiliation especially in the presence of persons who shone through their quality of mind and who had, as it were, triumphed over their birth by personal merit. To see himself set apart as a prince in such company was always deeply shaming to him, since he unfortunately believed that his princely title exempted him from any competition. All these things combined to convince him of the need to give his mind the cultivation it had so far lacked, in order to make up the five years' headstart which the educated and thinking world had of him.

To this end he chose the most up-to-date reading matter, to which he devoted himself with the seriousness he applied to everything he went about. But the unlucky hand which guided his choice of these works always led him to light on ones which were of little benefit either to his reason or his heart. And here too he was subject to his favourite propensity, which drew him irresistibly to things which were never meant to be understood. These and these only absorbed his mind and stayed in his memory; his reason and his heart remained empty, while these compartments of his brain were filled with confused ideas. On the one hand a dazzling style carried his imagination away, on the other his reason was entangled in sophistries. For both it was an easy matter to enslave a mind which was prey to any who could impose themselves upon him with sufficient forwardness.

One piece of reading which he had pursued with passion for more than a year, while hardly enriching his mind with a single profitable thought, had nevertheless filled it with doubts which, as was always the case given the consistency of his character, soon made their unhappy way into his heart. To make myself quite clear: he had entered this labyrinth a credulous zealot, and emerged from it a doubter and finally as a confirmed freethinker.

Among the circles into which he had allowed himself to be drawn was a certain private society calling itself the *Bucentaur,*[10] which under the outward appearance of a noble, rational independence of mind favoured in fact the most extreme licence of both opinion and conduct. As there were many clerics among its members and indeed several cardinals among its chief luminaries, the Prince was all the more easily persuaded to accept an introduction to it. Certain dangerous truths of reason, he thought, were nowhere safer than in the hands of men whose station in life itself enjoined moderation and who also had the advantage of having heard and weighed the arguments of the other side. The Prince had forgotten that depravity of mind and conduct finds all too easy access to persons of this station, because one less barrier restrains it and it is not dazzled by the appearance of saintliness which so often blinds the eyes of the multitude. And this was the case with the Bucentaur, the great majority of whose members, through a damnable philosophy and through conduct worthy of such a guide, were a disgrace not just to their calling, but to the whole of humanity.

The society had its secret grades, and honouring the Prince as I do, I will not believe he was ever admitted to its holy of holies. Everyone who became a member of this society had, at least as long as he remained one, to cast off his rank, his nationality, and his religious confession and to enter a state of universal equality. The selection of members was indeed rigorous, because only distinction of mind could qualify one for it. The society prided itself on the greatest refinement and the most cultivated taste, and this was the reputation it indeed enjoyed throughout Venice. This, as well as the appearance of equality which ruled within it, was irresistibly attractive to the Prince. Sophisticated and witty company, informative conversation, the best elements of the learned and the political world, which all met here as in their focal point, concealed from him for a long time all that was dangerous in this association. When gradually the true spirit of the institution began to show through the mask, or when indeed the members tired of being on their guard towards him, it was dangerous to turn back, and both false shame as well as concern for his safety forced him to conceal his inner distaste.

But even mere familiarity with men of this kind and their attitudes, though he was not led to follow their example, robbed him of the beautiful pure simplicity of his character and the delicacy of his moral feelings. His mind, lacking the support of sound knowledge and without outside help, could not unravel the subtle falsehoods with which he had been ensnared, and imperceptibly this terrible corrosive had eaten away almost all the foundations of his moral conduct. The supports on which his happiness should naturally have rested he surrendered in exchange for sophistries which deserted him at the decisive moment and forced him to clutch at whatever straws he was offered.

Perhaps a friendly hand might have succeeded in holding him back at the last minute from this abyss — but apart from the fact that I only became acquainted with the inner circles of the Bucentaur long after the damage had been done, an urgent matter had already summoned me away from Venice at the beginning of this period. Lord Seymour, too, a valuable acquaintance of the Prince's, whose cool head was proof against every kind of deception and who would undoubtedly have proved a solid support, left us at this time to return to his own country. Those in whose hands I left the Prince were honest but inexperienced men, very limited in their religion, who had neither insight into the nature of the evil which was at work nor sufficient standing in the Prince's eyes. They had nothing to oppose to his seductive sophistries but the dogmatic pronouncements of a blind untested faith, which either made him angry or merely amused him; he easily outclassed them, and his superior wit soon silenced these poor defenders of the good cause. The other men who subsequently gained his confidence were only concerned to enmesh him ever more deeply. When I returned to Venice in the following year — how different was everything that I found!

The influence of this philosophy soon showed itself in the Prince's conduct. The more rapidly he made his fortune in Venice and gained new friends, the more he began to lose in his old friends' estimation. Day by day I cared less and less for what I saw in him; indeed, we saw each other less often and I had altogether less of his time. The current of high society had caught him up. Never was his doorstep deserted when he was at home. One entertainment, one feast, one merriment followed another. He was the fair one courted by all, the king and the idol of every circle. Hard though he had found it, in the stillness of his previous restricted life, to imagine life in this social whirl, to his amazement he now found himself easily at home in it. Everyone was so obliging, every word that fell from his lips met with such acclaim, and if he had nothing to say, the company felt it had been robbed. And this good fortune that followed him everywhere, this universal success, made of him something more than he really was, because it gave him courage and self-confidence. The heightened opinion that he thus gained of his own merit gave him faith in the exaggerated and almost idolatrous adulation that was paid to his mind, an adulation which, but for this enhanced and to some extent justified confidence in himself, must surely have been suspect to him. Now, though, this general reputation was simply the confirmation of what his self-satisfied pride told him in silence — a tribute which, as he believed, was his by right. He would undoubtedly have escaped this snare if he had been allowed to pause for breath, and able calmly to compare his own merits with the image that was held up to him in such a flattering mirror. But his existence was a constant state of intoxication, a whirl of giddiness. The higher he had been set up, the more he had to exert himself to maintain this state of exaltation; the perpetual strain was slowly consuming him; even in his sleep he knew no rest. His weaknesses had been recognised and the passions which had been aroused in him had been well calculated.

Soon the honest gentlemen of his entourage had to bear the consequences of their master's new reputation. Serious sentiments and venerable truths which had always been dear to his heart now became objects of mockery to him. On the truths of religion he vented his revenge for the delusions which had so long oppressed him; but because a voice in his heart which was not to be completely stifled continued to battle the giddy thoughts in his head, there was more bitterness than good humour in his wit. His nature began to change, and he became capricious. The finest ornament of his character, his modesty, disappeared; flatterers had poisoned his trusty heart. The tact and delicacy which had formerly made those honest gentlemen quite forget that he was their master now all too frequently gave way to a brusque and imperious tone which pained them all the more because it rested not on the outward distinction of birth, which is easily disregarded and which he himself held of little account, but on an offensive presumption of his personal superiority. And because at home he was often given to reflections of a kind which he barred from his mind in the whirl of society, his own people rarely saw him other than gloomy, brooding, and miserable, while he enlivened the company of strangers with a false gaiety. We sympathised even as we grieved to see him following this dangerous course; but in the tumult in which he was plunged he no longer heard the gentle voice of friendship, and he was now too far lost in pleasure to be capable of understanding it.

It was in the very first weeks of this period that an important matter, to which even the warmest interests of friendship had to take second place, recalled me to my own sovereign's court. An invisible hand, which only long afterwards revealed itself to me, had found means of introducing confusion into my affairs at home and of spreading rumours about me which I had quickly to refute by my immediate presence. Parting from the Prince was hard for me, but all the easier for him. The bonds which had drawn him to me had long since slackened. But his fate had engaged my deepest sympathy, and so I made Baron von F*** promise that he would keep me constantly informed about it in writing — which promise he most conscientiously kept. From this point on I therefore ceased for a considerable period to be an eyewitness of these events, so I hope I may be permitted to let Baron von F*** speak for me and to fill in these gaps in my story by extracts from his letters. Although my friend F***'s view of these matters is not always my own, I have chosen to alter nothing in his words, from which the reader will have no difficulty in perceiving the truth.

*Baron von F*** to Count von O***
First Letter

May, 17**.

Thank you, my respected friend, for allowing me to continue in your absence the familiar communication which was my greatest pleasure during your time here. You know that there is no one here to whom I dare unburden myself about certain matters; whatever you may say about it, these people are hateful to me. Since the Prince has become one of them, and above all since you were called away from us, I feel completely abandoned in this teeming city. Z*** does not take it so hard, and the Venetian beauties know how to help him to forget the injuries which he has to share with me at home. And indeed, what cause has *he* to complain? He sees and desires to see nothing in the Prince but his master, and he could find another anywhere — but I! You know how close the Prince is to my heart in weal and woe, and for what good reasons. It is now sixteen years that I have lived with him, have lived only for his person. I entered his service as a nine-year-old boy, and since that time fate has never parted us. I have become what I am under his tutelage; a long association has moulded my personality to his; I have shared with him all his adventures, great and small. His happiness is my life. Until this unhappy year I have seen in him only my friend, my elder brother; I have lived in his eyes as in the bright summer sun, with not a cloud to mar my skies; and now, here in this miserable Venice, I have to see all this fall in ruins.

Since you left us, many things have changed here. The Prince of **d** arrived here last week with a large retinue and has brought a new, tumultuous animation into our circle. As he and our Prince are so closely related and are now on such good terms with each other, they will be keeping each other's company for most of the time that he remains here, which I hear will be until Ascension. They have started as they mean to go on; in the last ten days the Prince has scarcely had time to draw breath. The Prince of **d** has set his sights high from the beginning, which is all very well for him, as he will be leaving again before very long; but the worst of it is that he has infected our Prince, because he was virtually obliged to join him, and because, given the particular relationship between their two houses, he feels he must not allow his own to take second place here. Also, we shall ourselves be leaving Venice in a few weeks, which in any case will make it unnecessary for him to continue this extravagance.

The Prince of **d**, they say, is here on some errand for the *** Order, and thinks he is playing a part of great importance. You will readily imagine that he has immediately established himself with all our Prince's acquaintances. In particular, he had himself introduced to the Bucentaur with a great show, as he has for some time enjoyed playing the part of a wit and a freethinker, for as you know, in the correspondence which he keeps up with all the world he likes to be called the *Prince philosophe*. I do not know whether you have ever had the pleasure of seeing him. A very attractive appearance, an animated look, an expression of connoisseurship, a great display of reading, much studied naturalness (if I may so express it), and a princely condescension to feelings of humanity, together with a heroic self-confidence and the ability to out-talk all comers. Who could fail to pay homage to a Royal Highness with such brilliant qualities? How the quiet, taciturn, and solid worth of our Prince will fare beside such glittering excellence, we must wait and see.

Our arrangements have in the meanwhile undergone numerous and extensive changes. We have moved into a grand new house, opposite the new Procuratoria, because the Prince found the Moor's Head too cramped for him. Our company has also grown by a dozen new bodies — pages, blackamoors, heiducks and so on — everything on a grand scale. You used to complain of extravagance when you were here — but you should see us now!

Our more intimate relationships are still the same, except that the Prince, now that he is no longer kept within bounds by your presence, has become even more cold and monosyllabic towards us, if that were possible, and that we now see very little of him apart from dressing and undressing him. Under the pretext that we speak bad French and no Italian, he has managed to exclude us from most of the society he keeps, which I personally take as no great offence; but I think the truth of the matter is that he is ashamed of us, and that does grieve me, that is something we have not deserved.

Of our people (since you want to know all these small details) it is now hardly anyone but Biondello whom he uses. You will remember that he took him into his service after we lost our old attendant, and he has become indispensable to him in his new way of life. The fellow knows everything that is going on in Venice, and knows how to make use of it. It is just as if he had a thousand eyes to see and a thousand hands to work with. He arranges all this with the help of the gondoliers, he says. He is particularly useful to the Prince by making him acquainted in advance with all the new faces that he will meet in his social circles; and the Prince has always found his secret notes about them to be accurate. He also speaks and writes both Italian and French very well, and so has already got himself promoted to be the Prince's secretary. And I must tell you about one instance of selfless loyalty of a kind which is not often seen in people of this kind. Not long ago a respected merchant from Rimini asked the Prince for an audience. He had a particular complaint to make about Biondello. The Procurator, his former master, who must have been a strange sort of saint, had maintained an irreconcilable hostility to his family, and intended that if possible it should continue when he was dead. Biondello had his complete and exclusive confidence and was the repository of all his secrets, and on his deathbed he made Biondello promise to keep them faithfully and never to let the family draw any advantage from them; he was promised a considerable legacy in return for his silence. When his will was opened and his papers examined, great gaps and confusions were found, which only Biondello could explain. He denied all knowledge about them, let the very substantial legacy go to the heirs and kept his secrets. The relatives made him generous offers, but to no avail; finally, to escape their persecution, because they were threatening to take him to law, he entered the Prince's service. This merchant, who was the principal heir, now turned to the Prince and made even greater offers than before if Biondello would change his mind. But even the Prince's advocacy was fruitless. Biondello did confess that he had been entrusted with secrets of that kind, and did not deny that the deceased had perhaps taken his hatred of his family rather too far; "but," he added, "he was a good master to me and treated me well, and died implicitly trusting my honesty. I was the only friend he had left in the world, and for that I cannot betray his last hopes." He also gave us to understand that any revelations would do his late master's memory no credit. Was that not a mark of nobility and refinement?

And you can readily imagine that the Prince made no very great effort to dissuade him from such a praiseworthy resolution. And the rare loyalty which he displayed to his deceased master earned him the complete confidence of the living one.

May you be happy, my dear friend. How I long for that peaceful life in which you found us here, and for which you offered us such pleasant compensation! I am afraid my happy days in Venice are a thing of the past, and let it be enough for me if the same is not true for the Prince. The atmosphere he is now living in is one in which he cannot remain happy for long, if after sixteen years' experience I am not much mistaken. Farewell!

*Baron von F*** to Count von O***
Second Letter

May 18th

I had never thought that anything good would come out of our stay in Venice. But now it has saved someone's life, and I am reconciled to it.

Recently the Prince had himself carried home late at night from the Bucentaur, with two servants, one of them Biondello, accompanying him. I don't know how it happened, but the sedan chair which they had hastily taken came to grief, and the Prince found himself obliged to make the rest of the journey on foot. Biondello was walking ahead of him, their way led through some dark and remote streets, and as it was approaching daybreak the street-lamps were burning low or had already gone out. They had been going for about a quarter of an hour when Biondello discovered that he had got lost. The fact that one bridge looked much like another had deceived him, and instead of crossing over to St Mark's Square they found themselves in the Castello district. They were in one of the remotest alleys, and there was no sign of life anywhere around them; they would have to turn back to one of the main streets to get their bearings. They have only gone a few paces when in an alley not far away they hear someone shouting murder. The Prince, unarmed as he was, seizes a stick from one of the servants and runs off, brave as you know him, in the direction of the cry. Three fearful ruffians are on the very point of knocking down a fourth man, who can only feebly defend himself with the help of his companion; the Prince appears in the nick of time to save him from the fatal blow. His shouts and those of the servants startle the murderers, who are not expecting to be surprised in such a remote place, so that they leave their victim with only a few light dagger-blows and take to their heels. Half unconscious and exhausted by his struggles, the wounded man sinks into the Prince's arms; his companion explains to the Prince that he has saved the life of the Marchese di Civitella, nephew of Cardinal A***i. As the Marchese has lost quite a lot of blood, Biondello hastens to the best of his ability to perform the office of surgeon, and the Prince saw to it that the Marchese was carried to his uncle's palace, which was situated close by and to which he accompanied him himself. Here he quietly left him, without having revealed his identity.

But a servant who had recognised Biondello gave him away. The very next morning the Cardinal appeared, an old acquaintance from the Bucentaur. The visit lasted an hour; when they emerged the Cardinal was in great agitation, with tears in his eyes, and the Prince too was moved. That same evening he visited the wounded man, of whose recovery the surgeon is, by the way, entirely confident. The cloak he was wearing had deflected the dagger-blows and cushioned their impact. After this incident, not a day passed without the Prince's making or receiving visits in the Cardinal's house, and a strong friendship began to form between that house and him.

The Cardinal is a venerable man in his sixties, majestic in appearance, serene and in the best of health. He is believed to be one of the richest prelates in the whole territory of the Republic. He draws on his immense fortune as if he were still a young man, scorning no worldly pleasure, while at the same time observing a sensible degree of economy. The nephew is his sole heir, but is said not always to enjoy the happiest of relations with his uncle. Even though the old man is in no way an enemy of pleasure, his nephew's conduct is said to strain his tolerance to the limits. His free and easy principles and his abandoned way of life, unfortunately aggravated by everything that can beautify vice and inflame sensuality, make him the terror of every father and the curse of every husband; indeed, he is said to have provoked this last attack as a result of a relationship he had begun with the wife of the **an ambassador; not to mention various other disreputable affairs from which the Cardinal's wealth and reputation have only with difficulty been able to extricate him. But for this, the Cardinal would be the most envied man in all Italy, for he possesses everything that can make life desirable. But through this one black sheep of the family, fortune revokes all its blessings and embitters all the Cardinal's enjoyment of his wealth by the constant fear that he will have no heir to leave it to.

All this information I have from Biondello. This man has proved a real treasure to the Prince. Every day he makes himself more indispensable, every day we discover some new talent that he possesses. Recently the Prince was feverish and could not sleep. His nightlight had been extinguished, and no ringing could awake his valet, who had left the house to pursue some amorous adventure. The Prince therefore decided to get up himself to summon another of his servants. He had not gone very far when he heard some sweet music in the distance. He follows the sound as if spellbound and finds Biondello in his room playing the flute, with all his comrades around him. He cannot believe his eyes or ears and orders him to continue. With admirable delicacy Biondello extemporises the same melting adagio and adds the happiest variations and all the refinements of a virtuoso. The Prince, who as you know is a connoisseur of music, declares that he is worthy to play in the very best company.

"I shall have to let this man go," he said to me the next morning; "I cannot afford to reward him as he deserves." Biondello, who had heard him say this, came up to us. "Your Highness," he said, "if you do that, you will deprive me of my best reward."

"You are meant for better things than service," said the Prince. "I cannot stand in the way of your good fortune."

"Do not compel me to seek any other fortune, Your Highness, than the one I have chosen for myself."

"But to let a talent like that go to waste — no! I cannot allow it."

"Then permit me, my lord, to exercise it sometimes in your presence."

And so arrangements were immediately made to allow this. Biondello has been given a room immediately adjacent to his master's bedroom, where he can lull him to sleep with music and wake him with music again in the morning. The Prince wanted to double his wages, but he refused this, asking to be allowed to leave this intended favour on deposit with the Prince, as he might one day quite soon have need to draw on it. The Prince is now expecting him to come any day with some request; and whatever it may be, it is granted in advance. Fare you well, dear friend. I look forward impatiently to receiving news from K***n.

*Baron von F*** to Count von O***
Third Letter

June 4th

The Marchese di Civitella, who has now completely recovered from his injuries, had himself introduced to the Prince last week by his uncle, and since that day has been following him like his shadow. Biondello was not telling me the truth about the Marchese; at all events he was exaggerating greatly. He is very attractive in appearance and quite irresistible in company. It is impossible to dislike him; he conquered me at first sight. Just imagine the most enchanting physical presence, carried with both dignity and grace, a face full of spirit and soul, an open and inviting manner, an ingratiating tone of voice, the most eloquent fluency of speech, the finest flowering of youth wedded to the graces of the most refined upbringing. He has nothing of the haughty pride, the solemn stiffness which we find so unbearable in the other Nobili. Everything about him proclaims youthful gaiety, benevolence and warmth of feeling. His extravagances must have been greatly exaggerated to me, for I never saw a more perfect, handsome picture of good health. If he really is as bad as Biondello tells me, then he is a siren whom no one can resist.

To me he immediately spoke quite openly. He admitted to me with the most engaging frankness that he did not enjoy the best of reputations with his uncle the Cardinal and that he may well have done much to deserve this. But he was seriously determined to mend his ways, and for this the Prince could claim full credit. He also hoped that the Prince would help to reconcile him and his uncle, as the Prince had a great influence on the Cardinal. All he had lacked till now was a friend and guide, and he hoped that he had now found both in the Prince.

The Prince indeed exercises all the rights of a guide over him, and watches him closely and strictly like a mentor. But this relationship also gives him certain rights over the Prince, which he knows very well how to exploit. He never leaves his side now, he is present at all the Prince's engagements, only for the Bucentaur — and that is his good fortune! — is he still too young. Everywhere he goes with the Prince, he draws him away from the company by the refined way in which he manages to engage him and to keep him by his side. No one, people say, has ever been able to control him, and the Prince's reputation will be legendary if he can succeed in such a formidable task. But I am very much afraid that the tables may be turned and the master begin to learn from his pupil, and indeed everything seems already to be pointing in that direction.

The Prince of **d** has left now, and, it must be said, to our general satisfaction, including my master's. What I prophesied to you, my dear O**, has indeed come about. Given such different characters and the collisions these were bound to lead to, their relationship could not remain on the same footing for long. The Prince of **d** had not been long in Venice when an ominous schism arose in the sophisticated world, which threatened our Prince with the loss of half his admirers. Wherever he appeared, he found this rival in his path, who possessed just the necessary amount of low cunning and selfish vanity to exploit even the slightest advantage which our Prince might yield to him. And as he commanded all the petty tricks which our Prince's sense of noble pride forbids him to employ, he could not fail in a short time to have all the empty heads on his side and to flaunt himself as the leader of a party which was indeed worthy of him.[11] The sensible thing would of course have been not to engage in any competition with an opponent of this kind, and a few months earlier this would certainly have been the Prince's chosen course. But by now he had been carried off too far by the current to be able quickly to reach the shore again. These trivialities had, if only through the force of circumstances, gained a certain importance for him, and even if he had really despised them his pride would not now permit him to abandon them, at a time when to do so would have seemed not so much a free resolution on his part as an admission of defeat. Add to this the constant exchange of sarcastic remarks on both sides, and the spirit of rivalry which animated his supporters had also taken hold of him. And so, in order to secure his victories and to maintain the position which the general opinion accorded him, he felt himself obliged to multiply the occasions on which he could shine and win people to his side, and this could only be achieved by expenditure on a princely scale: feasts and banquets without end, extravagant concerts, presents and gaming for high stakes. And as this extraordinary madness soon spread to followers and servants on both sides, and since, as you know, these are in the habit of taking matters of honour even more seriously than their masters, he had to assist the good will of his people by further open-handedness. A long chain of pettinesses, all the inescapable consequences of a single relatively pardonable weakness to which the Prince in an unhappy moment allowed himself to succumb!

Well, we are now rid of our rival, but the damage he has done is not so easily reparable. The Prince's coffers are exhausted; the savings of many years of prudent economy have been spent; we must hurry to leave Venice if he is not to plunge himself into debt, which he has so far most carefully avoided doing. Indeed, our departure is now agreed upon, as soon as fresh letters of credit have arrived.

And who would grudge all this expenditure, if only my master had derived the slightest pleasure from it! But never was he less happy than he is now! He feels that he is no longer what he was — he tries to find himself — he is dissatisfied with himself and throws himself into new distractions to escape the consequences of the old ones. Every new acquaintance gives way to another which drags him ever further down. I cannot see what will become of us. We must leave — there is no other means of salvation — we must leave Venice.

But dear friend, still not a word from you! How am I to understand this long and obstinate silence?

*Baron von F*** to Count von O***
Fourth Letter

June 12th

Thank you, dear friend, for the token of your memory, which you sent to me through young B***hl. But what is this mention of letters which I am supposed to have received? I have received no letters from you, not a single line. What roundabout route can they have taken! In future, dear Count von O**, when you favour me with letters, send them via Trento and address them care of my master.

And now at last, dear friend, we have had to take that step which we have been fortunate to avoid for so long. Our letters of credit have failed to arrive, in this hour of urgent need have failed for the first time to arrive, and we have found ourselves forced to resort to a usurer, as the Prince is willing to pay a considerable price for secrecy. But the worst thing about this unpleasant state of affairs is that it has postponed our departure.

This gave rise to some expostulations between myself and the Prince. The whole business was arranged by Biondello, and the Hebrew was on our doorstep before I knew anything about the matter. Seeing the Prince brought to this extremity nearly broke my heart, and made me recall so vividly all my memories of the past, all my terrors for the future, that I must indeed have looked rather grim and gloomy when the usurer had left us. The Prince, whom this scene had in any case made very irritable, was pacing angrily up and down the room, the rolls of money were still lying on the table; I was standing at the window, occupying myself by counting the window-panes in the Procuratoria; after a long silence, he could finally contain himself no longer.

"Look here, F***!" he began, "I can't bear to see gloomy faces around me."

I said nothing.

"Why don't you answer? — Can't I see that your heart is bursting to pour out your resentment? And I *will* have you speak. Otherwise, heaven knows what wise secrets you are bottling up inside you."

"If I am gloomy, Your Highness," said I, "it is only because I can see that you are not happy."

"I know," he went on, "that I don't please you — that I haven't for a long time — that you disapprove of everything I do — that — What does Count von O** say?"

"Count von O** has said nothing to me."

"Nothing? How can you deny it? You pour out your hearts to each other — you and the Count! I know it very well. So you may as well admit it. I will not pry into your secrets."

"Count von O**," said I, "has yet to reply to the first of three letters that I have written to him."

"I have done a wrong thing," he went on. "Have I not?" (seizing one of the rolls of money). — "I should not have done this."

"I can see that it was *necessary*."

"I should not have exposed myself to such a necessity."

I said nothing.

"I know! I should never have tried to spread my wings, I should have stayed content with what I was and ended as a greybeard the way I had grown up as a man. But because I try for once to escape the drab uniformity of my previous life and look around me to see if I might not find some other source of enjoyment — because I —"

"If it was just an experiment, Your Highness, then I have nothing more to say — then the experiences it has gained you would be worth three times what it has cost you and more. But I must admit that it pained me to see that the world's opinion should have the right to decide where your happiness might lie."

"Count yourself fortunate that you can afford to despise the world's opinion! I am its creature, I must be its slave. What are we but opinion? Everything about us princes is opinion. Opinion is our wet-nurse and our governess when we are children, our legislator and our mistress when we are men, our crutch in our old age. Take away what we owe to opinion, and the meanest from the other ranks of society is better off than we are; for his fate has at least taught him a philosophy that can console him for that fate. A prince who mocks opinion undermines his very being, just as a priest does if he denies the existence of God."

"And yet, Your Highness —"

"I know what you are going to say. I can step outside the circle which my birth has drawn around me — but can I also rid my mind of all the illusions that education and early habit have planted there and a hundred thousand simpletons among you have stamped down deeper and deeper? Everyone wants to be *entirely* what he *is*, and our existence is nothing more than — *to appear to be happy*. And because we cannot *be* happy in your way, may we not be happy at all? If we are no longer allowed to draw joy directly from its true source, why should we not deceive ourselves with artificial pleasures, why not claim some meagre compensation from the very hand that robbed us?"

"You used to find that in your own heart."

"And if I can no longer find it there? — Oh, why are we talking like this? Why did you have to rouse these memories in me? — If I did take flight to this tumult of the senses to silence an inner voice that is the misery of my life — to silence this brooding reason that cuts swathe after swathe in my brain like a sickle and with every new investigation cuts off another branch of my happiness?"

"My dearest Prince!" — He had stood up and was pacing round the room in uncommon agitation.

"If everything sinks away before and behind me — if the past lies behind me in dismal monotony like a realm of petrifaction — if the future has nothing to offer me — if I see the whole circle of my existence closed in the narrow confines of the present — who can blame me if I embrace this moment, this meagre gift of time, ardently and insatiably as I would a friend whom I was seeing for the last time?"

"Your gracious Highness, there was a time when you believed in a more permanent good —"

"Oh, make that cloudy phantom hold firm, and I will embrace it with fiery arms! What joy can it be for me to gratify creatures of the moment who will be gone tomorrow as I shall myself? — Is not everything in flight about me? Everything thrusts and pushes its neighbour aside, to sip a hasty drop from the springs of life and go on its way still thirsting. Now, in the very moment when I am rejoicing in my strength, some other budding life waits to feed on my destruction. Show me anything that lasts, and I will be virtuous."

"What is it that has driven out the healing sensations that were once your pleasure and the lodestone of your life? To sow a seed for the future, to serve a higher, eternal order —"

"Future! Eternal order! — Take away what men have taken from their own breasts and attributed to their imaginary God as His purpose, to nature as its law — what is left to us then? What came before me and what will come after, I see as two dark, impenetrable curtains, hanging down over the two ends of human life, which no living being has ever drawn aside. Hundreds of generations have stood before them with their torches and tried to guess what lies behind them. Many have seen their own shadows, the figures of their passions, passing magnified across the curtain of the future and have shuddered at the sight of their own image. Poets, philosophers, and statesmen have painted their dreams on them, brighter or darker as the heavens above them were gloomier or more serene, and from a distance their pictures were convincing. And many a trickster exploited the general curiosity and astounded men's excited fantasies with his curious deceptions. And behind the curtain there was profound silence, no one — if there is anyone there — answered from behind; all there was to hear was a hollow echo of the question, as if it had been shouted into a grave. We all have to pass beyond that curtain, and shuddering we take hold of it, unknowing, who may be behind it waiting to receive us — *quid sit id, quod tantum perituri vident.*[12] Admittedly there were sceptics among them, who said that men were only fooled by the curtain and that there would be nothing to see behind it, because there was nothing there; but they were quickly despatched beyond it to convince them otherwise."

"But it was a hasty conclusion all the same, if they had no better reason than that they could not see anything."

"Look now, my dear friend, I will gladly content myself not to try to look beyond the curtain — and the wisest course will no doubt be to cure myself of all curiosity. But when I draw this uncrossable circle around me and close my whole being within the limits of the present, this little speck becomes all the more important to me that I was already in danger of neglecting in my vain dreams of conquest. What you call the purpose of my existence is no longer of any importance to me. I cannot escape it, I cannot advance it, but I know and I firmly believe that there is a purpose which I must and do fulfil. I am like a messenger carrying a sealed letter to the place of his destiny. What it contains is indifferent to him — all he can expect is his messenger's reward."

"Oh, how wretched you leave me standing here!"

"But what maze have we strayed into?" cried the Prince, and smiled as he looked at the table where the rolls of money were lying. "And yet not quite such a maze!" he added — "for perhaps you will now recognise me again in this new way of life. Nor could I wean myself so quickly from those imaginary riches, nor sever the pillars of my morality and my happiness so quickly from the pleasant dream with which everything in my earlier life was so inextricably bound up. I longed for the frivolity that makes life bearable for most of the people I see about me. Everything that took me out of myself was welcome to me. Shall I confess it to you? I wanted to *sink*, to destroy the source of my suffering together with the strength to bear it."

Here a visitor interrupted us[13] — Next I will give you a piece of news which you will scarcely be expecting after a conversation like today's. Farewell.

*Baron von F*** to Count von O***
Fifth Letter

July 1st

As our departure from Venice is now rapidly approaching, it was decided to devote this week to catching up on all the most important paintings and buildings — the sort of thing one always puts off during a long stay. Paul Veronese's *Wedding Feast at Cana* had been most particularly recommended to us, which is to be seen in a Benedictine monastery on the Isola San Giorgio. You must not expect me to give you a description of this extraordinary work of art, which made on the whole a very surprising but not very agreeable impression on me. We should have needed as many hours as we had minutes to take in a composition of a hundred and twenty figures, measuring more than thirty feet in width. What human eye can comprehend such a complex whole and appreciate in a single moment all the beauties that the artist has lavished upon it! It is also a pity that a work of such rich content, that ought to be gracing some public place where it could be appreciated by everybody, should have no better fate than to gratify a few monks in their refectory. The church of this monastery is no less worthy of a visit. It is one of the most beautiful in the whole city.

Towards evening we had ourselves rowed across to the Giudecca, to spend a pleasant evening in the delightful gardens. The company, which was not very large, soon dispersed, and Civitella, who had been looking all day for an opportunity of speaking with me, took me aside into one of the arbours.

"You are the Prince's friend," he began, "and I know on very good authority that he has no secrets from you. When I called in at his lodgings this morning, I met a man coming out whose trade is well known to me — and the Prince's brow was clouded over when I entered his rooms." — I was going to interrupt him — "You cannot deny it," he said, "I knew my man, I had got to the heart of him — and yet, could it be possible? The Prince surely has friends in Venice, friends who are obliged to him for their very lives, and is he really brought to such a pass that he is obliged to make use of creatures of that kind? Be honest with me, Baron! Is the Prince in difficulties? — It is no use your trying to conceal it. What you will not tell me I can surely find out from my man, who knows the price of every secret."

"Signor Marchese —"

"Forgive me. I have to appear indiscreet in order not to be ungrateful. I owe the Prince my life, and, what is more important than life itself, a sensible use of it. And am I to see the Prince taking steps he will have to pay for, steps which are beneath his dignity; it could be in my power to spare him such steps, and am I then to suffer in silence and do nothing?"

"The Prince is not in difficulties," I said. "Some letters of credit, which should have reached us via Trento, have unexpectedly failed to arrive. By chance, no doubt, — or perhaps because people did not know when we were leaving and were awaiting further instructions. These have now been sent off, and until then —"

He shook his head. "Do not mistake my intentions," he said. "It is not a matter of reducing my obligation to the Prince — would all my uncle's riches be enough for that? It is simply a matter of sparing him a momentary unpleasantness. My uncle has a large fortune, of which I can make use as if it were my own. A happy chance puts me in the unique position of being able to employ what is in my power to be of use to the Prince. I know," he went on, "what scruples the Prince must have — but these also apply to me — and it would be an act of magnanimity on the Prince's part to allow me this small satisfaction — even if it were only in appearance — to make me less sensible of the burden of obligation which is weighing upon me."

He would not desist until I had promised him to do all that I could in this, but I knew the Prince and had few hopes. Civitella would agree to any conditions the Prince might impose, though he confessed that he would be greatly offended if the Prince treated him as if he were a stranger.

In the heat of our conversation we had wandered away from the rest of the party, and were returning to join them when we saw Z*** coming to meet us.

"I thought the Prince was with you — is he not here?"

"We were just going to him. We thought he would be with the rest of the company."

"The company is all together, but we cannot find him anywhere. I don't know how we managed to lose sight of him."

At this Civitella remembered that the Prince might have had the idea of visiting the neighbouring church, which he had recently drawn to the Prince's attention. We immediately set off in that direction to look for him there. Even at a distance we recognised Biondello waiting at the entrance to the church. As we approached, the Prince emerged from a side door in some haste; his face was glowing, and he looked round for Biondello, whom he summoned to him. He seemed to be giving him some very important instructions, and all the time was keeping his eyes fixed on the door, which was still standing open. Biondello hurried away from him into the church — and the Prince, without seeing us, pressed though the crowd beside us and hastened back to our party, where he arrived before us.

It was decided to take our supper in one of the open pavilions of this garden, and the Marchese had also, without our knowledge, arranged a small concert, which was quite excellent. We were particularly impressed by a young female singer, who delighted us all both by her sweet voice and by her charming appearance. The Prince seemed not to notice anything; he said little and answered distractedly; his eyes were turned restlessly in the direction from which Biondello must appear; he seemed to be suffering some inner commotion. Civitella asked him whether he had liked the church; he could say nothing about it. A number of excellent paintings were mentioned, for which it was remarkable; he had not seen a single painting. We realised that our questioning annoyed him, and said no more. Hours passed, and Biondello still failed to appear. The Prince became more and more impatient; he left the table early and we saw him pacing up and down by himself in a remote avenue. No one could tell what might have happened to him. I did not dare to ask him what was the cause of such a strange transformation; I have for a long time now ceased to enjoy the confidences of old. All the more impatiently I awaited the return of Biondello, who would have to explain this mystery to me.

It was past ten o'clock when he returned. The news which he brought the Prince did nothing to break the Prince's taciturnity. He rejoined the company in ill temper, we ordered our gondola, and soon afterwards returned home.

I could find no opportunity all evening of speaking to Biondello, and had to go to bed with my curiosity unsatisfied. The Prince had dismissed us early; but a thousand thoughts were running through my head and kept me awake. For a long time I heard him pacing up and down above my bedroom; finally, sleep overcame me. Long after midnight a voice awakened me — I felt a hand touch my face; when I looked up, it was the Prince who was standing by my bed with a light in his hand. He could not sleep, he said, and asked me to help pass the hours of night with him. I was hastening to dress myself, but he told me to stay as I was, and sat down at my bedside.

"Something happened to me today," he began, "which I shall never be able to wipe from my mind. I left you, as you know, and went into the *** Church, which Civitella had made me curious to see, and which had already attracted my gaze from afar. As neither you nor he were at hand, I made my way alone; it was only a few steps. I told Biondello to wait at the entrance. The church was quite empty — a cool, ominous darkness enfolded me as I left the dazzling, sultry sunlight outside. I found myself alone in the wide vaulted space, as silent and solemn as the grave. I went to the centre of the cathedral and abandoned myself to the fulness of this impression; gradually the grand proportions of the majestic building became clearer to my eyes, and I lost myself in grave but pleasing contemplation. The evening Angelus rang out above me, its sound echoed gently away under the vaults as it did in my soul. Some of the altar-pieces had attracted my attention from a distance; I approached to look at them more closely; without realising it, I had gone the whole length of the church to the farthest end. Here a few steps lead behind a pillar to a side-chapel, where there are several small altars and statues of saints standing in niches. Now, as I enter the chapel on the right — I hear a gentle whispering quite close to me, as if someone was speaking softly to me — I turn towards the sound, and — two paces away from me, the figure of a woman meets my eyes — No, I cannot describe it, that figure! — Terror was my first reaction, but it soon gave way to the sweetest astonishment."

"And this figure, Your Highness — are you sure it was a living creature, something real, not just a painting, not a figment of your imagination?"

"Listen — It was a lady — No! Never till that moment had I set eyes upon a woman! — Everything was dark around us, only a single window admitted the fading daylight into the chapel, the sun shone no more but on that figure. In inexpressible grace — half kneeling, half lying — she was prostrating herself before an altar — the boldest, fairest, most perfect shape, unique and inimitable, the most beautiful outline in nature. Black was the robe which was gathered about the most enchanting body and the most delicate arms, and fell about her in spreading folds like a Spanish cloak; her long, light blond hair, braided into two broad plaits that had loosened themselves by their weight and escaped the cover of her veil, flowed far down her back in exquisite disorder — one hand touched the crucifix, and she sank down to rest gently on the other. But where can I find words to describe the heavenly charms of her face, where an angel's soul shone forth in all its glory as if seated on a throne? The evening sun played upon it, and its ethereal gold seemed to surround her like a halo in a painting. Can you remember our Florentine artist's Madonna? — Here she was, complete, even to the tiny irregularities that I found so attractive, so irresistible in that picture!"

I must explain to you what Madonna it was that the Prince was speaking of here. Shortly after you had left us, he got to know a Florentine painter, who had been brought to Venice to paint an altarpiece for a church whose name I cannot remember. He had brought three other paintings with him which he had intended for the gallery in the Palazzo Corner. These paintings were a Madonna, a Héloise, and an almost completely nude Venus — all three exceptionally beautiful, and so equal in merit that it was almost impossible to decide on any one to the exclusion of the others. Only the Prince did not hesitate for a moment; they had scarcely been set up before him when the Madonna claimed all his attention; in the other two he admired the genius of the painter, in this one he forgot the artist and his art and was lost in contemplation of what he had brought forth. He was quite extraordinarily moved by it; he could hardly tear himself away from the work. The artist, who as we could see heartily approved the Prince's judgement, had the curious notion of not wanting to see the three pieces separated, and asked for fifteen hundred zecchini for the three of them. The Prince offered him half the sum for this one alone — the painter insisted on his condition, and who knows what might have happened had not a more determined purchaser appeared. Two hours later all three pieces had disappeared; we never saw them again. This was the painting that now came to the Prince's mind.

"I stood there," he went on, "I stood there completely lost in contemplation of her. She did not notice me, she did not let my appearance disturb her, so deeply was she absorbed in her devotions. She was praying to her God, and I was praying to her — Yes, I idolised her — All those images of saints, all those altars, all those burning candles, had left me indifferent; now for the first time I felt as if I were in a sacred place. Shall I admit it to you? In that moment I felt a rock-like faith in the God she was holding fast in her beautiful hand. I could read His answer in her eyes. Thanks to her enchanting devotion! She made Him real to me — I followed her on her way through all His heavens.

"She stood up, and at last I came to myself. Confused and shy, I drew aside, and the noise I made revealed my presence to her. The unexpected proximity of a man must have surprised her, my presumption could have offended her, but there was no sign of either in the gaze she turned on me. There was a calmness in it, an inexpressible calmness, and a kindly smile played about her cheeks. She descended from her heaven — and I was the first fortunate creature that her benevolence encountered. She hovered still on the last steps of prayer — she had not yet touched the earth.

"Now there was a movement in another corner of the chapel. It was an elderly lady who now rose from a stall close behind me. I had not noticed her until now. She was only a few steps away from me, she had observed all my movements. I was taken aback — I cast my eyes down to the ground, and heard the rustle of garments passing by me.

"I saw them going down the length of the aisle. The beautiful figure is now upright — what enchanting majesty! What nobility in her carriage! The being that was is no more — new graces — a completely new apparition. Slowly they make their way. I follow them, hesitant, uncertain — do I dare to catch up with them? Shall I, shall I not? Will she not accord me one more look? Did she look at me when she passed by me and I was incapable of raising my eyes to her? — Oh, how I was tortured by these anxieties!

"They are standing still, and I — am rooted to the spot. The elderly lady, her mother, or whoever she is, observes the disorder in her beautiful hair and busies herself to tidy it, giving her her sunshade to hold as she does so. Oh, how disordered I would have wished to see that hair, how unskilful those hands!

"The task is completed, and they are approaching the door. I hasten my steps — the figure is half lost to sight — and now completely — now only the shadow of her dress as it flies behind her — She has gone. No, she is coming back. She had dropped a flower, she bends down to pick it up — she looks back once more — towards me? Who else is there for her eyes to seek in these dead walls? So I was no longer a stranger to her — I had been left behind too, like her flower — My dear F***, I am ashamed to tell you what childish interpretations I placed on that one look, that — perhaps was not meant for me at all!"

I felt able to reassure the Prince on this last point.

"How strange," continued the Prince after a profound silence, "that there can be something one never knew, never felt the lack of, and a few moments later one can live only for that? Can an instant of time divide a man into two beings so unlike each other? It would be as impossible for me to go back to the pleasures and wishes of yesterday morning as to the games of my childhood, now that I have seen *that,* now that this image dwells here — this powerful, living feeling in me: You can love nothing other now but *that,* and nothing other in this world can have any power over you."

"Consider, Your Highness, in what an impressionable mood you were when this apparition surprised you, and how many things combined to excite your imagination. To find yourself suddenly transplanted from the bright glare of day, from the bustle of the streets, into that silent darkness — given over entirely to the feelings which, as you yourself confess, the silence and the majesty of that place aroused in you — made more responsive to beauty by the sight of beautiful works of art — at the same time thinking yourself alone and lonely — and now all at once — close by — surprised by the figure of a young woman, where you thought you were unobserved — by a beauty, I grant you this, enhanced by flattering illumination, by a fortunate attitude, an expression of inspired devotion — what could be more natural than that your imagination, once aroused, made of all this something ideal, something of unearthly perfection?"

"Can imagination create something quite unprompted from without? — and in all that I could ever picture to myself, there is nothing which I could set beside that image. Complete and unaltered, as in the moment of contemplation, it lies in my memory; I can see nothing but that image — though you offered me a world in exchange for it!"

"Your gracious Highness, that is love."

"Must it necessarily have a name, this sum of my happiness? Love! — Do not debase my emotions with a name which thousands of feeble souls abuse! Who else can have felt what I feel? Such a being never existed before, how can the name exist before the sensation? It is a new feeling, unique, new-born with this unique being, for this being only to be felt! — Love! Love is something I am proof against."

"You despatched Biondello — no doubt to follow the track of your unknown lady, to make enquiries about her? What report did he make to you?"

"Biondello discovered nothing — as good as nothing. He found her still waiting at the church door. An elderly, well-dressed man, looking more like a citizen of Venice than a servant, came to escort her to her gondola. A number of poor people lined up as she passed, and left with very contented expressions. While this was happening, said Biondello, he caught sight of a hand adorned with several valuable jewels. She spoke a few words to her companion which Biondello did not understand; he claims that it was Greek. As they had some distance to go to reach the canal, people began to congregate; the sight was so extraordinary that all the passers-by were stopped in their tracks. No one knew her — But beauty is like a born queen. Everyone respectfully made way for her. She let fall a black veil over her face, covering half her dress, and hastened to board her gondola. Biondello was able to keep the vessel in sight all the way along the Giudecca canal, but the crowds kept him from following it any farther."

"But he must at least have noticed the gondolier, so that he would recognise him another time."

"He is sure he can find the gondolier, but it is not one of those he has regular dealings with. The poor people whom he questioned could tell him no more than that the signora has appeared every Saturday evening for some weeks now and has also dispensed some gold among them every time. It was a Dutch ducat, that he had exchanged for them and brought to show me."

"A Greek lady, then, and of rank, as it seems, wealthy at any rate, and given to charity. That is enough to be going on with, Your Highness — enough and almost too much! But a Greek lady, in a Catholic church?"

"Why not? She may have changed her religion. And yet — there is something mysterious about it all the same — Why only once a week? Why only on a Saturday, when the church is usually empty, as Biondello tells me? — Next Saturday at the latest must decide everything. But till then, my dear friend, help me to bridge this abyss of time! But it is no use! The days and the hours go on their steady pace, and my longings have wings."

"And when that day arrives — what then, Your Highness? What is to happen then?"

"What is to happen? — I shall see her. I shall find out where she lives. I shall find out who she is. — Who she is? — Why should that concern me? What I *saw* made my happiness, and so I already know everything that *can* make it!"

"And our leaving Venice, which we have fixed for the beginning of next month?"

"Could I know in advance that Venice would hold such a treasure for me? — You are asking the person that I *was*. I tell you that I *am* and will be only from this day on."

Now I believed I had found the opportunity to keep my word to the Marchese. I explained to the Prince that the diminished state of his finances would not allow us to stay in Venice any longer, and that if he were to prolong his stay beyond the time already agreed he would not be able to count on any further support from his own court. In this connection I discovered what had hitherto been kept from me, that his sister, the ruling *** of ***, had been paying him substantial subsidies, in secret and to the exclusion of his brothers, and that she was happy to double them if his own court should leave him without means. This sister, who as you know is something of a religious devotee, thinks that she can make no better use of the considerable sums she saves by keeping a very modest court than by making them over to her brother, whom she knows to be wise and charitable and whom she enthusiastically reveres. I had known for a long time that there was a close relationship between the two and that they frequently corresponded, but as the Prince's expenses had up to now been adequately met by the sources you know about, I had never suspected this hidden source of support. It is clear, then, that the Prince has been making further dispositions of money, which were and still are kept secret from me, and which, if I may judge from his character as I know it, must be such as do him nothing but credit. And to think that I could have imagined that I knew everything about him? — But after this discovery I felt myself all the more freed from any scruple in revealing the Marchese's offer to him — which, to no little surprise on my part, was accepted without difficulty. He gave me full authority to agree the matter with the Marchese as I saw fit and then immediately to settle with the usurer. His sister was also to be written to without delay.

It was morning when we parted. Unpleasant though this affair is and must be to me for a number of reasons, the most annoying thing of all is that it is threatening to prolong our stay in Venice. But of this newly aroused passion I expect much more good than evil. It is perhaps the most powerful means of saving the Prince from his metaphysical fantasies and bringing him down to earth again; it will, I hope, come to the usual crisis and then, like an artificial infection, take the old one away with it.

Farewell, my dear friend. I have written all this down immediately after the event. The post is just leaving; you will receive this letter on the same day as the preceding one.

*Baron von F*** to Count von O***
Sixth Letter

July 20th

This Civitella is the most obliging fellow in the world. The Prince had scarcely left me the other day when a letter was already there from the Marchese, urging the matter on me most strongly. I immediately sent him a promissory note in the Prince's name, for the sum of six thousand zecchini; in less than half an hour it was returned together with double the amount, in letters of credit as well as in ready money. The Prince himself finally agreed to this increase in the sum, but insisted that the Marchese accept the note, which was payable in a mere six weeks.

This whole week has passed in enquiries after the mysterious Greek lady. Biondello has put all his contacts to work, but up till now all has been fruitless. He did manage to find the gondolier, but he could get nothing out of him beyond that he had set the two ladies ashore on the island of Murano, where two litters had been waiting for them, into which they had disappeared. He thought they must be English, as they spoke a foreign language and paid him in gold. Nor did he know their companion; he thought he looked like one of the Murano looking-glass makers. At least we now knew that she was not to be sought on the Giudecca and that she was in all probability living on Murano; but it was our misfortune that the description the Prince gave of her was simply not good enough to enable a third party to recognise her. The passionate intensity with which he had, as it were, devoured the sight of her had itself made him incapable of *seeing* her; he had been blind to everything that others would have particularly paid attention to; from his description you would rather be inclined to look for her in the pages of Tasso or Ariosto than on one of the Venetian islands. Also, these enquiries have had to be conducted with the greatest discretion in order not to arouse any offensive impressions. As Biondello was the only person apart from the Prince who had actually seen her, at any rate through her veil, and so might be able to recognise her, he has tried as best he could to be at once in all the places where she might be supposed to be; the poor fellow's life all this week has been nothing but a constant running to and fro in all the streets of Venice. Especially in the Greek church no investigations have been spared, but all of them have been just as useless; and the Prince, whose impatience has risen with every frustrated expectation, has had finally to resolve to be patient until next Saturday.

His restlessness has been terrible. Nothing could distract him, nothing could hold his attention. His whole being was in a state of feverish agitation, he was lost to all society, but solitude only made matters worse. Now, as it happened, he has been this week of all weeks more than ever besieged by visitors. It was known that he would soon be leaving, and everyone has been pressing to see him. We have had to occupy these people in order to divert their suspicious attentions from him; we have had to occupy *him* in order to distract him. In this awkward situation, Civitella suggested faro, and in order at least to keep the crowds away, the stakes had to be high. At the same time he hoped to arouse in the prince a passing taste for the game, which would soon stifle this romantic turn of his passions and which we should still be able to wean him away from again. "Cards have saved me," said Civitella, "from a good many follies I was about to commit, or put right many that I had already committed. If a pair of beautiful eyes have robbed me of my senses or my peace of mind, I have often found them again at the card-table, and women have never had more power over me than when I didn't have enough money to gamble with."

I will leave aside the question of how far Civitella was right — but the means we had hit upon soon began to be more dangerous than the evil they were supposed to cure. The Prince, who could only find a fleeting pleasure in the game by playing for very high stakes, soon knew no limits or restraints. He was after all thrown quite off balance. Everything that he did took on a passionate character; everything happened with the violent impatience that now possessed him. You know his indifference towards money; here it became a complete lack of awareness. Gold pieces ran through his fingers like drops of water. He lost almost constantly, because he paid no attention whatsoever when he was playing. He lost enormous sums, because he took desperate risks. — Dear Count von O**, my heart trembles as I write this — in four days the twelve thousand zecchini were lost — and more besides.

You need not reproach me. I blame myself quite enough. But could I prevent it? Did the Prince ever listen to me? Could I do anything beyond uttering warnings? I did all that was in my power. I cannot believe myself responsible.

Civitella also lost considerable sums; I won about six hundred zecchini. The Prince's unparalleled bad luck attracted attention; he was all the less able to stop playing. You could see Civitella's pleasure in making him obliged to him, as he lent him the money straight away. The gap has been plugged; but the Prince owes the Marchese twenty-four thousand zecchini. Oh, how I long for the pious sister's savings! — Are all princes like this, my friend? The

Prince behaves just as if he were doing the Marchese favour upon favour, and the Marchese — is at all events playing his part well.

Civitella tried to pacify me by telling me that this very excess, this extraordinary ill luck of the Prince's, was the best means of bringing him to his senses. There was no shortage of money. He himself was hardly aware of the loss and would oblige the Prince at any time with treble the sum. The Cardinal too assured me that his nephew's intentions were honest and that he himself was ready to stand surety for him.

The saddest thing was that these huge sacrifices did not even have any effect. One might have thought the Prince would at least have been absorbed by his play. Not in the least. His thoughts were far away, and the passion which we were trying to damp down seemed only to be fed all the more by his ill-luck at the gaming table. If some decisive coup was awaited and everyone was gathering expectantly around his table, he would be looking for Biondello, to see if his face betrayed the news he might be bringing. But Biondello brought nothing — and he lost again and again.

The money found its way, I must tell you, into hands that were most needful of it. Some Excellencies who, as the wicked world likes to report of them, carry their frugal luncheon home with them themselves in their senator's bonnets, have entered our house as beggars and left it as wealthy men. Civitella pointed them out to me. "Look," he said, "how many poor devils profit by it, when a clever man chooses not to keep his wits about him! But I like that. It is princely, kingly! A great man, even in his aberrations, must still make others happy, and fertilise the fields like a river breaking its banks."

Fine and noble thoughts of Civitella's — but the Prince owes him twenty-four thousand zecchini!

Saturday, so anxiously awaited, arrived at last, and my master could not be dissuaded from making his way to the *** Church immediately after midday. He took up his place in the very same chapel where he had first seen his unknown beauty, but in such a way that he would not immediately be seen by her. Biondello was ordered to keep watch at the church door and to engage the lady's companion in conversation. I had taken it upon myself, as a passer-by who would be beyond suspicion, to make my return in the same gondola, so as to follow the unknown lady's trail a little further, if these other measures should not succeed. Two sedans were reserved at the same place where according to the gondolier she had disembarked on the previous occasion; for good measure the Prince had Chamberlain Z*** follow in another gondola. The Prince himself would venture everything on seeing her and if possible try his fortune with her in the church. Civitella was to keep well away, as his reputation with the fair sex in Venice stands so low that the lady's suspicions could not fail to be aroused if he were involved. You can see, dear Count, that it would be no fault of our precautions if the fair Unknown should escape us.

Never can more ardent wishes have been made in any church than in this one, and never have they been more cruelly frustrated. The Prince stayed at his post till after sunset, his expectations roused by every sound that approached his chapel, by every creak of the church door — seven full hours — and no fair Grecian. I say nothing of his state of mind. You will know what it is to cherish a vain hope — and a hope which for seven days and seven nights has almost been a man's sole nourishment.

*Baron von F*** to Count von O***
Seventh Letter

July

The Prince's fair Unknown reminded the Marchese Civitella of a romantic encounter he himself had experienced some time ago, and in order to distract the Prince he consented to tell us about it. I will repeat it to you in his own words. But the merry spirit with which he imbues everything he says will, I fear, not come across in my account.

"Last spring," said Civitella, "I had the misfortune to arouse the hostility of the Spanish ambassador, who in his seventieth year had been so foolish as to marry an eighteen-year-old Roman girl and to want to keep her for himself alone. His vengeance pursued me, and my friends advised me to get away quickly to escape its consequences, until either the hand of nature or an amicable settlement should have rid me of this dangerous enemy. But I really could not bear to leave Venice completely behind me, and so I decided to take lodgings in an unfrequented corner of Murano, where I lived in a lonely house under a false name, kept myself hidden during the daytime, and devoted the night to my friends and my pleasures.

"My windows looked out on a garden, which on the western side abutted on to the walls of a convent, but on the east projected into the lagoon like a small peninsula. The garden was laid out in the most charming way, but was very little visited. In the morning, when my friends had left me, I had the habit, before I went to bed, of spending a few moments at the window, to watch the dawn coming up over the Gulf before wishing the sun good night. If you have not yet had this pleasure, Your Highness, then let me recommend this viewpoint, perhaps the most exquisite in Venice for enjoying this magnificent spectacle. Purple night lies over the face of the deep, a golden haze announces the sun from the distant edge of the lagoon. Sky and sea rest in expectation. Two moments, and there it is, in full view, and all the waves on fire — an entrancing sight to behold!

"One morning, as I am abandoning myself as usual to the pleasure of this view, I suddenly discover that I am not the only one to be witnessing it.

I think I hear human voices in the garden, and turning towards the sound I see a gondola drawing up on the shore. A few moments more, and I see people emerging into the garden and slowly, as if taking a leisurely walk, approaching up the avenue. I observe that it is a man and a woman, accompanied by a small Negro boy. The woman is dressed in white, and a diamond sparkles on her finger; but in the half-light I can distinguish nothing more.

"My curiosity is aroused. For sure, a rendezvous and a pair of lovers — but in this place and at this quite unaccustomed hour! — for it was barely three o'clock, and everything still veiled in twilight gloom. This seemed a novelty to me, and to have the makings of a romantic affair. I decided to wait and see what might happen.

"I soon lose sight of them in the tree-lined walks of the garden, and it is a long time before they emerge again. Meanwhile the neighbourhood is filled with melodious singing. It was the gondolier, passing the time in his gondola in this way, and a colleague was answering him from some way off. They were singing verses from Tasso; time and place harmonised with them, and the melody faded sweetly away in the general silence.

"Meanwhile day had broken, and things could be more clearly distinguished. I look for my two people. They are now walking hand in hand up a wide avenue, often pausing to stand still, but their backs are turned to me and their way is leading them away from my lodging. From the dignity of their carriage, I infer persons of rank, and from an angelic bearing an uncommon beauty. They spoke little, as it seemed to me, but the lady more than her companion. They seemed to take no notice of the spectacle of the sunrise, which was now spreading itself in all its glory about them.

"As I fetch my telescope and train it so as to bring this remarkable apparition as close to me as possible, they suddenly disappear once more into a side-alley, and a long time passes before I see them again. The sun has now fully risen, they appear close below me and look up directly towards me —— What heavenly form do I espy! — Was it the play of my imagination, was it the enchantment of the light? I thought it was a supernatural being I beheld, and my eye started back, dazzled by the blinding light. — Such grace combined with such majesty! So much nobility of spirit with such a flower of youth — It is useless for me to try to describe it to you. Before that moment I had never known what beauty was.

"The interest of their conversation detains them close below me, and I have every leisure to immerse myself in the miraculous sight. But scarcely have my looks turned to her companion than even this beauty can no longer call them back. He seemed to me a man in the prime of life, rather lean and tall and noble in stature — but I have never seen a brow which radiated such spiritual presence, such nobility, such divinity. Though I was safe from any detection, I could not endure the penetrating gaze which shot like lightning from beneath the darkness of his eyebrows. There was a silent, touching sadness about his eyes, and a hint of benevolence about his lips which softened the pensive seriousness that overshadowed all his features. But something in the cut of those features which was not European, combined with clothing which seemed a mixture of various styles of dress, but boldly and successfully combined with inimitable taste, gave him a strange and unfamiliar appearance which enhanced in no small measure the extraordinary impression made by his whole being. Something wild in his look might have suggested the zealot, but his gestures and outward dignity bespoke a man schooled in the academy of life."

Z***, who as you know cannot help bursting out with whatever he is thinking, could here contain himself no longer. "Our Armenian," he cried, "our Armenian to the life! It can be no one else."

"What Armenian was that, may I ask?" said Civitella.

"Have you not heard about that farce?" said the Prince. "But no interruptions! I am beginning to take an interest in this man of yours. Go on with your story."

"There was something incomprehensible in his manner. His eyes rested significantly, passionately upon her when she looked away, and were cast down to the ground when it met hers. 'Is this man in his right mind?' I wondered. For an eternity I could only stand and look at nothing else.

"They were lost to me in the bushes again. I waited an age, an age, to see them emerge again, but it was in vain. Finally I discovered them again, from another window.

"They were standing by a fountain, at some distance from each other, both rapt in profound silence. They must have been standing like this for quite a long time. Her frank and soulful gaze rested questioningly on him and seemed to be reading every thought that formed on his brow. He, as if he did not feel bold enough to receive it at first hand, looked furtively to find *her* reflection in the mirroring water, or gazed fixedly at the dolphin from which the waters spurted into the basin. Who knows how much longer this pantomime might have lasted, if the lady could have borne it? But with the most enchanting tenderness the beautiful creature drew near to him, threw her arm about his neck, seized one of his hands and guided it to her lips. Calmly the impassive man submitted, but her caress remained unanswered.

"But there was something in this scene which touched me. It was the man who touched me. A violent passion seemed to be raging in his breast, an irresistible force to draw him towards her, an invisible hand to tear him away again. Silent but painful the struggle was, and so beautiful the peril at his side. No, I thought to myself, it is too much for him. He will, he must succumb.

"At a discreet sign from him, the little Negro disappears. Now I expect a sentimental scene, a kneeling apology, a reconciliation sealed with a thousand kisses. Nothing of the kind. The incomprehensible fellow takes from a wallet a sealed package and puts it in the lady's hands. Sadness overflows her features as she looks at it, and a teardrop glistens in her eye.

"After a brief silence, they move away. From a side-alley they are joined by an elderly lady, who had been accompanying them at a distance and whom I had not noticed until now. Slowly they walk away, the two ladies in conversation with each other, while *he* takes the opportunity of remaining behind them unnoticed. Indecisively, gazing fixedly towards her, he stands still, goes on and stands still again. All at once he disappears into the bushes.

"The two ahead look round at last. They seem agitated not to see him any longer, and stand still where they are, as it seems, to wait for him. He does not come. Their looks are cast anxiously around them, they set off again and double their pace. My eyes help them to search the whole garden. He disappoints us. He is not here.

"Suddenly I hear a noise by the canal, and a gondola casts off from the bank. There he is, on board — and with difficulty I restrain myself from calling it out to her. Now all is revealed — It was a scene of parting.

"She seemed to *sense* what I *knew*. Too quickly for the others to follow, she hurries to the shore. Too late. Swift as an arrow the gondola shoots away, with only a white handkerchief fluttering in the air from afar. Soon afterwards I see the ladies also being ferried across.

"When I woke again after a short sleep, I had to laugh at my own delusions. In my dreams my imagination had continued the encounter, and now truth itself turned into a dream. A young girl, enchanting as a houri, strolling with her lover in a distant garden beneath my window, a lover who is incapable of making any better use of an hour like this, seemed to me to make a picture which might at best be ventured — and excused — by the fantasy of a dreamer. But the dream had been too beautiful not to be renewed as frequently as possible, and the garden too had now become dearer to me, since my imagination had peopled it with such enchanting figures. A few unfriendly days which followed upon that morning drove me away from the window, but on the first fine evening I found myself drawn there again, almost unknowingly. But judge my amazement when after a brief search the shimmering white dress of my Unknown met my gaze. It was she herself. She was real. I had not merely been dreaming.

"The same matron was with her, leading a little boy by the hand; but she herself walked apart and self-absorbed. All the stations were visited which were made significant to her by her escort of the previous occasion. She lingered especially by the fountain, and her concentrated gaze seemed to seek in vain the beloved image.

"If on the first time I had been enraptured by that elevated beauty, today she exercised a gentler power on me, but one which was no less strong. I now had complete freedom to observe the heavenly image; the astonishment of that first sight now yielded imperceptibly to a more delicate emotion. The halo which had surrounded her disappears, and I see nothing in her but the most beautiful of women, who sets my senses on fire. In this moment it is decided. She must be mine.

"While I am pondering whether I shall go down now and approach her, or make enquiries about her before I am so daring, a small gate in the monastery wall opens, and a Carmelite monk emerges. Hearing the noise, the lady leaves her place, and I see her walking with swift steps towards him. He takes a paper from his breast, which she greedily seizes, and a joyous animation seems to fly over her features.

"In this very moment the arrival of my regular evening visitors drives me from the window. I take care to stay away from it, because I do not want anyone else to share in my conquest. I have to endure a whole hour of painful impatience, before I can finally rid myself of their burdensome company. I hurry back to my window, but everything has disappeared!

"The garden is quite deserted when I go down. Not a vessel in the canal. Not a sign of human presence. I know neither where she came from nor where she has gone. As I wander, my eyes seeking in all directions, I see something white in the distance before me. Approaching, I find it is a paper, in the form of a folded letter. What could it be but the letter that the Carmelite had brought her? 'A lucky find,' I cry. 'This letter will reveal the whole mystery to me, it will make me the master of her fate.'

"The letter was sealed with a sphinx, there was no address and it was in cipher; but that did not deter me, for I have some skill in decoding. Quickly I copy it, for it was to be expected that she would soon be missing it and be coming back to look for it. If she could no longer find it, this would prove to her that other people visited the garden, and such a discovery could easily frighten her away from it for ever. Could anything worse happen to my hopes?

"What I had supposed would happen, did. I had scarcely finished my copying when she returned with her former companion, both of them anxiously searching. I fasten the letter to a slate which I loosen from the roof and drop it in a place which she has to pass. The beauty of her joy when she finds it rewards me for my magnanimity. She examined it from every side with sharp and curious eyes, as if to discover what profane hand might have touched it; but the look of satisfaction with which she tucked it away proved that she had no suspicions. She went, and with a backward glance of her eyes took a grateful leave of the garden's guardian spirits, who had so loyally kept the secret of her heart.

"Now I hastened to decipher the letter. I tried with several languages; finally I succeeded with English. Its contents were so remarkable that I have remembered them word for word." —

Someone has interrupted me. The rest another time.

*Baron von F*** to Count von O***
Eighth Letter

August

No, my dear friend. You do the good Biondello an injustice. You are entertaining false suspicions. I will grant you every other Italian, but this one is honest.

You find it strange that a man of such remarkable talents and of such exemplary conduct should demean himself to the role of a servant, unless he has some secret end in view; and from this you conclude that this end must be a suspicious one. Why? Is it really such a novelty that a man of wit and merit should seek to please a Prince who has it in his power to make his fortune? Is it in any way dishonourable to serve him? Does Biondello not make it clear enough that he feels a personal loyalty to the Prince? He has confessed to him that he has a request which he wishes to confide to him. This request will undoubtedly explain the whole mystery. He may have some secret ends in mind, but may these not be quite innocent?

You are worried by the fact that this Biondello, in the early months — those in which you still favoured us with your presence — kept hidden all the remarkable talents which are now coming to light, and did nothing to attract attention to himself. That is true; but when at that time would he have had the opportunity to distinguish himself? The Prince had as yet no need of him, and we had to discover his other talents by chance.

But only the other day he gave us a proof of his devotion and honesty which will sweep away all your suspicions. The Prince is being watched. Enquiries are being made in secret about his way of life, about his acquaintances and his circumstances. I do not know who it is who is being so curious. But now listen.

Here on San Giorgio there is an establishment which Biondello often visits; perhaps he has a lady-friend there, I do not know. A few days ago he was there again; he finds a company assembled, lawyers and government officials, merry brothers and acquaintances of his. They are surprised and pleased to see him again. Old acquaintances are renewed, everyone tells what he has been doing till now, Biondello must also tell his story. He does so in a few words. He is congratulated on his new position, everyone has heard of the Prince of ***'s brilliant life-style, in particular of his generous treatment of those who know how to keep a secret; everyone knows of his connection with Cardinal A***i, he is fond of the card-table, and so on. Biondello is taken aback. — They tease him, tell him not to act so mysteriously, everyone knows that he is the Prince of ***'s agent; the two lawyers make him sit between them; the bottles are busily emptied — they urge him to drink; he excuses himself, saying that wine does not agree with him, but he takes a drink and pretends to get drunk.

"Yes," says one of the lawyers at last, "Biondello knows his job; but he hasn't learnt it all, he only knows the half of it."

"What's left to learn?" asks Biondello.

"He knows the art," replied the other, "of keeping a secret, but he doesn't yet know how to dispose of it to his advantage."

"Is there anyone here who'd like to buy it?" asked Biondello.

The other guests left the room at this, leaving him tête-à-tête with those two fellows, whose tongues were now loosened. In short, he was to find out for them about the relations of the Prince with the Cardinal and his nephew, tell them where the Prince got his money, and pass on to them any letters addressed to Count von O**. Biondello put them off for the moment; but who they were acting for, he could not make them tell him. To judge by the very handsome offers they made to him, the enquiries must be coming from a very rich man.

Yesterday evening he told my master the whole story. The Prince at first wanted simply to lay hold of the two middlemen, but Biondello made objections. They would after all have to be let loose again, and then he would have lost all credit with people of that kind, perhaps even put his life in danger. They all stuck together, all for one and one for all; he would rather make enemies of the Council of the Republic than be known for a traitor among *them;* he would also no longer be able to be of use to the Prince if he lost the confidence of that class of men.

We have been turning over in our minds who might be at the bottom of all this. Who is there in Venice who can be so anxious to know what my master's income and expenses are, what are his dealings with Cardinal A***i and what I am writing to you? Is this something we owe to the Prince of **d**? Or could it be that the Armenian is at work again?

*Baron von F*** to Count von O***
Ninth Letter

August

The Prince is floating on a sea of love and joy. He has found his Grecian beauty again. Let me tell you how it happened.

A foreign visitor, who had come by way of Chioggia and had a lot to say about the beautiful situation of that town on the Gulf, made the Prince curious to see it. It was arranged for yesterday, and in order to avoid all fuss and expense, he would have no one to accompany him but Z*** and me, together with Biondello, and my master wanted to remain incognito. We found a ship that was just leaving in that direction, and they were happy to take our fares. The company was very mixed, but of no particular interest, and the journey was uneventful.

Chioggia is built like Venice on piles rammed into the sea-bed, and is said to have about forty thousand inhabitants. There are few nobles, but you meet fishermen or sailors at every step. Anyone with a wig and a fine coat is called a rich man; a cap and a rough cape are the sign of a poor one. The situation of the town is beautiful, provided that you have never seen Venice.

We did not stay for long. Our captain, who had more passengers to carry, had to be back in Venice in good time, and there was nothing to detain the Prince in Chioggia. All had already taken their places when we arrived. As the company on the way over had been so annoying, this time we took a cabin for ourselves. The Prince enquired who else there might be on board? A Dominican, was the answer, and a number of ladies who were returning to Venice. The Prince was not curious to see them, and took to his cabin immediately.

The Grecian lady had been the subject of our conversation on the way over, and so too she was on the way back. The Prince recalled her appearance in the church with ardour; plans were made and discarded, the time passed as if in an instant, and before we were expecting it, Venice lay before us. Some of the passengers disembarked, the Dominican among them. The captain went to the ladies, who as we only now discovered were separated from us only by a thin partition, and asked where they wanted him to land. "On Murano," they answered, and named their address. "Murano!" cried the Prince, and a shudder of intimation seemed to run through his soul. Before I could reply to him, Biondello came rushing in. "Do you know whose company we have been travelling in?" — The Prince leapt up — "She is here! The lady herself!" Biondello went on. "I have just come from her travelling companion."

The Prince rushed out. The cabin was suddenly too small for him, at this moment the whole world would have been. A thousand emotions were raging in him, his knees were trembling, his face flushed and turned pale by turns. I trembled with him in expectation. I cannot describe this state to you.

The ship docked on Murano. The Prince leapt ashore. She came. I read in the Prince's face that it was she. The sight of her left me in no doubt. I have never beheld a more beautiful creature; all the Prince's description fell far short of the reality. Her face flushed a fiery red when she saw the Prince. She must have overheard all our conversation, and she could not doubt that she had been its subject. She turned a meaningful glance on her companion, as if to say, there he is! and cast her eyes down in confusion. A narrow gangplank was laid from the ship to the shore for her to walk on. She seemed hesitant to step on it — but not so much, as it seemed to me, because she was afraid of slipping, as because she could not do it without help and because the Prince was already reaching out his arm to support her. Necessity conquered her doubts. She accepted his hand, and came ashore. The violent turmoil in which the Prince found himself made him forget his courtesy; the other lady who was awaiting the same assistance was ignored — what would he not have ignored at that moment? At length I performed this office for her, and in doing so missed the opening of a conversation which had begun between my master and the lady.

He was still holding her hand in his — out of distraction, I imagine, and without realising it.

"Signora, this is not the first time that I —— that —" He could not say it aloud.

"I ought to remember," she murmured —

"In the *** Church," he said —

"In the *** Church, it was," she said —

"And could I have thought today that I was —— so near to you —"

At this she gently drew her hand away from his — He was instantly lost in confusion. Biondello, who had meanwhile been speaking with her servant, came to his rescue. "There is a garden here nearby, where you can go to be away from the crowd."

His proposal was accepted, and you can imagine how readily on the part of the Prince. They stayed in the garden until evening. We succeeded, Z*** and I, in occupying her companion, so that the Prince and the young lady could talk undisturbed. And you can tell from the fact that he obtained her permission to visit her that he made good use of their time together. He is there at this very moment, as I am writing to you. I shall learn more when he returns.

When we returned to our lodgings yesterday we also found the expected letters of credit from our court, but accompanied by a letter which roused my master to fury. He is being summoned home, and in a tone to which he is not accustomed. He replied immediately in the same manner and intends to stay here. The money is just enough to pay the interest on the capital that he has borrowed. We are eagerly awaiting an answer from his sister.

*Baron von F*** to Count von O***
Tenth Letter

September

The Prince has quarrelled with his court, and all income from that quarter has been cut off.

The six weeks after which my master was due to repay the Marchese were already over by a few days, and still no credit either from his cousin, from whom he had urgently and repeatedly asked for an advance, or from his sister. As you may imagine, Civitella did not press us; but the Prince remembered all the more clearly. Yesterday afternoon we received a reply from the court.

We had shortly before this taken out a new lease on our lodging, and the Prince had made it publicly known that he would be staying longer. Without a word he handed me the letter. His eyes were aflame, and I could read its contents from the expression of his brow.

Can you imagine, my dear O**? Back in *** they are informed of all my master's doings, and slander has spun a fearful web of lies about them. It has been learnt with displeasure, we are told among other things, that the Prince for some time has been betraying his previous character and adopting a form of conduct completely opposed to his former commendable attitudes. It is known that he has been abandoning himself most extravagantly to women and to the gaming table, plunging himself into debt, lending his ear to visionaries and conjurers of spirits, associating in a suspicious manner with Catholic prelates and holding court in a fashion exceeding both his rank and his income. It is even rumoured that he is on the point of crowning this appalling behaviour with apostasy and converting to Rome. In order to clear himself from this last allegation he is required to return home without delay. A banker in Venice, to whom he is to declare the state of his finances, has been instructed to satisfy his creditors *as soon as he has left Venice,* for it is not thought desirable in the present circumstances to place the money in his own hands.

What accusations, and in what a tone! I took the letter, read it again, trying to find something in it to lighten its import; there was nothing. It was quite incomprehensible to me.

Z*** now reminded me of the secret enquiries that had been made of Biondello a little while ago. The time, the contents, all the circumstances were in agreement. We had falsely put them down to the Armenian. Now it was clear who was responsible. Apostasy! — But in whose interest can it be to libel my master so hideously and so crudely? I am afraid it is a trick of the Prince of **d**'s to get us away from Venice.

The Prince was still silent, gazing fixedly ahead of him. His silence worried me. I threw myself at his feet. "In God's name, Your gracious Highness," I cried, "do not decide anything rash. You shall, you will receive the fullest possible satisfaction. Leave this matter to me. Send me back to ***. It would be beneath your dignity to answer to such allegations; but allow *me* to do it for you. The slanderer must be named and ***'s eyes opened."

This was the state of affairs in which Civitella found us. He asked with astonishment what was the cause of our dismay. Z*** and I said nothing. But the Prince, who for a long time now has made no distinction between ourselves and the Marchese, and was still far too agitated to hear the counsels of prudence in this moment, ordered us to give him the letter. I was hesitant, but the Prince snatched it from my hand and passed it to the Marchese.

"I am in your debt, signor Marchese," began the Prince, after Civitella had read the letter with astonishment, "but do not let this cause you any disturbance. Give me just another three weeks, and you shall be satisfied."

"Your Highness," cried Civitella in great agitation, "have I deserved this?"

"You did not want to remind me of it; I recognise your delicacy and thank you for it. In three weeks, as I said, you shall be completely satisfied."

"What is this?" Civitella asked me in amazement. "What is the meaning of it all? I do not understand."

We explained to him as much as we knew. He flew into a rage. The Prince, he said, must demand satisfaction; the insult was unheard of. Meanwhile he urged the Prince to make unlimited use of his fortune and his credit.

The Marchese had left us, and the Prince had not yet said a word. He was pacing furiously up and down the room; something extraordinary was going on in him. Finally he stood still and muttered to himself between his teeth: "Congratulations, he said — He died at nine o'clock."

We stared at him, overcome with fear.

"Congratulations," he went on, "congratulations — I am to be congratulated — Is that not what he said? What did he mean by it?"

"What makes you think of that?" I cried. "Why does that matter now?"

"I did not understand then what the man meant. Now I understand him. — Oh, it is unbearable to have a master above one!"

"Your gracious Highness!"

"Who can make us feel it. — Ah! It must be sweet!"

He paused again. His manner frightened me. I had never seen him looking like that.

"The most wretched of his subjects," he began again, "or the prince next to the throne! It is all one and the same. There is one distinction only between men — to obey or to rule!"

He scanned the letter again.

"You have seen the man," he went on, "who can have the impertinence to write this to me. Would you greet him in the street, if fate had not made him your master? By God! it is a fine thing to wear a crown."

He went on in this tone, and words were spoken which I dare not entrust to any letter. But in this connection the Prince revealed a fact to me which caused me no little amazement and terror and which may have the most dangerous consequences. We have until now been grossly mistaken about the state of family relations at the court of ***.

The Prince answered the letter immediately, despite all my protestations, and the manner in which he did so leaves no hope that the matter can be amicably resolved.

But you will also be curious, my dear O**, to hear something definite about the fair Grecian at last; but this is just the thing about which I am still not in a position to give you any satisfactory information. Nothing can be got out of the Prince, because he has been drawn into the secret and, I imagine, has been made to swear not to reveal it. But we have at least discovered that she is *not* Greek, as we had thought. She is German, and of the most noble descent. A certain rumour which I managed to follow up says that her mother is of the highest rank and that she is the fruit of an unhappy love affair which was much talked about all over Europe. Secret moves against her from a powerful quarter have forced her, so the story goes, to seek refuge in Venice, and these are also the reason for her concealment, which made it impossible for the Prince to find out where she was living. The reverence with which the Prince speaks of her and certain considerations regarding her on his part would seem to support these suppositions.

He is devoted to her with a terrible passion, which grows more intense day by day. To begin with she allowed him only infrequent visits; but after only a week the intervals grew shorter, and now not a day passes when the Prince is not there. Whole evenings pass without our having as much as a glimpse of him, and even if he is not in her company, *she* is all he is thinking of. His whole being seems to be transformed. He goes about as if in a dream, and none of the things which used to interest him arouse even the slightest attention in him.

Where can all this lead us, dear friend? I tremble for the future. The rupture with his court has left my master humiliatingly dependent on a single person, the Marchese Civitella. That man now holds the key to our secrets, to our whole destiny. Will he always be so magnanimously disposed to us as he now seems? Will this favourable understanding last for ever, and is it good to allow a single person, even the most nobly disposed, so much importance and power in our lives?

Another letter has been sent to the Prince's sister, with what success I hope to be able to report in my next letter.

*(The story continued by Count von O**)*

— But no next letter came. Three whole months passed before I received any news from Venice: an interruption whose cause was soon to become all too evident. All my friend's letters to me had been kept back and suppressed. Imagine my amazement, when this December I finally received the following missive, which only a lucky chance (because Biondello, to whom it had been entrusted, was suddenly taken ill) delivered to my hands.

"You have not written. You do not answer. Come — oh come, on the wings of friendship. Our hopes are dashed. Read the letter I have enclosed. All our hopes are dashed.

"The Marchese's wounds are said to be fatal. The Cardinal is plotting revenge, and his assassins are pursuing the Prince. My master — oh, my unhappy master! — Has it come to this? Hideous, unworthy fate! Like miserable wretches we have to hide from robbers and murderers.

"I am writing to you from the *** Monastery, where the Prince has found refuge. At this moment he is lying on a hard bed beside me and sleeping — oh, the sleep of deathly exhaustion, which will only rouse him to renewed awareness of his sufferings. For the ten days that *she* was ill, his eyes knew no sleep. I was there when they opened the body. They found traces of poisoning. She is to be buried today.

"Oh, my dear O**, my heart is torn to shreds. I was the witness of a scene which I shall never be able to erase from my memory. I stood at her deathbed. She passed away like a saint, and with the last powers of speech that remained to her as she died she urged her beloved to follow her on the path which was leading her to heaven. — All our fortitude was shaken to its foundations, the Prince alone stood firm, and even though he suffered the pain of her death three times over, he still retained enough strength of mind to refuse the pious zealot her last dying wish."

Enclosed with this letter was the following:

> *To the Prince of ***, from his sister.*
>
> "The One True Church, which has made such a glittering conquest in the Prince of ***, will surely not leave him without the means to continue the way of life which it has to thank for its conquest. I have tears and prayers for one who has gone astray, but no further charity for one unworthy to receive it.
>
> *Henrietta* ***."

I set out immediately by mail-coach, travelled day and night, and after three weeks I was in Venice. Haste though I might, I came too late. I had come to offer help and consolation to an unhappy man; I found a happy one, who had no further need of my feeble help. F*** was sick and could not speak to me when I arrived; I was brought the following note in his hand. "Go back, dear O**, to where you have come from. The Prince no longer needs you, nor me. His debts are paid, the Cardinal is reconciled, the Marchese restored to health. Do you remember the Armenian who caused us such confusion last year? You will find the Prince in *his* arms — five days ago he went to Mass for the first time."

I nevertheless tried to force my way to the Prince, but was turned away. At my friend's bedside I heard at last the whole extraordinary story.

End of Part One[14]

Translator's Notes

British spelling and idioms have been retained in Francis Lamport's translation. (Editor's note.)

[1] A province in the Baltic, now part of Latvia; in the eighteenth century part of the Kingdom of Poland, but with a substantial German population.

[2] Presumably a club or coffee-house.

[3] In its original sense, the man who 'punts' or wagers against the bank in faro, a popular card game at the time (cf. page 133).

[4] Pope Clement IV, who died in 1774. He was rumoured to have been poisoned by the Jesuits, whose Order he had suppressed two years previously.

[5] In 1757, during the Seven Years' War. The French (allied to the Austrians) defeated a Hanoverian army led by the Duke of Cumberland.

[6] A first-century Pythagorean, alleged to possess prophetic powers.

[7] *Le Comte de Gabalis ou Entretiens sur les sciences secrètes,* an occult tale by the Abbé Montfaucon de Villars, first published in 1670 and much reprinted, tells of the intercourse of "adepts" with spirits such as "sylphs and salamanders."

[8] In earlier editions, Schiller himself adds a footnote, "Perhaps the [glass] harmonica is meant." Invented by Benjamin Franklin in the 1760s, the instrument was sometimes used at séances, etc., on account of its strange, ethereal tones.

[9] David Garrick, famous English eighteenth-century actor, noted for the psychological realism of his performances.

[10] Named after the famous state galley of the Republic of Venice.

[11] Schiller here himself adds: "Note by Count von O**: The severe judgments which Baron von F*** permits himself to pass here and in certain passages of his first letter on an accomplished prince will be found exaggerated (as I find them myself) by all those who are fortunate enough to know the latter, and they will no doubt attribute them to the writer's youthful prejudices."

[12] "What it is that only those about to perish see" (slightly modified from Tacitus, *Germania,* ch. 40). The reference is to Langobardic slaves who had the privilege of

seeing the fertility goddess Nerthus in human form and washing her sacred carriage, but had to pay for this honour with immediate death by drowning.

[13] In the original 1789 version, Count von O**'s report of this philosophical dialogue continues for another twenty pages. See Helen Kilgallen's translation of "Das philosophische Gespräch" (The Philosophical Dialog) in this volume.

[14] Part Two never appeared. See further the Notes on the Translations section in this volume.

7: The Philosophical Dialog from *The Spiritualist*

Friedrich Schiller (1789)
Translated by Helen Kilgallen

I NEVER SHOULD HAVE VENTURED to follow my desires — I should have entered old age as indifferent as I entered manhood! But because I for once attempt to escape the drab uniformity of my previous life and look to see if I might not find some other source of pleasure — because I —"

"If it was an experiment, Your Highness, then I have nothing more to say — for the experiences that it has provided you with would not be expensive at three times the price. It caused me pain, I admit, that the world should decide the question that belongs only to your own heart — the question of *how* you should find happiness."

"You are fortunate that *you* can scorn the opinion of the world! I am her creature, I must be her slave. What are we other than opinion? Everything surrounding us as princes is opinion. Opinion is our nurse and governess in childhood, our legislator and lover once we are men, and our crutch in old age. Take from us what we owe to opinion, and the worst off amongst the lower classes is better off than we are, for his fate has at least taught him a philosophy to comfort him as he faces his fate. A prince who mocks opinion undermines his own being as much as the priest who denies the existence of God."

"And yet, Your Highness —"

"I know what you will say. I can step outside the circle that my birth has drawn around me — but can I also tear away all the illusions from my mind, those planted by upbringing and early habit and that a hundred thousand fools among you have set ever firmer and firmer? Everyone wants to be *entirely* what he is, and our existence is nothing more than *appearing happy*. Since we cannot *be happy* in your way, shall we therefore forgo being happy at all? If we can no longer draw joy from its pure source, should we also forgo deceiving ourselves with artificial pleasure — not be allowed some small compensation from the very hand that robbed us?"

"You once found such compensation in your heart."

"And if I no longer find it there? — Oh, how have we arrived at this? Why must you wake these memories in me? — When I took refuge in this very sensory tumult in order to silence an inner voice that is the misery of my existence — to calm the brooding reason that, like a scythe, drives back and forth in my brain and with each new investigation, cuts off another branch of my happiness?"

"Your Highness!" — He had risen to his feet and was pacing around the room in uncharacteristic agitation.

"When everything before me and behind me sinks away — the past in sad monotony like a kingdom of stone behind me — when the future offers me nothing — when I see the entire circle of my existence confined in the narrow space of the *present* — who would blame me that I passionately and insatiably embrace this meager gift of time, as if it were a friend I was seeing for the last time? And if I hasten to hoard this transient good, like the eighty-year-old man with his diadem? — Oh I have learned to treasure it, the moment! The moment is our mother, and let us love it as we would a mother!"

"Your Highness, you used to believe in a more lasting good —"

"Oh, make the vision in the clouds stay fixed for me, and I will embrace it with passionate arms. What joy can it give me to gratify creatures of the moment that will be gone tomorrow, just as I shall be gone? Is not all about me in flight? Everything struggles and pushes its neighbor away to hurriedly drink a drop from the well of existence and to leave it still longing. Now in the very moment when I rejoice in my vitality, already a new life depends upon my destruction. Show me anything that lasts and I will be virtuous."

"What has suppressed the generous emotions that were once the pleasure and guiding precept of your life? To sow seed for the future, to serve a high, eternal order —"

"Future! Eternal order! — If we take away that which man took from his own breast and attributed to his imagined God as purpose, and to nature as law — what are we left? —"

"To serve! Certainly to serve, so certainly as the least important brick in the wall serves the symmetry of the palace that rests upon it! But also as one sharing in decisions, sharing in enjoyment? The dear, well-meaning delusion of mankind! You wish to dedicate your energies to serve the eternal order? Is there any way you can refuse to do so? What you are and what you possess, you are and possess only to serve that order. Once you have given what you have to give and what only you could give to the eternal order, then you are nothing more. Your frailty delivers your judgment, and it is your frailty that executes the sentence. But who is then this nature, this order against which I bear my accusations? It is all the same! Would that she were to devour her own children, like the Greeks' Saturn, *were* only nature herself to be, even if she only survived that passing second! — She stands, an immeasurable tree, in an immeasurable space. The wisdom and virtue of entire generations run like sap in her veins, millennia and all the nations who made themselves heard in all those years fall like withered blossoms, like wilted leaves from her branches, which she stretches out with inherent, immortal fertility. Can you demand what she herself does not possess? Can you, a mere wind-blown ripple on the surface of the ocean, dare wish to ensure the mark of your existence there?"

"The history of the world refutes this dismal proposition. The names Lycurgus, Socrates, and Aristides have outlived their works."

"And the useful man who created the plough? — what was his name? Do you trust a distributor of rewards who does not distribute *justly*? They live in history, like mummies in balsam, to pass away with their stories only somewhat later."

"And this drive to eternal perpetuation? Can or may its necessity be *wasteful*? Can there be *something* in a force to which nothing corresponds in effect?"

"Oh, everything lies in this very effect. Waste? Does not the spout of water in the cascade also rise into the air with a force that could also propel it through infinite space? But already in the first moment of its leap upwards, gravity pulls against it, thousands of columns of air press down upon it, which, sooner or later, drive it in a higher or lower arch back to earth? In order to fall so *late,* it had to rise up with this exuberant force — almost an elastic force, such as the drive to immortality, was necessary, if the appearance of mankind was to maintain space for itself in the face of ever-encroaching necessity. I will concede my defeat, dear friend, if you can demonstrate to me that this drive toward immortality in humans does not end just as completely with the temporal end of human existence as do the most sensual of human drives. Indeed, our pride seduces us to pit energies — that we have solely *for* and solely *through* necessity — against necessity, but would we have this pride then, if necessity did not also obtain some advantage from *it*? If she were a rational being, she would have to find pleasure in our philosophies in a similar fashion to the wise commander who gloats over his warlike youths' courage, which promises him heroes in the battle."

"You would propose that thought serves only to generate motion? That the whole could be dead while the pieces were alive? That the end were so *base* and the means so *noble?*"

"We should never have said *end.* In order to enter into your mode of thinking, I will borrow this concept from the moral world, since we are accustomed to calling the results of an action its end. In the soul itself, the end does indeed go before the means; however, when its inner effects extend to the outside, this order is reversed, and the means acts toward the end as the cause to its effect. In this last sense, I permitted myself to make imprecise use of this term, which, however, need not exert any disturbing influence on our current analysis. Instead of means and end, insert cause and effect — where does that leave the difference between *base* and *noble*? What can be noble about the cause, other than that it fulfills its effect? Noble and base only indicate the relationship in which a circumstance stands opposed to a *certain principle in our soul* — it is therefore a concept that is to be used within the soul, not outside it. Can you see then how you are taking for granted what we must first articulate through our conclusions? Why else do you call the *thought,* in contrast with *motion,* noble, if not because you already presuppose that the thinking being is the central focus under which to order all categories of things? Enter into *my* system of thought, and this hierarchy will disappear, the thought is the effect and cause of the motion and an indispensable link in the chain of necessity, like the beat of the pulse that accompanies it."

"You will never make me accept this paradoxical, unnatural sentence. Through our reason, we can see the end of physical nature almost everywhere, even in human beings. Where do we even once see this order reversed and human ends subordinated to physical laws? And how will you reconcile this *external* determination with the drive toward happiness, which directs all of its efforts *inward* toward its own ends?"

"Do let us try. To express myself more concisely, I must again make use of your language. Let us assume that moral phenomena were necessary, as light and sound. In that case, beings must have existed who were created for this special calling, just as ether and air must be designed just so and no differently to be capable of such a number of vibrations that allow us to perceive color and harmonious sound. Beings must therefore exist who put themselves into motion, because freedom is the prerequisite of moral phenomena; what therefore in the case of air and ether, mineral, and plant is achieved by the original form, must in this case be preserved through some *inner* principle, against which the motives or the motivating forces of this being act approximately in the same way as do the motivating forces of the plant against the constant regulating type of its construction. Just as nature directs a simple mechanical being through unchanging mechanics, so must she move the thinking and feeling being through pain and pleasure."

"Quite right."

"We see her then in the moral world leave her former order behind, actually even engage in what appears to be a conflict with herself. In every moral being, she places a new center, a state within the state, even as if she had completely lost sight of her general purpose. All of the activities of this being are inclined to the center by a force analogous to that exerted in the physical world by gravity. In this sense, this being is grounded in itself, a true and real whole, constructed around its center through this circumstance, just as the planet earth became a sphere through gravity, and remained a sphere. Up to this point, nature seems to have completely forgotten herself.

"But we have heard that this creature is only present in order to bring forth the moral phenomena that she necessitated; the freedom of this being, or its power of independent motion, must therefore be subordinated to the end that she had specified for it. If in fact she wanted to remain master over the effects that it achieved, then she would have had to take control of the principle according to which the moral being moved. What else could she do, but conflate *her own* end for this being with the principle through which it is ruled, or in other words, make all of this being's purposive activities the necessary condition of its happiness?"

"This much I can follow."

"Therefore, if the moral being fulfills the conditions of its happiness, in the same step it enters into the plan of nature from which it would seem to have been removed through this separate plan, just as the planet earth is made capable of tracing the ecliptic of its orbit through its elements' fall toward their center. Thus, through pain and pleasure, the moral creature experiences each time only the relationship of its present state to the state of its highest perfection, which is one and the same as the end of nature. The organic being does not have and does not need this direction, for, in and of itself, it can neither approach nor distance itself from the state of its perfection. The moral being therefore has the advantage of the pleasure of its perfection, that is to say, its happiness, but at the same time, should it go astray from this course, it has the warning, suffering. If an elastic sphere were to be conscious of its condition, the pressure of a finger forcing a flat form upon it would cause it pain, and it would return with a feeling of pleasure to its most beautiful curvature."

"Its elasticity serves it in place of such emotion."

"But, so little as the fast movement that we call fire has in common with the sensation of burning, or the cubic form of salt has with its bitter taste, just as little does the feeling we call happiness have in common with the state of our inner perfection, which it accompanies, or with the purpose of nature, which it serves. Both, one might say, are bound to each other just as arbitrarily, as the laurel wreath to victory, or as stigma to a dishonorable transaction."

"So it seems."

"Man therefore need not be *privy* to the end that nature is pursuing through him. Should he never know of any principle other than that through which he rules in his little world, even if in his complacent delusion he should attribute the relationships of this little world of his to laws of nature herself — through his serving his structure, her ends are likewise ensured."

"And can anything be more perfect than having all pieces of the great whole promote only nature's end in that they remain true to their own ends, that they are not able to *want* to contribute to harmony, but instead they *must.* This concept is so beautiful, so captivating that one is already persuaded by that alone —"

"To attribute it to a spirit, you were going to say? Because egotistical humankind would like to attribute all that is good and beautiful to its own race, because it would so dearly like to have the creator in its own family. Give crystal the power of thought and its highest plan for the world would be crystallization, its God would be the most beautiful form of crystal. And is this not inevitable? If every drop of water did not hold so strong and true to its center, no ocean would ever have come into motion."

"But do you also know, Your Highness, that you have, up to now, only provided evidence against yourself? If it is true, as you say, that man cannot go astray from his center point, what is the source of your own presumption to determine the course of nature? How can you then hope to take on the task of ascertaining the law by which she acts?"

"Nothing is farther from the case. I determined nothing; I am only removing what human beings have taken from their own breasts and decorated with ostentatious titles, what they have then confused with *her.* What preceded me and what will follow me, I see as two dark, impenetrable curtains, which hang at either limit of human existence and which no living human has yet drawn aside. Many hundreds of generations have already stood with the torch before it, and guessed and guessed what might stand behind it. Many see their own shadows, the reflections of their passion, moving, magnified, projected on the curtain of the future, and they shudder in horror before their own image. Poets, philosophers, and nation builders have painted them with their dreams, smiling or more sinister if the sky above them was gloomier or more cheerful, and at a distance the perspective was convincing. Some frauds also exploited this general fascination and, through rare acts of trickery, astonished excited imaginations. A deep silence rules behind this curtain; no one, once he is behind it, answers from beyond; all that one heard was a hollow echo of the question, as if one had called into a crypt. All must eventually find their way behind this curtain, and with horror they take hold of it, unsure who might well stand behind it and receive them; *quid sit id, quod tantum morituri vident.*[1] Of course, there were also unbelievers amongst them, who claimed that this curtain only made fools of mankind, and that nothing had yet been observed because there was nothing behind the curtain to see; in order to convince them, they were sent behind it all the more quickly."

"It was always a rash conclusion, when they had no better reason than that they did not see anything."

"Look, dear friend, I am happy to resolve not to look behind this curtain — and the wisest course would surely be to wean myself of all curiosity. Yet in drawing this impermeable circle around myself and confining my entire existence within the limits of the present, this small speck becomes so much more important to me, this that I was so long in danger of neglecting for vain thoughts of conquest. What you call the end of my existence is no longer my affair. I cannot escape from it; I cannot help influence its course. I know, however, and firmly believe that I must and do fulfill such an end. But the means, which nature has chosen in order to fulfill her end through me, is therefore that much holier to me — it is everything that is mine, namely, my morality, my happiness. Everything else I will never know. I am like a messenger who carries a sealed letter to its destination. What the letter contains is of no importance to him — his only profit from the task will be his payment for the delivery."

"Oh, how poor you leave me standing!"

"But where have we led ourselves astray?" cried the Prince, looking with a smile at the table where the rolls of money lay. "And yet not so far astray!" he added — "for maybe you will now find me again in this new lifestyle. I too was not able to easily wean myself from those imaginary riches, the pillars of my morality and my happiness, from the dear dream with which everything that up till then had lived in me was so tightly intertwined. I longed for the carelessness that had made existence so bearable for the great majority around me. Everything that seduced me away from myself was welcome to me. Shall I confess to you? I wished to *sink* away in order to destroy this source of my suffering together with the capacity to suffer."

I was not yet ready to see the conversation end.

"Dear Prince," I began anew, "have I understood you correctly? The final end of mankind lies not in mankind, but outside? Mankind only exists for the sake of its consequences."

"Let us agree to avoid this expression, which leads us off course. Say mankind is there because the causes of its existence were there and because its effects exist, or, which says just as much, because the causes that preceded mankind had to have an effect, and the effects that mankind brought forth need to have a cause."

"If I wish to assign mankind a value, therefore, I can only weigh it according to the quantity and importance of the effects of which it is the cause."

"According to the *quantity* of its effects. We only call an effect important because it contributes to a larger number of effects. Mankind has no other worth aside from its effects."

"The human being, then, who provides the source of more effects would therefore be the more perfect human being?"

"Undeniably."

"What? Then there is no longer any difference between the good and the bad! Then the whole concept of moral beauty is lost!"

"I am not afraid of that. If it were so, then I would immediately want to concede you the argument for lost. The feeling of moral difference is a far more important authority to me than my reason — and I only began to believe in the latter when I found it in harmony with that former unalienable feeling. Your morality requires a support; mine rests on its own axis."

"Does experience not teach us that often the most important roles are played by the most mediocre players, that nature brings about the most constructive revolutions through the most destructive of individuals? A Mohammed, an Attila, or an Aurangzeb[2] is as effective a servant of the universe as storms, earthquakes, and volcanoes are valuable tools of physical nature. The despot on his throne who marks every hour of his reign with blood and suffering therefore would be a far worthier element of her creation than the farmer in his fields, because the despot is more effective — yes, what is saddest is that he would be even more excellent as a result of *that* which makes him the object of our disgust, through the larger sum of his deeds, that are all worthy of being cursed — he would have more rights to be called an excellent man, even as he sank below the level of mankind. Vice and virtue —"

"See," cried the Prince in vexation, "how you allow yourself to be deceived by superficial appearance, and how easily you concede my victory! How can you propose that a *destructive* life is an *active* life? The despot is the least useful creature in his state because he ties up the most active energies and suffocates the joy of creativity with terror and worry. His entire existence is a terrible negative, and when he takes hold of the noblest, holiest life and destroys freedom of thought — a hundred thousand active people do not compensate in a century for what a Hildebrand[3] or a Philip of Spain[4] manages to lay to waste in a few years. How could you honor these creatures and creators of decay by comparing them with those charitable and constructive tools of life and fertility?"

"I confess the weakness of my example — but if in place of Philip we set a Peter the Great on the throne, you cannot deny that this latter was more effective in his monarchy than the private man with that measure of energy and all of the activity of which he is capable. It is fortune, then, that according to your system decides the grade of excellence, for it is fortune that distributes the opportunity to cause effect."

"In your opinion, then, the throne in particular would present such an opportunity? Do tell me — if the king governs, what does the philosopher do in his kingdom?"

"He thinks."

"And what does the king do when he governs?"

"He thinks."

"And when the vigilant philosopher sleeps, what does the vigilant king do?"

"He sleeps."

"Take two burning candles, one of them standing in the room of a farmhouse, the other illuminating a merry company in a magnificent hall. What becomes of each?"

"They will shine. But even that supports me — both candles, let us assume, burn equally long and equally bright, and if one confused their destinies, no one would notice the difference. Why should one therefore be more excellent because chance privileged it to present itself in a sparkling hall of grandeur and beauty, why should the other be any worse because chance damned it to make poverty and affliction visible in a farmer's hut? And yet this inevitably follows from your assertion?"

"Both are equally excellent, but are both also *equal* in their achievements?"

"How is that possible? Because the one in the wide hall gave out so much more light than the other? Because it spread so much more pleasure than the other?"

"But consider that in this case, only the first effect is relevant — not the entire chain. Only the immediately subsequent effect belongs to the immediately preceding cause; only so many particles receptive to light as the candle directly touched were activated by it. And what then does one have to favor it over the other? Can you not draw an equal amount of rays from each source? Just as many from the sparkle of your eye as from the center of the earth? Abandon the habit of assuming that the large masses — which reason can only abstract and conceive of as such a whole — actually exist as such a whole in the actual world. The spark of fire that drops into a store of gunpowder, blows up a tower and flattens a hundred houses, has nonetheless only ignited one small grain."

"Very good, yet —"

"Let us apply this to moral actions. We go on a walk, and two beggars happen to meet us. I give one of them a piece of money, you give the other an equal amount; mine gets drunk on the money and commits, in this state of drunkenness, a murder; yours buys a dying father refreshment and in so doing, rescues his life. Had I then, through *the* very action through which you granted a life, taken a life? — Nothing could be farther from the case. The effect of my deed, like yours, ceases to belong to me as soon as it is no longer the immediate effect of *my* action."

"Yet if my reason predicts this chain of events and it is this insight that leads me to this deed — if I gave this beggar the money in order to rescue the life of a dying father, then all of the results are mine, if they come to pass as I predicted."

"Nothing could be less so. Never forget that *one* cause can only have *one* effect. The entire effect that you brought forth lay in bringing the piece of money from your hand into the hand of the beggar. This, in the long chain of effects, is the only one that can be credited to you. The medicine worked as medicine, and so forth — you appear bewildered. You believe that I am propounding paradoxes, perhaps a single word could help us agree, but we should rather seek this through our conclusions."

"From what has been said, I can very well see, it follows that a good deed is not responsible for its negative effects and a bad deed is not responsible for its happy effects. But at the same time it follows that neither the good deed is responsible for its good effect, nor the bad deed to blame for its negative effect, and that therefore both in their effect are exactly the same. — You must want to exclude the rare cases where the immediate effect is at the same time intended."

"Such an immediate effect does not exist, for between any effect that the human being brings forth outside of himself, and the inner cause or the will, a chain of indifferent effects will insert itself, even if no more than the movement of a muscle. You can therefore say, without apology, that both in their effect are morally one and the same, that there is no difference. And who would deny this? The stab of the dagger that ended the life of Henry IV[5] and that which ended the life of a Domitian,[6] are both entirely the same action."

"Correct, but the motive —"

"The motives therefore determine the moral action. And of what do motives consist?"

"Of conceptions."

"And what do you call conceptions?"

"Inner actions or activities of a thinking being, which correspond to external activities."

"A moral action then is the consequence of inner actions that correspond to external changes?"

"Entirely correct."

"If I therefore say, the event ABC is a moral action, I am then saying that the chain of external changes that this event ABC consists of is preceded by a chain of inner changes abc?"

"So it is."

"The actions abc in that case had already been decided, when the actions ABC began?"

"Necessarily."

"Even if ABC had not begun, that would make abc no less a fact. If morality was characteristic of abc, it would remain so, even if we were to completely eliminate ABC."

"I understand you, my Prince, and thus that which I had held for the first element in the chain would be the last within it. When I gave the beggar the money, my moral action was already entirely over, its entire worth or lack of worth already decided."

"That is what I mean. Were the results to occur as you predicted, that is, were ABC to follow abc, it would be nothing more than a *successful* good action. In this external stream of events, the individual has nothing more to say, nothing more belongs to him than his own soul. You see in this anew that the monarch has nothing over the private man, for he is as little master of this stream as the other; even in his case the entire realm of his effectiveness is limited to within his own soul."

"But this does not change anything, my Prince, for even the evil action has its motives like the good, that is, its inner activity, and it is only because of these motives that we call it evil. If you place the end and worth of man in the sum of his activities, I am therefore unable to see how you can separate morality from his end, and my earlier objections return."

"Listen to what we have established; *bad* or *good*, we have come to agreement, are categories first assigned to an action in the soul."

"That is established."

"Let us therefore lower a wall of separation between the exterior world and the thinking being; the specific action external to the being then appears morally indifferent; within the thinking being we refer to it as good or bad."

"Correct."

"Morality is therefore a relationship that can only be conceived of within the soul, never without, just as, for example, honor is a relationship that can only be conveyed within civil society."

"Quite right."

"As soon as we consider an action to be present in the soul, it appears to us as a citizen of a completely different world, and we must judge it according to entirely different laws. It belongs to a whole that contains its center point within itself, from which flows all it gives out, and toward which streams all that it receives. This center point or this principle is, as we earlier established together, nothing other than the inner drive to realize all of its drives in effects, or, in other words, to achieve the greatest demonstration of its existence. Into this state we place the perfection of the moral being, just as we call a clock perfect when all of the elements from which the artist created it correspond with the effect for which he created them; as we call a musical instrument perfect when all of its pieces make the greatest contribution to the greatest effect of which they are capable and for the sake of which they have been united. The relationship, then, in which the activities of the moral being stand to this principle, we label with the title *morality,* and an action is morally good or morally bad according to whether it approaches or distances itself from this, promotes it or hinders it. Are we in agreement?"

"Perfectly."

"Since this principle is no other than the most perfect activity of all the energies of man, is then a good action that in which more energies were active and a bad action that in which fewer energies were active?"

"Here, my Prince, let us pause. According to this, in a moral hierarchy, a small good deed that I do would fall far below the year-long plot of the St. Bartholomew's Day Massacre[7] or Cueva's conspiracy against Venice."[8]

At this, the Prince lost his patience. "When will I be able to make it fathomable for you," he began, "that nature knows no whole? Place together that which belongs together. Was that conspiracy *one* action, or not rather a chain of a hundred thousand actions? — and a chain of a hundred thousand *flawed* actions, against which your small good deed still stands superior? The drive of love of humanity, which was active in your deed, lay dormant in all of those actions. But we are becoming distracted. Where was I?"

"A good action would be that where more energies were active, and the reverse."

"And accordingly therefore, should fewer energies be active in it, a bad action would be bad, and the reverse?"

"Entirely conceivable."

"In the case of a bad action, therefore, only that would be *negated* that in a good action would be *affirmed?*"

"So it is."

"I therefore cannot say, an evil heart was necessary to commit this deed, any more than I can say, a child and not a man would be needed to lift this stone?"

"Very true. I would rather say that much of a good heart must be missing, in order to commit this deed."

"Vice is therefore only the absence of virtue, foolishness the absence of reason, a concept approximately similar to the concept of shadow or silence?"

"Quite right."

"No more, therefore, than one can say with correct logic that there is emptiness, silence, or darkness present, — even so little is there vice in mankind or in the entire moral world at all?"

"That is evident."

"If therefore there is no vice in mankind, then everything that is active in him, virtue, that is, is good, just as everything that makes sound is not quiet, and that does not stand in shadow is lit?"

"It follows."

"Every act, therefore, that the human being commits, is by virtue of its being an action, something good?"

"According to all that we have concluded."

"And if we witness a human being commit a bad action, this action is in that moment precisely the single good thing that we observe in him."

"That sounds peculiar."

"Let us use a comparison for our aid. Why do we call a dreary, misty winter day an unhappy sight? Is it because we find the snowy landscape unappealing in itself? Not in the least, if one were able to transplant the same sight into summer, it would elevate summer's beauty. We call it unhappy because this snow and misty air could not be present if the sun had shone to dissipate them, because they are incompatible with the greater attractions of summer. The winter is therefore a source of displeasure not because it is missing all pleasure, but because it excludes greater pleasures."

"Perfectly clear."

"It is just the same in the case of moral beings. We despise a person who flees from an encounter and in doing so, escapes death — not because the effective drive to self-preservation displeased us, but because he would have been less carried away by this drive had he possessed the marvelous quality of *courage*. I can admire the boldness, the cleverness of the robber who robs me, but I call him himself depraved, for in him there is a lack of the far more beautiful quality, *justice*. In this way a project that is the product of a year of restrained, active desire for vengeance can leave me astounded, but I call it repugnant, because it shows me a person who could live for years without loving his fellow man. I step with reluctance over a battlefield, not because so many lives are decaying there — pestilence and earthquakes could have done even more without rousing me against them — nor because I did not recognize the excellence of the energy, the skill, and the heroic courage that struck these warriors to the ground — but instead because this sight reminds me of so many thousands of human beings who lacked humanity."

"Excellent."

"The same applies to the *grades* of morality. A very cunning, finely conceived, and persistently pursued act of wickedness, courageously executed, has something magnificent in it that often draws weak souls to emulate it, for one finds so many great and beautiful energies in abundance at work there. And yet we call this act worse than a similar one of a lesser degree of spirit, and punish it more severely, because it more often allows us to recognize the lack of justice in its greater chain of motives. Should the act be committed especially against a benefactor, then it offends our entire sensibilities, for there were more frequent opportunities for the drive of love to be set into motion, and thus here we repeat with greater frequency the discovery that this drive was without effect."

"All this is clear and plausible."

"To return to our question. You concede, then, that it is not the activities of energies that make vice a vice, but their lack of activity."

"Entirely."

"Motives however are such activities; it is therefore falsely spoken to call an action depraved because of its motives. Nothing is less so! The motives are the only *good* that it has, it is only evil because of those motives that it lacks."

"Undeniably."

"But we could have demonstrated this proof even more simply. Would the depraved subject act according to these motives if they did not provide him pleasure? *Pleasure* alone is that which sets moral beings into action, and only the good, as we know, can provide pleasure."

"I am satisfied. From what has been established follows undeniably that, for example, a person of bright intellect and a well-meaning heart is only therefore better than another of equal intellect and a less well-meaning heart because he comes closer to the maximum inner activity. But another concern occurs to me. If you give a human being the qualities of intelligence, courage, bravery, and so forth, in a high degree of excellence, and let him only lack the single quality that we call a good heart — would you place him above one who has these former characteristics to a lesser degree, but the latter in its greatest amplitude? Unarguably the first person is far more active than the second, and as according to you the activity of the energies determines the moral worth, your judgment would therefore fall against the second man, and find itself in contradiction with the common judgment of mankind."

"It would, without fail, be very much in agreement with the common judgment. A person whose intellectual powers are active to a high degree would just as certainly possess an excellent heart, since he cannot love a quality in himself and hate it in another. If experience seems to conflict with this, then the subject's intelligence has either been judged too generously, or his moral goodness judged too reservedly. A great intellect with a feeling heart stands just as high above the brilliant villain in the order of beings as the stupid man with a soft, perhaps better put, *tender* heart stands below the latter."

"But an enthusiast with a stormy disposition is indeed clearly a more active being than the ordinary person with phlegmatic blood and limited perception?"

"In the case of even such a phlegmatic, limited, ordinary person, every energy comes indeed into effect, for no one is suppressed by any another. He is a human being in a state of healthy sleep; the enthusiast is like the frantic lunatic who throws himself into raging convulsions when the life force of even the most external arteries comes to a stop. — Do you have any other objection?"

"I am convinced, *with* you, that the morality of man is more or less comprised of the greater or lesser degree of his inner activity."

"Remember now," the Prince continued, "that we have set up this entire analysis in the confined realm of the human soul, that we have set it apart from the outer categories of things through a wall of separation, and within this circle, which we have never overstepped, we have staged the entire construction of human morality. At the same time, we have found that the happiness of a man corresponds perfectly with his moral excellence, that therefore his morality remains no more something to be supported, that no more could a pleasure precede a yet-to-be-achieved perfection, than could a rose blooming today be judged beautiful only a year later, or could a false note at the piano first contribute its false tone at the following performance. It would be equally thinkable that the light of the sun should shine this afternoon and its warmth fall during the next, as to think that the perfection of mankind could fall in this world and his happiness in the other — has this been proven to your satisfaction?"

"I can think of no argument against it."

"The moral being is therefore complete and determined in itself, like that which we differentiate from it with the label organic. The moral being is determined by its morality as the organic is determined through its construction, and this morality is a relationship that is thoroughly independent of that which occurs outside of the moral being."

"That has been demonstrated."

"Whatever else might surround me, then, the moral difference remains."

"I sense where this is leading, but —"

"Let there be then a rationally ordered whole, endless justice and goodness, a constancy of personality, eternal progress — this can at any rate no more conclusively be demonstrated in the moral world than it is in the physical. In order to be perfect, to be happy, the moral being needs no new authority, and if it expects one, then this expectation can at any rate no longer be grounded in any *demand*. What will become of him must in terms of his perfection be of no importance to him, just as the rose, in order to be beautiful — must be indifferent whether it blooms in a desert or in a royal garden, whether it is destined for the breast of a pretty girl or for the devouring worm."

"Is this comparison fitting?"

"Perfectly; I'll say *here* expressly, in the latter case in order to be *beautiful*, in the *former* in order to be *happy* — not in order to be *present!* This latter belongs to another analysis, and I do not wish to prolong the discussion."

"I cannot yet release you, Your Highness. You have — and it seems to me incontrovertibly — proven that man is only moral insofar as he is active in himself — but you claimed earlier that he only possesses morality in order to have effect outside of himself."

"You should say he is only active outside of himself because he has morality. Your *in-order-to*'s only confuse us. I have no tolerance for your constant invocation of ends."

"It comes down to a single point. You would say, then, that a man possesses the basis for the greatest number of effects outside of himself only insofar as he has achieved the highest degree of his own morality. And you have yet to prove this to me."

"Can you not derive such a proof yourself from what we have already concluded? The state of the highest inner productivity of man's energies, is it not the same state in which he can be the cause of the most effects outside himself?"

"*Can*, but not *must* — for did you yourself not concede that the ineffectiveness of a good deed does nothing to take away from its moral worth?"

"Not just conceded, but stipulated as most necessary! — How difficult you are to save from a misguided idea once it has taken hold of you. This apparent contradiction, that the external results of a moral deed are most irrelevant for its worth, and that the entire end of its being nevertheless only lies in its outward consequences, constantly confuses you. What if a great virtuoso were to play before a large but coarse society and a dilettante should intervene and abduct his entire audience — which of the individuals would you declare the more *beneficial*?"

"The virtuoso, of course, for the same artist will go on to entertain finer ears at another time."

"And would he indeed, if he did not possess the skill that at that time was wasted and that he had practiced at that time?"

"Hardly."

"And would his competitor ever achieve the same effect that he had brought forth?"

"Not that one, but —"

"But maybe a greater effect before his greater crowd, you wish to say? Can you in seriousness doubt whether an artist, who knew how to bewitch a circle of sensitive people and intelligent connoisseurs, did more than that dilettante in his whole life? That perhaps *one* emotion that the virtuoso aroused elevated itself in a fine soul to deeds that would afterwards be of benefit for a million? That perhaps that one emotion linked itself to an important chain as the single missing link and set the crown upon a beautiful design? — Even that dilettante, I concede, can make people happy —. The human being who has lost his moral crown will also continue to have effect, just as a piece of fruit, upon which rot has already taken hold can still be a meal for birds and worms, but will never again be thought worthy of the touch of a beautiful mouth."

"But let that artist play in a desert, live there and die. *I* may say his art rewards him; even where there is no ear to catch his notes, he is his own audience and enjoys in the harmonies that he brings forth the yet-more-beautiful harmony of his being. But *you* may not say this. *Your* artist must have an audience, or he is there in vain."

"I understand you — but your sample scenario can never occur. No moral being is in a desert; wherever it lives and moves, it touches an omnipresent universe. The effect that it achieves, were it only this single one, as we know, could only be achieved by *this* being and no other, and only given its full properties could it achieve this effect. Even if our virtuoso was only able to play a *single* time, concede to me that he would have to be precisely this artist, which he was, and that he, in order to be this, would have had to have gone through precisely that degree of practice and artistic preparation that he had completed, and that therefore his entire previous life as an artist participated in this moment of triumph. Was the first Brutus of no use for twenty years because for twenty years he played the fool? His *first* deed was to found a republic that even today stands as the greatest phenomenon in world history. And so would it be conceivable that my *necessity* or your providence should have prepared a man over an entire lifetime in silence for a deed that only in his final hour would be demanded of him."

"As obvious as this may sound — my heart cannot grow accustomed to the idea that all the energies, all the efforts of a man should only work for his influence in this temporality. The great experienced patriotic statesman who today is cast from the helm carries all of his earned knowledge, his practiced skills, and his productive plans into his forgotten private life, in which he dies. Maybe he had only the *final* stone to place upon the pyramid that fell to pieces behind him and that his successors had to begin from the ground up. Over fifty years of life, during the most taxing years of the governance of the kingdom, was he only building up for the sedentary quiet of his private life? You cannot answer me that he fulfilled his effect through this administration. If a man's entire calling is exhausted by his influence in the world, then his existence must end together with his influence."

"I refer you to the illustrative example of physical nature, from which you will have to concede to me *that she* only works for the passing moment. How many seeds and embryos, which nature prepared for future life with so much skill and care, are again dispersed in the kingdom of elements without ever having the chance to develop? — Why did she create them? In every human couple there sleeps, just as in the first couple, an entire human race; why did she allow only one individual to *come into being* out of so many millions? As certainly as she incorporates these decaying seeds, just as certainly moral creatures, in whose cases she seems to have abandoned a higher purpose, will sooner or later enter into the same. To want to fathom how she propagates a single effect through the entire chain of being would betray a childish presumptuousness. Often, we see, she suddenly drops the threads of a deed, an event, which she afterwards picks up just as suddenly three thousand years later, buries the arts and manners of the *eighteenth* century in Calabria, in order, perhaps, to display them to a transformed Europe in the *thirtieth* century, nourishes the hordes of nomads on the Tartar Steppes over many ages in order one day to send them as fresh blood for the languishing South, how she throws the ocean over Holland and Zealand's coasts during her physical course, in order perhaps to expose an island in distant America! But also at the smallest scale, such displays are not completely absent. How often does the *temperance* of a father, long since passed away, do wonders in a genius son, how often might an entire life be lived in order to earn an epitaph that will cast a firebolt into the soul of a late successor! — Because hundreds of years in the past a displaced bird dropped grains of seed there, a harvest blossoms for a newly arrived people on a desert island — and could a moral seed be lost in such fertile ground?!"

"O Best of Princes! Your eloquence only inspires me to return your fire. You are willing to grant so much perfection to your unfeeling necessity, and would rather not bestow this happiness on a God! Look around in all of creation. Wherever a pleasure lies ready, you find a being taking pleasure — and this endless pleasure, this feast of perfection, should stand empty through all of eternity!"

"How strange!" said the Prince after a deep silence. "That upon which *you* and *others* base their hopes, that is the very thing that toppled mine — precisely this faith in the perfection of things. If everything were not so self-contained, if I saw even a single blemish, a sliver, jutting out of this beautiful circle, that would prove to me immortality. Yet everything, everything that I see and observe falls back to this *visible* center point, and our most noble spirituality is such a completely indispensable machine for driving this wheel of transience."

"I cannot understand you, Your Highness. Your own philosophy judges and condemns you; truly, you are like the rich man who starves in the midst of his treasure. You admit that the human being encompasses everything in himself for finding happiness, that he can only achieve happiness through that which he possesses, and yet you yourself seek the source of your unhappiness outside of yourself. If your conclusions are correct, then it is indeed impossible that with even a single wish you can aim beyond this ring in which you hold mankind captive."

"Precisely that is the worst part, that we are only morally perfect, only blissful, in order to be useful, that we enjoy our *effort* but not our *works.* Hundreds of thousands of hands carried the stones of the pyramid together — but the pyramids were not their reward. The pyramids amused the eye of the kings, and the industrious slaves were compensated with their daily sustenance. What does one owe the worker, if he can no longer work, or there is no work left for him? What does one owe a human being, if he no longer can be used?"

"He will always be needed."

"And always as a thinking being?"

At this we were interrupted by a visit — and not a moment too soon, you will be thinking. Forgive me, dear O***, for this eternally long letter. You wanted to know all the small details about the Prince, and among them I can surely also count his moral philosophy. I know that his mental state is important to you, and it is only because of this that you are interested in his actions. It is for this reason that I have faithfully written down everything that remained in my mind from this conversation.[1]

In the near future I will write to you of a recent piece of news that you will hardly expect after a dialog such as today's. Farewell.

1.) And I also beg the forgiveness of my reader for having so faithfully copied the good Baron von F***. If the excuse that the latter had for his friend is not enough to satisfy the reader, I have another, which the Baron von F*** did not have, and which must excuse everything in the eyes of the reader. The Baron von F*** could namely not have predicted what sort of influence the philosophy of the Prince would have on his future fate, yet I do know, and for this reason I have wisely left everything as I found it. I promise the reader, who hoped to see ghosts here, that more will come, but as the reader himself sees, in the case of such an unbelieving man as the Prince von *** still is for now, such ghosts would be of no avail.

Notes

[1] "What it is that only those destined to die can see." Tacitus, *Germania,* ch. 40; see also 148 n. 12.

[2] Aurangzeb (1618–1707) was a Mughal ruler in India who imprisoned his father and had two of his brothers executed in order to ensure his succession to the throne.

[3] Hildebrand became Pope Gregory VII (1073–85). He repeatedly entered into conflict with Emperor Henry IV and was eventually exiled.

[4] Philip II of Spain (1527–98) ruled Spain during the Revolt of the Netherlands and the defeat of the Spanish Armada. His reign was marked by the persecution of Protestants and Spaniards of Muslim ancestry.

[5] Henry IV (1553–1610) of France enacted the Edict of Nantes in 1598, which granted a larger degree of religious tolerance to Protestants. He was assassinated in 1610 in Paris by Ravaillac.

[6] Domitian ruled as Roman Caesar from 81 A.D. until 96 A.D., when he was assassinated by enemies in the Senate. According to some historians, he was responsible for persecution of early Christians.

[7] The execution of Protestants in Paris on August 24, 1572, carefully planned by Maria von Medici and Charles IX.

[8] Alfonso de la Cueva led a conspiracy attempting to overturn the Venetian republic in 1618.

8: Haoh-Kiöh-Tschuen (The Tale of a Perfect Match)

Friedrich Schiller (1800–1801)
Translated by Carrie Collenberg

Book One

IN *TAMING*, A GREAT CITY OF THE CHINESE EMPIRE, there lived a noble young man named *Tiehtschongu,* who applied himself to scholarship. His figure was handsome, his soul magnanimous and pure; justice was his passion and it was a joy for him to stand up for the oppressed. Here he was swift and bold and not concerned about reputation; nothing could contain his fervor when he had an act of violence to avenge.

His father, named *Tieh-ying,* was a mandarin of justice and administered a judicial office at the court of the emperor in Peking. Because he feared the fiery disposition of his son, he had him pursue his studies at a safe distance from the court. When Tiehtschongu had reached his sixteenth year, his parents thought that the time had come for him to marry; however, he declared that he could not commit himself to such an indissoluble bond until he had found a woman in whom all the virtues of body and spirit were combined.

He was twenty years old when he read in a history book about an emperor who had demanded that the heart of one of his mandarins be removed in order to prepare a medicine out of it for the empress, who was sick. A mandarin named Pikang immediately offered himself for the operation. This great selflessness astounded the young man and reminded him of the obedience that he owed his parents and had hitherto so little shown. The reproaches of his conscience kept him awake the entire night; he decided to travel to them at once and beg them for forgiveness for his previous obstinacy.

With this resolved, he awoke early and set forth on his way, accompanied only by a single servant, *Siautan.* After he had a two days' journey behind him, nearly without resting, he found himself in the evening outside of a large village and stopped in front of a shabby hut. An old woman came out and, when she saw him in the traditional dress of a student, said to him: "Young Lord, certainly you have come to visit our young scholar Wey." — He said he knew no such person, but had lost his way and requested lodging for the night. The old woman took him in most willingly and regretted only that she could not accommodate him in a manner befitting his class. His servant, Siautan, then had to carry his bed and the rest of the luggage into the house; she herself went to cover his room with straw and to prepare him tea.

Tiehtschongu then inquired about the young scholar whom she had mentioned earlier. "You may not know," answered the old woman, "that this village was not always called *Wey-tsioün,* as it is now, but has its name from a family that lives here, which had otherwise always been in good standing, but now has fallen on hard times. Thank heaven at least one of them was able to study, even though he, too, is now in great misery. He traveled to court to take his examinations, where a learned man named *Hanyuen* met him and was so won over that he gave him his daughter's hand in marriage. But a noble mandarin fell in love with her and wanted to make her his concubine; when the parents did not give their consent, he had the daughter taken by force and afterwards seized the parents as well. No one knows where they have gone to; Wey is in despair and wants to take his own life."

She was still speaking when a crowd gathered on the street. Standing there among the people, they saw a young man who was dressed in blue and cried bitterly. "There he is," said the old woman. Tiehtschongu then asked whether the wife of the student was abducted by day or at night. By day, was the answer. Several people had witnessed it happen, but no one wanted to testify against him because he was such a powerful mandarin. —

"Perhaps," said Tiehtschongu, "you do not know what really took place and your report is nothing but lies." — "By no means," answered the old woman, annoyed with his disbelief. "A cousin of mine, who was bringing straw to the city, was present when the young woman along with her parents were carried into the mandarin's palace." — "Why did you not inform the young husband about this?" asked Tiehtschongu. — "How would that have helped?" she answered. "All resistance is in vain. The palace to which she was brought is a gift of the emperor; it is untouchable and holy, and no one is allowed to enter it unless he has permission from the emperor."

On the following morning, Tiehtschongu took leave of the old woman and had her paid five tsien (one guilder of our money). At parting, she begged him most urgently not to get her into any trouble by betraying what she had confided in him. "Why should this concern me?" he replied. "Your courteous reception is what I will keep in my memory."

He had hardly ridden out of earshot when he . . .

The Critical Essays

9: (A fragment of) A True Story (from most recent history): The *Truth* in Schiller's Literary Prose Works

Jeffrey L. High

> *His whole tale is nothing but a series of fabrications designed to string together the few truths that he found it in his interest to reveal to us.*
> — The Prince in Schiller's *The Spiritualist*[1]

WHILE SCHILLER COULD ENVISION himself as one of Germany's leading historians, an important aesthetic theorist, and a poet and dramatist for the ages, ironically — considering the impact and resonance of his prose works — he himself laid no such claim to a place in the history of literary prose. According to Schiller, it was the necessity of broad and colorful life experience, which he believed he lacked, that distanced him from literary prose works:

> The author of narrative prose cannot get by with the world within himself. He needs to be familiar with and have experience in the world outside him. This is exactly what I lack, and in my opinion, it might as well be everything.[2]

His stated belief that the prose genres demand broad familiarity with the external world, and that he lacked precisely this, very strongly implies that Schiller envisioned a very brief career as an author of literary prose. However, it must be countered that it was precisely his peculiar, if limited, true life experiences — absolutist Württemberg, the proximity to the Duke, his malaria and lung ailment, his dramatic escape and exile, his patrons and friends — that provide the sources for and personally inform each of his original prose works.

Although Schiller's actual life experiences largely inform if not dictate the contents of his original prose works, it is the Schillerian selection criterion of "familiarity" combined with "inner truth," "philosophical and artistic truth," and his adherence to the portrayal of "truth" as a narrative strategy, that provide the hallmark of his prose works, a concept Schiller described during his prose period in 1788:

> The advantage of *truth* that history has over novels could alone elevate it above them. The question is, however, whether the *inner truth*, which I call philosophical and artistic truth . . . does not have as much value as historical truth. That a person in *such* situations feels, acts, and expresses himself in *such a way* is a great, significant fact for humanity, and the novelist or dramatist has to get that across. The inner correspondence, the truth, will be felt and acknowledged without the actual occurrence of the event. The usefulness is not to be missed: this way one comes to know *mankind* and not simply *one man*, the species and not the elusive individual.[3]

Accordingly, the "truth" in Schiller's works is not necessarily historically accurate, but regards psychological-causal motivation,[4] the correspondence of character, situation, and reaction. A strategy emerges in Schiller's prose works that molds remarkable historical events and real-life experiences through an inductive, self-aware, reader-reception trialog between author, text, and reader, toward deduction based on "reason and the eternal laws of nature" (see p. 100).[5] Schiller selects and rewrites isolated individual "true" characters and events, often extreme or aberrant characters and conflicts, and anchors their stories in a more universal socio-historical validity with a focus on psychological plausibility, in order to demonstrate their universal significance: the deepest behavioral and moral truths about humanity.

Schiller's predilection for the combination of "inner truth" and extreme or aberrant characters and situations is by no means restricted to his prose works. He specifically deals with *Verirrung* (aberration) as a source of moral learning in the foreword to his first drama, *Die Räuber* (1781, The Robbers, NA 3:6), at the beginning of the "Philosophische Briefe" (1786, Philosophical Letters, NA 20:107) and in the introduction to "Der Verbrecher aus verlorener Ehre . . ." (1786, The Criminal of Lost Honor, NA 16:7; see p. 39). Indeed, Schiller's quest for stories suited to expose the inner truth about the "immutable structure of the human psyche" (see p. 40)[6] via actual unusual characters and events does not make Schiller's prose works any different from his dramatic works, almost all of which are based on remarkable if not imbalanced historical characters. Rather, it is his personal familiarity with the sources, the true characters, and the details of the particular extreme characters and situations selected for his original prose works that distinguishes them. This familiarity results in portraits of the individual in the most poignant, yet plausible, moments of truth — faced with unavoidable fate, armed only with fragmented knowledge and flawed character, "a human being like we are" (see p. 40).[7]

Schiller's first published prose work, "Eine großmütige Handlung aus der neusten Geschichte" (1782, A Magnanimous Act from Most Recent History), attributed to "Z. Z.," appeared in the second edition of the journal *Wirtembergisches Repertorium der Litteratur* (Württemberg Literary Repertorium), edited by Schiller with his professor Jakob Friedrich Abel and his classmates Johann Wilhelm Petersen and Johann Jakob Atzel. The very short moral tale on the love of two brothers for the same woman, close to an anecdote at less than four pages in the edition cited here, was published when Schiller was twenty-two years old, just after his sensational debut with the drama *The Robbers,* and during the early work on his next dramas *Die Verschwörung des Fiesko zu Genua* (1782–83, The Conspiracy of Fiesco at Genoa) and *Kabale und Liebe* (1782–84, Intrigue and Love). While the narrative is not based on actual personal experience, Schiller nonetheless knew his sources well. The story is based on that of the actual brothers Friedrich and Ludwig von Wurmb, the brothers of Schiller's future mother-in-law, Luise von Lengefeld. The woman in question, Christiane von Werthern, was a friend of Henriette von Wolzogen, the mother of Schiller's classmate and future brother-in-law, Wilhelm von Wolzogen. Schiller probably heard the story from Henriette von Wolzogen, who harbored the fugitive Schiller in Bauerbach during his flight from the Duke of Württemberg in 1782.

The fact that Schiller's first prose work, a moral tale, is based, whether largely or loosely, on a true occurrence from his personal circle of friends is significant for the understanding of Schiller's prose sources and his stated selection criterion of truth. Here, Schiller sets the tone theoretically and structurally for his later prose works and begins the story with a brief theoretical introduction explicitly addressing his readers[8] and appealing to their moral sense while contending that his story is true — "sie ist *wahr*" (NA 16:3; see p. 9) — a truth claim common to both his more famous novellas, "Der Verbrecher aus verlorener Ehre" (1786, The Criminal of Lost Honor. A True Story) and "Spiel des Schicksals. Ein Bruchstück einer wahren Geschichte" (1788–89, Game of Fate. A Fragment of a True Story), and the novel-fragment *Der Geisterseher. Aus den Memoires des Grafen von O*** (1786–89, The Spiritualist. From the Memoirs of Count von O**). In the same introductory paragraph, Schiller criticizes the artificial moral fantasy world of the drama and in particular the novel, citing Johann Timotheus Hermes' novel *Sophiens Reise von Memel nach Sachsen* (1770–72) and Samuel Richardson's *Grandison* (1753) and *Pamela* (1740), and dismissing all three for an unrealistic polarization of good and evil. Schiller's foreword thus provides a programmatic point of departure for the moral laboratory of his prose works, where real people — "humanity" — and "true" stories, which he contrasts with "künstliche" (artificial) and "idealistische" (idealistic) novels of his day, provide mostly painful subjects of study: "Who can say whether this same artificial existence in an idealistic world might not undermine our existence in the real one? We hover here, as it were, around the two poles of morality, angel and devil, and we leave the middle — humanity — lying in the breach" (see p. 9).[9] Here, a series of three "magnanimous acts" frame the story: 1) the elder brother's departure and return, 2) the younger brother's permanent self-exile, and 3) the lady's deathbed confession that she had loved the younger brother more, and that she had thus sacrificed her own happiness to avoid interfering in the brothers' goodness toward each other. Consequently, although the three acts become increasingly more generous, they culminate in a painful, realistic irony, characteristic of the particular anti-idealist and ruefully realist tendency of Schiller's prose works.

In November 1785, during his work on his fourth drama, *Don Karlos* (1783–87), and the "Philosophical Letters" (1786), Schiller delivered the tale "Verbrecher aus Infamie. Eine wahre Geschichte" (1785–86, Criminal of Infamy. A True Story) to his publisher Göschen in Leipzig, where it appeared anonymously in his journal *Thalia* in February of 1786. Again, Schiller's source is close to home. The psychological study of the development of a criminal, "Der Verbrecher aus verlorener Ehre" (The Criminal of Lost Honor), as it has become better known since its republication in the volume *Kleinere prosaische Schriften von Schiller* (1792, Schiller's Short Prose Works),[10] was inspired by his professor Jakob Friedrich Abel either while Schiller was a student at the Karlsschule Academy or during Abel's visit to Schiller in Mannheim in November of 1785 (NA 16:402). Abel's father had arrested and interrogated the historical "criminal," the bandit leader and murderer Fridrich Schwan from Ebersbach in Schiller's home state of Württemberg, who was executed in Vaihingen in 1760. Abel himself wrote a history of the "Sonnenwirt" (Innkeeper of the Sun) Schwan two years after Schiller, though it remains unclear which work was conceived first or whether Schiller was familiar with Abel's version.[11]

As was the case in his first published prose work, "A Magnanimous Act from Most Recent History," Schiller introduces the tale as a "true story," situating himself and his narrator as moral historians, similar to the narrational position in his historical works, which he began in the same period.[12] The text likewise begins with an explicit authorial introduction, this time substantially longer, and with a much broader articulation of focus. Here Schiller engages with two topical discourses of the 1780s, the anthropological anomaly of the outsider and historical theory,[13] expanding on them to propose the pedagogical benefits of *Seelenkunde* (NA 16:9; psychology, see p. 40). Again, similar to the criticism of the gulf between reader and subject in the foreword to "A Magnanimous Act" — "our imagination is ignited, our heart remains cold" (see p. 9)[14] — Schiller defines the failure of the specifically German bourgeois study of history as the "irreconcilable contrast that exists between the heated emotional state of an acting human being and the quiet mood of the reader" (see p. 39)[15] for all practical purposes. (The introduction to "Criminal" is clear about the scientific approach and moral education agenda of Wolf's case history. Schiller situates the narrator in the role of a Linnaeus, who classified organic life from kingdom to species — here as the scientific analyst of the human realm, who classifies "drives and inclinations"[16] — concluding that whereas "captivating rendering"[17] has failed to uncover the truth of "the human heart," the psychological approach will reveal that the criminal is "a human being like we are," as the "autopsy of his depravity"[18] should demonstrate (see p. 41).

Schiller's deceptive stated goal of purely objective analysis gives way to a "captivating rendering" almost as soon as Wolf assumes narration, and the dialogue form of the 'final act' ending in sublime sacrifice bears all the hallmarks of Schiller's tragedies and is just as painful and riveting. When Wolf recognizes that his judge wants to talk to him as an individual, entitled to the same respect any unknown person should receive, and when Wolf betrays — reclaims — his identity, he clearly does so with the awareness that this will result in his (deserved) execution: "Write to your prince how you found me, and that I betrayed myself of my own free will . . . plead for me, old man, and shed a tear on your report: I am the Innkeeper of the Sun" (see p. 55).[19] An author insightful enough to craft such a viscerally painful, human scene was no doubt aware that any narrative pretence of "cold" disinterest had disappeared along with the moral historian narrator, whose final comments introduce this final dialogue, which is several pages in length. Ironically, it is precisely the initial painstaking scientific analysis of the making of the criminal that ultimately makes his emotional recognition of the law — and his guilt — so effective.[20]

Schiller's "Criminal" is a remarkable early study in environmental psychology and the mechanisms of gang mentality that remains relevant after over two hundred years. In the tradition of the *moralische Erzählung* (moral tale or exemplary tale), the struggle between "virtue and vice" ends in the ultimate triumph of virtue, the free confession of the sublime criminal,[21] and his recognition of the social contract in spite of his mistreatment. On the other hand, the critical preoccupation with the role of the "variable conditions" of environment — the guilt of the state and local population in Schiller's Württemberg — in the predictable response of the "immutable structure of the human psyche" (see p. 40),[22] explodes the parameters of the moral or exemplary tale. At the time of the republication in 1792, Schiller also edited a collection based on François Gayot de Pitaval's anthology of crime stories with the telling subtitle, "As a Contribution to the History of Humankind,"[23] which along with Schiller's own "Criminal" and *The Spiritualist* has given Schiller the reputation as the founder of the German crime story[24] and as the first German author to fuse the realism of the crime story with the modern novella form.[25]

"Spiel des Schicksals. Ein Bruchstück einer wahren Geschichte" (1788–89, Game of Fate. A Fragment of a True Story) appeared in the January 1789 edition of Christoph Martin Wieland's journal *Der Teutsche Merkur* (The German Mercury) and then again with minor changes in the 1792 *Schiller's Short Prose Works.* During this same period, while Schiller also continued to struggle writing *The Spiritualist,* most of his energy was devoted to historical research for *Die Geschichte des Abfalls der vereinigten Niederlande von der Spanischen Regierung* (1788, The History of the Revolt of the United Netherlands from Spanish Rule,) and *Die Geschichte des Dreißigjährigen Krieges* (1791–92, The History of the Thirty Years' War). As the subtitle of "Game of Fate" implies — "A Fragment of a True Story" — Schiller's starting point is once again his own personal knowledge, the story of one of his godparents, General Philipp Friedrich Rieger, who spent four years locked in the Hohentwiel prison from 1762–66. Rieger, a talented but unscrupulous upstart, was imprisoned by his erstwhile friend Duke Karl Eugen of Württemberg on conspiracy charges, but after his release became the Commandant of the Hohenasperg prison just outside Ludwigsburg.

As was the case in "Criminal," Schiller focuses more on character study than on the fate mentioned in the title, which results in a biographical study and psychological profile that explains rather than portrays fate,[26] tracing the development from innate greatness and modesty to ruthless ambition and arrogance.[27] Aside from the story of Rieger, a second autobiographical thread runs through "Game of Fate," namely that of the pro-American poet and editor of the Stuttgart newspaper *Schubarts Deutsche Chronik,* Christian Friedrich Daniel Schubart (1739–91), who, unlike Rieger, and like the protagonist Aloysius von G***, actually did spend an entire decade in prison from 1777–87.[28]

Schubart, the father of Schiller's classmate Ludwig Schubart, served as a model for Schiller both as an author and as a character.[29] Schubart's "Zur Geschichte des menschlichen Herzens" (Toward the History of the Human Heart), the main source for Schiller's *The Robbers,* had appeared in Bathasar Haug's *Schwaebisches Magazin* in 1775.[30] In 1777, Schubart, already excommunicated, was subsequently imprisoned by Schiller's Duke Karl Eugen for ten years in the same Hohenasperg prison where the pardoned Rieger was then commandant, in part for his support of the American War of Independence, and in particular for his criticism of Karl Eugen's rumored sale of some 3000 Württembergian mercenaries to the British.[31] Facilitated by Commandant Rieger, Schiller and his school friend von Hoven illegally paid Schubart a visit in prison in November 1781, and Schiller took with him unpublished works by Schubart on his escape from Württemberg in September 1782, including Schubart's anti-feudal poem "Die Gruft der Fursten" (1780, The Crypt of Princes), the inspiration for Schiller's "Die schlimmen Monarchen" (1782, The Terrible Monarchs).[32] Schiller's portrayal of this contradictory character, Rieger, corroborates that of Schubart, who characterized his jailer Rieger as "a rare combination of manly greatness and childish pettiness, of the sublime and lowliness, from magnanimous goodness and destructive anger, capacity for mercy and revenge, for blazing fear of God and entirely unholy deeds."[33]

Schiller's portrayal of the fates of Rieger and Schubart has still further autobiographical overtones. Had he not succeeded in his escape from Württemberg, Schiller would very likely have landed in the same prison as Schubart. Later, in December 1788, Schubart's son, Ludwig, visited Schiller in Weimar, evidently inspiring Schiller to revisit fate under absolutism and Duke Karl Eugen in Württemberg, and the prison life of both his complicated godfather Rieger and his fellow political-literary rebel Schubart. The story appeared anonymously only three weeks later.

Schiller's interest in political conspiracy, first articulated in *Fiesko,* turned toward secret societies with his next projected drama *Friedrich Imhoff,* which never progressed beyond a plan. In a letter to Wilhelm Friedrich Hermann Reinwald of 1783, Schiller reported that he ordered books on "Jesuits, confessional conversion, bigotry, bizarre corruption of character, unfortunate victims of gambling."[34] This research appears to have found its expression in *Der Geisterseher. Aus den Memoires des Grafen von O*** (1786–89, The Spiritualist. From the Memoirs of the Count von O**). Here, Schiller consolidated his reputation as the author of political intrigue, a thematic leitmotif beginning with his earliest theoretical works and the early drama *Fiesko* and ending with his final drama fragment, *Demetrius* (1805).[35] *The Spiritualist,* Schiller's most popularly received prose work, appeared in his third journal *Thalia* in five installments from 1787 to 1789.[36] Inspired by the story of the con man Count Cagliostro (1743–95), the story is also informed by recent events such as Pope Clement XIV's disbanding of the Jesuits in 1773 and the plentiful contemporary conspiracy theories regarding secret societies' pursuit of political power. *The Spiritualist* appeared on the heels of two likely source publications of note, Elise von der Recke's *Nachricht von des berüchtigten Cagliostro Aufenthalt in Mitau* (1786, Report on the Infamous Cagliostro's Stay in Mitau) and an essay on the possibility of supernatural powers written by Prince Friedrich Heinrich Eugen of Württemberg.

As was the case with his first three original prose works, Schiller is able to draw on his oft-belittled personal experience. Schiller's close circle of acquaintances and his familiarity with the Württemberg court in particular inform the characters and situation from the outset. His frequent contact with Duke Karl Eugen and his family at the Karlsschule Academy from the age of fourteen to twenty-one made him intimately familiar with the daily comings and goings of the court, and at the same time his lower social status cast him early in the role of observer.[37] The likely inspiration for the tale was a response in defense of the possibility of supernatural powers written by Prince Friedrich Heinrich Eugen of Württemberg, the nephew of Schiller's own Duke Karl Eugen, like the Prince in Schiller's story, third in line to the throne, and thus without serious political aspirations.[38] Similarly, early in *The Spiritualist,* at a party on Brenta, a group of partygoers debate the reality of the spirit world, and the protagonist, the Prince, defends belief in the supernatural. Further description applies to Prince Friedrich in the first book: "He read a good deal, but indiscriminately; a neglected education and early military service meant that his mind was still immature. . . . He was a Protestant, like the rest of his family . . . As far as I know he had never become a Freemason." (NA 16:46; see p. 68). In "Book Two," the Count notices a change in the Prince that invokes the religious climate of Württemberg during Schiller's youth:

> This black nocturnal character dominated the whole of our Prince's youth; even from his games all joy was banished. All notions of religion had something fearful about them . . . And so there grew a silent resentment against it in his heart, forming . . . a resentment against a Lord for whom he felt in equal measure reverence and revulsion. (NA 16:103; see p. 108)

Schiller lends documentary-style appearance of veracity to the story through a series of authorial strategies. Changes of narrative perspective and disruptive factual commentary from the narrator, here in the form of footnotes, support the introductory statement that the story is based on facts. The ostensibly "true" story is attributed to a (fictitious) source, "the Memoirs of Count von O**," a device that reveals both the rhetorical nature as well as the insistence on the Schillerian "truth" *device* — as opposed to the mere inclusion of true materials — as relative to the socio-historical and psychological plausibility and validity of the conflict. Thus, although the story is by no means true as told, it is plausible and exhibits behavioral, moral, and philosophical truths about humanity, if in the story of a mostly fictional prince. At the same time, it is important to establish that, as was the case with the other original literary prose works, the fictional truth disembarks from a vortex of actual characters from recent history, preeminently, one whom Schiller knew personally.

As was the case with the earlier prose works, Schiller's first narrator begins with a brief foreword, conceding the fantastic nature of the tale, "I am going to tell you about a series of occurrences which many will find incredible,"[39] — but quickly employing the usual battery of truth claims in rapid succession, allusions to current affairs, invocation of possible witnesses, as well as a promise that even those who cannot understand the historical truth involved will see the human truth in the events described:

> that I largely witnessed with my own eyes. Those few who are familiar with a certain affair in the political world, if they should still be alive to read these papers, will find that they cast a welcome light on that matter, and even those others who lack this key to the story will perhaps find in it a significant contribution to the history of treachery and of the aberrations of the human spirit. They will be astonished at the *daring purposes* wickedness is capable of conceiving and pursuing, and they will be amazed at the extraordinary *means* which it contrives in order to achieve those aims. (see p. 68)[40]

Schiller ends the opening paragraph with yet another dramatic truth claim, invoking the de facto death of the narrator as guarantee for authenticity: "Truth pure and simple will guide my pen, for if these papers ever reach the public, I shall by then be no more and shall have nothing either to gain or to lose on account of what I have to report" (see p. 68).[41]

Driving the plot throughout is a series of attempts to manipulate perception of the truth, followed by partial uncovering of the "keys" to the truth behind deceptive "veils,"[42] followed by new stratagems designed to build upon the confused "truths" arrived at through a flawed dialectic process of truth-seeking. In the midst of this quest for truth, the Prince delivers a Schillerian thesis on the inscrutable nature of truth itself, without ever abandoning the method of the pursuit, namely, to seek it through "reason and the eternal laws of nature" (see p. 100),[43] and disembarking from an inquiry into the mechanisms of the human psyche: "Even if I cannot see his reasons, does that mean that he does not have them?" (see p. 100)[44] The Prince's low expectations for his prison interrogation of the conjurer — "let me assume for the moment that the things he told us really happened"[45] — foreshadow the dubious results: "I admit that I do not yet fully understand the workings of his deception" (see p. 100).[46] Nor will he. Contrasting drama to prose, Schiller's English lord invokes drama tradition to question the boundaries of the plausible: "Really, Your Highness, I don't think that even a playwright worried about his three Aristotelian unities would have crammed so much action into a single interval, or expected his audience to suspend their disbelief so completely" (see p. 102).[47] Echoing the theoretical introductions of "A Magnanimous Act" and "Criminal," Schiller's Prince concedes that dramatic effect (more than prose) is more likely to blur the lines between objective analysis and subjective emotion: "I have seen Garrick play Richard the Third — And were we cold and detached enough at that moment to be totally unbiased observers? Could we have put this man's [the Sicilian's] passions to the test, when we were so overwhelmed by our own?" (see p. 104–5).[48]

Schiller's adherence to his position that literary prose must stem from plausible truth, ergo in some part from personal experience, or in his case, personal experience and the experiences of the acquaintances of his inner circle, is remarkable in its consistency. Of the original prose works, three moral tales that belong to the early history of the German novella and a novel fragment (not a novel) that remains a frame novella,[49] two are based closely on the true-life experiences of relatives of two of his most intimate acquaintances, while the third features a main character whose social and personal history so closely parallels those of his acquaintance, Prince Friedrich Heinrich Eugen of Württemberg, that it is reasonable to assert that the story is based to some extent on his character. In the rare cases where personal experience is not the source for Schiller's prose works — in the adaptations and historical anecdotes — the same interest in the plausibility of character and situation overrides. In the final paragraph of his Diderot adaptation, "Ein merkwürdiges Beispiel einer weiblichen Rache" (1785, A Remarkable Example of Female Revenge), Schiller explains his attraction to the plot in familiar terms, praising Diderot's original for "the bold novelty of the intrigue" and the "unmistakable truth of the narrative" (see p. 37).[50]

Schiller's preferred prose point of departure, first-hand accounts or actual experience, fairly dictated that his production be limited to the few tales discussed here. As a result, Schiller's literary prose is more specifically related to contemporary occurrences and culture than his works in other genres. In addition to his perceived lack of personal experience, Schiller was clearly uncomfortable with the transparency of his own prose: "where one coolly and consciously follows every step the writer takes in the human heart."[51] By the time Schiller's struggle with *The Spiritualist* began, literary prose had become a menial task, and the novelist the unloved "half-brother of the poet,"[52] as he complained to his fiancée Charlotte von Lengefeld and her sister Caroline on 20 November 1788: "I long for the time when I can choose my work with more consideration for my actual feelings."[53] Nonetheless, Schiller's role in the evolution of the German novella from the "playfulness of Boccacio"[54] and from Diderot's parody of Parisian decadence to tragic moral studies is unmistakable, and the history of German novella classics bears out a Schillerian heritage in the most prominent genre-defining conventions,[55] though perhaps nowhere more obviously than in the thematic common ground of remarkable truth on the outer edge of plausibility, but within the realm of personal experience — a step toward the "uncanny" and the "anthropological fantastic."[56] Schiller's adherence to his own verisimilitude doctrine is significant for the truth and reality aspect, as well as the psychological realism that informed the nascent German novella. His pursuit of unusual occurrences — (Goethe's later "unerhörte Begebenheit") — that demonstrated the "truths that he found it in his interest to reveal to us" (see p. 100),[57] is guided by the final nexus of very real considerations that converge in all of his novellas, "the problem of free will, and behind the psychological question . . . the ethical, behind the social question the existential one," as Bernhard Zeller described it (Zeller, 64). The psychological realism of Schiller's "Criminal,"[58] characteristic of Schiller's short prose works in general, is rooted in the plausibility of real characters in realistic, extreme, and current situations. The same verisimilitude doctrine can be argued of the common novella feature of artificially reinforcing the historical urgency of the tale by disguising names and places through omission, or, conversely, for reinforcing historical credibility by providing actual names, dates, places, and historical events.

"A true story" ("Criminal"), "a fragment of a true story" ("Game of Fate") the "truth pure and simple," even in what is largely a "series of fabrications" (*Spiritualist*): Schiller's prose consistently comprises studies of remarkable or aberrant behaviors exemplary for their singular focus and articulation of plausible "character and situation" (Zeller, 69). Prefiguring Poe, Dostoyevsky, and 200 years of detective and mystery authors, Schiller and his narrators practice analytical empiricism on the edge of the fantastic, where "the immutable structure of the human psyche"[59] confronts the worst of the "variable conditions that externally determine the state of the psyche" (see p. 40).[60] It is precisely the overriding focus on the Schillerian idea of "realism and truth" (Zeller, 51) in the portrayal of human nature, plausibility, and universality of the reaction of character to situation that has been largely ignored in the scholarly pursuit of German Classicism and classicity. When legend would have it that German Classicism was at the apex of its flight from reality toward the wooden pursuit of beautiful form, Schiller wrote to Goethe on 7 July 1797 that the art term *Schönheit* (beauty) itself had become such a hackneyed falsification that it would serve art well to replace it entirely with *Wahrheit* (truth) (NA 29:98). Hardly surprising then that Schiller's main characters expose "inner," "philosophical and artistic truth," in the most plausible extreme; criminals, con men, and despots, or remarkably morally resolute heroes situated in apparent ethical dead-ends, often at the hands of the former. Criminal, victim, or hero in the extreme, but real, intersections of character and situation in life on earth — they were "human being[s] like we are" (see p. 40).[61] On the eve of the 250th anniversary of his birth (1759–2009), Schiller's original prose works are still in this sense "true stories," or, in some cases, only the most extreme "fragments of true stories" (if no longer "from most recent history").

California State University Long Beach

Notes

The function of "truth" in Schiller's literary prose works is a recurring theme in an earlier article: Jeffrey L. High, "The Author of Literary Prose," in *Friedrich Schiller. Playwright, Poet, Philosopher, Historian,* ed. Paul Kerry (Oxford: Peter Lang, 2007), 117–51.

[1] "Seine ganze Erzählung ist offenbar nichts als eine Reihe von Erfindungen, um die wenigen Wahrheiten aneinander zu hängen, die er uns preiszugeben für gut fand." *Schillers Werke. Nationalausgabe,* ed. Julius Petersen et al. (Weimar: Herrman Böhlaus Nachfolger, 1943ff.), 16:91–92. Subsequent citations as "NA" with volume and page number.

[2] "Der epische Dichter reicht mit der Welt, die er in sich hat nicht aus, er muß in keinem gemeinen Grad mit der Welt außer ihm bekannt und bewandert sein. Dies ist was mir fehlt, aber auch alles wie ich glaube" (NA 26:113).

[3] Letter to Caroline von Beulwitz of 10 [and 11] December 1788: ". . . der Vorzug der *Wahrheit,* den die Geschichte vor dem Roman voraushat, könnte sie schon allein über ihn erheben. Es fragt sich nun ob die *innre Wahrheit,* die ich die philosophische und Kunstwahrheit nennen will, und welche in ihrer ganzen Fülle im Roman oder in einer andern poëtischen Darstellung herrschen muß, nicht eben soviel Werth hat als die historische. Daß ein Mensch in *solchen* Lagen *so* empfindet, handelt, und sich ausdrückt ist ein großes wichtiges Factum für den Menschen; und das muß der Dramatische oder Romandichter leisten. Die innre Uebereinstimmung die Wahrheit wird gefühlt und eingestanden, ohne daß die Begebenheit wirklich vorgefallen seyn muß. Der Nutzen ist unverkennbar. Man lernt auf diesem Weg den *Menschen* und nicht *den* Menschen kennen, die Gattung und nicht das sich so leichtverlierende Individuum" (NA 25:154). Translation by Gail Hart.

[4] "Die psychologisch-kausalistische Motivation." Herbert G. Göpfert in Friedrich Schiller, *Gesamtausgabe,* ed. Herbert G. Göpfert (Munich: Deutscher Taschenbuch Verlag, 1966), vol. 16: *Erzählungen,* 203.

[5] "Menschenvernunft und ewige Naturordnug" (NA 16:91).

[6] "in der unveränderlichen Struktur der menschlichen Seele" (NA 16:9).

[7] "Mensch [. . .] wie wir" (NA 16:8).

[8] "Die Erzählungen heben fast durchwegs mit einer Einleitung an, die sich deutlich von der eigentlichen Geschichte trennen lässt. Diese Einleitungen liessen sich unterdrücken, ohne dass die Geschichte dadurch unverständlich würde." Heinrich Keller, *Schillers Prosa* (Winterthur: Keller, 1965), 5.

[9] "Wer weiß, ob nicht eben diese gekünstelte Existenz in einer idealischen Welt unsre Existenz in der wirklichen untergräbt? Wir schweben hier gleichsam um die zwei äußersten Enden der Moralität, Engel und Teufel, und die Mitte — den Menschen — lassen wir liegen" (NA 16:3).

[10] *Kleinere prosaische Schriften von Schiller* (Leipzig: Crusius, 1792).

[11] *Geschichte eines Räubers,* in Jakob Friedrich Abel, *Sammlung und Erklärung merkwürdiger Erscheinungen aus dem menschlichen Leben* (Stuttgart: Erhard, 1787), 2:1–86.

[12] Benno von Wiese, "Friedrich Schiller, Der Verbrecher aus verlorener Ehre," in *Die deutsche Novelle von Goethe bis Kafka* (Düsseldorf: August Bagel, 1967), 1:33–46, here 33.

[13] See Helmut Koopmann, "Schillers Erzählungen," in *Schiller-Handbuch,* ed. Helmut Koopmann (Stuttgart: Kröner, 1998), 703.

[14] "unsre Phantasie wird entzündet; unser Herz bleibt kalt" (NA 16:3).

[15] "widriger Kontrast der heftigen Gemütsbewegung des handelnden Menschen und der ruhigen Stimmung des Lesers" (NA 16:8).

[16] "Trieben und Neigungen" (NA 16:7).

[17] "hinreißenden Vortrag" (NA 16:8).

[18] "die Leichenöffnung seines Lasters" (NA 16:9).

[19] "Schreiben Sie es Ihrem Fürsten, wie Sie mich fanden und daß ich selbst aus freier Wahl mein Verräter war [. . .] bitten Sie für mich, alter Mann, und lassen Sie dann auf Ihren Bericht eine Träne fallen: Ich bin der Sonnenwirt" (NA 16:29).

[20] Schiller later acknowledged the similarity to Karl Philipp Moritz's psychological novel *Anton Reiser.*

[21] The recognition of the law, moral or civic, parallels Schiller's description of *Die Räuber* in his foreword of 1781 ("Vorrede zur ersten Auflage"): "Der Verirrte tritt wieder in das Gelaise der Geseze. Die Tugend geht siegend davon" (NA 3:8).

[22] "in der *unveränderlichen* Struktur der menschlichen Seele, und in den *veränderlichen* Bedingungen, welche sie von außen bestimmen" (NA 16:9).

[23] "als ein Beitrag zur Geschichte der Menscheit." Friedrich Schiller, ed., *Merkwürdige Rechtsfälle als ein Beitrag zur Geschichte der Menscheit. Nach dem französischen Werke des Pitaval durch mehrere Verfasser ausgearbeitet,* 4 parts (Leipzig: Crusius, 1792–95).

[24] Friedrich Schiller, *Gesamtausgabe,* ed. Herbert G. Göpfert (Munich: Deutscher Taschenbuch Verlag, 1966), 7, 994.

[25] Rainer Schönhaar, *Novelle und Kriminalschema. Ein Strukturmodell deutscher Erzählkunst um 1800* (Bad Homburg: Gehlen, 1969), 78.

[26] Helmut Koopmann, *Friedrich Schiller I: 1759–1794* (Stuttgart: Metzler, 1966), 66.

[27] Koopmann 1998, 705.

[28] See Benno von Wiese, *Friedrich Schiller* (Stuttgart: Metzler, 1959), 300–301.

[29] See Ursula Wertheim, "Der amerikanische Unabhängigkeitskampf im Spiegel der zeitgenösischen deutschen Literatur," in *Deutschlands literarisches Amerikabild,* ed. Alexander Ritter (Hildesheim: Georg Olms, 1977), 50–91, here 63–70.

[30] See Gerhard Kluge, "Kommentar," in *Friedrich Schiller, Werke und Briefe in zwölf Bänden,* ed. Gerhard Kluge (Frankfurt am Main: Deutscher Klassiker Verlag, 1988), II: *Dramen I* (1988), 903.

[31] Between 1774 and 1777, Schubart published some 185 news items and commentaries on the American War of Independence, overwhelmingly anti-tyrannical in tone. See Jeffrey L. High, "Edinburgh — Williamsburg — Ludwigsburg: From Teaching Jefferson and Schiller Scottish Enlightenment Happiness to the 'American War' and *Don Karlos,*" in *Jahrbuch für internationale Germanistik* (Bern: Peter Lang, 2005), 281–314, here 303.

[32] In 1782, still in prison, Schubart wrote the poem "To Schiller" ("An Schiller"), in which Schiller appears as an avenging angel of the politically oppressed. *C. F. D. Schubarts, des Patrioten, gesammelte Schriften und Schicksale,* vol. 4, *C. F. D. Schubarts sämmtliche Gedichte,* vol. 2 (Stuttgart: Scheible, 1839), 62–64. On 23 September

1782, during his escape from Württemberg, Schiller read Schubart's unpublished poems, likely written in prison, to his friend Andreas Streicher.

[33] "eine seltene Mischung von männlicher Größe und kindischer Kleinheit, von Erhabenheit und Niedrigkeit, von menschenbeglückender Güte und Zerstörungsgrimm, von Fähigkeit des Erbarmens und Rachsucht, von hellodernder Gottesfurcht und ganz ungottseligen Taten." Cited as in *Der Verbrecher aus verlorener Ehre und andere Erzählungen,* mit einem Nachwort von Bernhard Zeller (Stuttgart: Reclam, 1964), 67. Subsequent citations as "Zeller" with page number.

[34] "über Jesuiten, Religionsveränderungen, Bigottismus, seltne Verderbnisse des Charakters, unglückliche Opfer des Spiels." *Der Geisterseher,* in *Hauptwerke der deutschen Literatur, Einzeldarstellungen und Interpretationen,* ed. Manfred Kluge and Rudolf Radler (Munich: Kindler, 1974), 275.

[35] Gerhard Storz, *Der Dichter Friedrich Schiller* (Stuttgart: Klett, 1959), 178–96.

[36] Koopmann 1966, 213.

[37] Robert Minder, "Schiller, Schwaben, Frankreich und die Herrlichkeit der Väter," in *Schiller. Reden im Gedenkjahr 1959* (Stuttgart: Klett, 1961), 170–200, here 173.

[38] See Kindler 275.

[39] "Ich erzähle eine Begebenheit, die vielen unglaublich scheinen wird" (NA 16:45).

[40] "von der ich großenteils selbst Augenzeuge war. Den wenigen, welche von einem gewissen politischen Vorfalle unterrichtet sind, wird sie — wenn anders diese Blätter sie noch am Leben finden — einen willkommenen Aufschluß darüber geben; und auch ohne diesen Schlüssel wird sie den übrigen, als ein Beitrag zur Geschichte des Betrugs und der Verirrungen des menschlichen Geistes, vielleicht wichtig sein. Man wird über die Kühnheit des Zwecks erstaunen, den die Bosheit zu entwerfen und zu verfolgen imstande ist; man wird über die Seltsamkeit der Mittel erstaunen, die sie aufzubieten vermag, um sich dieses Zwecks zu versichern" (NA 16:45).

[41] "Reine, strenge Wahrheit wird meine Feder leiten; denn wenn diese Blätter in die Welt treten, bin ich nicht mehr und werde durch den Bericht, den ich abstatte, weder zu gewinnen noch zu verlieren haben" (NA 16:45).

[42] Dennis Mahoney notes that Schiller repeatedly employs the terms "Schlüssel" (key) and "Decke" (veil, cover) in the pursuit of truth in *The Spiritualist* (see p. 236).

[43] "Menschenvernunft und ewige Naturordnung" (NA 16:99).

[44] "Wenn ich diese Gründe auch nicht einsehe, soll er sie deswegen weniger haben?" (NA 16:91).

[45] "lassen Sie mich einstweilen annehmen, daß die erzählte Begebenheit sich wirklich ereignet habe" (NA 16:91).

[46] "Ich gestehe, daß ich das ganze Gewebe seines Betrugs noch nicht ganz durchschaue" (NA 16:91).

[47] "Wahrlich, gnädigster Herr, selbst nicht einmal ein dramatischer Schriftsteller, der um die unerbittlichen drei Einheiten seines Aristoteles verlegen war, würde einem Zwischenakt soviel Handlung aufgelastet, noch seinem Parterre einen so starken Glauben zugemutet haben" (NA 16:94).

[48] "Ich habe Richard den Dritten von Garrick gesehen — Und waren wir in diesem Augenblick kalt und müßig genug, um unbefangene Beobachter abzugeben? Konnten wir den Affekt dieses Menschen prüfen, da uns der unsrige übermeisterte?" (NA 16:98).

[49] "Although *Der Geisterseher* is commonly referred to as a novel or novel-fragment, it will in fact never be finished, and remains a frame novella comprising shorter novellas, each told by a new narrator. The central novella in Book One of the conned noble family is introduced with the familiar critical term 'unusual occurrence' and is peppered with phrases like 'unexpected turn.'"

[50] "die kühne Neuheit dieser Intrige" and "unverkennbare Wahrheit der Schilderung" (NA 16:223–24).

[51] Schiller's letter to Caroline von Beulwitz and Charlotte von Lengefeld of 12 February 1789: "wo man jedem Schritt, den der Dichter im menschlichem Herzen tut ruhig und aufmerksam nachgeht" (NA 25:202).

[52] "Halbbruder des Dichters." In *Ueber naïve und sentimentalische Dichtung* (NA 20:462). See Koopmann 1998, 699.

[53] "Ich sehe mit Sehnsucht der Epoche entgegen, wo ich meine Beschäftigungen für mein Gefühl besser wählen kann" (NA 25:141).

[54] Johannes Klein, *Geschichte der deutschen Novelle von Goethe bis zur Gegenwart* (Wiesbaden: Franz Steiner Verlag, 1956), 34.

[55] See "Introduction" (p. 3–4).

[56] Markus Müller, "Reconsidering the Fantastic: An Anthropological Approach," *Anthropoetics* II, 2 (January 1997).

[57] "wenigen Wahrheiten aneinander zu hängen, die er uns preiszugeben für gut fand" (NA 16:91–92).

[58] Klein 33.

[59] "der *unveränderlichen* Struktur der menschlichen Seele" (NA 16:9).

[60] "*veränderlichen* Bedingungen, welche sie von außen bestimmen" (NA 16:9).

[61] "Mensch[en] war[en] wie wir" (NA 16:8).

10: Playing with the Rules: Schiller's Experiments in Short Prose Fiction, 1782–1789

Nicholas Martin

SCHILLER'S CAREER AS A WRITER OF PROSE FICTION was short lived. It lasted only seven years, from 1782 (when he was twenty-two years of age) until 1789. Schiller's short stories of this period have begun to attract significant critical attention in recent years.[1] However, even the texts that are today considered to be Schiller's major prose-writing achievements of the 1780s, notably "Der Verbrecher aus verlorener Ehre" (1786, The Criminal of Lost Honor) and *Der Geisterseher* (1786–89, The Spiritualist), remain to a large extent overshadowed by his simultaneous achievements as a dramatist and lyric poet.[2] The period during which Schiller composed all of his published prose fiction coincided with the writing of his important early dramas *Die Räuber* (1781, The Robbers), *Die Verschwörung des Fiesko zu Genua* (1782–83, The Conspiracy of Fiesco at Genoa), *Kabale und Liebe* (1782–84, Intrigue and Love), and *Don Karlos* (1783–87).

The overshadowing of Schiller's prose writing by his dramas is truer still in the case of his shortest short stories, which will be the focus of this essay: "Eine großmütige Handlung aus der neusten Geschichte" (1782, A Magnanimous Act from Most Recent History); "Herzog von Alba bey einem Frühstück auf dem Schlosse zu Rudolstadt. Im Jahr 1547" (1788, Duke Alba's Breakfast at Rudolstadt Castle in the Year 1547); and "Spiel des Schicksals. Ein Bruchstück einer wahren Geschichte" (1789, Game of Fate. A Fragment of a True Story).

The relatively low esteem in which Schiller's short stories are still held is attributable, at least in part, to the brevity of his career as prose writer, to the relatively meager output (in terms of quantity) of this career, as well as to Schiller's later, disparaging remarks on his own prose fiction in particular, and on the genre in general. He dismissed the Alba anecdote, for example, as something "of little consequence,"[3] and he appears to have regarded even the more substantial and far superior story, "Game of Fate," as "insignificant."[4] More damning still, as far as the reputation of his prose fiction is concerned, is Schiller's remark in *Über naïve und sentimentalische Dichtung*

(1795–96, On Naïve and Sentimental Poetry) that the novelist is a mere "half-brother of the poet."[5]

Schiller's short stories of the 1780s are at once late variants on a long-established tradition of prose fiction writing in eighteenth-century Germany and fledgling experiments in what was to become the peculiarly German tradition of the novella from Goethe to Kafka and beyond. While it did not enjoy anything like the prestige of (classical) drama in eighteenth-century Germany, the epic genre had nevertheless acquired a degree of respectability, thanks in large measure to the writings and journals of Gottsched, Wieland, and others. Gottsched's weekly journals of the 1720s owed much, in their turn, to English models and precursors such as Addison and Steele's *Spectator* and *Tatler*. Their primary function was educative, publishing short stories that made tangible the abstract maxims contained in the more theoretical contributions to the journals and weeklies in question.[6]

From the middle of the eighteenth century, however, and largely under the influence of French writers such as Jean François Marmontel, whose *Contes moraux* (*Moral Tales*) appeared from 1755 onwards in the journal *Mercure de France,* a new type of prose writing began to emerge on the German literary scene — the *Moralische Erzählung* (moral tale). Marmontel's successful recipe was to mix entertaining "human interest" stories with morally improving maxims and warnings. In Germany this recipe was imitated, with considerable popular success, in the 1770s and 1780s in the satirical prose writings of Johann Carl Wezel (1777–78), the short texts by Johann Heinrich Merck, which were published from the late 1770s in Wieland's *Der Teutsche Merkur,* and in prose fiction published by Sophie von La Roche and Christian Lebrecht Heyne in the early 1780s. In the words of Jürgen Jacobs:

> Marmontel, and his many later German imitators, are concerned above all with feminine virtue, false ambition and the mistakes made by parents when raising children. Although the short stories often deal with members of the nobility, they nevertheless preach the burgherly moral virtues of family values, thrift, duty, and the cult of sensibility.[7]

While the young Schiller was aware of these developments and acutely conscious of the morally didactic animus of contemporary prose fiction, a more immediate, formative influence on the themes of his prose writing was the work of Christian Garve, to which he had been introduced by his Karlsschule professor and mentor, Jakob Friedrich Abel. In his *Gedanken über das Interessirende* (1779, Thoughts on What Interests Us), Garve sets out a theory of intellectual perception based on the division and co-existence in man of mind (or soul) and body. An individual's interest is engaged, Garve argues, when his sensuous or intellectual curiosity is aroused or, ideally, when both are aroused simultaneously. Garve's conviction that sensuous and moral drives guide man in equal measure lead him to demand that, if literature is seriously to engage the interest of the reading public, it must shape and present gripping stories taken from real life. This belief that only a careful examination of the interaction of body and soul can reveal the true workings of an individual is precisely the anthropological and psychological perspective of the late Enlightenment that will govern Schiller's experiments in short prose fiction.[8]

Equally powerful influences on the concerns and methods adopted by Schiller in his short prose fiction, with Abel once again acting as mediator, were the creative reworkings of psychological and criminal case studies in Karl Philipp Moritz's *Magazin zur Erfahrungsseelenkunde* (1783–93, Journal for Psychological Case Studies) and the fourteen volumes of August Gottlieb Meißner's *Skizzen,* published between 1778 and 1796.[9] When discussing plans for a new journal with Christian Gottfried Körner in 1788, for example, Schiller declared that material similar to the dialogues in Meißner ("Meissnerische Dialoge") should be included in the new publication.[10] Meißner's and Moritz's collections had begun to move away from the concerns of the traditional "moral short story." Admittedly, the representations of characters' passions and drives remained largely faithful to the Enlightenment aspiration of educating the reader, but these representations or fictional reworkings of actual events tended to privilege the psychological dimension of their subjects over the moral.[11] It was this psychological dimension, and the human and narrative possibilities it opened up, which particularly appealed to the young Schiller, who was simultaneously investigating the division and co-existence in man of mind (or soul) and body in his medical studies.[12]

The prose fiction published by Meißner and Moritz had begun to problematize the notion of moral education. While not questioning its inherent value, texts published in their collections had started to explore the limits or efficacy of an individual's moral education, once s/he is placed in an extreme situation. Schiller was to take up and pursue this type of exploration in his short stories of the 1780s by confronting "enlightened," burgherly characters with extreme situations and cruel blows of fate in order to test their psychological (and moral) resilience. Much like his early dramas, Schiller's short stories become a creative psychological laboratory, in which the limits of human autonomy and freedom of action — cherished tenets of Enlightenment — are tested by exposing a fictional(ized) character to inner and/or outer crises.[13]

Theoretical considerations are naturally important when interpreting Schiller's short stories, as is an awareness of the literary-historical context in which he was writing. However, we must not overlook the practical, personal context. Schiller did not write in an ethereal realm, free of mundane concerns. For most of his career he was driven by the urgent need to earn a living from his writing. As he wrote to Körner in 1788: "I must make a *living* from *writing* and be on the look-out for things that will be *lucrative*."[14] Peter-André Alt's description of the type of contribution Schiller needed for his journal (*Rheinische*) *Thalia*, launched in 1784, and of the (economic) motives underlying this need, applies equally well to the motivation behind all of Schiller's prose fiction in the period under review here (1782–89): "[Schiller's] *Thalia* required contributions that would grip the reader's interest and satisfy the entertainment needs of as wide a circle as possible. This meant that abstract theoretical treatises as well as dry, didactic writing had to be excluded. The urgent need was to maximize the journal's appeal by publishing short, pithy, and exciting texts."[15]

Schiller makes this imperative clear in the foreword to *Thalia*. Of the eight types of material he lists as desirable for inclusion in the journal, the first is headed "Portraits of Remarkable People and Actions."[16] Under this heading Schiller states that he wishes to include "newly discovered cogs in the unfathomable clockwork mechanism of the soul." (This is already an implicit subversion of the Enlightenment notion of the "divine watchmaker.") Schiller continues: "individual phenomena which resolve themselves as a curious improvement or deterioration are, I confess, more important [to me] than the dead treasures in the antiquarian's cabinet or a newly discovered neighbour of Saturn."[17]

The first of Schiller's short stories to be published, "A Magnanimous Act from Most Recent History," appeared in October 1782 in the second number of the journal *Wirtembergisches Repertorium der Litteratur*, which was edited by Schiller himself, his Karlsschule professor Jakob Friedrich Abel, and his schoolfriends Johann Wilhelm Petersen and Johann Jakob Atzel. The first two numbers appeared before Schiller's flight from Württemberg, and he was the major contributor to both. It seems likely that he wrote "A Magnanimous Act from Most Recent History" during the summer of 1782.[18] The story is so short — barely four pages long in the edition cited here — that it is almost an anecdote. Indeed, it is referred to as such at the beginning of the second paragraph (NA 16:3; see p. 9). The tale deals with the love of two brothers for the same woman, the decisions and courses of action of these three characters as well as the catastrophic consequences for all three of them of their respective decisions and actions.

The story is framed in the style of a contemporary morality tale, though Schiller is at pains both in the title and in his opening, theoretical address to the reader to stress that the story is true: "The present anecdote of two Germans — which I write with both pride and happiness — has an indisputable merit: *it is true.* I hope that it will leave my readers warmer than all of Richardson's novels about Grandison and Pamela."[19] Schiller's claim that the story is true, and the fact that he makes little attempt to disguise the real identities of his characters, make it relatively easy to identify the story's historical basis. It is based on the lives of Friedrich and Ludwig von Wurmb, the brothers of Schiller's future mother-in-law, Luise von Lengefeld. The woman to whom they were both attracted, initially without each other's knowledge, was Christiane von Werthern, a friend of Henriette von Wolzogen's, the mother of Schiller's schoolfriend and future brother-in-law, Wilhelm von Wolzogen. According to Alt, Henriette von Wolzogen — who harbored the fugitive Schiller in Bauerbach during his flight from Württemberg in 1782 — had heard Christiane von Werthern's deathbed confession, which forms the ironic climax to the story, and later confided it to Schiller.[20]

The plot of this very short story is quickly summarized. As already indicated, it deals with the love of two brothers, the "Barons von Wrmb." for the same young woman, "Fräulein von Wrthr." Each brother is initially unaware that the other is also in love with the woman, and she chooses not to enlighten either of them on this score. When the truth emerges, the elder brother performs the first "magnanimous act" of the tale by leaving Germany for Holland. However, he is unable to deal with the pain of separation, withers and almost dies. He returns to Germany in a precarious state of health, collapsing into the arms of his beloved. At this point the second "magnanimous act" occurs. The younger brother sacrifices himself, and his love for the woman, by going to live in self-imposed exile in Batavia in the East Indies, where, as he writes in a letter to his brother, he vows to start a new life despite the pain of separation that he is now experiencing in his turn. The elder brother marries the young woman but, after just one year of what in light of later revelations is ironically termed "the most blissful of marriages" (see p. 11)[21] the woman falls terminally ill. On her deathbed, in what is arguably the third "magnanimous act" of the tale (at least toward the reader) she confesses to her dearest friend — presumably, Henriette von Wolzogen — that she had always felt a stronger love for the younger brother, the one who had fled to the East Indies.

Although "A Magnanimous Act from Most Recent History" is constructed and narrated in the manner of a conventional "moral short story," by its end no unambiguous, improving moral has emerged. The young woman's deathbed confession is related without comment, and it is left up to the reader to draw her/his own conclusions from the three "magnanimous acts" which frame the tale. In the words of Jeffrey L. High: "The painful irony of the lady's deathbed confession is typical of the particular anti-idealist tendency of Schiller's prose works. Here, three virtuous acts of Enlightenment morality vie for the reader's awe, and nobody wins but the reader."[22] A number of possible conclusions suggest themselves, all of which point to genuine skepticism on Schiller's part concerning the practical consequences of self-denying moral acts. The younger brother's "magnanimous act" — removing himself to the East Indies — is seen not only to deepen his own misery but also, arguably, to hasten the young woman's death. His "magnanimity" is, in fact, a disastrous and self-defeating repression of his emotions. The attitude of the young woman is also implicitly criticized. By withholding her true feelings until the end, seemingly to avoid interfering in the brothers' magnanimity toward each other, she appears to have denied herself, quite literally, a life-saving opportunity to make herself and at least one of the brothers genuinely happy. An element of social criticism can also be detected here. As Gert Vonhoff has suggested, the woman's submissiveness and quiescence is a product of the contemporary social order, which assigned to women the role of helpless victims.[23]

The psychologically gripping, yet, in conventional didactic terms, negative and unsatisfactory ending of this "moral short story" indicates the extent to which Schiller is here deliberately playing with and subverting traditional expectations of the genre in order to reveal its shortcomings in terms of narrative perspective as well as its underlying ideological flaws. As Ulrike Rainer has commented on the ending of "A Magnanimous Act from Most Recent History": "This 'moral' short story reveals itself on closer inspection to be highly questionable. Perhaps it does not leave the reader 'warmer' than 'all the volumes of [Richardson's] *Grandison* and *Pamela*' but s/he will certainly feel more unsettled and more reflective."[24]

Of the three short stories under discussion here, "The Duke of Alba's Breakfast at Rudolstadt Castle in the Year 1547," first published in October 1788 in *Der Teutsche Merkur,* is the slightest, both in terms of its length and its significance — as either a short story in its own right or as part of the larger story of Schiller's development as a writer of prose fiction. The text which, like "A Magnanimous Act from Most Recent History," is characterized in the opening lines as an "anecdote," was probably inspired by Schiller's visit, together with Wilhelm von Wolzogen and the Lengefeld sisters, to Rudolstadt Castle on July 7, 1788. The text can also be read in the context of Schiller's intensive engagement at this time with the history of Imperial Spain in the sixteenth century, as seen above all in his *Geschichte des Abfalls der vereinigten Niederlande von der spanischen Regierung* (Revolt of the Netherlands), published in the same year (1788). Schiller's source, which is also referred to in the opening paragraph, was a chronicle of 1670 by the Thuringian theologian Söffing, which Schiller had consulted in the library of a Rudolstadt privy councilor. Schiller's text presents a character portrait of Countess von Schwarzburg. In 1547, during the brief Schmalkaldic War between the forces of Emperor Charles V and those of the Schmalkaldic League of Protestant German princes, the courageous Thuringian countess prevented Spanish troops from plundering her land and her subjects' property by holding hostage in her castle the commander of the Spanish army, the legendary Duke of Alba, and threatening to kill him, until she received assurances that his soldiers would return any stolen property and leave peacefully.

"Duke Alba's Breakfast at Rudolstadt Castle in the Year 1547" stands out among Schiller's prose fiction of the 1780s, precisely because it is such an unremarkable text. However, as Alt has pointed out, the story is perhaps worthy of a footnote in the history of German prose fiction writing. According to Alt, it anticipates in some respects the type of anecdotal short story that would be cultivated and developed later by Heinrich von Kleist, which is characterized by tension and terseness, aimed at maximizing the reader's sense of surprise.[25] The surprise in Schiller's text, for Duke Alba and for the reader, is that breakfast should turn into a matter of life and death. None the less "Duke Alba's Breakfast at Rudolstadt Castle in the Year 1547" remains little more than an uplifting anecdote, with a straightforward moral message. Perhaps for this reason it is slightly disappointing because, unlike Schiller's other prose fiction of the 1780s, it does not play with or challenge the rules of the sub-genre of the morality tale. As we have already seen, Schiller himself thought the tale to be "of little consequence," though it is unclear whether this was a judgment on the text's literary shortcomings or on the fact that it was conceived, at least in part, as a eulogy to the ruling house of Thuringia by way of praising a famous ancestor, a motive which Schiller later came to regret.[26]

The story "Game of Fate" (Spiel des Schicksals), which was published anonymously in the January 1789 number of *Der Teutsche Merkur,* is of a different order of magnitude to the two texts discussed thus far, in terms of both its length (it occupies some twenty pages in the edition cited here) and its literary quality. It is also the only one of these three texts which Schiller chose to re-publish in his collection *Kleinere prosaische Schriften* (Schiller's Short Prose Works) of 1792, which would tend to confirm that the author himself held "Game of Fate" in relatively high regard, despite that negative remark to his future wife quoted above.[27] Like the two earlier texts it rests on the twin foundations of (claimed) authenticity and a psychological examination of characters *in extremis.* However, and this makes comparison with the other two texts invidious perhaps, in "Game of Fate" Schiller allows himself far more space in which explore the psychological dimension. Specifically, he gives himself more scope to investigate how characters' behavior is conditioned by the socio-political structures within which they are forced to live, and how one character in particular behaves when he suffers a sudden reversal of fortune and finds himself in an unaccustomed, extreme situation.

The text relates the story of Aloysius von G***, a talented member of the middle classes, who serves with distinction in the army and whose potential is soon noticed by the Prince. G***'s character is impetuous, fiery and stubborn. Not unlike the Prince, G*** possesses an element of grandeur and majesty, tempered by a degree of humility. Under the Prince's affectionate patronage G*** enjoys a meteoric career and by the age of twenty-two he is effectively in control of most of the affairs of state. The Prince is more than happy to delegate his authority to his faithful underling, so that he can enjoy more aristocratic pursuits. Meanwhile, G***'s now more or less unfettered power causes his behavior to become increasingly harsh, arbitrary and contrary. In his lust for and enjoyment of power, G*** is shown to be deeply capricious. He is capable of acts of both extraordinary kindness and vicious revenge. G*** is now no longer the Prince's friend, merely his very able chief functionary. Joseph Martinengo, a Piedmontese count, becomes one of G***'s numerous enemies. G***, who appointed Martinengo, fails to notice the threat posed by the seemingly mild-mannered and submissive count, while Martinengo makes himself invaluable by encouraging the Prince's excesses, only to save him repeatedly from embarrassment.

Martinengo plots G***'s downfall. Martinengo succeeds in undermining G*** by showing the Prince real letters (or perhaps falsely concocted ones) from G*** to a rival court, which "prove" the chief minister's unpardonable treachery. Martinengo has G*** humiliatingly arrested without charge at the parade ground, demanding his sword and badges of rank in front of five hundred silent onlookers. G*** is thereupon led away and cast into a dungeon. When he is given bread and water the next day, G*** asks what offence he has committed but receives no answer. Moreover, he discovers that he is languishing in a pit he had himself designed to punish an innocent man, and that this same man is now his jailer. More humiliating still, the jailer is too magnanimous to exact any revenge on G***. Eventually, after G*** has spent sixteen months in solitary confinement, a garrison preacher asks the Prince's permission to see the prisoner. Upon seeing G***'s deplorable condition, the minister pleads with the prince to grant the prisoner more humane conditions. Long after Martinengo has fallen from grace, and after a ten-year sentence, G*** is pardoned and ordered to leave the state forever. Over the next twenty years G*** begins a new career elsewhere as a soldier and quickly works his way back to a position of power similar to the one he had enjoyed earlier under the Prince. Shortly before his death, the Prince begins to yearn for his erstwhile friend and invites G*** to return. The Prince restores G*** to his former position and there he happily remains for nineteen years as warden of the *** prison. Having apparently learnt little from his own experience, G*** is harsh and unjust to his prisoners, and dies of a stroke at the age of eighty while raging at one of them.[28]

"Game of Fate" has not only a verifiable grounding in authentic, historical fact — it is a creative reworking of the fate of General Philipp Friedrich Rieger, one of Schiller's godparents — it also possesses strong autobiographical elements.[29] Indeed, the story contains marked traces of a reckoning on Schiller's part with aspects of the feudal, autocratic regime in Württemberg, which had to a large extent shaped (or scarred) his upbringing and education. Rieger, on whom Schiller's character Aloysius von G*** is based, was born in 1722. He was a ruthless careerist and protégé of Karl Eugen (1728–93), Duke of Württemberg, rising to become chief of the ducal military staff.

Rieger fell from grace in 1762 as a result of the intrigues of a Count Montmartin (on whom Schiller modeled his character Martinengo), and was imprisoned for four years in Hohenentwiel fortress, before being rehabilitated by the Duke in 1766. In 1771 the Duke appointed him General Commandant of the Hohenasperg fortress, a few miles north of Ludwigsburg and not far from Schiller's birthplace in Marbach. The fortress complex housed a notorious prison, in which the dissident writer Christian Friedrich Daniel Schubart was later to be incarcerated during Rieger's tenure as commandant. General Rieger died in 1782 of a stroke, precipitated it seems by his raging rebuke of one of the Hohenasperg's garrison soldiers, whom Rieger suspected of malingering.

The young Schiller was required to compose a conventional *Trauergedicht* (poem of mourning) in remembrance of Rieger.[30] His true feelings about Rieger, and the system that made him what he was, were not to emerge until the publication of "Game of Fate" in 1789. Schiller knew something of Rieger already; indeed he had met him in 1781 when paying a clandestine visit to Schubart at Hohenasperg. He would also have been familiar with Friedrich Nicolai's view of Rieger. After visiting Hohenasperg in July 1781, Nicolai characterized its commandant as an impetuous, astute but also rather cold individual.[31] In his autobiography *Leben und Gesinnungen* (1793, Life and Attitudes), published shortly before the death of his tormentor Duke Karl Eugen, Schubart characterized his jailer Rieger as "a rare combination of manly greatness and childish pettiness, of the sublime and the base, of magnanimous goodness and destructive anger, of capacity for mercy and revenge, of blazing fear of God and entirely unholy deeds."[32]

The most striking formal feature of "Game of Fate" is its furious yet controlled tempo which, as Alt points out, is contained with a five-part structure not unlike that of a classical tragedy: exposition, tension, climax, retardation and resolution.[33] G***/Rieger also resembles a tragic hero in some respects. He is presented at the outset as one on whom the gods smile, before his hubristic ambition takes over, and this is followed, inevitably, by downfall and nemesis. In presenting G*** as a man who believes he is untouchable, but who is, in fact, sleepwalking to disaster, Schiller may be well be echoing an important theme of Goethe's *Egmont,* a text which Schiller had recently reviewed. Like G***, Egmont is naively or arrogantly insouciant, refusing to believe that he is any danger. As a result he falls into the clutches of his executioner Alba.[34] For similar reasons G*** falls foul of Martinengo's intrigues. (Martinengo bears more than a passing resemblance, of course, to the jealous, scheming character Wurm in Schiller's play *Intrigue and Love.*) The cruel and arbitrary nature of G***'s subsequent imprisonment in the story deliberately recalls the fate of Christian Friedrich Daniel Schubart. Schubart, who had been incarcerated without trial by Duke Karl Eugen in Hohenasperg from 1777 to 1787, was a dissident writer and something of a political and literary hero to Schiller. Schubart's son, Ludwig, visited Schiller in Weimar in December 1788, and it seems likely that the memories and associations inspired by this visit were the catalyst for the writing of "Game of Fate."

The principal interest and focus of the story lies in its psychological investigation of G***'s character. However, unlike the psychological experiments Schiller had conducted in "A Magnanimous Act from Most Recent History" and the Alba anecdote, which are largely playful, on this occasion the psychological examination has a serious, political purpose. As Michael Hofmann has recently pointed out:

> The psychological analysis [in the short story] exposes the mechanisms through which careers are made and destroyed in the feudal system of governance and control; on the one hand, the analysis exposes fundamentally the perversity of this political system, but on the other hand indicates pressingly that the individuals caught up in this system become to some extent infected by this perversity, such that they themselves become collaborators, even perpetrators.[35]

Like his real-life counterpart, Rieger, G***'s character and temperament have become so corrupted by his identification with the values and ethos of the absolutist system that, even after he has become a victim of this system and been imprisoned by it in inhuman conditions for a decade, he is unable to change his ways or learn from his experience. Schiller's perhaps depressing, but psychologically persuasive, conclusion is his skeptical insight that people caught up in any system that survives on instrumentalization will be unable to learn from their experiences or to transcend the exploitative mechanisms that have made them what they are.[36] In this sense, as Gerhard Kaiser has argued, the heroes of Schiller's short stories are, in fact, not heroes at all, because they are no longer the focus of the poetic world. They are presented as inseparable from a complex constellation of socio-political events, which is in turn a specifically modern mode of experience.[37]

As this essay has tried to indicate, it is not possible to argue that Schiller's shortest stories of the period 1782 to 1789 should be ranked alongside his achievements as a dramatist and lyric poet. It is possible, however, to argue that, as well as being entertaining and challenging in their own right, they can be read as important complements to the anthropological and social concerns of Schiller's early dramas and as pointers to the more sophisticated anthropological pessimism that Schiller develops in his theoretical writings of the mid-1790s, and in his dramas from *Wallenstein* (1796–99) onwards. Specifically, Schiller mounts successful challenges to the tradition of the *Moralische Erzählung* (moral tale) by playing with and undermining the assumptions of this sub-genre. Underlying these experiments is Schiller's belief in a fundamental dualism in man, not only of an inner kind

— the divide and interaction between our physical and moral natures — but also of an outer kind — the interaction between man and his (socio-political) circumstances, which casts doubt on the practical efficacy of much conventional moral wisdom. In the words of Benno von Wiese:

> As a story-teller [Schiller] interprets the dualism of person and situation [. . .] This is not "realism" in the sense of mimesis (a representation of reality soaked in the detail of individuals and things), but an "analytical realism" which deals with fixed, general constants and brings them into contact, experimentally, with ever-changing external conditions.[38]

The outcome of these experiments, as we have seen, is often surprisingly pessimistic, as well as entertaining and enlightening, though not always in ways which Enlightenment, in the narrow sense, would necessarily endorse.

Commenting on Schiller's decision to give up writing prose fiction after 1789, T. J. Reed has observed that "Schiller is one of the eighteenth century's great lost novelists, lured away by the traditional cultural prestige of tragic drama."[39] In a sense, however, Schiller's early short stories form part of this dramatic achievement, at least thematically. Whether Schiller's motives for abandoning prose fiction writing after 1789 were cultural, personal, financial, or political (his attention was, after all, distracted by events elsewhere in 1789), it is nevertheless the case that Germany perhaps lost her first great modern novelist as a result — and acquired her foremost dramatist.

University of Birmingham

Notes

[1] See, for example: Christa Bürger, "Schiller als Erzähler? Von der Kunst des Erzählens zum Erzählen als Kunst," in *Friedrich Schiller. Angebot und Diskurs: Zugänge, Dichtung, Zeitgenossenschaft,* ed. Helmut Brand (Berlin and Weimar: Aufbau, 1987), 33–48; Ulrike Rainer, *Schillers Prosa. Poetologie und Praxis* (Berlin: Erich Schmidt, 1988); Achim Aurnhammer, "Engagiertes Erzählen: 'Der Verbrecher aus verlorener Ehre,'" in *Schiller und die höfische Welt,* ed. Achim Aurnhammer, Klaus Manger, and Friedrich Strack (Tübingen: Niemeyer, 1990), 254–70; Peter-André Alt, *Schiller: Leben — Werk — Zeit,* 2 vols. (Munich: Beck, 2004, 2nd rev. ed.), 1:467–99; Gert Vonhoff, "'Die Macht der Verhältnisse': Schillers Erzählungen," in *Friedrich Schiller,* ed. Heinz Ludwig Arnold and Mirjam Springer (Munich: Edition Text + Kritik, 2005), 71–81; Jeffrey L. High, "Schiller, the Author of Literary Prose," in *Friedrich Schiller: Playwright, Poet, Philosopher, Historian,* ed. Paul Kerry (Oxford and Berne: Peter Lang, 2007), 117–51. Subsequent citations as "High 2007" with page number.

[2] In *Schillers Werke. Nationalausgabe,* ed. Julius Petersen et al. (Weimar: Hermann Böhlaus Nachfolger, 1943ff.), 16:7–29, 45–184. Subsequent citations as "NA" with volume and page number.

[3] "von wenigem Belang" (To Körner, 1 Oct. 1788: NA 25:112).

[4] "Daß Sie einen Aufsatz von mir ["Spiel des Schicksals"] verkannt oder doch fast verkannt haben, sollte ich Ihnen als Autor und als Ihr Freund nicht vergeben; denn auch bey unbedeutenden Produkten, wie an diesem z.b. nicht viel ist, auch nicht seyn soll, bildet sich doch der Autor ein, daß man seine Manier kennen müsse" (to Charlotte von Lengefeld, 5 Feb. 1789: NA 25:198).

[5] "Halbbruder des Dichters" (NA 20:462).

[6] See Alt, 1:467–68.

[7] "Es geht bei Marmontel — wie später bei seinen zahlreichen deutschen Nachahmern — vor allem um weibliche Tugend, um falschen Ehrgeiz und um elterliche Erziehungsfehler. Obwohl die Erzählungen häufig adliges Personal bemühen, predigen sie die bürgerlichen Tugenden des Familiensinns, der Sparsamkeit, des Pflichtbewußtseins und des empfindsamen Gefühlskults." Jürgen Jacobs, "Die deutsche Erzählung im Zeitalter der Aufklärung," in *Handbuch der deutschen Erzählung*, ed. Karl Konrad Polheim (Düsseldorf: Bagel, 1981), 56–71, here 58. For further discussion of these developments, see Alt, 1:468.

[8] See Alt, 1:469.

[9] See Alt 1:470. Alt also mentions François Gayot de Pitaval's *Causes célèbres et intéressantes* (1734–43) in this context. For further discussion of Pitaval's importance to Schiller, see Alexander Košenina, "Schiller's Poetics of Crime," in *Schiller: National Poet — Poet of Nations. A Birmingham Symposium*, ed. Nicholas Martin (Amsterdam and New York: Rodopi, 2006), 201–17.

[10] To Körner, 12 June 1788: NA 25:70.

[11] See Alt 1:470.

[12] See Kenneth Dewhurst and Nigel Reeves, *Friedrich Schiller: Medicine, Psychology and Literature* (Oxford: Oxford UP, 1978).

[13] See Alt, 1:472–73. In this context Alt also stresses Schiller's debt to the "psychological" concerns of eighteenth-century French and English novelists, including Rousseau, Fielding, Prévost, Richardson, Laclos, Sterne and, above all, Diderot, whose novel *Jacques the Fatalist and his Master* (*Jacques le fataliste et son maître*, 1771) was one of Schiller's favorite texts. He translated and published an episode from the novel in the *Thalia* in 1785 and later recommended it enthusiastically to Goethe (Alt, 1:473).

[14] "Ich muß von *Schriftstellerei leben*, also auf das sehen, was *einträgt*" (To Körner, 18 Jan. 1788: NA 25:5).

[15] "die *Thalia* verlangt nach Beiträgen, die das Interesse der Leser fesseln und das Unterhaltungsbedürfnis möglichst breiter Kreise befriedigen. Das schließt tiefgründige theoretische Abhandlungen ebenso wie spröde Lehrdichtung aus. Dringend geboten bleibt die Veröffentlichung spannungshaltiger Texte, die durch Kürze und Prägnanz zu wirken vermögen" (Alt, 1:467).

[16] "Gemälde merkwürdiger Menschen und Handlungen" (*Ankündigung der Rheinischen Thalia:* NA 22:95).

[17] "Neugefundene Räder in dem unbegreiflichen Uhrwerk der Seele — einzelne Phänomene, die sich in irgend eine merkwürdige Verbesserung oder Verschlimmerung auflösen, sind mir, ich gestehe es, wichtiger als die toten Schätze im

Kabinett des Antikensammlers oder ein neu entdeckter Nachbar des Saturnus" (NA 22:95). All translations by the author, unless otherwise noted.

[18] See Michael Hofmann, "Eine großmütige Handlung aus der neusten Geschichte," in *Schiller-Handbuch: Leben — Werk — Wirkung,* ed. Matthias Luserke-Jaqui (Stuttgart and Weimar: Metzler, 2005), 299–301, here 299.

[19] "Gegenwärtige Anekdote von zween Teutschen — mit stolzer Freude schreib' ich das nieder — hat ein unabstreitbares Verdienst — *sie ist wahr.* Ich hoffe, daß sie meine Leser wärmer zurücklassen werde als alle Bände des *Grandison* und der *Pamela*" (NA 16:3). Schiller is here aligning himself with late Enlightenment skepticism concerning the practical and moral efficacy of the type of sentimental and entirely fictional prose, which was thought be exemplified in Samuel Richardson's novels. The story is narrated in a sober, sparse style quite unlike Richardson's and, indeed, quite unlike the at times extravagantly rhetorical and pathos-ridden style of Schiller's early dramas.

[20] See Alt 1:477.

[21] "die seligste der Ehen" (NA 16:6).

[22] High 122.

[23] See Vonhoff 73.

[24] "Diese 'moralische' Erzählung entpuppt sich bei näherer Betrachtung als höchst fragwürdig. Sie läßt vielleicht den Leser nicht 'wärmer' zurück als 'alle Bände des *Grandison* und der *Pamela,*' doch sicherlich beunruhigter und nachdenklicher" (Rainer 98).

[25] See Alt 1:478.

[26] See note 3 above. See also Alt 1:478. Schiller had met Ludwig Friedrich von Schwarzburg-Rudolstadt, the ruling hereditary prince of Thuringia, on May 29, 1788.

[27] See Michael Hofmann, "Spiel des Schicksals. Ein Bruchstück aus einer wahren Geschichte," in *Schiller-Handbuch: Leben — Werk — Wirkung,* ed. Matthias Luserke-Jaqui (Stuttgart and Weimar: Metzler, 2005), 315–19, here 316. See also High 128. The negative comment to Charlotte von Lengefeld concerning "Game of Fate" (see note 4 above) reflects Schiller's annoyance at her failure to recognize his authorship rather than any fundamental dissatisfaction with the text itself.

[28] This plot summary is indebted to the synopses provided by High 2007 (128–29) and Hofmann (317–18).

[29] According to the commentary in the edition cited here, "Game of Fate" does not seek to provide an historically accurate account of the events it relates. Rather, the short story is concerned with "the poetic shaping of an historical case" ("Es ist die poetische Gestaltung eines historischen Vorgangs" [NA 16:411]).

[30] See Alt 1:525–26, and Hofmann 315–16.

[31] "Obgleich sein äußeres Ansehen etwas ernsthaft und auch sein Diskurs meist ernsthaft war; so war doch alles was er sagte, mit Scharfsinn, Witz und Laune gewürzt. Dabey sprach er über manches mit seltner Offenherzigheit." Friedrich Nicolai, *Gesammelte Werke,* ed. Bernhard Fabian and Marie-Luise Spieckermann, 20 vols. (Hildesheim, Zürich and New York: Georg Olms, 1984), Vol. 19, III.9, 162.

[32] "eine seltene Mischung von männlicher Größe und kindischer Kleinheit, von Erhabenheit und Niedrigkeit, von menschenbeglückender Güte und Zerstörungsgrimm, von Fähigkeit des Erbarmens und Rachsucht, von hellodernder Gottesfurcht und ganz ungottseligen Taten." Quoted in Friedrich Schiller, *Der Verbrecher aus verlorener Ehre und andere Erzählungen,* mit einem Nachwort von Bernhard Zeller (Stuttgart: Reclam, 1964), 66–67.

[33] See Alt 1:523.

[34] See Alt 1:523–24.

[35] "Die psychologische Analyse [in der Erzählung] verdeutlicht die Mechanismen, nach denen im feudalen Herrschaftssystem Karrieren gemacht und wieder zerstört werden; sie verdeutlicht dabei einerseits und grundlegend die Perversität dieses politischen Systems, andererseits wird aber eindringlich darauf verwiesen, dass die Personen, die sich in dem System bewegen, von dieser Perversität gewissermaßen angesteckt und so zu Kollaborateuren, ja Tätern werden" (Hofmann 317). This syndrome is what Vonhoff calls, more succinctly, "die Verstrickung des Bürgertums in das Machtsystem des Absolutismus" (Vonhoff 75).

[36] For further discussion, see Hofmann 317.

[37] "ein epischer Held, der eigentlich gar kein Held ist, nicht in der Sinn-Mitte der dichterischen Welt steht, sondern als Glied einer Konstellation begegnet, die ihrerseits den Sinn trägt. Denn der Mensch als Moment einer Konstellation — das ist ja wohl eine spezifisch moderne Erfahrungsweise der Person." Gerhard Kaiser, "Der Held in den Novellen: 'Eine großmütige Handlung aus der neusten Geschichte' und 'Der Verbrecher aus verlorener Ehre,'" in Gerhard Kaiser, *Von Arkadien nach Elysium. Schiller-Studien* (Göttingen: Vandenhoeck und Ruprecht, 1978), 45–58, here 46.

[38] "[Schiller] interpretiert als Erzähler den Dualismus von Person und Situation [. . .] Es ist dies zwar kein 'Realismus' im Sinne dinglich gesättigter, individualisierter Wirklichkeitsdarstellung, sondern ein 'analytischer Realismus,' der mit festen, allgemeinen Konstanten rechnet und sie experimentell mit jeweils wechselnden äußeren Bedingungen zusammenbringt." Benno von Wiese, *Friedrich Schiller* (Stuttgart: Metzler, 1959), 308–9.

[39] T. J. Reed, *The Classical Centre: Goethe and Weimar 1775–1832* (London: Croom Helm, 1980), 105.

11: Diderot and Schiller's "Revenge": From Parisian Parody to German Moral Education

Otto W. Johnston

AT THE CONCLUSION OF HIS SHORT STORY, "Ein merkwürdiges Beispiel einer weiblichen Rache" (A Remarkable Example of Female Revenge), Schiller adds a postscript in which he identifies his source. An unpublished manuscript by Diderot was making the rounds, he tells us, a novel, which Schiller calls, "Jakob und sein Herr oder Fatalismus" (Jacob and His Master or Fatalism).[1] The theater director in Mannheim, Heribert von Dalberg, owned a copy, which he gave to Schiller. The "bold novelty of the intrigue," the "unmistakable truth of the narrative," and the "unadorned elegance of the description" persuaded him to attempt what he labels "a translation" for publication in his literary magazine, *Die Rheinische Thalia* in 1785 (see p. 37).[2] But is what he produced a translation? A closer look will reveal that Schiller's work is best described as an adaptation of a segment of Diderot's novel. Contrary to what Schiller suggests in his postscript, he didn't merely translate, but rather restructured the story in such a way as to tell a different tale. As we shall see, Diderot's rendition is a piece of juicy gossip told by an innkeeper's wife about one of her aristocratic patrons. Schiller's version, by contrast, is meant as an example of unbridled vengeance, the ultimate intrigue against an unsuspecting ex-lover, in short: the work of a monster.

Schiller changes Diderot's original in four significant ways. First, he isolates this particular incident and in so doing exaggerates its importance outside the context of Diderot's novel. Second, he deletes the numerous interruptions in the landlady's narrative as well as the commentary provided by other characters in the story and thereby lays all the blame for the intrigue at the feet of his "Frau von P***," whom Diderot identifies as "Madame de La Pommeraye." These interruptions are significant because they allow Diderot's landlady to start the story again, each time from a slightly different narrative perspective. The comments of her listeners tend to point a finger at the supporting cast, whose complicity makes the dirty little intrigue possible. Third, Schiller changes the language. The landlady's account, though eloquent and not what one would expect from a simple innkeeper's wife, is full of colloquialisms, idiomatic expressions, and language common to a French bourgeois when talking about aristocrats. Schiller dispenses with those expressions peculiar to the middle class, when voicing astonishment at the immorality of the nobility, and raises the narration to the level of aristocratic discourse. In other words, his narrative persona, unlike Diderot's, uses upper-class language to mirror his aristocratic players, invoking their own ethical code. With his unequivocal, princely High German, he condemns the behavior of the upper class according to its own rules, not those of the middle class. Fourth, he omits Diderot's subsequent depictions of the victim of the plot, who reappears later in the novel to tell an equally bizarre tale of his servant's victimization. The return of the Marquis d'Arcis is meant to show how well the deceived survived the deception, and to emphasize that this incident of female revenge is just one of many illustrations in the ongoing battle between the sexes. It is outrageous, maybe even unique, but it is in no way unparalleled. Beyond these four major variants are smaller changes that give the tale a coherence Diderot didn't intend and an intensity he sought to diffuse because his intention was to satirize Parisian society in his day, experiment with the novel as a literary form, entertain the reader by commenting on Madame de La Pommeraye's quest for vengeance from a variety of perspectives, and then demand that the reader form his or her own opinion. Schiller's narrator incites his reader to moral indignation by deviating from the initial justification for the Marquis' cruel-hearted treatment of his mistress, then presenting step-by-step the wicked impulses of a spiteful soul bent on a retaliation that borders on the criminal. Diderot's narrative voice participates in the story by making fun of the characters, pointing out their foibles and ill-conceived plans. His characters supply the proof that Parisian society can only be parodied, never understood or excused. Schiller's more serious teller of the tale is determined to recreate characters who probe the depths of human depravity. In short, Diderot used the novel to caricature his Parisian milieu, to illustrate the hypocrisy, violence, and thirst for revenge inherent in the human condition, and as a means to get even with his opponents. Schiller saw literature as a vehicle for the moral education of his reader.

For the most part, Schiller studies have overlooked these major differences because scholars have taken Schiller at his word. When he prepared the first major authoritative edition of Schiller's works in 1868, Karl Goedeke set the stage for the inquiry for years to come, when he stated unabashedly, "I've only compared [Schiller's version] with the original at random."[3] Not all scholars fit this description, of course. In an essay for the *Marbacher Schillerbuch* in 1905, Ludwig Geiger found enough differences between the German and French versions to fill ten pages.[4] But Geiger, like those who followed, concentrated on those passages he believed he could translate more accurately than Schiller. In other words, he understood Diderot's text much better than Schiller, who was allegedly less proficient. Richard Weissenfels, who prepared the Säkular-edition of Schiller's short stories, noted many of those discrepancies discovered by Geiger, and added a few of his own, but focused on one humorous example of Schiller's occasional dyslexia: he had mistaken the French "les indigens" (native) for "indignes" (unworthy, undeserving) and therefore rendered a passage in Diderot's text inaccurately.[5] But this scholarly hubris, this desire to improve upon the work of the writer presumed less skillful, obscures the fact that Schiller and Diderot worked at cross-purposes. Unfortunately, this same pretentious urge to correct was practiced *ad nauseam* by those metaphysically oriented *Geisteswissenschaftler* (literary scholars) of the past century who were determined to show that they understood the philosophical systems of the period far better than the German poet. It will be shown that Schiller, the "translator," changed the French wording on occasion, but altered more emphatically the structure, emphasis, and purpose of Diderot's novel. Schiller states as much in his postscript when he notes, "All of Diderot's eloquence can hardly reason away the disgust that this unnatural deed must by necessity arouse."[6] He adapted Diderot's text to illustrate an unnatural and tragically immoral *exemplum*, not to translate a witty social satire. This is especially important when we look at Schiller's utilization of source material in general. We tend to overlook the impact of French liberalism on his literary creativity. Virtually all of his dramas and most of his short stories and essays are based in part on French sources, which he treats in much the same way. It will be shown that French caricature and parody, once in Schiller's hands, become genuine German tragedy and an experiment in moral umbrage.

Before examining the four major differences in detail, we must contend with an uncomfortable suspicion. Could the manuscript in Dalberg's possession have been different from the standard text we have today? His original may have been closer to Schiller's text, thus explaining the wording of those passages in the German text at variance with the French edition that has come down to us. Misgivings are justified because, first, Schiller misquotes the title and, second, he abbreviates the characters' names. By citing his source as "Jacob and his Master or Fatalism," which is a faulty rendition of *Jacques le fataliste et son maitre*, Schiller prompts us to ask whether the rest of his text differs from ours. However, despite the discrepancies, it is highly unlikely that Schiller worked from a manuscript at variance with Diderot's text in the modern authoritative edition.[7] Copies of this segment in Diderot's novel found in the libraries at Gotha and Weimar vary only in minor details from the authoritative texts of Diderot's works prepared from the St. Petersburg (Leningrad) manuscripts that his heirs had sent to Catherine the Great.[8] Goethe saw a copy in 1780 and quotes the full title as we know it.[9] Eight years after Schiller adapted the story for his own purposes, Wilhelm Mylius translated the entire novel into German with the same title Schiller used but with none of his variants. A more likely explanation for the discrepancy in title and character names is that Dalberg had received a copy of this segment of Diderot's novel as a supplement to the *Correspondance littéraire,* edited and circulated by Melchior Grimm and the Abbé Guillaume Raynal. Diderot, who died in 1784, was hesitant to publish the novel in France because in it he had attacked many powerful and influential politicians, clerics and writers. For that reason, he preferred to protect his work and himself from reprisals by sending it out of the country in installments, which his friends Grimm[10] and Raynal simply added to their wide-ranging literary correspondence. A catalogue of the Diderot collection in the National Library at Paris also lists the *Correspondance littéraire* as the novel's handwritten source. In all likelihood, the Dalberg "*Originalschrift,*" as Schiller calls it, didn't differ in any significant way from the text we regard today as the definitive version. The manuscripts reposed at St. Petersburg (Leningrad) serve as the basis for more recent authoritative editions only because they contain Diderot's last comments and occasional emendation in his own handwriting. This means, of course, that Schiller's variances represent his own reworking of the story intended to suit a different narrative purpose.

To understand why Schiller abbreviated the names, we need not look at Diderot's novel, but rather at Schiller's other short stories, where almost all the characters are identified as ***, thereby adding to the mystery. The subtitle to *Der Geisterseher* (1787–89, The Spiritualist), for example, is "From the Memoirs of Count von O**." In "Spiel des Schicksals" (1789, Game of Fate) we encounter Aloisius von G*** in the service of the Prince of ***. Obviously, Schiller used this shorthand as a stylistic technique to add an aura of suspense and enigma to his version.[11] For this reason, his abbreviations do not suggest that he copied them from Dalberg's manuscript. We are, therefore, safe to assume that what Dalberg gave Schiller differed only slightly from the text we consider the last, best version approved by Diderot.

Shortly before the account of Madame de La Pommeraye's revenge, Diderot's narrative persona recounts an equally spiteful example of male retaliation against a woman. A pastry cook (*le Pâtissiere*), who spent more time looking into his oven than into his wife's conduct,[12] discovers in a roundabout way that his wife has been deceiving him with the steward of Monsieur de Saint-Florentin, a prominent Parisian.[13] The steward, in order to get the husband completely out of the way, had falsely accused him of beating her and had a warrant (*une lettre de cachet*) sworn out for his arrest. But the police constable (*l'Exempt*) charged with serving the warrant was a friend of the pastry cook. Together they hatch a complex scheme to catch the wife *in flagrante delicto* and throw the steward in jail, using the same warrant issued for the arrest of the pastry chef. The wife in her nightgown is caught in bed with the steward (captured brilliantly in a drawing by Maurice Leloir in 1884), who is first brought to the city's prison and later to the *Bicêtre,* a prison hospital for lunatics and those suffering from venereal disease. When even Monsieur Saint-Florentin, the minister responsible for policing the capital, approves of the police officer's handling of the whole sordid affair, the wife is so thoroughly disgraced that she is left completely at the mercy of her husband. Having given this account of male revenge, Diderot's narrator moves on to that striking incident of female revenge against a man designed and executed by Madame de La Pommeraye. It is obvious that Diderot intends both of these remarkable examples as counterpoints that show the hypocrisy and thirst for reprisal endemic to Parisian society in his day.

In order to make the point even more clearly, Diderot has the landlady break off the story of Madame de La Pommeraye's vendetta because of urgent business that requires her immediate attention. Having recounted about 8 percent of the narrative amid constant interruptions, she leaves and thereby gives Jacques and his master the opportunity to comment. Jacques begins a wholesale attack on the institution of marriage by reciting the fable of the Sheath and the Dagger (*la Gaîne et du Coutelet,* 150). Since a sheath can accept many daggers and many knives fit into a variety of sheaths, Jacques contends, monogamy and marriage are absurd societal constructs that run counter to human instincts. After presenting this argument in the form of a fable, Jacques narrates an example, just as bizarre as the preceding ones, of the unrelenting quest for retribution in the military. The account of the countless duels[14] between Monsieur de Guerchy and an officer he had wrongly accused of cheating at dice illustrates the absurdity of the *point d'honneur* in the army's code of ethics. After the wronged man runs his sword through the body of his accuser, he picks him up off the field, sees to his wounds, and invites him to duel again as soon as his wound has healed. The two take such pleasure in reproducing the duel that the whole notion of reprisal or "satisfaction" is shown to be ludicrous.

The landlady then returns with two bottles of champagne and picks up the story line not where she left off, but with the Marquis and the Madame embracing and expressing their relief that now the truth was out. Before she was interrupted, the landlady had left the pair discussing the fickleness of the human heart, the emptiness of lovers' pledges, and the bonds of marriage, which, in turn, prompted Jacques' outburst against marriage. When she returns, she describes the pain Madame had felt and her violent reaction to the news that she was no longer the object of the Marquis' love. Once *l'hôtesse* ends her tale of female scheming, Jacques and his master quarrel over reprisals taken against servants and counter-retribution exerted by servants against their masters. A short time later in the novel, the Marquis des Arcis reappears and narrates another weird tale of retribution, this time within the religious community. By the end, every social institution has been shown to be corrupt, their standard-bearers spiteful and manipulative. "Don't get mad, get even" has become a way of life and the meaning of existence in this culture.

On the metaphorical level, a great deal more is being said. A tradesman can turn the tables on a false witness only if he knows the right people and those in authority take his side. The institution of marriage serves to separate men and women, not bring them together. The military code of honor is a travesty perpetrated by sadists and masochists, who fight incessantly because they derive some demonic pleasure in wearing a uniform that permits them to engage in violence against one another. Aristocrats hide their true feelings behind masks and seek revenge in intrigue and labyrinthine complots. Jacques' quarrel with his master parallels the king's struggle against an unruly Parliament at Paris bent on regaining that power usurped by Louis XIV. Priests, abbots, monks have lost all pretensions of leading a godly life and practice tit-for-tat just like everyone else. Parisian society, indeed French life, is dominated by feuds and recrimination, revengefulness and reprisals, intrigue and retaliation. The symbols intensify the message at the surface level and the implications of the metaphors. A baker who delights the palate with the finest pastries can turn sour and spiteful with the help of police authority, which, in turn, helps those friends who prepare its pleasures. Marriage is an empty institution working against true love and the natural attraction between men and women because it stifles genuine feelings. Military officers, who are responsible for the nation's defense, fight no enemy — they fight and wound each other. The king doesn't lead; he seeks to get even with those who want to share in his power and weaken his prerogatives. The church no longer signifies sacrifice, neither God's will for his creation nor contrition and repentance. On the contrary, it, too, is corrupt and power hungry, full of souls looking forward only to the day of reckoning with their own contemporaries. Here the Furies rule supreme. This is social satire at its finest, caricature at the hands of a skillful artist, a parody of every aspect of societal life in mid-eighteenth-century France.

None of this is contained in Schiller's plot line. The vengeance of his Frau von P*** is not contextualized, not remarkable in the sense of a clever intrigue that outshines all the others. As in other early works (*The Robbers),* Schiller is drawn instead to the aberrant behavior of a tormented soul so hurt, so damaged, that its ethical imperatives are tuned out and shut down. Unlike Diderot, whose interruptions, digressions, and stories-within-stories represent playful experiment with the novel as a genre, Schiller exploits each sordid detail, inserts each to heighten the drama and increase the suspense. He is not interested in caricature or the burlesque elements in the novel; his focus is on the violation of moral principles, the dishonesty, the villainy. If Diderot's narrator shrugs his shoulders and scoffs, Schiller's text exposes the degeneracy of the human mind and spirit. In the eyes of Diderot's narrative persona, "everybody's doing it"; for Schiller the deep descent of this woman is an individual tragedy from which we must learn so that we do not repeat it.

Schiller not only restructures the tale but also dismisses the many perspectives on the events voiced by the other characters. Jacques pities the poor Marquis who is completely taken in by the scam.[15] "Not me," retorts his master,[16] as he finishes a long tirade against the Marquis whose wickedness prompted Madame to scheme against him in the first place. In a clever *tour de force,* Diderot has Jacques and his master switch philosophical perspectives. The master, who up to now has advocated free will, remarks to Jacques, "Do you know what I think? I fear the marriage of the Marquis to a whore was written up there, on high" to which Jacques at first agrees, but then retorts, "The bitch! The scheming, raging shrew! Why did he ever have anything to do with her?"[17] His question implies that the Marquis had possessed enough free will to avoid his fate, a position Jacques, the Fatalist, has denied throughout the novel. His master, still incensed at the Marquis, asks pointedly with regard to Madame de La Pommeraye, "And why did he seduce her and then abandon her?"[18] The landlady sides with Jacques' master and finds fault with the Marquis, "Why stop loving her without rhyme or reason?" A strange twist occurs after the landlady recounts the conclusion: the Marquis d'Arcis and his new wife, the former Mlle. Duquenoi, leave for his estate and remain there until the injurious scandal and idle rumors subside. At this point, Jacques' master takes issue with the behavior of the daughter, Mlle. Duquenoi, for her part in the machinations of her mother and the Madame against her future husband, "Not afraid for even a moment, no sign that she was uncertain or felt any remorse. I have seen her without the slightest repugnancy take part in the whole horrible affair."[19] Yet the landlady defends her by pointing out that we don't really know what went on in her heart; she may have been full of remorse. At any rate, she made a good wife with whom the Marquis was happy as a king.

The irony in all these attitudes is that they are all self-serving. Jacques, who would have been much happier doing all the talking himself, eggs the landlady on because he's drinking her champagne and proposes yet another toast to one of the characters whenever his glass is empty. The landlady delights in the telling and the attention she receives because she gets little or none from her husband, whom she admits she doesn't love. The master expresses his exasperation at all of the characters, but winds up taking a position that is countered in depth by Diderot's narrative persona. There is outrage in all the voices, but no real textual position on what is right and what is wrong in the unfolding of such events. In fact, the landlady claims she is neither adding to nor subtracting from the plot, but simply telling it as it happened. Yet in the telling she reminds her listeners of a scandal her aristocratic patron had hoped would be forgotten.

Schiller skips all of this and moves on to the defense of Madame de La Pommeraye presented by Diderot's persona, who sees in this incident merely "a less common sort of betrayal."[20] Schiller translates this passage with a more intense expression, "a betrayal that doesn't happen every day."[21] For Schiller's narrator, the whole intrigue evokes nothing but "Abscheu" (disgust or loathing, NA 16:223). He finds nothing to mitigate the guilt of his Frau von P*** and is not concerned with those who facilitate her actions. With these deletions, Schiller's text differs profoundly from the French original. His narrator is the more traditional omniscient, omnipresent moralist, a surveillance camera in the heavens, which records and judges the deeds of mere mortals. By analyzing the conduct and complicity of each of the characters in the scheme, Diderot's narrative persona shifts the blame in accordance with the degree to which each figure participated; Schiller's narrator, by contrast, tells a coherent and lucid tale of one woman's scorn and revenge that probes the depths of immorality. By presenting so many differing perspectives on the characters' conduct, Diderot makes the reader the arbiter. The one holding the book must exercise his or her moral judgment as to who is right and who is wrong. Schiller will adopt that same technique later in his plays, in order to include his audience in the moral decision-making. In *Die Braut von Messina* (1801/02, The Bride of Messina),[22] for example, the chorus will comment on the dramatic action from so many perspectives that the audience is compelled to decide where guilt and innocence, atonement and retribution lie. But in this story, his morally superior narrator passes sole judgment and condemns the guilty party without chance of reprieve or a thought to mitigating circumstances. The difference between Diderot's and Schiller's narrative perspective becomes especially vivid when Diderot's storyteller addresses the reader directly and asks, "Do you want me to break off this eloquent and loquacious gossip of a landlady and return to Jacques' love affairs? As for me, I don't care one way or the other."[23] He could care less about the "bavarde," this incessant chatter or gossip of the landlady. That's all it is for him: scandal, rumor, babble. For Schiller such a perverse reversal of love and hatred calls forth revulsion that is reflected in the different level of language in his adaptation.

Schiller's discourse is both perplexing and revealing. On the one hand, it is striking that he avoids the middle-class jargon of Diderot's original; on the other hand, his highbrow idiom bears witness to his different purpose. Just weeks before he started work on Dalberg's manuscript, another of Schiller's adaptations of a Diderot original had its premier in the theater at Frankfurt am Main (13 April 1784) and was performed two days later at Mannheim. *Kabale und Liebe* (Intrigue and Love) owes so much to Diderot's *Le Père de famille* (first performed at Paris in February 1761) that one can easily see the source for the German middle-class tragedy in the French theatrical farce. We shall have more to say about these parallels when we examine the way Schiller uses French sources in general and what his rendering of the landlady's tale tells us about that process. Here we merely draw attention to the opening scene of Schiller's play, which is full of idioms and phraseology common to Germany's bourgeoisie. While scolding his wife for promoting their daughter's relationship to a prince, Miller, the musician, protests in one turn of phrase after another that echo middle-class speech patterns.[24] The aristocrats we encounter later in Schiller's stage production, by contrast, speak in their own more voluble idiom. This confirms that Schiller was capable of, even ingenious in, exploiting the differences and deep divisions in the German social hierarchy by showing that the segregated ranks even speak differently. The gulf separating the emerging bourgeoisie from the ruling elites is not only visible in the way they behave toward one another but also audible in the manner in which they speak.

Yet none of these differing linguistic characteristics are in evidence anywhere in *A Remarkable Example of Female Revenge*. In Diderot's original, the innkeeper's wife lapses into middle-class phraseology when she is interrupted, when she returns, and sometimes in the middle of her narration. Geiger includes several of these idioms among those expressions he insists Schiller did not translate accurately. Nevertheless, Schiller's more noble German does not bear witness to an improper rendering of those French idioms common to the bourgeoisie. On the contrary, Schiller avoids middle-class sentiments, prejudices, and linguistic patterns that would obscure the effect of this short story. Schiller's adaptation does not illustrate the class struggle he had already represented on stage, but confronts the nobility on its own terms, according to its own value system, and in its own language. By retelling the landlady's chatter in more high-class German, Schiller's elite-sounding narrator takes moral umbrage at the behavior of one from his own class. As we have seen, *l'hôtesse* revels in the telling, the attention her listeners pay her, and in her own talent for turning gossip into a general condemnation of aristocratic conduct from a middle-class point of view. But she hasn't a clue as to the implications or deeper meaning for the aristocratic characters she talks about. She really doesn't get the point of her own story. For the middle class to which she belongs, her idle gossip is an exercise in finger pointing and in muckraking. Even Diderot's persona scoffs at such an attitude whenever he shows how pervasive the urge for retribution is in all walks of French society.

However, from the standpoint of aristocratic ideology, the point of the episode is about losing face, embarrassing oneself in the sight of peers, in soiling the family line and lineage. An aristocrat who marries a whore doesn't just cross the line between two classes; he falls into the abyss of the lowest class in a highly delineated hierarchical social structure. His children are outcasts because the bloodline has been contaminated. They cannot be counted upon to muster courage in times of war, to show leadership when others fall behind, to defend the farmland and the country from all enemies. It simply isn't "in their blood." Because their genes have been compromised, they cannot be considered nobility. They can't farm, have no trade and no training as merchants. In fact, they are literally good for nothing. By aristocratic reckoning, the Marquis has fallen from the top to the bottom by his own blindness to the machinations of another, his total inability to discipline himself and keep passions under control. Nobility obliges. This Schiller's Marquis A*** has failed to honor and live by; as a result, the once-open doors to high society are slammed shut in his face.

Having been raised at the court of Duke Karl Eugen of Württemberg and educated at his Karlsschule, Schiller experienced firsthand the ways of the ruling class and the rules of conduct elites lived by. His chief objection was not to the quality of his educational experience, but rather to the conformity those rules demanded. The graduates of the Duke's school were clones, intellectual conformists, stuck in the same ill-fitted uniform. The system of elites demanded submission and stifled freedom.[25] Therefore, he recognized the implications of the story in terms of what's important to the nobility. A nobleman who takes a former prostitute for a wife would be the laughing stock of the entire court and couldn't show himself at any concert, theater performance, parade, or military review. For this reason, Schiller could dispense with that middle-class grumbling and finger pointing he had dramatized, with the aid of idiomatic language, in his play. Instead, he could accuse society's upper class in their own parlance of violating their own ethical norms by analyzing the indecent and demonic behavior exhibited by his Frau von P*** and her Marquis A***, both of whom are despicable. By telling the tale in a more ennobling German, his point could not be lost on any member of the upper class, even those at the courts of petty German princes where French was the preferred language. For his middle-class reader, such a rebuke of the machinations of aristocrats on their own terms was sheer delight. Schiller would use this same elevated language again a year later in "Der Verbrecher aus verlorener Ehre" (1786, The Criminal of Lost Honor) when he sought to dignify a poacher turned murderer, whose desperation heightens the more infamous he becomes.

There is yet another difference. Diderot builds on and borrows from a sub-genre that had almost no following in Germany — pornographic literature. French writers had already produced numerous novels that turned prostitution into a viable topic. The most famous of these was Abbé Antoine Francois Prévost d'Exiles' *Histoire du Chevalier des Grieux et de Manon Lescaut* (1738), his eighth volume in a series devoted to sexually explicit themes. Although indebted to Daniel Defoe's *Moll Flanders* (1722), Prévost's novel probes human sexuality in far more depth and detail. Manon Lescaut is the born courtesan, who delights in passionate eroticism, regards love as the basis for serial monogamy, lives with her lovers only as long as they can afford her, yet reviles any of those who leave her. Her saving grace is her *naïveté*, an attribute that upgraded this sub-genre in the eyes of the French reading public.[26] The subsequent literature of this kind in France showed the prostitute from every conceivable angle.[27] The impact of such writing and Diderot's intention of poking fun at it becomes especially transparent when he has mother and daughter Duquenoi take the professional names Madame and Mlle d'Aisnon (162), derived from *aine:* "groin" plus the relatively common suffix *-on,* as they begin to ply their trade "in Traversière street at the hotel Hamburg" (202).[28] The street name designates a crossing everyone goes through, implying that a lot of traffic came to the door of mother and daughter, while the hotel's moniker mirrors the reputation that German harbor city had among Parisians.

Aspects of Madame de La Pommeraye's web of deception that induced a nobleman to marry a lady of the night are foreshadowed in Jean-Baptiste Gimat de Bonneval's *Fanfiche ou les mémoires de Mademoiselle de. . . .* (1748), in which an impoverished aristocrat, an officer no less, still wants to marry the heroine after she confesses her illicit past to him and reveals the source of her income. But, in an unexpected turn of events, she declines this proposal for his sake and helps him find a match more suitable to his social standing. When he is killed in a foreign war, she withdraws from her sexual escapades to mourn for him. Diderot's Mlle. Duquenoi was certainly not the first *courtisane innocente,* whose mother recruits her into the world's oldest profession at a young age, but who doesn't take to it. Nor is she the first to begin life in a bordello, only to be rehabilitated by a Madame de La Pommeraye–like figure and become a model wife. That distinction belongs to the heroine Lucile in Nicolas Edme Restif de la Bretonne's novel *Lucile ou les progrès de la vertu* (1768) and to Zéphire in his *Le Pornographe, ou La prostitution réformée* (1769).[29] Diderot turns the Zéphir motif in Bretonne's novel on its head when he has an aristocrat reform and refine a young prostitute (Mlle. Duquenoi) initiated into prostitution by her mother. In *Le Pornographe,* that task had fallen to Edmond, a poor farm boy. A parallel to the motif of feigned pious charity, which Madame de La Pommeraye demands from mother and daughter, is found in *Les Liaisons dangereuses* (1782). But, once again, the motif is inverted. In Pierre Choderlos de Laclos' epistolary novel, the male character rather than the female pretends to act as a godly benefactor of the poor in order to entice and win the sympathy of the targeted, would-be lover. There is also a correspondence between the tactics of Madame de La Pommeraye and Leclos' Marquise de Merteuil, as outlined in Lettre LXXXI.[30] At any rate, Diderot probably did not know Laclos' masterpiece[31] while working on his *Jacques le Fataliste et son maitre* since it appeared only two years before his death and he had read portions from the unpublished manuscript of his own novel to his friends as early as 1770 and 1771.[32] Moreover, the segments of *Jacques le fataliste* included as supplements ("feuilletons") to the *Correspondance littéraire* were sent to Germany between November 1778 and June 1780,[33] which means that they were already in circulation before *Les Liaisons dangereuses* appeared in print, thus making it more likely that Laclos knew Diderot's work. Despite these congruities, Laclos was influenced more by Rousseau and Samuel Richardson than by Diderot, whose complete novel wasn't published in France until 1796.

Nevertheless, such plot lines fascinated French readers as much as they repulsed their counterparts in Germany, where literature of this kind in particular and novels in general were branded "Arsenik des Geistes" (intellectual arsenic).[34] The few libraries that lent out belletristic writing or German translations of this type of French fiction were berated as "brewers of moral poison"[35] or even "moral whorehouses."[36] Fearing a loss of power, clerics denounced prose narrative and promoted *Erbauungsliteratur* (devotional literature). This is especially evident in magazines and journals that published book reviews in these years: in 1785, almost two thirds of the *Jenaische Allgemeine Zeitung* or the *Allgemeine Literatur Zeitung* was devoted to religious tracts that attempted to deepen the spirituality of their readers. In this respect, Schiller's intense concentration on the ethical dimension of what Frau von P*** has done is prompted in part by the literary scene in the German-speaking territories, where moral edification was expected from the Muses and the *moralische Erzählung* (moral tale) was the dominant short prose form. The major writers of this period, known as *Sturm und Drang* (Storm and Stress), produced few novels but many stage productions, which steered clear of outright prostitution[37] but did illustrate the dilemma of the "fallen woman" and the consequences of unbridled passion. The theology student Läuffer in Jakob Michael Lenz's *Der Hofmeister* (1774, The Family Tutor), for example, seduces Gustchen, who bears his child, but tries to commit suicide by drowning. Filled with remorse and believing Gustchen is dead, Läuffer castrates himself. But the plot, rather than cater to prurient interests, is intended as a warning to the well-to-do against quartering private tutors in their homes, and as a plea for the establishment of public schools. Seduction and adultery rather than prostitution are the main themes in Friedrich Maximilian von Klinger's *Das leidende Weib* (1775, The Suffering Woman), which ends in despair and death for the lovers who are unable to resist the lure of passionate sexuality. Here again, it is not the carnality that serves as the focal point but rather the tragedy that uncontrolled sexual desire causes and the indictment of degenerate life at German courts. Infanticide is the subject of Heinrich Leopold Wagner's theater production *Die Kindermörderin* (1776, The Child Murderess), which is probably the best example of tragic seduction staged at this time, though the tragedy would not appear in print for another three years and only then with the first act deleted.

These examples illustrate the gap separating French belles-lettres, its thematic curiosity and creativity, from German stage productions and literary taste. There was still some enmity toward prose fiction in France, but not nearly as much as in Germany. Diderot's landlady confirms this lingering aversion when she tells Jacques that she was raised at the Royal Abbey at

Saint-Cyr, founded by Louis XIV and Madame de Maintenon for the daughters of impoverished noblemen. But her downfall came because she "read[s] little in the Gospels and many a novel."[38] In late eighteenth-century Germany, opposition to the genre was much greater and tales of prostitutes were disdained as the lowest form of rubbish. The closest any major dramatist of the period comes to the topic of "love for sale" is Lenz with his play, *Die Soldaten* (1776, The Soldiers), in which unscrupulous officers corrupt and betray the daughters of middle-class merchants. To alleviate the social misery engendered by moral weakness, Lenz proposes that the state establish a *Pflanzschule von Soldatenweibern* (institute for volunteer harlots) to take care of the sexual needs of soldiers whose regiments forbid them to marry. Needless to say, the play, initially billed as a comedy, would not premier in Germany for nearly a century. It was first performed at the Burgtheater in Vienna on 26 December 1863.

It is incongruous, to be sure, to contrast the plots of French novels with those themes brought to the much more public stage in Germany. Yet the prowess that invigorates French epic literature in this period is rivaled not by German novelists but only by the brilliance of German playwrights. There were German writers who followed the French narrative lead, yet they were castigated and their works shunned. The most famous German courtesan up to Schiller's day was Grimmelshausen's *Landstörtzerin Courasche* (1669, The Runagate Courage),[39] who discovers at a young age that she can't get pregnant and then uses her sexuality for survival and to get what she wants. Yet she remained in the shadow of her much better-known antagonist, *Simplicissimus* (1668/9), at least until she was resurrected as *Mutter Courage* (Mother Courage) by Bertolt Brecht in 1941. But even this runagate, who rails against her rival to no avail, ends up a gypsy queen and reappears in *Der seltsame Springinsfeld* (1670, That Odd Jump-in-the-Field), is a figure right out of French and Spanish picaresque novels. In fact, in the first episode, Courasche, in order to escape a horde of enemy soldiers who would surely rape her, disguises herself by putting on men's clothing. The entire representation corresponds closely to the thirty-eighth "Histoire" ("Le Chaste Strategem") in Jean Pierre de Camus-du Bellay's *Les Memoriaux Historique* (1643, Historical Memories, Paris). In other words, this vagabond is hardly a German literary creation. A more sympathetic figure is Christoph Martin Wieland's *Musarion* (1768), who is not really a prostitute, but rather a hetaera, a willing, sophisticated concubine who uses her charm and beauty to obtain wealth and social status.[40] This verse epic, which venerates Musarion as a "beautiful soul," and promotes a lifestyle based on the "philosophy of the graces," a happy, ironically wise outlook on life, seeks to unify intellect and sensuousness through poetic invention.[41] Despite Johann Jakob Wilhelm Heinse's valiant effort to promote Wieland's outlook on pleasure-seeking amid grace and style, his *Laidion oder die Eleusinischen Geheimnisse* (1774,

Laidion or the Eleusinian Mysteries), together with *Musarion,* was condemned as pagan and anti-Christian and consigned to an index of immoral readings as determined by narrow-minded priests and pastors.[42] Those who read these works anyway were attracted less to pornographic elements than to the purification such characters experience or to the chastening of others who eventually find true love in the course of such narratives.

These differences in French and German literary productivity help to explain why Diderot and Schiller assume such different attitudes toward their subject. When German writers reproduced situations and characters from French literature, they recast them to point out social problems peculiar to Germany or teach moral lessons with a solemnity seldom found among French writers of the period. When Schiller translates the motif of prostitution from Diderot's work, he presents his adaptation to an audience conditioned to scorn and repel depictions of any deviant sexual conduct that does not lead to sanction and repentance. For that reason, the saving grace of the story from a French point of view is largely inconceivable to the German reader: The Marquis forgives the prostitute who is now his wife and lives with her happily ever after. Schiller's Marquis doesn't just withdraw to his country estate; he makes hurried plans for a hasty *Abreise* (departure). Diderot's Marquis d'Arcis calculates that the whole business will have blown over in about three years and he can return to the capital "sans consequence" (207), meaning without embarrassment. Schiller's Marquis von A***, on the other hand, breaks away with his woman of easy virtue to escape the consequences of her former life to his reputation, and to forestall the disintegration of his social status. He doesn't even give her the time to pack, as Diderot's Marquis d'Arcis had granted his wife. While Diderot implies that none are so pious as a converted whore, who can give her man untold pleasure, Schiller widens and deepens the moral abyss into which his Marquis has fallen by referring to those former times Diderot hadn't mentioned. His Marquis von A*** will not return until, literally, "the trees of time [have] grow[n] bark over the injuries of the past" (see p. 35).[43] Schiller brings the image of the prostitute into a German literary context with its strong tradition of moral indignation at libidinous excess, where a nobleman who marries a prostitute will be censured much more severely than Diderot judged his Marquis d'Arcis. In tune with his audience, Schiller has his characters make a more contrite, speedy departure.

The rapid survey above has shown that contrasting political developments and variant units of cultural inheritance account in part for the two distinct narrative perspectives. In search of other factors which help explain these contrary outlooks, the particular literary environments in France and Germany as well as their differing religious predispositions were examined. Yet these factors, as significant as they are, do not account completely for Diderot's more casual vantage point and Schiller's serious moral fascination.

Both writers, it would seem, are driven by more innate impulses. Diderot uses every stylistic means at his disposal to reflect the human condition by exposing deeply troubling examples of retribution, especially prevalent in Paris at the time. Diderot's narrator rises above those human foibles by poking fun at them and suggesting that it's all just gossip, rumor, and idle chatter. All that his characters need do is move away, flee to their estates or to another country to avoid being caught up in plots and intrigues. His point is that no one is safe in this society. Schiller, on the other hand, reacts as an artist propelled by a more deep-seated, spontaneous compulsion, like someone kicked in the moral solar plexus. As disparate as these narrative points of view appear, there may be, on a more fundamental level, a common denominator. Ever since Robert L. Trivers first proposed it in evolutionary biology in 1985,[44] the theory of "reciprocal altruism" has attracted several proponents, who offer a fresh perspective on both ethical and aberrant behavior. Michael Shermer (1997), Robert Buckman (2000), Robert Hinde (2002), and Marc Hauser (2006)[45] have made the case for understanding our sense of right and wrong as an essential attribute, necessary for the continuation of the human race. In the days of hunters and gatherers, it was, according to them, a matter of life and death to know whom one could trust and who was untrustworthy. Gossip was the source for reputation that had survival value in as much as it identified who was a good reciprocator and who was an unreliable cheat. In the *Origins of Virtue,* Matt Ridley argues that morality is a by-product of the instinct to persevere that, at an earlier point in human development, necessitated self-fashioning as a kind and generous individual, if he or she was to remain in the group. Once ostracized, a man or woman alone could and would not endure for very long. It was likewise imperative to denounce and punish double-dealers, frauds and deceivers, lest primitive humans perish because they relied upon them.[46] In light of this theory as applied to Diderot and Schiller, we can understand our own fascination with this story as the result of stimulation that reaches us at the primary level. Diderot perceives the immoral event as deeply rooted in human nature. To illustrate this, he develops characters based on the conduct of his friends and foes.

Drawing instinctively the tragic conclusion from source material rich in perception is Schiller's strength. His uncanny ability to plumb the innermost regions of the psyche, to show what makes individuals good or bad, how they fall from honorable to immoral, or from idealist to traitor enables him to make major contributions to German culture. What others treated in a lighter vain, even as comedy, Schiller probed to deeper levels of life's vital force. He treats both historical source material and literary models in the same meticulous, probing way. His refashioning of historical events and personalities is well documented. In a letter to Caroline von Beulwitz, he states that he feels sorry for future generations who might mistake his fictional representations for historical fact because history was but an arsenal of reading materials for his own poetic imagination.[47] But, as we have seen, so were literary models. His adaptation of Diderot's Madame de La Pommeraye shows a pattern we can also detect in his reworking of *Le Père de famille*. In that play and in Schiller's *Intrigue and Love* the motives are the same: Aristocrats fall in love with women of lower social status. Both St. Albin and Ferdinand are forced by their fathers into marriages with women they don't love; neither of them will listen to or obey their parents. When they are threatened with extreme consequences, they draw swords against their fathers. In both plays, the young nobles plan to flee into a neighboring country with their bourgeois paramours. The women characters follow the same plot line: Sophie and Luise refuse to run away, even when Diderot's Commander and Schiller's President show up with soldiers and force their way into bourgeois homes in order to arrest their sons. Both middle-class women regard the gulf between the classes as far wider than do their aristocratic lovers. The actions of Schiller's Lady Milford mirror the commendable deeds of the Comtesse d'Amaldi. In short, the parallels are so numerous that there can be little doubt as to where Schiller ultimately got his idea for *Intrigue and Love,* whether directly from Diderot or via Otto von Gemmingen's loose translation.[48]

Nor was Schiller above capitalizing on the scandal surrounding *Le Père de famille,* one that made the plot, the motives, and the characters notoriously well known among theater audiences all over Europe. In 1761 the *Année Littéraire,* a magazine devoted to theater criticism, had accused Diderot of plagiarism, contending that he had pilfered these situations from Carlo Goldoni's *Padre di famiglia*. Despite Goldoni's insistence that such incrimination was unjust, the public remained convinced that the complaint was true.[49] Even Voltaire thought Diderot was guilty of literary piracy.[50] In *Jacques le fataliste et son maitre,* Diderot rewrites another of Goldoni's less than adequate plays, *Le Bourru bienfaisant* (The Benevolent Curmudgeon), which had been staged in Paris in 1771, insisting he was merely correcting the artistic deficiencies in a mediocre stage production. His point is that this could have been a good play, but Goldoni was simply not up to the task of making it great. He, therefore, begins rewriting the script with the words, "if I had written that play . . . "[51] which kept the whole question of Diderot's plagiarism alive and in front of the reading public. But if Diderot did appropriate situations from Goldoni's work, which was never proven beyond a reasonable doubt, then Schiller rewrites Diderot's *Le Père de famille,* in order to center on ethical issues and the resulting tragic implications. The situations, the characters, the abuse of power — in short, the whole class struggle — had, because of the scandal, heightened the sensitivity of Schiller's German middle-class audience to the issues he raises, which helps to explain the success of Schiller's play on the German stage.

Yet, as with his Madame and Marquis, Diderot offers a simple solution to the problems in *Le Père de famille,* one that avoids pain and misery. All that has to happen is that evidence emerges to confirm that Sophie has some noble blood in her veins, and all is forgiven, all can end well. Schiller shows what happens when no such evidence is forthcoming. Stimulated by Diderot's perception of the absurdity of class distinction and social rank, both of which impede the development of true love, Schiller reacts to the scenario on an instinctive level. Such base behavior, such immoral conduct as shown by these fathers against their own flesh and blood, such abuse of aristocratic power against those of lower rank can only lead to death and destruction. The French tale of retribution detailed by an incessant gossip becomes a German moral tragedy, one horrific example of the monstrous behavior of Frau von P*** told from the vantage point of a morally driven narrator's all-seeing eye. Determined to probe the depths of the psyche, Schiller shocks the reader to the core, where Diderot invites us to grin and smirk. Politically, Diderot's literary representation was dangerous and provocative to the powers that be, an integral part of the emerging class struggle between aristocrats and bourgeoisie, whereas Schiller focused on a specific act of aristocratic wrongdoing in a language specific to the elites, condemning them on their own terms by their own words. As heir to a distinct cultural legacy, the French writer could build on and borrow from a literary subset scorned in Germany, where readers looked more for moral guidance than for a parody of decadence. Diderot's and Schiller's respective cultural backgrounds in philosophy and religion as well as their respective audiences prompted different reactions to examples of revenge and atonement. For the French *philosophe* it's all part of the game we play with one another, all a characteristic of our human condition that he observes, points out, and tries to avert with an equally ludicrous solution. The response of the German poet is to unfold all the ethical dimensions, put the tragic consequences in the spotlight, and familiarize his readers with villains and liars, scoundrels and deceivers, who threaten the harmony of civilization and the freedom of the individual, and the conditions that create them.

University of Florida

Notes

[1] *Schillers Werke. Nationalausgabe,* ed. Julius Petersen et al. (Weimar: Hermann Böhlaus Nachfolger, 1943ff.); quotes from vol. 16 (ed. H. H. Borcherdt, 1954), referred to hereafter as NA with volume and page number, here 16:223.

[2] "Aber die kühne Neuheit dieser Intrige, die unverkennbare Wahrheit der Schilderung, die Schmucklose Eleganz der Beschreibung haben mich in Versuchung geführt, eine Übersetzung davon zu wagen . . ." (NA 16:223–24).

[3] "Das Original . . . habe ich nur hie und da verglichen." "Vorwort," in *Schillers Sämtliche Schriften,* ed. Karl Goedeke, 3rd ed. (Stuttgart: Cotta, 1868), 3:xiv.

[4] "Schiller und Diderot," in *Marbacher Schillerbuch,* Zur hundertsten Wiederkehr von Schillers Todestag, herausgegeben vom Schwäbischen Schillerverein (Stuttgart and Berlin: Cotta, 1905), 81–91.

[5] *Schillers Sämtliche Werke.* Säkular-Ausgabe, ed. Eduard von der Hellen and Richard Weißenfels (Stuttgart and Berlin: Cotta, 1904–5), 2:410. Subsequent citations as "SA" with volume and page number.

[6] "Diderots ganze Beredsamkeit wird dennoch schwerlich den Abscheu hinwegräsonieren, den diese unnatürliche notwendig erwecken muß" (NA 16:223).

[7] For more details, see my article, "Schiller, Diderot and the Dalberg Manuscript," *Germanic Review* 46 (May 1971): 167–81.

[8] For an overview of the history of Diderot's manuscript, see the introduction by Simone Lecointre and Jean Le Galliot to their edition, *Jacques Le Fataliste et son Maitre.* Edition critique. Texte et variantes établis sur le manuscript de Léningrad (Genève: Librairie Doz, 1977), xiii–lxxx. Quotes in parentheses in the text are from this edition.

[9] Letter to Merck, 7 April 1780, No. 228, in *Goethe. Briefe.* Hamburger Ausgabe. 2nd ed., ed. Karl Mandelkow and Bodo Morawe (Hamburg: Wegner, 1968), 1:300: "Es schleicht ein Manuscript von Diderot: Jacques le fataliste et son maitre herum, das ganz vortrefflich ist. Eine sehr köstliche und große Mahlzeit mit großem Verstand für das Maul eines einzigen Abgottes zugerichtet und aufgetischt."

[10] For details, see Joseph R. Smiley, *Diderot's Relations With Grimm* (Champagne/Urbana: U of Illinois P, 1950).

[11] Jeffrey L. High refers to Schiller's "practice of artificially reinforcing the historical urgency of the tale by disguising names and places through omission." Jeffrey L. High, "The Author of Literary Prose," in: Paul Kerry, ed., *Friedrich Schiller. Playwright, Poet, Philosopher, Historian* (Oxford: Peter Lang, 2007), 117–51, here 149.

[12] "qui regardait de plus près à son four qu'à la conduite de sa femme" (121).

[13] I have consulted the following translations, J. Robert Loy, *Diderot. Jacques the Fatalist and His Master* (New York/London: Norton, 1959); Wesley D. Camp and Agnes G. Raymond, *Jack the Fatalist and His Master. A New Translation from the French of Denis Diderot.* American University Studies. Series II: Romance Languages and Literature. Vol. 8 (New York: Peter Lang, 1984); David Coward, *Denis Diderot. Jacques the Fatalist. A New Translation.* Oxford World's Classics (London: Oxford UP, 1999). I am indebted to them all.

[14] "Ils se battent une seconde, une troisieme, jusqu'à huit ou dix fois . . ." (156).

[15] "Ce pauvre Marquis me fait pitié" (128).

[16] "Pas trop à moi" (128).

[17] "La chienne! La coquine! l'enragée! Et porquoi aussi s'attacher à une pareille femme?" (128).

[18] "Et pourquoi aussi la séduire et s'en détacher?" (128).

[19] "Pas un instant de crainte, pas le moindre signe d'incertitude, pas un remords; je l'ai vue se prêter sans répugnance à cette longue horreur" (208).

[20] "que des trahisons moins communes" (213).

[21] "eine Verräterei, die nur weniger alltäglich ist" (NA, 189).

[22] English title as trans. by Charles E. Passage (1962).

[23] "Voulez-vous que nous laissions là cette élégante et prolixe bavarde d'hôtesse et que nous reprenions les amours de Jacques? Pour moi, je ne tiens a rien" (149).

[24] For a brilliant analysis, see Erich Auerbach, "Musikus Miller," chapter 17 in *Memesis. Dargestellte Wirklichkeit in der abendländischen Literatur* (Berne: Francke, 1946), 404–21.

[25] Schiller says as much and offers a detailed explanation in his announcement on 11 Nov. 1784, concerning the publication of his literary magazine the *Rheinische Thalia*. ("Vermischte Schriften," SA 16:146–48).

[26] Another insightful analysis is offered in Erich Auerbach's *Memesis*, chapter 16: "Das unterbrochene Abendessen," 371–403.

[27] R. Frick, "Manon Lescault als Typus," *Germanisch-Romanische Monatsschrift* 7 (1915/16), 123–45.

[28] "en rue Traversiere à l'Hôtel Hambourg."

[29] Klaus Sasse, *Die Entdeckung der "courtisane vertueuse" in der Französischen Literatur des 18. Jahrhunderts: Rétif de la Bretonne und seine Vorgänger*. PhD diss., Hamburg, 1967.

[30] Anne Coudreuse, *Diderot. Jacques le Fataliste* (Paris: Gallimard, 1993); see "La marquise de Merteuil," 94–95.

[31] The version by Laclos remains the most popular. Christopher Hampton dramatized Laclos's novel for the London stage, after which it became a hit on Broadway. It has been filmed under various names eight times and adapted for television twice. Piet Swerts and Conrad Susa have both composed music for an opera based on the novel.

[32] Paul Vernière, "Diderot et l'invention littéraire: Jacques le fataliste," *Revue de l'histoire littéraire de la France* 59 (1959): 156–67.

[33] Jeannette Geffriaud Rosso, *"Jaques le fataliste": L'Amour et son Image* (Pisa: Libreria Goliardica Editrice, 1981), 117.

[34] The term, pertaining to libraries that lent such books, was coined by the book dealer Heinrich Wilhelm Fleischer in his *Über bildende Künste, Kunsthandel und Buchhandel in Hinsicht auf Menschenwohl: Glaubensbekenntnis eines Kunst- und Buchhändlers* (1792; repr., Munich: Kraus, 1981), 65.

[35] The term was used in the *Gothische Gelehrten Zeitungen* for the year 1793. Quoted by Alberto Martino and Marlies Stützel-Prüsner, "Publikumsschichten, Lesegesellschaften und Leihbibliotheken," in *Zwischen Revolution und Restauration: Klassik, Romantik,* ed. Horst Albert Glaser, Deutsche Literatur. Eine Sozialgeschichte, vol. 5 (Hamburg: Rowohlt, 1980), 49.

[36] See the article by Friedrich Karl von Moser in the *Neues Patriotisches Archiv für Deutschland* II (1794), 184–85.

[37] A few notable exceptions are surveyed by Fritz Landsittel, *Die Figur der Kurtisane im deutschen Drama des 18. Jahrhunderts.* PhD diss., Universität Heidelberg, 1923.

[38] "j'ai peu lu l'Evangile et beaucoup de romans" (170).

[39] Hans Jakob Christoffel von Grimmelshausen, *The Runagate Courage,* trans. R. L. Heller and J. C. Osborne (Lincoln: U of Nebraska P, 1965).

[40] Hans Hauschild, *Die Gestalt der Hetäre in der griechischen Komödie* (Leipzig: Vogel, 1933).

[41] Werner Bock, *Die ästhetischen Anschauungen C. M. Wielands* (Berlin, 1921); Karl-Heinz Kausch, "Die Kunst der Grazie," *Jahrbuch der deutschen Schillergesellschaft* 2 (1958): 12–42.

[42] Derek M. van Abbé, "Unfair to Wieland?" *Publications of the English Goethe Society* 32 (1962): 1–23.

[43] "die Zeit eine Rinde über das Vergangene gezogen hat" (NA 16:221).

[44] R. L. Trivers, *Social Evolution* (Menlo Park, CA: Benjamin & Cummings, 1985).

[45] Michael Shermer, *How We Believe: The Search for God in an Age of Science* (New York: W. H. Freeman, 1999); also *The Science of Good and Evil: Why People Cheat, Gossip, Care, Share and Follow the Golden Rule* (New York: Holt, 2004); Robert Buckman, *Can We Be Good without God?* (Toronto: Viking, 2000); Robert A. Hinde, *Why Good Is Good: The Sources of Morality* (London: Routledge, 2002); Marc Hauser, *Moral Minds: How Nature Designed Our Universal Sense of Right and Wrong* (New York: Ecco, 2006).

[46] Matt Ridley, *The Origins of Virtue* (London: Penguin, 1997).

[47] To Caroline von Beulwitz, 10/11 Dec.1788, NA 25:154.

[48] Schiller does not mention Diderot directly, but does refer to the title of his play. Instead he mentions Otto von Gemmingen's free form translation, *Der deutsche Hausvater.* For details, see Walter Schafarschik, *Friedrich Schiller. Kabale und Liebe.* Erläuterungen und Dokumente. Reclam Universal-Bibliothek, No. 33 (Stuttgart: Reclam, 1980), 68.

[49] In his memoirs (1787) Goldoni exonerates Diderot and tells of his visit with him. He was also very disappointed that Diderot kept up his criticism of Goldoni's work. See *The Memoirs of Carlo Goldoni Written by Himself,* trans. Jonathan Black (New York: Knopf, 1926), chapter 12, 157–60.

[50] Charles Palissot de Montenoy, who had attacked both Diderot and Rousseau in his comedies, informed Voltaire of the brewing scandal in a letter dated 28 May 1760. His reaction is recorded in *Œuvres complètes de Voltaire,* ed. Adrien J. Q. Beauchot and Georges Bengesco (Paris: Garnier Frères, 1880), Corr. p. 406, Note 1.

[51] "si j'en avais été l'auteur" (133).

12: True Crime and Criminal Truth: Schiller's "The Criminal of Lost Honor"

Gail K. Hart

AS A YOUNG MAN, FRIEDRICH SCHILLER was vitally interested in crime and criminals, not merely for the excitement of the illicit but also for the moral complications that lawbreakers and their judges presented to the thoughtful reader or spectator. His highly successful play, *Die Räuber* (1781, The Robbers), was built around the figure of Karl Moor, a charismatic criminal who was driven to become a robber captain by a scheming brother and a weak father. Karl did in fact rob, murder, and burn communities to the ground, but he became and remains one of the German stage's most popular heroes. As Schiller put it: "They will admire my incendiary bandit, yes even almost love him."[1] German audiences loved him without any qualification and the apotheosis of the lawbreaker at the beginning of Schiller's career set the tone for further investigations of criminality as a legitimate response to intolerable circumstances.

Schiller himself lived in intolerable circumstances as a cadet in the personal military school of Duke Karl Eugen of Württemberg, into which he was literally drafted by the Duke at the age of fourteen. Schiller had done especially well in the state examinations and Karl Eugen, reviewing the results, decreed that he should be enrolled against his parents' wishes and against his own. Schiller had hoped to study theology, which was not offered at the Karlsschule (literally "Karl's school"), but he was inducted anyway and ordered to study law and then allowed to study medicine. Discipline was severe and surveillance was unrelenting as cadets marched through their regimented days in robotic unison. Families were kept at a distance and the young men were obliged to regard the Duke as their father. Indeed, a number of them could actually claim him as father biologically, if illegitimately, because Karl Eugen frequently exercised his "right" to the young women of his duchy and stashed their male issue at the school.[2] Schiller also studied alongside several castrati whom Karl had had altered for the court opera. It was a repressive, controlling environment, organized around blind obedience to the solipsistic Duke, who had created the school to train future servants of the state. However, while attending to his physical, representative, and administrative needs, Karl Eugen had also recruited a staff of accomplished teachers, and the Karlsschule, despite its military emphasis, provided Schiller with a good classical education. This education was extended because he had to write two dissertations and a practical paper before he was awarded his doctor of medicine and then, deemed ripe for civil service, he was assigned to a regiment of mostly elderly men as the company physician.

While still working on his doctoral theses, Schiller wrote *The Robbers* in secret and sneaked out of Württemberg to witness the triumphant premiere in Mannheim. There, Schiller was celebrated as the author of the moment and he witnessed the explosive impact of his play in a full professional production. When he tried to attend another performance (one has to imagine the contrast between accepting the adulation of an enthusiastic audience and ministering to the regiment), he was apprehended, placed in military jail for a short period, and forbidden in perpetuity to write any further "comedies." Thus Schiller was himself something of a criminal, having sat out a jail sentence and having continued to practice his now-criminalized writing profession. He also became a fugitive shortly thereafter, running for the border and fleeing Württemberg for the freedom of Mannheim and a career as dramatist, poet, and occasional writer of prose. The regiment's loss was posterity's gain.

Not much was made of the fictional prose by the author of great dramas like *The Robbers, Don Carlos, Wallenstein,* and *Mary Stuart* and the writer of dozens of famous poems that are still today memorized by German school children. Consequently, the exquisite tale of Christian Wolf and his encounters with the law has never had the full notoriety it deserved — though it is probably the best known of the prose pieces. "Der Verbrecher aus verlorener Ehre. Eine wahre Geschichte" (The Criminal of Lost Honor. A True Story) appeared anonymously in 1786 as "Criminal of Infamy. A True Story" (Verbrecher aus Infamie. Eine wahre Geschichte) in Schiller's journal *Thalia* — it was hoped that the crime theme would entice readers to buy and read the journal. The final version was published under the author's name in 1792 with a few very minor changes. This slightly altered later version forms the basis for the translation in our volume.

Schiller's or the narrator's challenge in the story of Christian Wolf — a name that has both pious and feral associations — is to elicit and earn empathy for the young man who crossed legal lines in a series of desperate acts. In German absolutist societies, legal lines were locally determined by a dizzying array of princes, dukes, counts, and other minor nobles who ruled the more than three hundred principalities that occupied the area now known as Germany. The eighteenth-century poet Friedrich Hölderlin commented on the arbitrariness of the contemporary legal and penal systems in a haunting aphorism about the slippery ontology of crime and punishment: Punishment is the infliction of just deserts and the consequence of criminal actions. Criminal actions are those that result in punishment. And punishment results where criminal actions are committed."[3]

The determining factor in Hölderlin's circular attempt to define crime via punishment and punishment via crime is the ruler's will. Inasmuch as law defines crime, our understanding of legal right and wrong is here dependent on the caprice of hereditary rulers and the interests of the ruling. In Schiller's tale, empathy for or identification with the criminal is an exercise in testing shared human emotions and inclinations and an internal sense of right against the legal systems of the petty tyrants of the eighteenth-century German principalities.

There are conditions under which we all might transgress or consider doing so and Schiller was attempting an *explanation* for criminal aberration that implicates the audience in the mental processes that lead *or could lead* to illicit action. This is a gesture that has been repeated by writers for over two centuries; indeed, it is almost impossible to imagine television and film without it. The need to ground and explain criminal activity, even where law is relatively stabilized, leads us to scrutinize the circumstances of the crime and also of the criminal as *delinquent* — that is, as a person with a past whose formative years disposed and positioned him for a particular antisocial act. At the root of such scrutiny is the conviction that humanity is basically good. This conviction is endangered by abhorrent crime and the need arises to absorb an apparent contradiction, the crime, into this belief system. Faced with evidence of an abhorrent crime, we can either denounce the perpetrator as something other than decent and human, thus rescuing humanity by excising the criminal, or we can acknowledge the perpetrator's humanity and address the riddle of his apparently indecent or aberrant, or even deviant behavior, a popular literary exercise that was only beginning in Schiller's time.

Joining with other contemporary practitioners of *Seelenkunde* (literally "soul knowledge"),[4] Schiller addressed this riddle by looking at his subject's social and economic circumstances and at his formative years, toward a larger examination of the human soul under the influence of eighteenth-century absolutism and its institutions. One of these institutions, which may require some explanation for the reader who puzzles at Schiller's mention of "stealing honorably," is the feudal lord's control of the beasts of the forests. These animals were the property of the land-owning nobility and in many regions; farmers, townspeople, and laborers were not allowed to hunt or kill them without permission. To do so was to steal from the lord who owned the forests and everything within. The reason why such theft might be designated honorable is that these edicts were oppressive to hunters, who needed the game for food and most especially to farmers, whose fields were ravaged and trampled by animals that they were not allowed to kill. This also diminished the supply of food and thereby complicated the satisfaction of a basic human need. Thus poaching or illegal hunting was something of an ambiguous crime inasmuch as it often contributed to the well-being of the oppressed and did no significant damage to the victims, who were well-off and had not catalogued or inventoried the contents of their forests. They were unlikely to feel the absence of the contested animals but were threatened and provoked by the subversion practiced by poachers as the feudal clock ticked toward 1789 and the ultimate defiance of inherited dominion.

Indeed, in this atmosphere of relatively helpless subjection to absolutism, poachers were even celebrated by the common people, precisely because of their scorn for questionable laws and, it seems, because their motivations were accessible to and shared by those who were law-abiding. One of the most popular bandits of the time was Matthias Klostermayer (1736–71), the Bavarian Robin Hood, a poacher who also troubled various tax collectors and petty officials of the crown, whose job it was to enforce unwelcome legislation. Klostermayer was a genuine miscreant, who also robbed and roughed up innocent citizens, but the legend presents him as a hunter and benefactor of the people and he is frequently cited as one of the historical models for Schiller's beloved Karl Moor (The Robbers). Poaching was illegal but apparently morally acceptable and Christian Wolf's illicit hunting — done for perceived love of his Hanne — was a very minor transgression, a liminal crime, that would not have taken him to the slippery slope had it not been for the excessive punishment that followed. Schiller's social criticism (the logical conclusion of his primary anthropological and psychological interests) focuses on the justice system of his time, specifically on the practice of looking at the statute or the letter of the law and not at the human circumstances that brought about the transgression. He portrays a tendency to condemn and ostracize the offender and argues for a more empathic understanding of crime and what leads to it. Excessive punishment, here intended to re-define and magnify a minor crime with subversive implications, is itself a crime in Schiller's view.

In Wolf's story, the facts of the fictional case are particularly egregious. His rival for Hanne was, of all things, a forester and game warden who deliberately hunted him down for the sake of personal animus rather than justice. An especially severe edict against poaching had just been renewed at the time of Wolf's first arrest and it prescribed a prison sentence for this lesser crime. He was able to avoid prison by sacrificing his entire financial base and paying a large fine, but this left him still in love, but now without means. Poverty compelled him to poach; Robert the Forester followed again, again advancing his own romantic and professionally ambitious agenda. This time Wolf was sent to the penitentiary for one year. Upon his release, he was both angry and unemployable and he again took to the forest, once again to be arrested, by Robert, for poaching. In no way was Wolf innocent of the crimes he was accused of, but the justice system failed him repeatedly by not considering the contributing factors. As Schiller puts it in a much-quoted and well-known formulation: "The judges looked into the book of laws, but not one of them looked into the psychological constitution of the accused" (NA 16:11-12; see p. 42). Wolf was branded and sentenced to three years at the state penitentiary, where he was housed with murderers. The recidivist poacher learned from the hardened inmates and in his own account, "I entered the dungeon . . . as a lost soul, and I left it as a criminal" (NA 16:12; see p. 42) This institutionally aggravated moral corruption is not new to the contemporary reader, who is familiar with "the crime of punishment"[5] and prisons as schools for criminals, but it was both daring and perceptive in 1786 to expose the need for a re-thinking of prison politics. Wolf is acutely aware of the injustice of his punishment and indeed considers himself "prepunished," that is, as having earned the right to commit the crimes that would retroactively justify the severity of the penalties assessed against him. This is a very important observation since it suggests that excessive punishment also tips the balance in the mind of the criminal who responds to the surplus penal attention as if it were license to commit further crimes. His debt to society overpaid, Wolf exits the penal institution ready to make good on his credit.

Thus the love-struck poacher is transformed into a truly dangerous malefactor. The intensification of slight anti-social tendencies, following on a lack of guidance in youth — Schiller makes much of Wolf's father having died early[6] — and complicated by the over-zealousness of the justice system, reaches the point where our subject is positioned for all manner of crime, including murder. Wolf's personality, his family background, and his misfortunes suffice to have placed him on the edge of decent society, but Schiller includes another social-critical factor here, possibly as a critique of elementary or unreflected physiognomy, the new "science" of judging character from physical, usually facial, appearance popularized by Johann Kaspar Lavater (1741–1801). Christian Wolf is exceptionally ugly, "pleasing to no one" physically, and teased and mocked by his classmates and peers. In a crucial scene, he is rejected by an attractive child, to whom he had shown kindness, solely on the basis of his appearance. The child's reaction speaks for his society, and the ugly son of a deceased innkeeper, himself to become infamous as the Innkeeper of the Sun, reacts to yet another exclusion with lawbreaking. The point is not that ugliness is a certain sign of inner or spiritual corruption (and bad intentions), but rather that any correlation between the two may be the result of injury done by society to those who deviate from established standards of beauty. It is for this reason that Schiller's tale is thought to have influenced Mary Shelley's *Frankenstein* (1818).[7] Shelley's monster is also rejected, abused, and ostracized because of his loathsome appearance and he too suffers deeply from the rejection. Like Wolf, the monster swears vengeance against the society that formed him and like Wolf, the monster murders. Wolf's failure of pulchritude is yet another element of the case Schiller has been assembling as he poses the very difficult question of why and how human beings turn to crime and why they kill.

"The Criminal of Lost Honor" is Schiller's focused and sustained attempt to make murder intelligible to his bourgeois readers, but we may question whether the attempt is successful. Wolf advances from morally tolerable transgressions to the act of taking another man's life, and Schiller investigates this act with an emphasis on the details of what has gone before. Cursed with ugliness, deprived of a father at an early age, the protagonist suffers a series of insults and injustices to which he responds with increasingly asocial and anti-social behavior. Schiller's appeal to the reader-judge to look into the delinquent's heart rather than into a law book facilitates a utilitarian argument that aligns him with Cesare Beccaria (1738–94)[8] and other penal reformers of the time who based their challenges to penal retribution on a more refined criminal psychology. However, it is the mystery of murder that prevails in this tale and, despite the near-excess of explanation that Schiller applies to the case, the homicidal moment remains inscrutable. As Wolf tells it, he returned from his three-year sentence, began poaching out of pure defiance, and ran into Robert alone in the woods:

> Of all people, the one person I hated more intensely than any living thing in the world, and this person was suddenly subject to the mercy of my lead ball. In this moment, it seemed to me as if the whole world was at stake in my shot and that all the hatred of my entire life had rushed into the one fingertip with which I was to apply the deadly pressure. (NA 16:15; see p. 45)

Yet the significant moment in which Wolf actually willed the killing and pulled the trigger is elided:

> My arm trembled as I left the dreadful decision to my shotgun—my teeth chattered as if in a fever chill, and my breath was frozen suffocating in my lungs. For an entire minute, the aim of my shotgun swayed undecided somewhere between the man and the deer—a minute—and another—and yet another. Vengeance and conscience wrestled unmercifully, uncertain—but vengeance won, and the forester lay dead on the ground. (NA 16:15–16; see p. 45)

In the description of this crucial moment, Wolf offloads the decision to finger, arm, shotgun, and the agencies of vengeance and conscience.[9] The murder, the actual triggering of the mechanism (another intermediary) that shoots the bullet into the enemy, is not a direct application of will, but more of an observation of the action that preceded it and the result that followed. The careful exploration of the movements of mind and development that result in crime brings us to the brink of the event but cannot take us any farther. This is the limit of the human truth that Schiller seeks in this "autopsy of his depravity." He can't explain or depict the essence of the act of killing another human being. He can only provide the context. Of course, the contributing factors are highly significant and can be addressed by readers receptive to Schiller's didacticism.

Schiller recognized several kinds of truth in his "True Story," confidently drawing the line between "inner" or human truth, what he considered the universals of the human psyche, and historical truth. As a historian, Schiller often worked on chronicling events that he treated very differently in his poetic works, such as the material surrounding the histories of *Don Karlos* and *Wallenstein*, one of the differences being that in drama he sought to demonstrate general species behavior where history, he believed, was limited to conveying the individual behavior of particular specimens. He made this dichotomy explicit in a letter to Caroline von Beulwitz, two years after publishing "Criminal":

> What you say of *history* is certainly right and the advantage of *truth* that history has over novels, could alone elevate it above them. The question is, however, whether the *inner truth*, which I call philosophical and artistic truth . . . does not have as much value as historical truth. That a person in *such* situations feels, acts, and expresses himself in *such a way* is a great, significant fact for humanity and the novelist or dramatist has to get that across. The inner correspondence, the truth, will be felt and acknowledged without the actual occurrence of the event. The usefulness is not to be missed: this way one comes to know *mankind* and not simply *one man*, the [human] race and not the easily [unrepresentative] individual.[10]

Inner truth trumps historical truth for Schiller in this instance, but "Criminal" also has historical roots and its inclusions and omissions are enlightening. In a sense, Schiller was transforming a single historical individual, the ruffian, bandit, and murderer Fridrich Schwan (1729–60), into a literary figure with whom readers could identify because of psychological similarities. The historical Schwan will always be surface and facts, but the fictional Wolf consists of emotions, motives, and reactions that speak to an audience that watches him deteriorate (or grow) into someone like Schwan. This opposition between historical truth and the more empathic truth of literary fiction is represented by Schiller's narrator in terms of heating (fiction) and cooling (history):[11]

> An irreconcilable contrast prevails between the heated emotional state of an acting human being and the quiet mood of the reader to whom the story is presented; such a broad gap separates them that it is difficult, indeed impossible, for the latter to recognize any relationship to the former. A gulf separates the historical subject at hand and the read-

> er that preempts any possibility of a self-comparison or practical usefulness[. . . .] If the story is to mean anything more to us, and achieve its noble end, then we must necessarily choose from one of the following two methods—either the reader must become as heated as the protagonist, or the protagonist must become as cold as the reader. (NA 16:8; see p. 40)

In Schiller's rendering, the choice between evoking either literary empathy or historical understanding seems to fall with literary warmth, but he does not neglect the historical and the career of the now-forgotten Schwan informs almost every page.[12]

Fridrich Schwan was a notorious criminal from Schiller's home province of Württemberg who was executed gruesomely (broken on the wheel) in 1760, a year after Schiller's birth. Schwan's family ran a prosperous guest house called the "Sun" and he, like Wolf, was known as the *Sonnenwirt* or Innkeeper of the Sun — a clear acknowledgment of the provenance or "truth" of the tale. Schiller's favorite teacher, Jacob Friedrich Abel (1751–1829) was the son of the magistrate who arrested Schwan and he had access to interrogation protocols and accounts of Schwan's behavior, including his own attempts to tell his shameful story. While awaiting sentencing and execution, Schwan would regale those who visited his cell with cautionary tales of his errant life and certain events were transmitted to Schiller through Abel. Abel published a biography of Schwan in 1787, a year after "Criminal" appeared,[13] but unlike Schiller's tale his book emphasized the criminal's remorse and return to Christian piety before death. For example, Abel describes a resigned and contrite killer on the scaffold:

> [Schwan], calm and resigned, said to those gathered around him: "Now it is my turn" and asked them to take him to the scaffold on which he was to be executed. Then, as soon as they untied him, he threw himself to the floor, prayed loudly and fervently, and warned the others not to follow his example, and thanked those who had been kind to him, most of them by name. This was his farewell to the world. As soon as it was finished, he asked the executioners how he should lie, laid himself down calmly and joyfully with their help and, praying and giving thanks, received the death blow.[14]

Abel's biography had a clear teleology as the criminal transgresses, confesses, repents, warns the crowd not to live as he did, and goes joyfully to his death in full expectation of everlasting redemption. Schiller's story, on the other hand, refers only briefly and very early on to Wolf's torture and execution and it ends with the criminal's arrest and self-identification: "I am the Innkeeper of the Sun." This may or may not be redemptive, but it is certainly suggestive of self-knowledge and recognition of his transgressions, a knowledge that the reader now shares to some extent.

Where Schiller ascribes some of Wolf's problems to the absence of a father, Schwan blamed his entire criminal career on his all-too-present father. As a young man, the fiery and passionate Schwan also desired women and needed money to realize his love or satisfy his lust. Since his father refused to give him any, Schwan began to hunt illegally, but he went further, stealing family money in his father's absence. His father reported the crime and Schwan was incarcerated locally, but broke out after a few days and fled. He was at large for some time but was finally apprehended, shot down from his horse, and sent to the district prison. "The prison had the effect that all prisons must have, as long as their current organization is maintained. [Schwan] came back ten times worse than when he went in,"[15] and Father Schwan was thus indirectly responsible for his son's criminal education. When he returned, Schwan terrorized the village and his family because his father would not allow him to marry the woman he loved — he was still under-age and needed permission. He was eventually re-incarcerated in the district prison for these many instances of brutality, but inasmuch as he broke out three times and continued his campaign of terror and vengeance against those who came between him and his beloved, he was finally sent to the Hohentwiel fortification for maximum security. There, the wild young man jumped from a high window, but broke a leg and was returned to his cell. Once it healed, he managed to gouge a hole in the wall of his cell with a single nail, and escaped once again.

Abel recounts Schwan's description of his first murder and here there is no ambiguity about agency. Like Wolf, Schwan killed a village rival, an old enemy, whom he happened to see in the forest just as he was aiming at a deer. Also like Wolf, Schwan described a situation of indecision where he tried mightily to control his hatred and turn away:

> He drew the rifle back, in order to aim at the deer again; but immediately the rage overcame him again; he aimed at his enemy again, and pulled back; he aimed again four times and four times he pulled back. Finally his senses were taken over by a complete confusion, struggle, rage, and terror clouded his mind, rage won, he shot, and committed his first murder.[16]

The derivation of Schiller's murder description is obvious, but the observation, "he shot," distinguishes the two passages and underscores Schiller's history-literature dichotomy. The historical figure shot an enemy, but the literary one who has our empathy considers shooting and then sees his enemy dead on the ground. The writer of fiction does not lead his warm readers to that wretched point where they are implicated in a homicide nor can he really convey the conscious act. Those who understand the protagonist's plight are not asked to understand or experience his (missing) will to kill. In the cold historical text, which Abel also uses to explain the psychological formation of a criminal and to criticize the justice system, Schwan shoots. The actual act is not elided or assumed, though Abel's effort to avoid it is evident. We can appreciate Schwan's humanity but the prose that conveys it is much colder than Wolf's first-person description of his emotions.

This, in brief, is the historical model for "The Criminal of Lost Honor," the true story that takes us beyond the criminal career of Schwan — who was described on wanted posters as good-looking — to the emotional development of his ugly counterpart, Christian Wolf. Wolf's conscience survives his years of crime and incarceration and he ultimately becomes dissatisfied with his life in the wild as the leader of a gang of thieves and murderers. He makes an attempt to join the military, writing several times to the sovereign and requesting pardon in exchange for military service, which would have allowed him to use the same skills he had developed with the gang under the mantle of legitimacy. "Criminal actions are those that result in punishment" and, according to this logic, since there is no punishment for killing and plundering in the service of the state, Wolf would have ceased to be a criminal. But his petitions were never heard — just as the fugitive Schiller's conciliatory letters to Duke Karl Eugen were never answered — and he resolved to try his luck in another province with another military unit.

As Wolf rides out to try to pursue a legitimate career and renounce his criminal past, he is apprehended at the gate of a small city where the gatekeeper, unlike the judges who sent him to prison, looks beyond his (stolen) papers and into his face, "on which so many raging emotions lay bare, much like the disfigured corpses on display at the site of a pilgrimage" (NA 16:26; see p. 53). The guard relies on his intuition and human understanding, but here to Wolf's disadvantage because he takes him to the court for further investigation. Wolf is ultimately detained but resists giving information about himself because the judge treats him rudely. On the next day, the judge apologizes for his behavior and treats Wolf with respect. Wolf identifies himself and confesses. This gesture of respect is often viewed as the restoration of the honor that Wolf had lost as an over-punished young man. The tale ends with this restoration, but the effect of Wolf's revelation is already known — both to Wolf and the reader. In confessing his identity to the judge, Wolf consents to be tortured and executed as a robber and murderer.

University of California, Irvine

Notes

[1] "Man wird meinen Mordbrenner bewundern, ja fast sogar lieben." *Unterdrückte Vorrede* [Suppressed Preface to *The Robbers*] in *Schillers Werke. Nationalausgabe,* ed. Julius Petersen et al. (Weimar: Herrman Böhlaus Nachfolger, 1943ff.), 3:244–45, my translation. Subsequent citations as "NA" with volume and page number.

[2] Peter Lahnstein, *Schillers Leben,* Munich: Paul List Verlag, 1981, 42–44.

[3] "Strafe ist das Leiden rechtmäßigen Widerstands und die Folge böser Handlungen. Böse Handlungen sind aber solche, worauf Strafe folgt. Und Strafe folgt da, wo böse Handlungen sind." "Über den Begriff der Strafe," in Friedrich Hölderlin, *Sämtliche Werke und Briefe,* II (Berlin: Aufbau Verlag, 1970), 362.

[4] See Peter-Andre Alt, *Schiller: Leben-Werk-Zeit* (Munich: Beck, 2000), 468–75 for thorough information on the contemporaries whose work on psychology and criminal psychology informed Schiller's narrative. These include Karl Philipp Moritz, Christoph Martin Wieland, Christian Heinrich Spiess, August Gottlieb Meissner, and Christian Garve.

[5] Karl Menninger's title for a seminal book that examined the anti-social effects of legal punishment (New York: Viking, 1968).

[6] Achim Auernhammer even suggests that it is as much the "lost father" as the lost honor that engenders his criminal career, in "Engagiertes Erzählen: *Der Verbrecher aus verlorener Ehre,*" in *Schiller und die höfische Welt,* ed. Auernhammer et al. (Tübingen: Max Niemeyer Verlag, 1980), 254–70, here 270.

[7] See Syndy McMillan Conger, "A German Ancestor for Mary Shelley's Monster," *Philological Quarterly* 59.2 (Spring 1980): 216–31.

[8] Cesare, Marquis of Beccaria-Bonesana (1738–94) was credited as the author of the highly influential pamphlet, *On Crimes and Punishments* (1764) that argued for, among other things, the uselessness of torture and the death penalty.

[9] Harald Neumeyer, noting the unconscious or non-conscious character of the actual act and Wolf's later statements that he did not himself understand how it had happened, argues that the narrator's careful causal sequence of ever-increasing anti-social sentiments cannot explain this crime. The narrator's causal argument fails, Neumeyer believes, because the act depicted was "incalculably unconscious." "Unkalkulierbar unbewusst — Zur Seele des Verbrechens um 1800" in *Romantische Wissenspoetik,* ed. Gabriele Brandstetter and Gerhard Neumann (Würzburg: Königshausen & Neumann, 2004), 151–77, here 163.

[10] Letter to Caroline von Beulwitz of 10 [and 11] December 1788: "Was Sie von der *Geschichte* sagen ist gewiß ganz richtig, und der Vorzug der *Wahrheit,* den die Geschichte vor dem Roman voraushat, könnte sie schon allein über ihn erheben. Es fragt sich nun ob die *innre Wahrheit,* die ich die philosophische und Kunstwahrheit nennen will, . . . nicht eben soviel Werth hat als die historische. *Daß* ein Mensch in *solchen* Lagen *so* empfindet, handelt, und sich ausdrückt ist ein großes wichtiges Factum für den Menschen; und das muß der Dramatische oder Romandichter leisten. Die innre Übereinstimmung die Wahrheit wird gefühlt und eingestanden, ohne daß die Begebenheit wirklich vorgefallen seyn muß. Der Nutzen ist unverkennbar. Man lernt auf diesem Weg den *Menschen* und nicht *den* Menschen kennen, die Gattung und nicht das sich so leichtverlierende Individuum" (NA 25:154), my translation.

[11] For an original and convincing discussion of the contrast between Schiller's narrator and Wolf, who narrates the greater part of the tale in the first person, see David Rosen, "Die Annalen seiner Verirrungen: The Divided Narrative of *Der Verbrecher aus verlorener Ehre,*" *New German Review* 10 (1994): 11–27.

[12] "Schiller's deceptive stated goal of purely objective analysis gives way to a 'captivating rendering' almost as soon as Wolf assumes narration, and the dialogue form of the 'final act' ending in sublime sacrifice bears all the hallmarks of Schiller's tragedies and is just as painful and riveting" (High 177).

[13] Jakob Friedrich Abel, *Lebensgeschichte Fridrich Schwans* (Stuttgart: Ernst Klett Verlag, 2001), 36. All translations from this book are mine.

[14] "[Er] sagte zu den Umstehenden ganz ruhig und gelassen: Jezt ist die Reyhe an mir, und bat, ihn zu dem Gerüste, auf dem er hingerichtet werden sollte, hinzuführen. Hier warf er sich, sobald er entbunden war, nieder, betete laut und eifrig, ermahnte die Umstehenden, sich an ihm zu spiegeln, und dankte allen Personen, die ihm bisher Gutes gethan hatten, meistens namentlich. Diß war sein Abschied von der Welt. So bald dieser vollendet war, gieng er muthig auf das Gerüste hinauf, fragte die Henkersknechte, wie er sich legen müsse, legte sich dann mit ihrer Hülfe ruhig und freudig nieder und empfieng betend und dankend den tödtlichen Stoß" (Abel 71).

[15] "Das Zuchthaus hatte bey Schwanen die Folgen, die durchaus alle Zuchthäuser haben müssen, so lange ihre bisherige Einrichtung beybehalten wird. Er kam zehnmal schlimmer zurück, als er hineingegangen war" (Abel 38–39).

[16] "Er zog die Flinte zurück, um sie wieder gegen den Hirsch zu richten; aber sogleich übermannte ihn die Wuth aufs neue, er zielte wieder gegen seinen Feind und zog wieder zurück, viermal ziehlt er also aufs neue, und viermal zog er wieder zurück. Endlich bemeisterte sich eine gänzliche Verwirrung seiner Sinne, Kampf und Wuth und Schrecken umnebelten seinen Geist, die Wuth siegte, er schoß, und vollbracht war sein erster Mord" (Abel 45).

13: *Der Geisterseher:* A Princely Experiment or, the Creation of a "Spiritualist"

Dennis F. Mahoney

IN MAY OF 1786, ELISE VON DER RECKE published in the *Berlinische Monatsschrift* an exposé of the occultist deceptions of the Sicilian adventurer Guiseppe Balsamo, alias Count Cagliostro, during his stay at the court of Courland in 1779. Shortly thereafter, Prince Friedrich Heinrich Eugen of Württemberg wrote for that same monthly journal — in which Kant's definition of Enlightenment had appeared only two years previously — a response defending the possibility of communication with the spirit world. A member of the Protestant side of the ruling ducal family in Schiller's Württemberg, the young Prince had two sisters who already had converted to Catholicism. His essay was taken as a sign that he, too, was considering a conversion, thus raising the possibility that Duke Karl Eugen (best known today for his complicated relationship with the young Schiller), who had no direct male heirs, might one day be succeeded by a nephew who was a fellow Catholic. Schiller, acquainted with the political situation in his native land and looking for a sensational subject that would attract more readers to his journal *Thalia,* began working on a story that appeared in five installments between 1787 and 1789 before being published in book form as *Der Geisterseher. Aus den Memoires des Grafen von O**** (1789; 3rd rev. ed. 1798, The Spiritualist. From the Memoirs of Count von O**). The term *Geisterseher* is not Schiller's invention. Kant had employed it in *Träume eines Geistersehers, erläutert durch Träume der Metaphysik* (1766, Dreams of a Ghost-seer, elucidated through Dreams of Metaphysics), his critique of Emanuel Swedenborg's theosophical-cosmological speculations that attempts to regulate the products of the imagination through the beginnings of his own critical philosophy.[1] Karl Philipp Moritz likewise published *Fragmente aus dem Tagebuch eines Geistersehers* (1787, Fragments from the Diary of a Ghost-seer) that serve as a link between the rationalism of the earlier eighteenth century and the beginnings of Romanticism. But it is Schiller's story that not only seized the interests of readers throughout Europe but also provided a seismographic analysis of the political, religious, and psychological fissures of the late 1780s — features of the text and its reception that make his novel fragment fascinating to this day.

Already in 1765, one year before Kant's treatise on Swedenborgian spirit-seeing, Horace Walpole had published the prototype for the Gothic novel, namely *The Castle of Otranto,* whose setting in medieval Italy and alleged origin as a translation from an old manuscript helped make palatable to a modern, enlightened audience its depictions of supernatural intervention into human affairs. Ann Radcliffe continued this development in works like *A Sicilian Romance* (1790) with its tales of imprisonment in castles and convents from the sixteenth century. In both novels, the "Gothic" ruins testify to the end of a period of tyranny and superstition, while the foreign setting allows Walpole's and Radcliffe's readers to indulge in travels to an imaginary Middle Ages, set comfortably far away from their present situation. In the case of Schiller's *Spiritualist,* however, the action takes place in the recent past in the area around Venice, just over the Alps from German territories, and the main character is a German who becomes entrapped in the prisons of his own imagination. In Schiller's text, Venice is the meeting place for aristocrats from all over Europe who are there to view the churches and works of art, frequent the gaming tables, and indulge in sexual tourism. What for most of them is just one more stop on the Grand Tour becomes for the Prince an entry into the sinkholes of depravity just below the glittering surface of late-Enlightenment culture, including areas of his own psyche that have been inhibited or suppressed. Horror is coming uncannily closer to home, as E. T. A. Hoffmann — a great admirer of Schiller's *The Spiritualist,* which is mentioned explicitly in his tale "Das Majorat" (1817, The Entail of Succession) — will demonstrate in "Der Sandmann" (1816, The Sandman).[2]

From the very onset, Schiller's narrator makes it clear that his friend, the prince of an unnamed German principality, has been subjected to malicious deception. Although *The Spiritualist* was never completed, by the end of its second book it has become increasingly evident that unscrupulous manipulators are intent upon inducing this potential successor to the throne to convert to Catholicism and thereby expose his land to their machinations. Not only that — through a combination of enormous gambling debts, romantic infatuation, and the belief in his supposed intellectual and personal superiority, the Prince has been led to the point where he appears ready to murder the one remaining relative standing between himself and succession to the throne. Shortly before the end of Book Two, he is heard murmuring to himself the cryptic words that the so-called Armenian, a mysterious masked man, had uttered at the beginning of the tale: "Congratulations, Prince [. . .] *he died at nine o'clock*" (see p. 68)[3] Like the figure of Macbeth, Schiller's Prince is tempted by the embodiments of Fate to pursue what they suggest is his pre-ordained role in life, thereby throwing to the winds his earlier reputation for virtue and probity. In the case of Shakespeare's play, the "Weird Sisters" are not only malevolent, but also genuine figures from the world of witchcraft and magic. In *The Spiritualist,* by contrast, Schiller devotes the second half of Book One to exposing all the parlor-game tricks employed by the Armenian and his confederates to win the confidence of the Prince, and it is the Prince himself who unmasks a number of these deceptions. This section of the novel anticipates Ann Radcliffe's employment of the "Explained Supernatural" at the conclusion of her Gothic romances, with one crucial difference. Whereas this latter procedure brings the reader back to a comfortable, "enlightened" reality after having enjoyed a suspenseful ride through the haunted house of the plot, the Prince's ability to see through the first set of deceptions practiced upon him is in fact the prelude to his ensnarement in the even more carefully contrived plan of manipulation within Book Two of the novel.

Throughout the text, words like *Schlüssel* (key) and *Decke* (veil, cover) are employed repeatedly in terms of unlocking or uncovering the truth, but there are so many different tellers of tales with various degrees of reliability and trustworthiness that it becomes difficult, if not impossible, to ascertain the "truth pure and simple" (see p. 67)[4] that Count von O** proclaims as the guiding light of his narrative in the opening paragraph of the novel. In addition, the tale's location in Venice, particularly during the time of Carnival, lends a sensory dimension to the motif of masks and unmasking, leading to a profound uncertainty as to who the characters in the story actually are and what reality is. Carnival, we should not forget, is a "Catholic" and heavily ritualized festival that would have seemed foreign and even upsetting to eighteenth-century visitors from Protestant territories, yet the longer the Prince remains in Venice, the more at home he becomes, and the less willing to return to his previous life. As Victor Sage observes:

> The literary narrative of "black Venice" is itself, in the transitional period between Gothic and high Romantic, a labyrinth of epistemological doubt and disorientation, and evidently some specifically Venetian thematics — masquerade, for example, and the notion of a labyrinthine architectural space — enter the formal arrangement of these Gothic texts.[5]

There is, for example, a Chinese puzzle quality to Schiller's novel in installments, with one mystery being cleared up, but others still to be explained, and with enough plot teasers to encourage readers (and, eventually, other writers) to imagine how things will continue.[6] In this regard, we as readers are placed in a conundrum analogous to that of the Prince, which encourages us to empathize with him and to refrain from any overly hasty condemnation of his character.

Ultimately, Schiller's novel challenges its readers to question what could have induced an inhabitant of the supposed Age of Reason to fall prey to necromancers and conspirators against his own better judgment. In addition to his own pecuniary interests in enticing readers to buy the next installment of *Thalia,* Schiller put considerable effort into exploring the psychological predispositions and institutional mechanisms that made the Prince innately prone, as the narrator states, "to be dominated by others, though he was not weak" (see p. 68).[7] Kant's famous definition describes Enlightenment as *"der Ausgang des Menschen aus seiner selbstverschuldeten Unmündigkeit"* (mankind's exit from its self-incurred immaturity); it is a lack of courage — "laziness and cowardice" ("Feigheit und Faulheit") — that explains why the vast majority of people gladly remain immature for life.[8] Schiller, by contrast, makes a point of emphasizing the Prince's personal bravery and active desire to employ his critical faculties, which would seem to make him an exemplary representative of what for Kant is the motto of the Enlightenment: *"Sapere aude"* (dare to know). As Gert Vonhoff has demonstrated with regard to other tales by Schiller, it is the negative impact of societal pressures upon the minds and bodies of individuals that brings about their malformation.[9] Nowhere in Schiller's oeuvre does this process receive more extensive and intensive treatment than in *The Spiritualist,* whose exposé of how education, rationality, and art (in the widest sense of the term *Kunst*) can be used to ensnare and entrap, not to enlighten, makes this tale an eighteenth-century preview of the Culture Industry's employment of "Aufklärung als Massenbetrug" (Enlightenment as Mass Deception).[10]

Before launching his tale, Count von O** provides an overview of the political and personal circumstances that hitherto have induced the Prince to lead so quiet and modest a life. Wanting to keep his independence and to live within the restrictions of his court allowance, the Prince is traveling in strict incognito with a small entourage, avoiding extravagance, and showing no interest in the various allurements of Venice during Carnival. At the age of thirty-five, he hitherto has remained indifferent to women. Protestant by birth rather than by conviction, he never has undertaken a serious review of the grounds for his belief, although at one point in his youth he had been a religious enthusiast. Key reasons for this lack of foundations in his intellectual and moral development are the "neglected education and early military service" (see p. 68)[11] — not personal irresponsibility — that have kept his mind from advancing to maturity. As we shall see later in the story, the Prince has the unfortunate tendency to read indiscriminately whatever writings come his way, which explains "the confusion of his ideas" (see p. 68)[12] that will leave him open to manipulation. A product of the military, he is accustomed to obeying orders, which gives added poignancy to the count's observation that his friend was "equally courageous whether in fighting one recognised prejudice or in facing death in the cause of another" (see p. 68).[13]

Yet another character trait proves particularly significant in the light of future developments: "In the midst of noisy crowds of people he walked alone; rapt in the world of his own imagination, he was often a stranger in the real one" (see p. 68).[14] At the beginning of Book Two of the novel, the reasons for such a psychic disposition are spelled out in more detail: To a large degree, this is a result of a brutal and bigoted Protestant religious upbringing that has made the supernatural simultaneously an object of fear and attraction. Religious matters, the Prince admits to his friend the Count, are like "an enchanted castle" (that he would rather pass by (see p. 108),[15] and yet he finds himself drawn to explore its twisting passages. These images are taken directly from the repertoire of the Gothic novel, where the castle represents the malformed mind of the protagonist; one need only think of Poe's "The Fall of the House of Usher," whose title refers both to the domicile and to the family's sole remaining descendants, Roderick and Madeline Usher. The chief inhabitant of the Prince's castle, however, is the image of a monstrous God that has been impressed into his lively imagination, with religion serving as the prohibitory agent of all his childhood and youthful inclinations. Thus, his religious faith is intermingled with "resentment against a Lord for whom he felt in equal measure reverence and revulsion" (see p. 108).[16] In a striking analogy, the Prince is compared to a serf who has fled a harsh master with the chains of servitude still dragging behind him, and thus a prey to any charlatan who discerned these chains and knew how to make use of them (NA 16:103; see p. 108).

As soon becomes clear, the Count is not the only person in Venice to have conducted a study of the Prince's character, which he got to know during their years of common military service. The mysterious appearance and cryptic words of the black-robed "Armenian" — who may or may not be a clergyman with ties to the Roman Catholic Church — are calculated to evoke the sentiment of another literary prince — Shakespeare's Hamlet — that "there are more things in heaven and earth than are dreamt of in our philosophies" (see p. 70),[17] once the melancholic protagonist learns that his cousin, the only son of the old and infirm ruler, had died on the same day and at the same time as the Armenian's first words to him. For the Prince, the sudden elevation of his prospects for succession to the throne is, at least initially, a minor consideration compared with the possibility that the Armenian might be in possession of supernatural knowledge. Count von O** observes at this juncture: "to make contact with the spirit world had once been the fantasy dearest to his heart, and since that first encounter with the Armenian all those ideas which his maturer reason had meanwhile dismissed had once again risen to his mind" (see p. 75).[18] In other words: Whoever gains control of the Prince's imagination will be able to control him entirely — body, mind, and soul. The remainder of Book One of *The Spiritualist* consists of prophecies, séances, and tales within tales that are designed to reinforce the Prince's supposition that the Armenian is a figure unbound by the normal constraints of time and space and also in control of hidden forces watching over his destiny. As Jeffrey Sammons points out in his introduction to the reprint of a nineteenth-century English translation of *Der Geisterseher:*

"It has often been observed that the Age of Reason was also an age of credulity. Experiments in spiritism, alchemy, the occult, ancient wisdom, and the like were endemic in the late eighteenth century. But these interests need not be incompatible with the Enlightenment, for they are impelled by the same desire to stretch the limits of the known universe."[19] Hence, the pursuit of knowledge undertaken by the Prince makes him willing to see whether he can learn through a séance conducted by a Sicilian adventurer — a Cagliostro figure — what his friend and fellow soldier, the Marquis de Lanoy, had been trying to convey to him before he died of wounds suffered at the Battle of Hastenbeck during the Seven Years' War.[20]

To be sure, the Prince soon learns from the so-called Sicilian the entirely natural means employed to simulate spectral appearances (magica laterna, a disembodied voice emanating from a confederate hidden in the chimney, etc.) and rightly suspects that this Sicilian conjurer and the Armenian are in league with one another. Nonetheless, the report that his friend the Marquis has an illegitimate daughter living in a convent on the Flemish border provides fuel for an imagination that will be stoked to fever pitch in Book Two of the novel, when the Prince encounters a beautiful female stranger praying fervently in the half-lit recesses of a Venetian church — an apparition that proves more successful in winning over the Prince than did the hocus-pocus in Book One. Although never explicitly stated, this encounter with a beautiful "Grecian" woman — who turns out not to be Greek at all, but rather a German who reputedly is the fruit of an unhappy love affair and with a mother of the highest rank (NA 16:156, see p. 146) — suggests a secret connection between the Marquis' daughter and what becomes the Prince's first great love. Is this meeting a chance occurrence, was it ordained by fate, or has it been pre-arranged by the Armenian and the new circle of acquaintances around the Prince? By the end of Book Two, this figure has died by poison before we as readers have learned much about her, but the report of her deathbed conversation with the Prince suggests that she has been used as a tool to induce a religious conversion. Indeed, this plot detail was so well received that *Geheimbundromane* (secret-society novels) written in the wake of Schiller's *Der Geisterseher* had as one of their stock elements a so-called *Bundestochter,* or daughter of the Society, who was responsible for enticing the leading male figure to become a member. In the years immediately preceding the French Revolution, outgrowths of Masonic orders such as the Illuminati and the Rosicrucians were accused of aspiring to control over rulers across Europe; in fact, the 1786 accession to the Prussian throne by Frederick Wilhelm II, the pleasure-loving nephew of Frederick the Great who had fallen under the spell of Rosicrucian ministers, provided a real-life analogue to the plot of *The Spiritualist.*[21] Recent critics have argued that the figure of Marquis Posa, the friend and advisor of the title character in Schiller's drama *Don Karlos* (1787), represents Illuminist theory and practice, with the figure of the Armenian serving as its ideological opposite.[22] In *The Spiritualist,* the secret society in question seems to be the Society of Jesus, which had been banned by Pope Clement IV in 1773 but was rumored to still have its hand in machinations across Europe.[23] And what could be more "Jesuitical" than to conjure up the appearance of a female figure that the Prince explicitly compares to the image of the Madonna in a painting he recently has been shown (NA 16:131; see p. 127)? Consciously or not, he receives his first instruction in Catholic theology in Palladio's Church of Il Redentore (The Redeemer), with this unknown beauty serving as Mediatrix: "In that moment I felt a rock-like faith in the God she was holding fast in her beautiful hand [i.e., a crucifix] . . . She made Him real to me" (see p. 128).[24] Both the 1792 and 1798 editions of *The Spiritualist* use title-page engravings of the fair Grecian in the church — one in which the Prince observes her kneeling in prayer, crucifix in hand; one in which she gazes Madonna-like at the reader — as elements of marketing strategy, which suggests that this scene exerted a particularly powerful fascination on Schiller's readers as well.[25]

What the Prince neglects to mention, to be sure, is that he also had seen two other paintings — "a Héloise, and an almost completely nude Venus" (see p. 127)[26] — which the artist regarded as inseparable, refusing to sell one without the inclusion of the others. At this juncture in the Prince's career, he is capable of apprehending only a spiritualized depiction of femininity — as opposed to the pagan carnality of Venus and the amorous, but also intellectual religiosity of Héloise, the medieval scholastic Abelard's mistress. Such selective discernment, however, makes him all the more susceptible to the manipulation of the sensual desires that his rigidly Calvinistic upbringing had suppressed. Mirjam Springer compares the Prince's enchantment with Faust's first glimpse of Helena, the embodiment of female beauty, in the magic mirror of the Witch's Kitchen — a scene in *Faust,* incidentally, that Goethe wrote during his Italian journey at the same time that Schiller was living in Weimar and working on *The Spiritualist* — but then observes that Schiller's staging is even more akin to the use of the automaton Olimpia in E. T. A. Hoffmann's "The Sandman" as the means for enchanting Nathanael.[27] If one wished to look for an immediate literary antecedent for this scene in the church, Peter-André Alt points out that in Lessing's *Emilia Galotti* (1772), the heroine is accosted by Prince Hettore Gonzaga while praying on the morning of her impending marriage to another (who later is murdered in the course of the Prince's abduction of Emilia);[28] Lessing's Prince, one might add, has just had his passion for Emilia further inflamed by viewing the portrait done by Conti, the court painter. Regardless of whichever literary parallels one favors, they all underscore Springer's contention that Schiller's *The Spirtualist* is "ein moderner Medienroman" (a modern novel about the media), in which tales and tableaux are used to ensnare their intended victim, and the "medium" governing all these intrigues is the inscrutable, anonymous Armenian, whom Springer characterizes as the complete technization of reason — modern times, indeed![29]

First, though, the ease with which the Prince uncovered the Sicilian's deceptions has led him to become a member of a freethinking Venetian society, the Bucentaur, whose licentious practices exercise a corrosive effect on him. Having freed himself, or so he thinks, from one set of false beliefs, he now looks with disdain on conventional precepts and mocks his retainers for their sincere, but untested faith (NA 16:108, see p. 111). In addition, he begins to lord it over those whom he had hitherto treated more as friends than servants, not because of his elevated social ranking, but due to the exaggerated self-confidence in his own intellectual superiority that his new acquaintances in high society have encouraged. This portion of *The Spiritualist* exemplifies Rousseau's critique of the moral corruption of contemporary European society, which Rousseau saw increasing with the advancement of the arts and sciences[30] and which already has found expression within Part One of the novel in the Sicilian's tale of the fall of the del M**nte family, where one brother secretly murders the other in order to marry his fiancée. As the Prince plunges into a giddy, never-ending round of social engagements, he never is given the opportunity to rest and recollect himself, which in turn saps his energies and makes him a sullen and gloomy companion in his private life. So as not to appear ridiculous in the sophisticated circles he now frequents, the Prince feels compelled to seek out the most up-to-date reading matter. Judging from the opinions he now espouses, Peter-André Alt identifies them as the writings of the French materialist *philosophes* Helvétius and d'Holbach.[31] Regardless of the specific authors or works, Count von O** makes clear their effect on the Prince: "And here too he was subject to his favourite propensity, which drew him irresistibly to things which were never meant to be understood. These and only these absorbed his mind and stayed in his memory; his reason and heart remained empty, while these compartments of his brain were filled with confused ideas" (see p. 110).[32] For the 1792 and 1798 editions of *The Spiritualist,* Schiller radically reduced in scope the "Philosophical Dialog" that he printed in 1789, both within issue six of *Thalia* and also in the first edition of his novel, but a key portion of it that is retained provides a vivid portrayal of the crisis of an aristocracy that has lost a sense of its innate self-worth.[33] In the Fourth Letter of Baron von F*** to Count von O**, whom calumny has induced to return to his home court of Courland and who therefore is unable to play any role in bringing his friend the Prince back to his senses, the latter openly proclaims his enslavement to whatever the world considers valid:

> Everything about us princes is opinion. Opinion is our wet-nurse and our governess when we are children, our legislator and our mistress when

> we are men, our crutch in our old age. Take away what we owe to opinion, and the meanest from the other ranks of society is better off than we are; for his fate has at least taught him a philosophy that can console him for that fate. A prince who mocks opinion undermines his very being, just as a priest does if he denies the existence of God. (see p. 122)[34]

The Prince's radical skepticism and frenetic pace of life, however, only imperfectly disguise a longing for certainty. The Prince tells the Baron somewhat later within this same conversation: "Show me anything that lasts, and I will be virtuous" (see p. 123).[35] As the Prince's encounter with the fair Grecian occurs in the very next chapter of Book Two, the logic of Schiller's narrative suggests that the Prince's journey from naïve belief to joyless doubt is part of the plot to lead him back into the fold of the Catholic Church, but only after all ties with his previous life have been severed. For this purpose, the Prince has become so obsessed with learning the identity of this beautiful stranger that he spends money with reckless abandon and becomes indebted to the Marchese di Civitella, the nephew of a Venetian cardinal who is a fellow member of the Bucentaur. It is Civitella who suggests to the Prince that he visit the church where he first meets the fair Grecian, and it is a story that Civitella tells about his own wordless encounter with a mysterious and ravishingly beautiful young woman that establishes in the Prince's imagination a connection between the girl of his dreams and the Armenian. Ulrike Rainer observes that the Prince falls prey to the pantomime he experiences or hears about, which in contrast to the Sicilian's wordy and elaborate deceptions in Book One allows him to become entrapped in his own imaginings.[36] As the Prince tells one of his retainers, Baron von F***, on the night after his first encounter: "She did not notice me, she did not let my appearance disturb her, so deeply was she absorbed in her devotions. She was praying to her God, and I was praying to her — Yes, I idolised her" (see p. 128).[37] But his notion of religiosity is now allied with the wish to possess his beloved — something his earlier religious upbringing had forbade him — and anything standing in the way of his attaining these earthly delights will be met with violence. From the hints Schiller provides his readers in the final pages of Book Two, the Prince and the Cardinal's nephew become rivals in love and fight a duel in which the Marchese is wounded, although seemingly not as seriously as Baron von F*** reports in a letter that finally does reach Count von O**, who for months has been kept unaware of developments by a conspiracy that intercepts his correspondence. By the time the latter journeys in all haste to Venice, hoping to help and console his friend, the Marchese has recovered, the Prince's debts have been paid — although not by his German relatives, from whom he now has irrevocably broken — and the Prince is in the company of the Armenian, with whom he has heard his first mass (NA 16:158–59; see p. 148).

These plot developments accord well with the conspiracy theory proposed in 1786 by the Weimar court official Ernst Anton von Göchhausen that Jesuits, of all people, had infiltrated the Illuminati and were employing an excess of Enlightenment in order to blind the populace and induce a return to Catholicism.[38] In 1795, the English translator of the first two installments of Schiller's novel in *Thalia* establishes an explicit link between the Illuminati and the forces of obscurantist Catholicism in his summary of what we know as Book Two of *The Spiritualist,* and — unbeknownst to readers not acquainted with Schiller's original — his own speculative conclusion:

> Insnared in this manner, by the united artifices of a woman and a priest, the Prince was soon completely perverted. He embraced the Catholic faith, and under the ridiculous pretence of gaining millions of deluded Protestants to the true Church, he was brought to consent to the murder of the Prince who barred his ascent to the throne. The attempt however did not succeed, and the same persons who engaged him in the crime, inflicted his punishment. To avoid the danger of a discovery, they dispatched him by poison, and he died in the bitterest agonies of contrition and remorse.[39]

In 1800, the Reverend William Render published a four-volume edition of *The Armenian; or the Ghost-seer. A History founded on Fact,* of which only the first two volumes are Schiller's text, with the rest being Render's own work. Once again, the Iluminati are mentioned, whom by this point conspiracy theorists in Germany and Great Britain were accusing of having brought about the French Revolution.[40] E. J. Clery has drawn attention to the importance of the 1795 translation of Schiller's text in encouraging a new development in Gothic fiction, whose objective was "the demystification of metaphysical appearances, but only in order to leave the reader in the most horrible reality."[41] Clearly, the proliferation of editions (authorized and unauthorized), translations, and continuations of Schiller's novel in the years after 1789 attests to its international appeal during an era of profound turmoil and uncertainty.

How the story actually would have proceeded is anyone's guess, unless some necromancer more skillful than I can persuade Schiller to arise from the dead and complete his novel.[42] Despite the public's clamoring for a conclusion to the tale, the subject matter of *The Spiritualist* had lost its attraction for him. Upon resuming work in March of 1788 on what became the second part of Book One, Schiller complained in letters to his friend Körner that this scribbling was a sinful waste of time.[43] After its enthusiastic reception in the fifth issue of *Thalia* in May of that year, to be sure, Schiller began thinking of a separate book edition that would contain material not to be included in the *Thalia* installments. As late as the beginning of 1789, statements in letters to Körner and to Charlotte and Caroline von Lengefeld, his future wife and sister-in-law, indicate his interest in elements such as the "Philosophical Dialog" and the introduction of the beautiful Grecian, which appeared in the March and May 1789 issues of *Thalia*. But this enthusiasm was soon dampened by preparations for his move to the University of Jena and the need to prepare lectures in history. By the fall of 1789, Schiller had time only for a hasty conclusion to the book version of the novel and also for one final installment in *Thalia* — Civitella's account of *"Der Abschied"* (The Farewell) that he had witnessed on the island of Murano between a beautiful woman and an imposing older man — that was not included in his publisher Göschen's first and second editions. The third and final edition of *The Spiritualist* includes this narrative, but otherwise no new material, and further pares down the "Philosophical Dialog" from the editions of 1789 and 1792. Given his temporary change of focus from drama and prose to history and aesthetic theory, coupled with his low estimation of the novelist as a mere *"Halbbruder"* (half-brother) of the poet (NA 20:462), Schiller decided to devote his main energies to aesthetic treatises such as *Über naïve und sentimentalische Dichtung* (1795–96, On Naïve and Sentimental Poetry), from which the above quote comes, and then — with Goethe's aid and encouragement — to poetry and drama. As T. J. Reed observes, "Schiller is one of the eighteenth century's great lost novelists, lured away by the traditional cultural prestige of tragic drama."[44]

One should not forget, of course, that not only Schiller's focuses changed during the years after 1789. By 1797, the state of Venice itself had disappeared from the map of Europe, having been amalgamated into Napoleon's conquests during his Italian campaigns. And compared to the Reign of Terror and the French Revolutionary Wars — which eventually resulted in Pope Pius VI being carried into French exile in 1798, raising the very real possibility that the Catholic Church might not survive as an institution — was the conversion of a prince to Roman Catholicism still such an object of horror? With regard to Ann Radcliffe's novel *The Italian, or the Confessional of the Black Penitents* (1797), which is set in eighteenth-century Italy, E. J. Clery discerns a tempering of attitudes toward Roman Catholicism, including even the Inquisition, which she interprets as "a symptom of the collective loss of nerve among the Protestant elite in Great Britain" in the wake of the French Revolution.[45] By analogy, it may well have been a prudent decision on Schiller's part to cease work on a "Princely Experiment" more suited to the concerns and fears of the pre-revolutionary European Enlightenment.

That having been said, there are indications that the effort Schiller devoted to developing the psychological profile of the Prince bore fruit within his dramatic output after 1798, the date of the third edition of *The Spiritualist*. There is, for example, the figure of Wallenstein in the drama trilogy of the same name (1799), another character whose ambitions are fed by his belief that he has been predestined by heaven to ascend to the throne; like the Armenian and other calculating schemers within Schiller's oeuvre, of course, Wallenstein also does not shrink from manipulating people like his daughter Thekla and her beloved Max Piccolomini if this suits his plans. Similarly, the character of Mortimer — tool and victim of the Catholic Church in *Mary Stuart* (1800) — demonstrates the power of art, combined with real feminine beauty, to ensnare a youthful enthusiast. Mortimer, like the Prince, has been subjected to a rigid Protestant upbringing, which makes him all the more susceptible to the art, music, and architecture of Counter-Reformation Italy that inspires his conversion to Catholicism, as he reveals to Maria in act one, scene six. Inspired by a portrait of her that he sees in the home of one of her exiled Scottish supporters, the Bishop of Ross, Mortimer volunteers to return to England and free the Queen from her imprisonment. Once acquainted with Maria's physical presence, though, this plan turns into a resolve not only to rescue her but also to make her his own, with a willingness to kill his uncle and anyone else standing in his way, including Queen Elizabeth herself. Betrayed by his self-serving rival, Lord Leicester, Mortimer commits suicide rather than surrender, with his final words suggesting an inability to distinguish between the earthly and the heavenly Maria: "O holy Mary, pray for me, / Let me for ever dwell in Heaven with You."[46] Through this depiction of religious fanaticism, Schiller provides his audience with a frame of reference for considering the ideological conflicts of their own day; one might think of the beheading of another monarch, Louis XVI of France, but instances of human cruelty and duplicity unfortunately do not end with the eighteenth century. In his introduction to *The Ghost-Seer*, Jeffrey Sammons draws attention to Schiller's much less partisan treatment of Catholicism in his latter plays, with more attention paid to the miraculous and supernatural in *Die Jungfrau von Orleans* (1801, The Maid of Orleans) than the historical sources warranted.[47] Although Schiller himself was never friendly to organized religion, his portrayal of Maria's acceptance of her fate in act five with the help of her Catholic faith suggests the benefits of mature, considered religious belief — a level that Schiller's Prince never reached in *The Spiritualist.* Although this latter tale never was brought to a conclusion, its impact on German Romantic writers like E. T. A. Hoffmann and even, one might argue, Thomas Mann's *Der Tod in Venedig* (1912, Death in Venice) testifies to its ability to challenge and inspire future generations of readers and writers.[48]

University of Vermont

Notes

[1] For a representative example of Emanuel Swedenborg's writings, see *Heaven and Its Wonders and Hell: from Things Heard and Seen* (New York: Swedenborg Foundation, 1952). For a discussion of the fears unleashed by Kant's readings of Swedenborg, which reminded him uncomfortably about his own earlier cosmological

speculations, see Hartmut Böhme and Gernot Böhme, "The Battle of Reason with the Imagination," trans. Jane Kneller, in *What is Enlightenment? Eighteenth-Century Answers and Twentieth-Century Questions,* ed. James Schmidt (Berkeley & Los Angeles: U of California P, 1996), 426–52, originally published as chapter 4 of *Das Andere der Vernunft: Zur Entwicklung von Rationalitätsstrukturen am Beispiel Kants* (Frankfurt am Main: Suhrkamp, 1983).

[2] E. T. A. Hoffmann, "Das Majorat," in *Werke* (Frankfurt am Main: Insel, 1967), 2:48. At the beginning of "Der Sandmann," Nathanael assures his friend Lothar that he is no "aberwitziger Geisterseher" (superstitious ghost-seer, 2:7). Although Nathanael, like Schiller's Prince, suffers from an overactive imagination, there are numerous indications within the text that sinister forces actually are persecuting him. For a succinct and lucid discussion of Hoffmann's use of the Uncanny, as compared with Freud's interpretation within his 1919 essay of the same name, see Hoffmann, *The Golden Pot and Other Tales,* translated with an Introduction by Ritchie Robertson (Oxford and New York: Oxford UP, 1992), xvi–xxi.

[3] Future quotes from this translation will be accompanied by parenthetical references to Francis Lamport's translation in this volume. The German text is from volume 16 of the *Nationalausgabe* (= NA) of Schiller's works: "Wünschen Sie sich Glück, Prinz . . . *Um neun Uhr ist er gestorben.*" *Schillers Werke. Nationalausgabe,* ed. Julius Petersen et al. (Weimar: Herrman Böhlaus Nachfolger, 1943ff.), 16:47. Subsequent citations as "NA" with volume and page number.

[4] "*reine, strenge Wahrheit*" (NA 16:45).

[5] Victor Sage, "Black Venice: Conspiracy and Narrative Masquerade in Schiller, Zschokke, Lewis, and Hoffmann," *Gothic Studies* 8 (2006, no. 1): 52–72, here 55.

[6] On the never-ending succession of illusions and disillusionment, interuptions and continuations, see Monika Schmitz-Emans, "Zwischen wahrem und falschem Zauber: Magie und Illusionistik als metapoetische Gleichnisse. Eine Interpretation zu Schillers *Geisterseher,*" in *Zeitschrift für deutsche Philologie* 115 (1996, Special Issue): 33–43, esp. 42, and Ursula Regener, "Zufall oder Intention: Zum verborgenen Plan von Schillers *Geisterseher,*" in *Critica Poeticae: Lesarten zur deutschen Literatur,* ed. Andreas Gossling and Stefan Nienhaus (Würzburg: Königshausen & Neumann, 1992), 125–38.

[7] "sich beherrschen zu lassen, ohne schwach zu sein" (NA 16:46).

[8] Immanuel Kant, *Ausgewählte kleine Schriften* (Hamburg: Meiner, 1969), 1–9, here 1, and "An Answer to the Question: What Is Enlightenment?" in Schmidt, *What is Enlightenment?,* 58–64, here 58; the italics are Kant's.

[9] Gert Vonhoff, "'Die Macht der Verhältnisse': Schillers Erzählungen," in *Friedrich Schiller,* ed. Heinz Ludwig Arnold and Mirjam Springer (Munich: Edition Text + Kritik, 2005), 71–81.

[10] Max Horkheimer and Theodor Adorno, *Dialektik der Aufklärung* (Frankfurt am Main: Fischer, 1974), 108–50. On page 75 of the aforementioned essay, Vonhoff alludes to Schiller's depiction of the instrumentalization of reason in a way that anticipates Horkheimer and Adorno, but without developing the point any further.

[11] "eine vernachlässigte Erziehung und frühe Kriegsdienste" (NA 16:46).

[12] "die Verwirrung seiner Begriffe" (NA 16:46).

[13] "gleich großen Mut, ein erkanntes Vorurteil zu bekämpfen und für ein anderes zu sterben" (NA 16:46).

[14] "Mitten in einem geräuschvollen Gewühle von Menschen ging er einsam; in seine Phantasiewelt verschlossen, war er sehr oft ein Fremdling in der wirklichen" (NA 16:46).

[15] "ein bezaubertes Schloß" (NA 16:103).

[16] "Widerwillen gegen einen Herrn, vor dem er in gleichem Grade Abscheu und Ehrfurcht fühlte" (NA 16:103).

[17] "Es gibt mehr Dinge im Himmel und auf Erden, als wir in unsern Philosophien träumen" (NA 16:49). Andrew Brown points out this allusion to *Hamlet* (act 1, scene 5: 168–69) at the conclusion to the introduction of his translation of *The Ghost-seer* (London: Hesperus, 2003), xi–xvii, here xvii.

[18] "Mit der Geisterwelt in Verbindung zu stehen, war ehedem seine Lieblingsschwärmerei gewesen, und seit jener ersten Erscheinung des Armeniers hatten sich alle Ideen wieder bei ihm gemeldet, die seine reifere Vernunft so lange abgewiesen hatte" (NA 16:56).

[19] Jeffrey L. Sammons, Introduction to Friedrich Schiller, *The Ghost-Seer,* trans. Henry G. Bohn (Columbia, SC: Camden House, 1992), v–xv, here vii.

[20] As Sammons states in his learned and informative introduction: "Schiller clearly means to allude to Cagliostro in his figure of the Sicilian, who is from Palermo, as Cagliostro was, and who appears in a foreign uniform, as Cagliostro often did" (vii). For further information on Cagliostro and his depiction in Goethe's dark comedy *Der Großkoptha* and Schiller's *Der Geisterseher,* see Uta Treder, "Wundermann oder Scharlatan? Die Figur Cagliostros bei Goethe und Schiller," *Monatshefte* 79 (1987): 30–43.

[21] For further information on the Masons, Illuminati, and the Rosicrucians, see the chapter of the same name in Klaus Epstein, *The Genesis of German Conservatism* (Princeton: Princeton UP, 1966), 84–111. For a case study of "A Rosicrucian on the Prussian Throne," see the corresponding chapter in Christopher McIntosh, *The Rose Cross and the Age of Reason: Eighteenth-Century Rosicrucianism in Central Europe and Its Relationship to the Enlightenment* (Leiden: Brill, 1992), 113–31. For a penetrating discussion of Schiller's novel in the context of the secret-society novels of the late Enlightenment, see Michael Voges, *Aufklärung und Geheimnis: Untersuchungen zur Vermittlung von Literatur- und Sozialgeschichte am Beispiel der Aneignung des Geheimbundmaterials im Roman des späten 18. Jahrhunderts* (Tübingen: Niemeyer, 1987), 343–98.

[22] See Hans-Jürgen Schings, *Die Brüder des Marquis Posa: Schiller und der Geheimbund der Illuminaten* (Tübingen; Niemeyer, 1996) and Marion Beaujean, "Zweimal Prinzenerziehung: *Don Carlos* und *Geisterseher*. Schillers Reaktion auf Illuminati und Rosenkreuzer," *Poetica* 10 (1978): 217–35.

[23] See Ritchie Robertson, "Schiller and the Jesuits," in *Schiller: National Poet — Poet of Nations,* ed. Nicholas Martin (Amsterdam: Rodopi, 2006), 179–200.

[24] "Ich glaubte in diesem Augenblick felsenfest an den, den ihre schöne Hand umfaßt hielt . . . Sie machte mir ihn wirklich" (NA 16:132).

[25] For reproductions of these two engravings, see NA 16:385 and 400. Mathias Mayer, in the afterword to his excellent edition of *Der Geisterseher,* likewise provides reproductions of these two illustrations from the 1792 and 1798 editions of the novel (Stuttgart: Reclam, 2005: 228 and 233).

[26] "eine Heloise und eine fast ganz unbekleidete Venus" (NA 16:131).

[27] Mirjam Springer, "'Das große Gewitter von Mscrpt.' Schillers *Geisterseher,*" in *Friedrich Schiller,* ed. Heinz Ludwig Arnold and Mirjam Springer (Munich: Edition Text + Kritik, 2005), 82–95, here 89–90.

[28] Peter-André Alt, *Schiller: Leben — Werk — Zeit* (Munich: Beck, 2004, 2nd rev. ed.) 1:580.

[29] Springer 86–87. I would argue that the manipulation exerted upon Nathanael by the diabolic Coppola/Coppelius and his henchman Spalanzani — the creator of the automation Olimpia whose appearance Nathanael explicitly compares to Chodowiecki's representation of Cagliostro (Hoffmann, *Werke* 2:18) — represents Hoffmann's creative homage to Schiller's tale.

[30] Jean-Jacques Rousseau, *Discours sur les Sciences et les Arts* (1750): "nos âmes se sont corrompues à mesure que nos sciences et nos arts se sont avancés à la perfection"; in *Schriften zur Kulturkritik* (Hamburg: Meiner, 1971), 14.

[31] Alt 583–84.

[32] "Und auch hier waltete sein Lieblingshang vor, der ihn immer zu allem, was nicht begriffen werden soll, mit unwiderstehlichem Reize hinzog. Nur für dasjenige, was damit in Beziehung stand, hatte er Aufmerksamkeit und Gedächtnis; seine Vernunft und sein Herz blieben leer, während sich diese Fächer seines Gehirns mit verworrenen Begriffen anfüllten" (NA 16:106).

[33] For a comparison of the 1789 version of this "Philosophical Dialog" with the 1798 version, please consult the respective translations by Helen Kilgallen and Francis Lamport within this volume.

[34] "Alles an uns Fürsten ist Meinung. Die Meinung ist unsre Amme und Erzieherin in der Kindheit, unsre Gesetzgeberin und Geliebte in männlichen Jahren, unsre Krücke im Alter. Nehmen Sie uns, was wir von der Meinung haben, und der Schlechteste aus den übrigen Klassen ist besser daran als wir; denn sein Schicksal hat ihm doch zu einer Philosophie verholfen, welche ihn über dieses Schicksal tröstet. Ein Fürst, der die Meinung verlacht, hebt sich selbst auf, wie der Priester, der das Dasein eines Gottes leugnet" (NA 16:122–23).

[35] "Zeigen Sie mir etwas, das dauert, so will ich tugendhaft sein" (NA 16:124).

[36] Ulrike Rainer, *Schillers Prosa: Poetologie und Praxis* (Berlin: Erich Schmidt, 1988), 128–29; see also Fritz Martini, "Erzählte Szene, stummes Spiel: Zum Siebenten Brief des Baron von F . . . in Schillers *Geisterseher,*" in *Untersuchungen zur Literatur als Geschichte: Festschrift für Benno von Wiese,* ed. Vincent Gunther et al. (Berlin: Erich Schmidt, 1973), 36–60.

[37] "Sie bemerkte mich nicht, sie ließ sich durch meine Dazwischenkunft nicht stören, so ganz war sie in ihrer Andacht vertieft. Sie betete zu ihrer Gottheit, und ich betete zu ihr — Ja, ich betete sie an" (NA 16:131).

[38] For details on the bizarre logic employed by von Göchhausen in advancing these claims, see Epstein 96–100.

[39] *The Ghost-seer or Apparitionist, an Interesting Fragment, Found among the Papers of Count O*****. From the German of Schiller.* I am quoting from the corresponding American edition (New York: Swords, 1796), 120. Judging from his summary of Schiller's plot from an "editorially preserved note, which is presumably from the author," Victor Sage appears to be using an edition based on this 1795 translation; see Sage, "Black Venice," 56 and 68 n. 15.

[40] On the conspiracy theory of the French Revolution, see Epstein 503–46. Many thanks to Francis Lamport for alerting me to these two early English "translations."

[41] See the chapter "Conspiracy, Subversion, Supernaturalism," in E. J. Clery, *The Rise of Supernatural Fiction 1762–1800* (Cambridge: Cambridge UP, 1995), 156–71, esp. 156–60. For a study of thematic and structural aspects to Schiller's novel within the tradition of the German secret-society novel and the attempts of other authors to complete it, see Walter Bußman, "Schillers Geisterseher und seine Fortsetzer: Ein Beitrag zur Struktur des Geheimbundromans" (PhD diss., Göttingen, 1960).

[42] This essay is dedicated to Hubert Zapf (Universität Augsburg), with whom I co-taught a seminar on "The Gothic Strain in English, German, and American Romanticism" in the summer of 2001 that included a reading of *Der Geisterseher,* and who also was a willing participant in the November 10, 2006, "Schiller Séance" at NEASECS in Salem, Massachusetts organized by Jeff High and myself. In addition, I would like to thank Jeff High, Francis Lamport, and Janet and Malcolm Whatley, who read the earlier versions of this manuscript and made many helpful suggestions for improvement.

[43] See Jeffrey L. High, "Schiller, the Author of Literary Prose," in *Friedrich Schiller. Playwright, Poet, Philosopher, Historian,* ed. Paul Kerry (Oxford: Peter Lang, 2007), 117–51, here 136.

[44] T. J. Reed, *The Classical Centre: Goethe and Weimar 1775–1832* (London: Croom Helm, 1980), 105.

[45] Ann Radcliffe, *The Italian,* ed. Frederick Garber, with a new Introduction and Notes by E. J. Clery (Oxford: Oxford UP, 1998), xxiii.

[46] Friedrich Schiller, *Mary Stuart,* translated with an Introduction and Notes by Francis Lamport (London: Penguin, 1998), 95. "Maria, heilge, bitt für mich / Und nimm mich zu dir in dein himmlisch Leben!" (NA 9:112, Verses 2819–20).

[47] Sammons viii.

[48] For a discussion of the significance of Schiller's work, including *Der Geisterseher,* for Mann's great novella, see Jeffrey L. High, "Goethe, Schiller, Kleist und Aschenbach: Thomas Manns Selbsterklärung zum Novellen-Klassiker in *Der Tod in Venedig,*" in *Thomas Mann (1875–1955),* ed. Walter Delabar and Bodo Plachta (Berlin: Weidler, 2005), 89–105.

Schiller's Literary Prose Works in English Translation

"Der Verbrecher aus verlorener Ehre"

"The Criminal." Translated by Anon. In *The German museum; or, monthly repository of the literature of Germany*. London: Geisweiler, 1800–1801.

"The Criminal become so from Lost Honour." Translated by L. Wapler. Augsburgh: priv. print, 1825.

"The Criminal, or Martyr to Lost Honour." Translated by Thomas Roscoe. In *The German Novelists: Tales selected from Ancient and Modern Authors in that Language*, vol. 3, 322–59. London: Colburn, 1826.

"The Dishonoured Irreclaimable." Translated by Richard Holcraft. In *Tales from the German: Selected from Popular German Writers*, 139–75. London: Longmans, 1826.

"The Criminal in Consequence of Lost Reputation." Translated by Anon. In *Romanticist and Novelist's Library*, ed. William Hazlitt. London: Clements, 1841.

"The Criminal from Lost Honour." Translated by J. Oxenford and C. A. Feiling. In *Tales from the German*, 34–50. New York: Harper, 1844.

"Herzog von Alba bey einem Frühstück auf dem Schlosse zu Rudolstadt. Im Jahr 1547"

"The Duke of Alva at a Breakfast in the Castle of Rudolstadt." Translated by Leigh Hunt. In *One Hundred Romances of Real Life*, 130–31 London: Whittaker, 1843.

"Spiel des Schicksals"

"The Sport of Fortune." Translated by Thomas De Quincey. In *Blackwood's Magazine*, VIII (January 1821): 375–81.

"The Sport of Destiny." Translated by Thomas Roscoe. In *The German Novelists*, 302–21. London: Colburn, 1826.

"The Sport of Destiny." Translated by Henry G. Bohn. In *The Works of Frederick Schiller,* 483–93. London: Bohn, 1849.

"The Sport of Destiny." Translated by Henry G. Bohn. In *Schiller's Works,* 483–93. London: Bell and Daldy, 1873.

"The Sport of Destiny." Translated by Percy Pinkerton. In *Aesthetic and Philosophical Essays.* Boston: Estes, 1902.

"The Sport of Destiny." Translated by Marian Klopfer. In *Great German Short Novels and Stories,* ed. Victor Lange, 100–109. New York: Random House, 1952.

Der Geisterseher

The Ghostseer. Translated by Anon. In *Weird Tales from the German,* ed. H. Weber. London: Paterson, n.d.

*The Ghost-seer or Apparitionist an Interesting Fragment, Found among the Papers of Count O*****. From the German of Schiller.* Translated by Daniel Boileau. London: Vernor, 1795; New York: Swords, 1796.

The Armenian; or the Ghostseer. A History founded on fact. Translated by William Render. London: Symonds, 1800.

The ghostseer! Translated by William Render. London: Bentley, 1831.

*The Ghost-seer. From the Pages of the Count O ****. A New Translation from the German of Schiller.* New York: Sun Office, 1843.

The Visionary: From the papers of the Count De O—. A Tale from the German of Schiller. In *Omnibus of Modern Romance.* New York: Ferrett, 1845.

The Ghost-seer. Translated by H. G. Bohn, in *Friedrich Schiller. Works, Historical and Dramatic.* London: Bohn, 1846–49; New York: Harper, 1855.

Ghost Seer. A Tale. Translated by Anon. *Blackwood's Edinburgh Magazine,* July 1857.

The Ghost-Seer. Translated by Henry G. Bohn, ed. Jeffrey L. Sammons. Columbia, SC: Camden House, 1992.

*The Man who sees Ghosts: From the Memoirs of the Count Von O****.* Translated by David Bryer. London: Pushkin, 2003.

The Ghost-seer. Translated and with an Introduction by Andrew Brown. Foreword by Martin Jarvis. London: Hesperus, 2003.

Works Cited

Abel, Jakob Friedrich. "Geschichte eines Räubers." In *Sammlung und Erklärung merkwürdiger Erscheinungen aus dem menschlichen Leben.* Stuttgart: Erhard, 1787. 2:1–86.

———. *Lebensgeschichte Fridrich Schwans.* Stuttgart: Ernst Klett Verlag, 2001.

Alt, Peter-André. *Schiller: Leben — Werk — Zeit.* Munich: Beck, 2000.

———. *Schiller: Leben — Werk — Zeit.* 2nd rev. ed. Munich: Beck, 2004.

Astbury, Katherine. *The Moral Tale in France and Germany 1750–1789.* Oxford: Voltaire Foundation, 2002.

Auerbach, Erich. *Memesis. Dargestellte Wirklichkeit in der abendländischen Literatur.* Berne: Francke, 1946.

Auernhammer, Achim. "Engagiertes Erzählen: *Der Verbrecher aus verlorener Ehre.*" In *Schiller und die höfische Welt,* edited by Achim Auernhammer, et al., 254–70. Tübingen: Max Niemeyer Verlag, 1980.

Aust, Hugo. *Novelle.* Stuttgart: Metzler, 1999.

Beauchot, Adrien J. Q., and Georges Bengesco, eds. *Œeuvres complètes de Voltaire.* Paris: Garnier Frères, 1880.

Beaujean, Marion. "Zweimal Prinzenerziehung: *Don Carlos* und *Geisterseher.* Schillers Reaktion auf Illuminati und Rosenkreuzer." *Poetica* 10 (1978): 217–35.

Beccaria, Cesare. *On Crimes and Punishments.* Translated by Henry Paolucci. Englewood Cliffs, NJ: Prentice Hall, 1963.

Bock, Werner. *Die ästhetischen Anschauungen C. M. Wielands.* Berlin, 1921.

Böhme, Hartmut, and Gernot Böhme. "The Battle of Reason with the Imagination." Translated by Jane Kneller. In *What is Enlightenment? Eighteenth-Century Answers and Twentieth-Century Questions,* edited by James Schmidt, 426–52. Berkeley & Los Angeles: U of California P, 1996. Originally published as chapter 4 of *Das Andere der Vernunft: Zur Entwicklung von Rationalitätsstrukturen am Beispiel Kants* (Frankfurt am Main: Suhrkamp, 1983).

Brown, Andrew, trans. *The Ghost-seer.* London: Hesperus, 2003.

Buckman, Robert. *Can We Be Good without God?* Toronto: Viking, 2000.

Bürger, Christa. "Schiller als Erzähler? Von der Kunst des Erzählens zum Erzählen als Kunst." In *Friedrich Schiller. Angebot und Diskurs: Zugänge, Dichtung, Zeitgenossenschaft*, edited by Helmut Brand, 33–48. Berlin and Weimar: Aufbau, 1987.

Bußman, Walter. "Schillers Geisterseher und seine Fortsetzer: Ein Beitrag zur Struktur des Geheimbundromans." PhD diss., Göttingen, 1960.

Clery, E. J. *The Rise of Supernatural Fiction 1762–1800.* Cambridge: Cambridge UP, 1995.

Conger, Syndy McMillan. "A German Ancestor for Mary Shelley's Monster." *Philological Quarterly* 59.2 (Spring 1980): 216–31.

Coudreuse, Anne. *Diderot. Jacques le Fataliste.* Paris: Gallimard, 1993.

Dewhurst, Kenneth, and Nigel Reeves. *Friedrich Schiller: Medicine, Psychology and Literature.* Oxford: Oxford UP, 1978.

Diderot, Denis. *Denis Diderot. Jacques the Fatalist. A New Translation.* Translated by David Coward. Oxford World's Classics. London: Oxford UP, 1999.

———. *Jack the Fatalist and His Master. A New Translation from the French of Denis Diderot.* Translated by Wesley D. Camp and Agnes G. Raymond. American University Studies. Series II: Romance Languages and Literature. Vol. 8. New York: Peter Lang, 1984.

Epstein, Klaus. *The Genesis of German Conservatism.* Princeton: Princeton UP, 1966.

Fleischer, Heinrich Wilhelm. *Über bildende Künste, Kunsthandel und Buchhandel in Hinsicht auf Menschenwohl: Glaubensbekenntnis eines Kunst- und Buchhändlers.* Frankfurt: Fleischer, 1792. Reprint, Munich: Kraus, 1981.

Frick, R. "Manon Lescault als Typus." *Germanisch-Romanische Monatsschrift* 7 (1915/16): 123–45.

Geiger, Ludwig. "Schiller und Diderot." In *Marbacher Schillerbuch.* Zur hundertsten Wiederkehr von Schillers Todestag, herausgegeben vom Schwäbischen Schillerverein. Stuttgart and Berlin: Cotta, 1905. 81–91.

Goethe, Johann Wolfgang von. *Goethe. Briefe.* Hamburger Ausgabe. 2nd ed. Edited by Karl Mandelkow and Bodo Morawe. Hamburg: Wegner, 1968.

Goldoni, Carlo. *The Memoirs of Carlo Goldoni Written by Himself.* Translated by Jonathan Black. New York: Knopf, 1926.

Grimmelshausen, Hans Jakob Christoffel von. *The Runagate Courage.* Translated by R. L. Heller and J. C. Osborne. Lincoln: U of Nebraska P, 1965.

Hall, Daniel. *French and German Gothic Fiction in the late Eighteenth Century.* Oxford, Berne, Frankfurt am Main: Peter Lang, 2004.

Hart, Gail K. *Friedrich Schiller: Crime, Aesthetics, and the Poetics of Punishment.* Newark: U of Delaware P, 2005.

Hauschild, Hans. *Die Gestalt der Hetäre in der griechischen Komödie.* Leipzig: Vogel, 1933.

Hauser, Marc. *Moral Minds: How Nature Designed Our Universal Sense of Right and Wrong.* New York: Ecco, 2006.

High, Jeffrey L. "The Author of Literary Prose." In *Friedrich Schiller. Playwright, Poet, Philosopher, Historian,* edited by Paul Kerry, 117–51. Oxford: Peter Lang, 2007.

———. "Edinburgh — Williamsburg — Ludwigsburg: From Teaching Jefferson and Schiller Scottish Enlightenment Happiness to the 'American War' and *Don Karlos.*" In *Jahrbuch für internationale Germanistik,* 281–314. Bern: Peter Lang, 2005.

———. "Goethe, Schiller, Kleist und Aschenbach: Thomas Manns Selbsterklärung zum Novellen-Klassiker in *Der Tod in Venedig.*" In *Memoria. Thomas Mann 1875–1955,* edited by Walter Delabar and Bodo Plachta, 89–105. Berlin: Weidler, 2005.

Hinde, Robert A. *Why Good Is Good: The Sources of Morality.* London: Routledge, 2002.

Hoffmann, E. T. A. *The Golden Pot and Other Tales.* Translated with an Introduction by Ritchie Robertson. Oxford and New York: Oxford UP, 1992.

———. "Das Majorat." In *E. T. A. Hoffmann, Werke.* Frankfurt am Main: Insel, 1967. 2:41–113.

———. "Der Sandmann." In *E. T. A. Hoffmann, Werke.* Frankfurt am Main: Insel, 1967. 2:7–40.

Hofmann, Michael. "Eine großmütige Handlung aus der neusten Geschichte." In *Schiller-Handbuch: Leben — Werk — Wirkung,* edited by Matthias Luserke-Jaqui, 299–301. Stuttgart and Weimar: Metzler, 2005.

———. "Spiel des Schicksals. Ein Bruchstück aus einer wahren Geschichte." In *Schiller-Handbuch: Leben — Werk — Wirkung,* edited by Matthias Luserke-Jaqui, 315–19. Stuttgart and Weimar: Metzler, 2005.

Hofmann, Michael, Jörn Rüsen, and Mirjam Springer, eds. *Schiller und die Geschichte.* Munich: Wilhelm Fink, 2006.

Horkheimer, Max, and Theodor Adorno. *Dialektik der Aufklärung.* Frankfurt am Main: Fischer, 1974.

Jacobs, Jürgen. "Die deutsche Erzählung im Zeitalter der Aufklärung." In *Handbuch der deutschen Erzählung,* edited by Karl Konrad Polheim, 56–71. Düsseldorf: Bagel, 1981.

Johnston, Otto W. "Schiller, Diderot and the Dalberg Manuscript." *Germanic Review* 46 (May 1971): 167–81.

Kaiser, Gerhard. *Von Arkadien nach Elysium. Schiller-Studien.* Göttingen: Vandenhoek and Ruprecht, 1978.

Kant, Immanuel. "An Answer to the Question: What is Enlightenment?" In *What is Enlightenment? Eighteenth-Century Answers and Twentieth-Century Questions,* edited by James Schmidt, 58–64. Berkeley: U of California P, 1996.

———. "Beantwortung der Frage: Was ist Aufklärung." In *Ausgewählte kleine Schriften.* Hamburg: Meiner, 1965. 1–9.

Kausch, Karl-Heinz. "Die Kunst der Grazie." *Jahrbuch der deutschen Schillergesellschaft* 2 (1958): 12–42.

Keller, Heinrich. *Schillers Prosa.* Winterthur: Keller, 1965.

Klein, Johannes. *Geschichte der deutschen Novelle von Goethe bis zur Gegenwart.* Wiesbaden: Franz Steiner Verlag, 1956.

Kleist, Heinrich von. *Sämtliche Werke und Briefe.* Vol. 2. Edited by Helmut Sembdner. Munich: Deutscher Taschenbuch Verlag, 1987.

Kluge, Gerhard. "Kommentar." In *Friedrich Schiller, Werke und Briefe in zwölf Bänden,* edited by Gerhard Kluge. Frankfurt am Main: Deutscher Klassiker Verlag, 1988.

Kluge, Manfred, and Rudolf Radler, eds. "Der Geisterseher." In *Hauptwerke der deutschen Literatur, Einzeldarstellungen und Interpretationen.* Munich: Kindler, 1974.

Koopmann, Helmut. *Friedrich Schiller I: 1759–1794.* Stuttgart: Metzler, 1966.

———, ed. *Schiller Handbuch.* Stuttgart: Kröner Verlag, 1998.

———. "Schillers Erzählungen." In Koopmann, *Schiller-Handbuch,* 699–710.

Košenina, Alexander. "Schiller's Poetics of Crime." In *Schiller: National Poet — Poet of Nations. A Birmingham Symposium,* edited by Nicholas Martin, 201–17. Amsterdam and New York: Rodopi, 2006.

Lahnstein, Peter. *Schillers Leben.* Munich: Paul List Verlag, 1981.

Lamport, Francis, trans. *Maria Stuart.* London: Penguin, 1998.

Landsittel, Fritz. "Die Figur der Kurtisane im deutschen Drama des 18. Jahrhunderts." PhD diss. Universität Heidelberg, 1923.

Lecointre, Simone, and Jean Le Galliot, eds. Introduction to *Jacques le Fataliste et son maitre,* xiii–lxxx. Edition critique. Texte et variantes établis sur le manuscript de Léningrad (Genève: Librairie Doz, 1977).

Loy, J. Robert. *Diderot. Jacques the Fatalist and His Master.* New York and London: Norton, 1959.

Martini, Fritz. "Der Erzähler Friedrich Schiller." In *Schiller. Reden im Gedenkjahr 1959.* Stuttgart: Klett, 1961. 124–58.

———. "Erzählte Szene, stummes Spiel: Zum Siebenten Brief des Baron von F . . . in Schillers *Geisterseher.*" In *Untersuchungen zur Literatur als Geschichte: Festschrift für Benno von Wiese,* edited by Vincent Gunther et al., 36–60. Berlin: Erich Schmidt, 1973.

Martino, Alberto, and Marlies Stützel-Prüsner. "Publikumsschichten, Lesegesellschaften und Leihbibliotheken." In *Zwischen Revolution und Restauration: Klassik, Romantik,* edited by Horst Albert Glaser. Deutsche Literatur. Eine Sozialgeschichte, vol. 5. Hamburg: Rowohlt, 1980.

Martinson, Steven D. "Friedrich Schiller's 'Der Verbrecher aus verlorener Ehre,' or the Triumph of the Moral Will." *Sprachkunst* 18 (1987): 1–9.

McIntosh, Christopher. *The Rose Cross and the Age of Reason: Eighteenth-Century Rosicrucianism in Central Europe and Its Relationship to the Enlightenment.* Leiden: Brill, 1992.

Meninger, Karl. *The Crime of Punishment.* New York: Viking, 1968.

Minder, Robert. "Schiller, Schwaben, Frankreich und die Herrlichkeit der Väter." In *Schiller. Reden im Gedenkjahr 1959.* Stuttgart: Klett, 1961. 170–200.

Müller, Markus. "Reconsidering the Fantastic: An Anthropological Approach." *Anthropoetics* 2, 2 (January 1997).

Moser, Friedrich Karl von. Article in *Neues Patriotisches Archiv für Deutschland,* edited by Friedrich Karl von Moser, 184–85. Frankfurt and Leipzig, 1794.

Murr, Christoph Gottlieb von, trans. *Haoh Kjöh Tschwen, das ist die angenehme Geschichte des Haoh Kjöh.* Ein chinesischer Roman in vier Büchern. Leipzig: Johann Friedrich Junius, 1766.

Neumann, Gerhard. "Die Anfänge deutscher Novellistik. 'Schillers Verbrecher aus verlorener Ehre' — Goethes 'Unterhaltungen deutscher Ausgewanderten.'" In *Unser Commercium. Goethes und Schillers Literaturpolitik.* Stuttgart: Cotta, 1984. 433–60.

Neumeyer, Harald. "Unkalkulierbar unbewusst — Zur Seele des Verbrechens um 1800." In *Romantische Wissenspoetik,* edited by Gabriele Brandstetter and Gerhard Neumann, 151–77. Würzburg: Königshausen & Neumann, 2004.

Nicolai, Friedrich. *Gesammelte Werke.* Edited by Bernhard Fabian and Marie-Luise Spieckermann. 20 vols. Hildesheim, Zürich and New York: Georg Olms, 1984. Vol. 19, III.9, 162.

Nutz, Thomas. "Vergeltung oder Versöhnung?: Strafvollzug und Ehre in Schillers 'Verbrecher aus Infamie.'" *Jahrbuch der Deutschen Schillergesellschaft* 42 (1998): 146–64.

Oettinger, Klaus. "Schillers Erzählung *Der Verbrecher aus Infamie.* Ein Beitrag zur Rechtsaufklärung der Zeit." *Jahrbuch der Deutschen Schillergesellschaft* 16 (1972): 266–76.

Polheim, Karl Konrad, ed. *Theorie und Kritik der deutschen Novelle von Wieland bis Musil.* Tübingen: Max Niemeyer Verlag, 1970.

Radcliffe, Ann. *The Italian,* edited by Frederick Garber, with a new Introduction and Notes by E. J. Clery. Oxford: Oxford UP, 1998.

Rainer, Ulrike. *Schillers Prosa: Poetologie und Praxis.* Berlin: Erich Schmidt, 1988.

Reed, T. J. *The Classical Centre: Goethe and Weimar 1775–1832.* London: Croom Helm, 1980.

Regener, Ursula. "Zufall oder Intention: Zum verborgenen Plan von Schillers *Geisterseher.*" In *Critica Poeticae: Lesarten zur deutschen Literatur,* edited by Andreas Gossling and Stefan Nienhaus, 125–38. Würzburg: Königshausen & Neumann, 1992.

Ridley, Matt. *The Origins of Virtue.* London: Penguin, 1997.

Robertson, Ritchie. "Schiller and the Jesuits." In *Schiller: National Poet — Poet of Nations,* edited by Nicholas Martin, 179–200. Amsterdam: Rodopi, 2006.

Rosen, David. "Die Annalen seiner Verirrungen: The Divided Narrative of *Der Verbrecher aus verlorener Ehre.*" *New German Review* 10 (1994): 11–27.

Rosso, Jeannette Geffriaud. *"Jaques le fataliste": L'Amour et son Image.* Pisa: Libreria Goliardica Editrice, 1981.

Rousseau, Jean-Jacques. *Discours sur les Sciences et les Arts.* In *Schriften zur Kulturkritik.* Edited and translated by Kurt Wiegland. Hamburg: Meiner, 1971.

Ryder, Frank G. *Die Novelle.* New York: Holt, Rinehart and Winston, 1971.

Sage, Victor. "Black Venice: Conspiracy and Narrative Masquerade in Schiller, Zschokke, Lewis, and Hoffmann." *Gothic Studies* 8 (2006, no. 1): 52–72.

Sammons, Jeffrey L. Introduction to *The Ghost-Seer,* by Friedrich Schiller, v–xv. Translated by Henry G. Bohn. Columbia, SC: Camden House, 1992.

Sasse, Klaus. *Die Entdeckung der "courtisane vertueuse" in der Französischen Literatur des 18. Jahrhunderts: Rétif de la Bretonne und seine Vorgänger.* PhD diss., Universität Hamburg, 1967.

Schafarschik, Walter. *Friedrich Schiller. Kabale und Liebe.* Erläuterungen und Dokumente. Reclam Universal-Bibliothek, No. 33. Stuttgart: Reclam, 1980.

Schiller, Friedrich. *Friedrich Schiller: Werke und Briefe in zwölf Bänden,* edited by Gerhard Kluge. Deutscher Klassiker Verlag: Frankfurt am Main, 1988–.

———. *Gesamtausgabe,* edited by Herbert G. Göpfert. Munich: Deutscher Taschenbuch Verlag, 1966.

———. *The Ghost-seer or Apparitionist an Interesting Fragment, Found among the Papers of Count O*****.* From the German of Schiller. Translated by Daniel Boileau. New York: Swords, 1796.

———. *Kleine prosaiasche Schriften von Schiller.* Leipzig: Siegfried Lebrecht Crusius, 1792.

———. *Mary Stuart.* Translated with an Introduction and Notes by Francis Lamport. London: Penguin, 1998.

———, ed. *Merkwürdige Rechtsfälle als ein Beitrag zur Geschichte der Menscheit. Nach dem französischen Werke des Pitaval durch mehrere Verfasser ausgearbeitet.* 4 parts. Leipzig: Crusius, 1792–95.

———. *Schillers Sämtliche Schriften.* 3rd ed. Edited by Karl Goedeke. Stuttgart: Cotta, 1868.

———. *Schillers Sämtliche Werke.* Säkular-Ausgabe. Edited by Eduard von der Hellen and Richard Weißenfels. Stuttgart and Berlin: Cotta, 1904–5.

———. *Schillers Werke. Nationalausgabe.* Edited by Julius Petersen et al. Weimar: Herrman Böhlaus Nachfolger, 1943ff.

———. *Der Verbrecher aus verlorener Ehre und andere Erzählungen,* mit einem Nachwort von Bernhard Zeller. Stuttgart: Reclam, 1964.

Schings, Hans-Jürgen. *Die Brüder des Marquis Posa: Schiller und der Geheimbund der Illuminaten.* Tübingen; Niemeyer, 1996.

Schmitz-Emans, Monika. "Zwischen wahrem und falschen Zauber: Magie und Illusionistik als metapoetische Gleichnisse. Eine Interpretation zu Schillers *Geisterseher.*" *Zeitschrift für deutsche Philologie* 115 (1996, Special Issue): 33–43.

Schönhaar, Rainer. *Novelle und Kriminalschema. Ein Strukturmodell deutscher Erzählkunst um 1800.* Bad Homburg: Gehlen, 1969.

Schubart, Christian Friedrich Daniel. *C. F. D. Schubarts, des Patrioten, gesammelte Schriften und Schicksale.* 4 vols. Stuttgart: Scheible, 1839.

Sharpe, Lesley. "*Der Verbrecher aus verlorener Ehre:* An Early Exercise in Schillerian Psychology." *German Life and Letters* 33 (1980): 102–10.

Shermer, Michael. *How We Believe: The Search for God in an Age of Science.* New York: W. H. Freeman, 1999.

———. *The Science of Good and Evil: Why People Cheat, Gossip, Care, Share and Follow the Golden Rule.* New York: Holt, 2004.

Silz, Walter. "Geschichte, Theorie und Kunst der Deutschen Novelle." In *Der Deutschunterricht* 11, 5 (1959): 82–100.

Smiley, Joseph R. *Diderot's Relations With Grimm.* Champagne/Urbana: U of Illinois P, 1950.

Springer, Mirjam. ""Das große Gewitter von Mscrpt': Schillers *Geisterseher.*" In *Friedrich Schiller,* edited by Heinz Ludwig Arnold and Mirjam Springer, 82–95. Munich: Edition Text + Kritik, 2005.

Storz, Gerhard. *Der Dichter Friedrich Schiller.* Stuttgart: Klett, 1959.

Strich, Fritz. *Deutsche Klassik und Romantik.* Bern: Francke, 1962.

Swedenborg, Emanuel. *Heaven and Its Wonders and Hell: From Things Heard and Seen.* New York: Swedenborg Foundation, 1952.

Treder, Uta. "Wundermann oder Scharlatan? Die Figur Cagliostros bei Goethe und Schiller." *Monatshefte* 79 (1987): 30–43.

Trivers, R. L. *Social Evolution.* Menlo Park, CA: Benjamin & Cummings, 1985.

van Abbé, Derek M. "Unfair to Wieland?" *Publications of the English Goethe Society* 32 (1962): 1–23.

Vernière, Paul. "Diderot et l'invention littéraire: Jacques le fataliste." *Revue de l'histoire littéraire de la France* 59 (1959): 156–67.

Voges, Michael. *Aufklärung und Geheimnis: Untersuchungen zur Vermittlung von Literatur- und Sozialgeschichte am Beispiel der Aneignung des Geheimbundmaterials im Roman des späten 18. Jahrhunderts.* Tübingen: Niemeyer, 1987.

Vonhoff, Gert. "'Die Macht der Verhältnisse': Schillers Erzählungen." In *Friedrich Schiller,* edited by Heinz Ludwig Arnold and Mirjam Springer, 71–81. Munich: Edition Text + Kritik, 2005.

Wertheim, Ursula. "Der amerikanische Unabhängigkeitskampf im Spiegel der zeitgenösischen deutschen Literatur." In *Deutschlands literarisches Amerikabild,* edited by Alexander Ritter, 50–91. Hildesheim: Georg Olms, 1977.

Wieland, Christoph Martin. Introduction to *Don Sylvio von Rosalva.* In *Wielands Werke,* XIV. Theil. Berlin: Hempel, 1772. 167–68.

Wiese, Benno von. *Friedrich Schiller.* Stuttgart: Metzler, 1959.

———. "Friedrich Schiller, Der Verbrecher aus verlorener Ehre." In *Die deutsche Novelle von Goethe bis Kafka.* Düsseldorf: August Bagel, 1967. 1:33–46.

Zeller, Bernhard, ed. *Der Verbrecher aus verlorener Ehre und andere Erzählungen,* mit einem Nachwort von Bernhard Zeller. Stuttgart: Reclam, 1964.

Contributors

IAN CODDING is a 2006 graduate of California State University Long Beach and an independent translator.

CARRIE COLLENBERG is a PhD Candidate in German Studies at the University of Minnesota. She has spoken and published on German cultural history, focusing on the relationship between visual culture and terrorism. Her publications include "Dead Holger" in *Baader-Meinhof Returns. History and Cultural Memory of German Left-Wing Terrorism* (2008) and *'Vorstellung des Terrors' — 9/11, RAF and the Sublime* in *Signs of War in Literature, Film and Media* (2008).

TANYA DOSS received her MA in German in 2006 from California State University Long Beach, and is currently a private language tutor.

ROBERT ELLIS DYE is Emeritus Professor of German at Macalester College. In addition to the numerous essays he has published on a variety of topics in the premier journals of his profession, he is the author of *Love and Death in Goethe, "One and Double"* (2004), President of the Goethe Society of North America, and was longtime review editor of the *Goethe Yearbook.*

GAIL K. HART is Professor of German at the University of California, Irvine. She is author of *Readers and Their Fictions in the Novels and Novellas of Gottfried Keller* (1989); *Tragedy in Paradise: Family and Gender Politics in German Bourgeois Tragedy 1750–1850* (1996); and *Friedrich Schiller: Crime, Aesthetics, and the Poetics of Punishment* (2005).

JEFFREY L. HIGH is Associate Professor of German Studies at California State University Long Beach. He is the editor of *Die Goethezeit: Werke — Wirkung — Wechselbeziehungen* (2001), coauthor of *Wende: Deutsch für das erste Jahr* (2002), and the author of *Schillers Rebellionskonzept und die Französische Revolution* (2004). He has published on Schiller, Goethe, Thomas Jefferson, Kleist, Georg Foster, and pedagogy.

OTTO W. JOHNSTON is Emeritus Professor of German at the University of Florida. His expertise is in Age of Goethe, Kleist, and nineteenth-century Realism. He is author of *Der Deutsche Nationalmythos. Ursprung eines politischen Programms* (Metzler, 1990) and *The Myth of a Nation: Literature and Politics in Prussia under Napoleon* (1989).

HELEN KILGALLEN received her MA in German from California State University Long Beach in 2006 and is a doctoral candidate and instructor of first-year German at the University of California, Irvine. Her current academic interests include the relationship of religion and politics in Romanticism, and Eighteenth and Nineteenth Century depictions of the Orient.

FRANCIS LAMPORT is Emeritus Fellow and tutor in German at Worcester College, Oxford University. His publications include *Lessing and the Drama* (1981); *German Classical Drama: Theatre, Humanity and Nation* (1990); and translations and articles on German literature and drama of the classical period (Lessing, Goethe, Schiller, Kleist etc.).

EDWARD T. LARKIN is Professor of German and Chair of the Department of Languages, Literatures, and Cultures at the University of New Hampshire. He is author of *War in Goethe's Writings: Representation and Assessment* (1992) and translator of Erich Hackl's *Narratives of Loving Resistance: Two Stories* (2006).

DENNIS F. MAHONEY is Professor of German at the University of Vermont. He is author of *Die Poetisierung der Natur bei Novalis: Beweggründe, Gestaltung, Folgen* (1980), *Der Roman der Goethezeit* (1987), *The Critical Fortunes of a Romantic Novel: Novalis's "Heinrich von Ofterdingen"* (1994), and *Friedrich von Hardenberg (Novalis)* (2001), and editor of *The Literature of German Romanticism,* volume 8 of the Camden House History of German Literature (2004). In addition to his articles and book chapters on German literature from Lessing to Büchner, he also has published on the German film and been guest editor of the journal *Historical Reflections* for special issues on the topics "The Eighteenth Century and Uses of the Past" (Fall 1992) and "The End of the Enlightenment" (Fall 2000).

NICHOLAS MARTIN is Senior Lecturer in European intellectual history and director of the Graduate Centre for Europe at the University of Birmingham. His publications include *Nietzsche and Schiller: Untimely Aesthetics* (1996) and, as editor, *Nietzsche and the German Tradition* (2003). He has recently edited a special issue of *Forum for Modern Language Studies* on literary reflections of modern war. He is currently researching German literary responses to the First World War during the 1920s and early 1930s.

LESLEY SHARPE is Professor of German at the University of Exeter. She is author of four monographs on aspects of Schiller's works: *Schiller and the Historical Character* (1982), *Friedrich Schiller: Drama, Thought and Politics* (1991), *Schiller's Aesthetic Essays: Two Centuries of Criticism* (1995), and *A National Repertoire: Schiller, Iffland and the German Stage* (2007). She has also written widely on Goethe and women writers of the eighteenth century. She edited *The Cambridge Companion to Goethe* (2002) and from 1994 to 2000 was Germanic Editor of the *Modern Language Review.*

Index

Abel, Jakob Friedrich, 175–76, 184, 189–91, 229–31, 233
Abelard, Peter, 240
aberration, 39, 67, 134, 174, 181, 183, 207, 216, 224
absolutism, xiii, 173, 179, 197, 201, 223–25
accomplice, 30, 51, 61, 80, 101–2, 103
action, ix, xiii, xxvi, 30, 36, 39, 102, 152, 158–63, 168, 181, 190–91, 209, 217, 224, 227, 231, 235. *See also* deed
adaptation, xi, xvii, xviii, 1, 3, 182, 202, 204, 209–10, 215, 217, 220
Addison, Joseph, 189
aesthetics, ix–x, xiii–xv, xvii, 173, 244
Alt, Peter André, 191–92, 194, 196, 198, 199–201, 232, 240–41, 248
anecdote, xvii–xviii, 1–2, 9, 56, 175, 182, 188, 191, 193–94, 197
anger, 34, 64, 66, 179, 196. *See also* rage
animal, 44–45, 65, 224–25
anthropology, 1, 176, 182, 187, 190, 197, 225
apparition, *The Apparitionist,* xxv, 47, 51, 78–81, 86–87, 95–98, 100–101, 105, 128–29, 136, 239, 249
angel, xiii, 9, 11, 16, 24–25, 65, 107, 127, 136, 176, 185
aristocracy, aristocrat, 69, 90, 194, 202–3, 207, 208, 210–12, 217–18, 235, 241
Armenian, xiii, 68–70, 72–75, 80–81, 84–85, 88–89, 95, 97, 99, 102–3, 105–7, 137, 141, 144, 148, 235–36, 238–43, 245
Arnim, Achim von, 3
Astbury, Katherine, 2, 5
attribute, 9, 211, 216
Atzel, Johann Jakob, 175, 191
Aust, Hugo, 2, 5

balance, 26, 133, 174, 226. *See also* harmony
band, gang, 50–52, 57, 177, 231
bandit, 176, 222, 225, 228. *See also* criminal
behavior, xii, 3, 29, 43–44, 55–56, 89, 144, 174, 180, 183, 194–95, 203, 207–8, 210–11, 216, 218, 224, 227–29, 231
betrayal, 37, 208–9
Boccaccio, Giovanni, 1–4
Bohn, Henry, xxv, 247
brain, 33, 50, 110, 122, 151, 241. *See also* mind
Brecht, Bertolt, 214
Brentano, Clemens, 3
Bretonne, Nicolas Edme Restif de la, 212, 220
Bucentaur, 110–11, 114, 116–17, 119, 241–42
Bürger, Gottfried August, xiv

Cagliostro, Count Alessandro di (Guiseppe Balsamo), xiii, 179, 234, 239, 247–48. *See also* Sicilian
Camus-du Bellay, Jean Pierre de, 214
capacity, 39, 156, 179, 196
carnival, 67, 236–37
case history, 177

Catholic, Catholicism, xiii, 83, 130, 144, 234–36, 238, 240, 242–45
Cervantes, Miguel de, 1–2, 4
chance, 2, 4, 18, 69, 89, 103, 106–7, 125, 140, 147, 158, 166, 209, 239. *See also* coincidence
church, 17–18, 25, 28, 37, 43–44, 58, 65, 124–27, 130, 132, 134–35, 142–43, 147, 207, 235, 238–40, 242–45
circumstance, x, xii, 32, 62, 65, 70, 99, 102, 105, 119, 140, 144, 153, 198, 209, 222, 224–25, 237. *See also* condition; state
city, 16, 32, 33, 41–42, 44, 52–54, 67–70, 72, 113, 124, 169–70, 205, 212, 231
class, 12, 141, 150, 170, 194, 203, 209–11, 214, 217–18. *See also* rank; status
Classicism, xvii, 183, 189, 196, 201, 223, 249
clergy, clergyman, x, 64–65, 238
Clery, E. J., 243–44, 249
Codding, Ian, vii, xxi, xxiv, 9–11, 56–58
Collenberg, Carrie, viii, xxi, xxvi, 169–70
coercion, 55, 61
coincidence, 86, 105
compassion, 9, 34, 52
condition, xiii, 10, 18, 27, 34, 40, 57, 63, 65–66, 76, 80, 87, 90, 92, 125, 128, 154, 177, 183, 194–95, 197–98, 203, 215–16, 218, 224. *See also* circumstance; state
confession, 9, 14, 17, 22, 28, 55, 79, 98, 105, 109, 176–77, 179, 192, 244
confusion, 1, 3, 68, 80–81, 96, 113, 115, 142–43, 148, 230, 237
conjurer, conjuration, xiii, 74, 78, 83, 86–87, 95, 99, 104–5, 144, 181, 239–40
conspiracy, ix, xiii, 4, 161, 168, 178–79, 242–43, 246, 249
Correspondance littéraire, 205
courage, xvii, 15, 20, 46, 48, 53, 57, 68, 88, 108, 112, 152, 162–63, 193, 210, 237
court (judicial), courthouse, 42, 52–54, 231
court (royal), 62, 65, 72, 113, 131, 143–45, 169–70, 179, 195, 211, 213, 222, 234, 237, 240–41, 243
courtesan, 211–12, 214, 220
crime, viii, xii, 4, 33, 35–36, 39–40, 46, 52, 62, 64, 80, 105, 177, 199, 222–27, 230–32, 243
crime story, criminal story, ix, xi–xii, 176, 177, 190, 199, 223
criminal, vii–ix, xi–xii, 41–42, 52–53, 65, 84, 107, 176–77, 183, 190, 203, 222–24, 226–27, 229–32. *See also* bandit; murderer; robber
crowd, xii, 36, 53, 63, 68–69, 73, 81, 97, 126, 130, 133, 143, 165, 170, 229, 237. *See also* mob
Crusius, Siegfried Lebrecht, xix, 184–85

Dalberg, Wolfgang Heribert von, xi, 37, 202, 204–5, 209, 219
danger, 10, 16, 19, 28, 40, 45, 51, 58, 62, 68, 70, 86–87, 92, 95–96, 105–7, 110–11, 113, 123, 133, 135, 141, 145, 156, 196, 212, 218, 224, 226, 243
death, x, 1, 10, 12, 16, 25, 43, 46, 50–53, 63, 65–66, 68, 71, 77–78, 80, 88, 92, 96, 98, 106, 115, 147, 149, 162, 176, 181, 192, 194–96, 212–13, 216, 218, 229, 232, 237, 239
death penalty, 232
debt, debtor, x, 31, 53, 82, 120, 144–45, 148, 199, 226, 235, 242
decency, 43, 54, 211, 224, 226

deception, deceit, 9, 14–16, 30, 35, 51, 84, 92, 100–5, 109, 111, 116, 122–23, 150, 157, 177, 181, 203, 205, 212, 216, 218, 233–37, 241–42
deed, 11, 30, 36–37, 40, 52, 65, 157–59, 161, 165–66, 179, 196, 204, 209, 217. *See also* action; misdeed
Defoe, Daniel, 211
demon, 82, 207, 211
depravity, xii, 41, 44, 51, 110, 162–63, 177, 203, 228, 235
desire, 28–29, 31, 35, 39, 50–51, 61, 66, 93, 113, 150, 162, 213, 230, 237, 239–40
destiny, 9, 45, 63, 90, 123, 146, 158, 164, 168, 238, 244. *See also* fate
detective story, 183
devil, 9, 22, 46, 51, 74–75, 83, 107, 134, 176
D'Holbach, Paul Henri Dietrich, 241
didactics, xii, 189, 191, 193, 228
Diderot, Denis, vii-viii, xi, xvii–xviii, xxiv, 1, 12–38, 182, 199, 202–21
Diderot, Denis, works by: *Jacob the Fatalist and His Master,* xvii, xxiv, 37, 199, 202, 204, 208, 212, 217, 219–20
disease, 44, 77, 106, 206. *See also* illness; sickness
disgrace, 21, 42–44, 50, 105, 110, 206
dishonor, dishonour, 45, 140, 154
Döblin, Alfred, 4, 6
Doss, Tanya, viii, xxii
dream, dreamer, 10, 29, 40, 66, 68, 70, 123–24, 138, 146, 155–56, 234, 238, 242. *See also* Kant, Immanuel, *Dreams of a Ghost-seer, elucidated through Dreams of Metaphysics*
drive, 39, 64, 152–53, 160–62, 177, 190, 216
dungeon, 42–43, 195, 226. *See also* prison
duty, 10, 28, 54, 65, 92, 189
Dye, Robert Ellis, vii, xxi, xxiv, 12–38

education, viii, 27, 57, 59, 68, 110, 122, 177, 180, 189–90, 195, 202–3, 211, 223, 230, 237
emotion, xiii, 9, 16, 35, 39, 53, 63, 65, 92, 108–9, 130, 139, 142, 151, 154, 165, 176–77, 181, 193, 224, 228, 231
enemy, 42, 46, 53, 60, 64, 87, 117, 135, 207, 214, 227, 230; foe, 216; opponent, 61, 119, 203. *See also* rival
Enlightenment, 2, 185, 190–92, 198, 200, 234–35, 237, 239, 243–44, 246–47
enthusiast, 163, 237, 245. *See also* zealot
envy, 41–42, 52, 60, 62. *See also* jealousy
eternity, eternal laws, eternal order, 20–22, 26, 32, 46–47, 55, 66, 79, 94, 100, 102, 123, 137, 151–52, 164, 167, 174, 181
event, xiii, xvii, 3, 22, 39, 53, 57, 63, 81, 84, 90, 104–6, 113, 118, 132, 134, 142, 158–60, 166, 174, 179–80, 183, 190, 197–98, 200, 208, 212, 216, 227–29
evidence, xii, 29, 89, 99–100, 109, 155, 210, 218, 224. *See also* proof
evil, 44, 46, 82, 92, 107, 111, 131, 133, 160–62, 175, 221
experiment, viii, xii, 1, 103, 121, 150, 188–90, 197–98, 201, 203–4, 207, 234, 239, 244

fact, factual, ix, xiii, 180, 195, 217, 243

fantastic, 40, 93, 95, 180, 182–83, 187
fantasy, 75, 95, 138, 175, 238. *See also* imagination
fate, 2–3, 10–11, 16–17, 23, 35–36, 40, 44, 53, 58, 64, 66, 84, 90–92, 94, 107, 113, 122, 124, 139, 145, 147, 150, 168, 174, 178–79, 190, 195–96, 208, 235, 239, 242, 245. *See also* destiny
fear, xiii, 10, 20, 34, 36, 43, 45–47, 51–52, 54, 60, 63, 66, 68, 71, 72, 74, 79, 84, 89, 91, 93, 98, 100, 103, 108–9, 116–17, 135, 144, 145, 179–80, 196, 208, 213, 238, 244–45
feeling, 3, 9, 10, 12, 14, 23, 27, 31, 35–37, 42, 61, 63, 90, 92, 108, 111, 114, 118, 129–30, 153–54, 156–57, 163, 167, 182, 193, 196, 207
feudal system, 178, 195, 197, 201, 224–25
fever, 10, 45, 72, 75, 106, 117, 133, 227
fiction, viii–xiii, xv, xviii, 1, 180, 188–91, 193–94, 198, 200, 213, 216, 223, 225, 228, 230, 243, 249
fortification, fortress, 63–66, 196, 230. *See also* prison
fragment, vii-viii, x–xi, xiv, xviii, xxiv, xxvi, 59, 63, 173–75, 178–79, 182–83, 187–88, 234, 249
frame novella, 2, 182, 187
free will, 39, 44, 52, 55, 177, 182, 208
freedom, 15, 40–43, 51, 68, 90, 101, 108, 139, 153–54, 157, 190, 211, 218, 223
Freemason, Mason, 68, 93, 180, 239, 247. *See also* secret society
Friedrich Heinrich Eugen, Prince of Württemberg, xiii, 179–80, 182, 234
friend, friendship, xi, xiv, 11, 13–15, 19–23, 25–32, 37–38, 40, 45, 47–49, 57, 59–62, 65–66, 71, 75, 77–79, 86, 88, 94, 98, 101, 104, 107, 109, 111–20, 122–25, 130, 132–33, 135, 138, 140, 146–48, 151–52, 155, 168, 173, 175, 178, 186, 191–92, 195, 205, 207, 212, 216, 235, 237–39, 241–43, 245–46

gambling, gaming, 16, 70, 120, 133–34, 144, 148, 179, 235
Garrick, David, 104, 148, 181, 187
garrison, 44, 64, 195–96
Garve, Christian, 189, 232
Geiger, Ludwig, 203–4, 210
genre, xi, 3–4, 40, 173, 182, 188–89, 193–94, 197, 207, 211, 214
ghost, *The Ghostseer, The Ghost-seer, Ghost Seer,* xxv, 94–95, 99–102, 168, 234, 243, 245–47, 249. *See also* Kant, Immanuel; Moritz, Karl Phillipp; Schiller, Friedrich: *The Spiritualist;* Swedeborg, Emanuel
Gimat de Bonneval, Jean-Baptiste, 212
Göchhausen, Ernst Anton von, 243, 249
God, gods, 10–11, 13, 18, 22, 25–26, 28–29, 35, 43–44, 46, 51, 55, 57, 62, 79, 87, 94, 99, 108, 122–23, 128, 144–45, 149–51, 155, 167, 179, 196, 207, 221, 238, 240, 242
Goedeke, Karl, 203, 219
Goethe, Johann Wolfgang von, x, xii, xiv–xv, 1–6, 182–84, 187, 189, 196, 199, 201, 204, 219, 240, 244, 247, 249
Goethe, Johann Wolfgang von, works by: "Conversations of German Refugees," 4–5; *Egmont,* xii, 196; *Faust,* 240; *Faust II,* 240;

Iphigenia on Tauris, xii; "Novelle," 3
Goldoni, Carlo, 217, 221
Göschen, Georg Joachim, xviii, 176, 244
Gothic, xi, xiv–xv, 235–36, 238, 243, 246, 249
Gottsched, Johann Christoph, 189
Grimmelshausen, Hans Jakob Christoffel, 214, 221

Hamburg, 33, 212
happiness, xvii, 9–13, 15, 17, 19, 21, 22, 24, 30–35, 38, 42–43, 47–48, 50, 52, 59–62, 66, 90, 93–94, 96–98, 110–11, 114, 116–17, 120–22, 124–25, 130–31, 134, 142, 146–47, 150–51, 153–56, 159, 161–65, 167, 176, 191, 193–95, 208, 214–15, 239
harmony, 59, 90, 93, 103, 136, 153–54, 157, 165, 218. *See also* balance
Hart, Gail K., viii, xxi, 184, 222–33
hatred, xi, 36, 45, 100, 113, 163, 227
Haug, Bathasar, 178
heart, 9–12, 14–16, 23–26, 28–29, 31–33, 35–36, 39–41, 43–44, 46–51, 61, 63–66, 73, 90, 92, 94, 108, 110, 112–13, 121–22, 125, 133, 139, 147, 150, 161, 163, 166, 169, 176–78, 180, 182, 203, 206, 208, 227, 238, 241
heaven, heavens, 10, 19, 21, 26, 28–30, 56, 65, 70, 74, 96, 121, 123, 127–28, 136, 139, 147, 170, 209, 238, 244–45
Heinse, Johann Jakob Wilhelm, 214
hell, 22, 43, 46–49, 245
Héloise, 128, 240, 248
Helvetius, Claude Adrien, 241
Herder, Johann Gottfried, x
Hermes, Johann Timotheus, 11, 175
Heyne, Christian Lebrecht, 189
Heyse, Paul, 3
High, Jeffrey L., iii–iv, vii–viii, xvii–xix, xxi–xxiv, xxvi, 1–6, 39–55, 173–87, 192, 198, 200, 219, 233, 249
history, xvii, 39, 56, 152, 166, 169, 173–74, 176–78, 180–83, 193, 217, 228, 230, 243–44; historiography, ix
history of the German novella, 1–2, 182
history of German prose, 6, 173, 194
Hoffmann, E. T. A., 4, 6, 235, 240, 245–46, 248
Hofmann, Michael, xv, 197, 200–201
Hohenasberg, 178, 196
Hohentwiel, 178, 196, 230
Hölderlin, Friedrich, 223–24, 232
honor, honour, 13, 14, 16–17, 19, 21, 24–25, 27, 29–30, 32, 35–36, 41, 43–45, 49–50, 52, 55, 58, 69, 77–78, 80, 90, 111, 120, 140, 149, 154, 157, 160, 207, 211, 216, 224, 231–32. *See also* dishonor, dishonour; Schiller, Friedrich: "The Criminal of Lost Honor"
Honor (Your Honor), 54–55, 93
human, human being, ix, xii–xiii, xxv, 2, 9, 16, 29, 39–40, 43–44, 47–48, 55, 58, 64–67, 73, 78, 81, 93–94, 123–24, 136, 139, 149, 152–53, 155–56, 159, 161–63, 165–67, 174, 176–78, 180–83, 189–90, 195, 197, 203, 206–7, 211, 216, 218, 224–25, 227–28, 231, 235, 245
humanity, humankind, human race, xii, 3, 9, 13, 39, 41, 43–44, 50–51, 65–66, 110, 114, 155, 161–62, 174–77, 180, 216, 224, 228, 231
hypocrite, hypocrisy, 28, 36, 108, 203, 206

identity, 17, 47, 80, 91, 117, 177, 191, 231, 242
identification, 197, 224, 229
illness, 106. *See also* disease, sickness
Illuminati, 239, 243, 247
imagination, 9, 12, 21–22, 24, 31, 36, 61, 64, 66, 68, 71, 87, 93, 95, 102, 108, 110, 112, 114, 116, 118, 123–24, 127, 129, 131, 136, 138, 143–44, 146–47, 151, 155–56, 176, 217, 234–35, 237–39, 242, 246. *See also* fantasy
impulse, 9, 20, 37, 39, 46, 108, 203, 216
inclination, 21, 30, 39, 59, 68, 107–8, 132, 153, 177, 224, 238
individual, xii, 3, 39, 157, 160, 165–66, 174, 177, 189, 190–91, 196–98, 201, 207, 216, 218, 228, 237
instinct, 46, 206, 216, 218
intellect, ix, xiii, xiv, 59, 109, 163, 189, 211, 213–14, 235, 237, 240–41
interrogation, 176, 181, 229
intrigue, 37, 179, 182, 196, 202, 207, 209, 216, 241
irony, 176, 192, 208, 214

Jacobs, Jürgen, 189, 199
jail, jailer, 64, 179, 195–96, 205, 223. *See also* fortification; penitentiary; prison
jealousy, 42, 51, 60, 196. *See also* envy
Jesuit, 148, 179, 186, 240, 243, 247
Jena, x, 213, 244
Jew, Jewish, 38, 81
Johnston, Otto W., viii, xxi, 202, 221
joy, 10, 21, 26, 49, 91, 97, 108, 122, 139, 141, 150–51, 157, 169, 180, 229, 242
judge, judgement, judiciary, xii, 28, 34, 40, 42, 47, 52–55, 71, 74–75, 79, 88–89, 95, 99, 104, 128, 131, 138, 141, 160, 163–64, 167, 177, 209, 215, 222, 226–27, 231. *See also* honor, honour
justice, injustice, xii, 20, 36, 41, 51–52, 54, 57, 60, 64, 66, 71, 82, 91, 98, 107, 140, 152, 162, 164, 169, 195, 223, 225–27, 231

Kafka, Franz, 184, 189
Kaiser, Gerhard, 2, 5, 197, 201
Kant, Immanuel, 234–35, 237, 245–46
Kant, Immanuel, works by: *Dreams of a Ghost-seer, elucidated through Dreams of Metaphysics,* 234; An Answer to the Question: What is Enlightenment?," 234, 237, 246
Karl Eugen, Duke of Württemberg, x, xiii, 178–80, 195–96, 211, 222, 231, 234
Karlsschule, 176, 179, 189, 191, 211, 222–23
key, 61, 67, 72–74, 77, 85, 100, 104–6, 146, 181, 186, 236
Kilgallen, Helen, vii, xxvi, 149–68, 248
Klein, Johannes, 2–5, 187
Kleist, Heinrich von, 2–4, 6, 38, 194, 249
Klinger, Friedrich Maximilian von, 213
Klostermayer, Matthias, 225
knowledge, 13, 39, 59, 61, 68, 71, 111, 115, 126, 166, 174, 178, 192, 224, 229, 238–39
Koopman, Helmut, 5, 184–87
Körner, Christian Gottfried, 190, 198–99, 243

La Roche, Sophie von, 189
Laclos, Pierre Choderlos de, 199, 212–13, 220
Lamport, Francis, vii, xxi, xxiii, xxv–xxvi, 67–149, 246, 248–49

language, xxiv, 12, 57, 68, 70, 93, 132, 140, 153, 202–3, 209–11, 218
Larkin, Edward T., vii, xxi, xxiv, 59–66
Lavater, Johann Caspar, 226
law, x, xii, 16, 37, 39, 41–45, 52, 54, 71, 80–81, 87, 100, 102, 105–6, 115, 123, 151, 153–55, 160, 174, 177, 181, 185, 222–27
lawbreaker, 42, 222
lawyer, 140–41
legal system, legality, xii, 10, 28, 36, 66, 178, 223–25, 230, 232
Leipzig, x, 176
Lengefeld, Charlotte von (Schiller) and Caroline (von Beulwitz) von, 182, 187, 200, 216, 228, 243
Lengefeld, Luise von, 178, 192–93, 199
Lenz, Jakob Michael, 213–14
Lessing, Gotthold Ephraim, 240
Lessing, Gotthold Ephraim, works by: *Emilia Galotti,* 240
letter, 25, 29–31, 33–34, 52, 56–57, 62, 65, 67, 69, 103, 106, 113, 116, 118, 120–21, 123–25, 132, 135, 139–41, 143–48, 156, 167, 192, 195, 231, 241–42. *See also* Schiller, Friedrich: "Letters on *Don Carlos*"
Linnaeus, Carl, (Carl von Linné), 39, 177
love, 9–16, 19, 23, 26–27, 29–30, 36, 39, 41, 44, 48, 53, 59, 62, 66, 90, 92–93, 96, 109, 129–30, 136, 138, 141, 146, 151, 161–63, 170, 175–76, 191–92, 202, 206–9, 212–18, 222, 225–26, 230, 239, 242, 245
Ludwigsburg, 178, 185, 196

Madonna, 73, 127–28, 240
magic, magician, magic lantern, magic mirror, 75–79, 81, 83, 85–86, 106, 236, 239–40
magnanimity, 64, 92–93, 125, 139, 146, 169, 176, 179, 192–93, 195–96. *See also* Schiller, Friedrich: "A Magnanimous Act from Most Recent History"
Mahoney, Dennis F., viii, xxi, xxvi, 186, 234–49
Mann, Thomas, 4, 6, 245, 249
Mannheim, x–xi, xvii, 37, 176, 202, 209, 223
Marbach, ix, 196, 203, 219
Marmontel, Jean François, 189, 199
marriage, 11, 12, 16, 18, 32–33, 97, 170, 192, 206–8, 217, 240
Martin, Nicholas, viii, xxii, 188–201, 247
Mason, Freemason, 68, 93, 180, 239, 247
mechanism, 3, 39, 153, 177, 181, 191, 197, 201, 227, 237
medicine, x, 3, 158–59, 169, 190, 199, 222–23
Meißner, August Gottlieb, 190
melancholy, xvii, 13, 15, 17, 22, 24, 51, 68, 83, 94, 108, 238
Merck, Johann Heinrich, 189, 219
mercy, 27, 29, 31, 33, 45, 52, 55, 65–66, 179, 196, 206, 227
military, x, 55, 59, 66, 68, 180, 195, 206–7, 211, 222–23, 231, 237–38
mimesis, 198
mind, xiii, 13, 15–17, 22, 25–26, 28, 39, 41, 48, 57, 59, 61, 66, 68–69, 74–75, 85, 90, 107–13, 115, 122, 126, 128, 133, 135, 137, 140–41, 147, 150, 168, 180, 189, 207, 221, 226–27, 230, 237–38, 241. *See also* brain
mirror, 74–75, 84, 112, 137, 240
misdeed, xii, 40. *See also* crime; deed

misery, 28, 31, 34–35, 44, 64–65, 94, 113–14, 122, 147, 151, 170, 192, 214, 218
mob, 36, 43, 53–54; multitude, 110; pack, 50–51. *See also* crowd
moderation, 18, 20, 54, 60, 110
moral tale, morality tale, xi, xvii, 1–3, 5, 175, 177, 182, 189, 191, 194, 197, 213
morality, viii–ix, xii–xiii, xvii, 1–4, 9, 39–40, 61, 111, 124, 152–54, 156–67, 174–77, 180, 182–90, 192, 194, 198, 200, 202–4, 206, 209–10, 213–16, 218, 221–22, 225, 226–27, 237, 241. *See also* moral tale
Moritz, Karl-Philipp, 185, 190, 232, 234
motif, ix, 3, 179, 212, 215, 236
motive, xii, 153, 159–60, 162–63, 191, 194, 198, 217, 228
Müller, Markus, 187
murder, murderer, xii, 34, 43, 45–46, 48–50, 52, 98, 100, 116, 147, 158, 176, 211, 213, 222, 226–28, 230–31, 235, 240–41, 243
Murr, Christoph Gottlieb von, xviii, xxvi
Musil, Robert, 4–5
mystery, ix, xiii, 39, 69, 76, 80, 88–89, 100, 104, 107, 126, 130, 132, 139–41, 183, 205, 215, 227, 235–36, 238, 242

narrative, narrative persona, ix, xii–xiii, 2, 4, 37, 173, 175, 180, 182, 190, 193, 202, 203, 205–8, 209, 213–16, 232, 236, 242, 244, 246. *See also* narrator
narrator, narration, xxv, 3, 4, 108, 176–77, 180–81, 183, 187, 192, 200, 203, 206–7, 209–10, 216, 218, 223, 228, 232–33, 235, 237
nature, xxv, 2, 18, 39, 41, 47, 51, 59, 61, 63, 93, 95, 97, 100, 102, 106, 111–12, 123, 127, 135, 151, 153–57, 161, 166, 174, 180–81, 183, 198, 216, 221
Neumann, Gerhard, 2, 5, 232
Nicolai, Friedrich, 196, 200
nobleman, 28, 90, 211–12, 214–15
nobility, Nobili, 69, 115, 118, 128, 136, 189, 203, 210–11, 224
novel, novelist, ix, xiv, xvii–xviii, xxvi, 9, 11, 174–75, 182, 185, 187, 189, 191, 198–200, 202–8, 211–14, 220, 228, 234–41, 243–44, 247–49
novella, vii, xxi, xxiii, 1–5, 175, 177, 182–85, 187, 189, 201, 249

obligation, x, 13, 23–24, 26, 32, 106, 112, 114, 116, 120, 125, 132–33, 134, 211, 222
occult, 51, 74, 148, 234, 239
occurrence, 3, 53–54, 57, 67, 74, 89, 98, 108, 174–75, 180, 182, 187, 228, 239
Oellers, Norbert, xxv
outrage, 43, 48, 50, 63, 203, 208

pain, 10–11, 16, 34, 36, 44, 61, 64, 66, 89, 112, 121, 137, 139, 147, 150, 153–54, 175–77, 192, 206, 218, 233
paint, painter, painting, 22, 29, 33, 95, 101, 123, 124, 126–28, 155, 240
pantomime, 72, 85, 102, 137, 242
Paris, viii, 16, 21–22, 28, 30, 35–36, 168, 182, 202–3, 205, 206–7, 209, 212, 214, 216–17
passion, 9–10, 15, 19, 26–27, 29, 31, 39, 45, 52, 59, 66, 68, 73, 92–93, 95, 104, 109–10, 112, 123, 131–34, 137, 146, 151, 155, 169, 181, 190, 211, 213, 230, 240
penal system, 223, 226–27, 232
penitentiary, 42, 44, 48, 225–26. *See also* fortification; prison

perfection, 101, 129, 154, 160, 164, 167, 248
Petersen, Johann Wilhelm, 175, 191
philosophe, 18, 37, 114, 218, 241
philosopher, ix, xxi, 10, 37, 93, 105, 123, 155, 157, 183, 198, 219, 249
philosophy, vii, ix, xiii, xiv, xvii, xviii, xxiii, xxv, 70, 110, 112, 122, 149–50, 152, 167–68, 173–74, 180, 183–84, 204, 208, 214, 218, 228, 234, 238, 242, 247–48
physiognomy, 53, 73, 97, 226
Pitival, François Gayot de, 177, 185, 199
plausibility, 2, 91, 162, 174, 180–83
pleasure, 12, 16, 24, 28, 50, 60–61, 66, 68, 94, 97, 109, 113–14, 117, 120, 122–23, 129, 133, 135, 144, 150–54, 158, 162, 163, 164, 167, 207, 214–15, 239
poacher, poaching, 41–42, 45, 48, 211, 225–27
Poe, Edgar Allan, 183, 238
politician, politics, ix, xiii, 2, 56, 67, 111, 179–81, 185, 194, 197–98, 205, 215, 218, 226, 234, 237–62. *See also* statesman
pope, 76, 148, 168, 179, 240, 244
popularity, ix, xi–xii, xiv–xv, xxv, 179, 189, 220, 222, 224–26
portrait, xiii, 33, 77, 86, 174, 191, 193, 240, 245
prayer, 21, 29, 73, 78–79, 92, 95, 128, 147, 229, 239–40, 242, 245
Prévost, Antoine François (d'Exiles), 199, 211
pride, 30, 42, 44, 60–61, 107, 111–12, 118–19, 152, 191
principle, 117, 153–54, 160, 207
prison, prisoner, xii, 43, 48, 54, 63–66, 71, 83–84, 91–92, 105, 168, 178–79, 181, 185–86, 195–97, 205–6, 225–26, 230–31, 235, 245. *See also* dungeon; fortification; jail; penitentiary
proof, 92, 101–2, 111, 130, 140, 163, 165. *See also* evidence
prostitute, 37, 211–15
Protestant, Protestantism, x, xiii, 57, 68, 168, 180, 193, 234, 236–38, 243–45
psyche, 40, 174, 177, 181, 183, 216, 218, 228, 235
psychology, ix, xii, 2–3, 6, 39–40, 42, 148, 174, 176–77, 180, 182, 185, 190, 193, 194, 197, 199, 225–28, 230, 232, 234, 237, 244
punishment, xii, 42, 223–26, 231–32, 243

Radcliffe, Ann, 235–36, 244, 249
rage, 16, 26, 33, 42–43, 46, 52, 57, 73, 145, 230. *See also* anger
Rainer, Ulrike, 193, 198, 200, 242, 248
rank, ix, 16, 31, 60, 62, 67, 72, 92, 109–11, 122, 130, 136, 144, 146, 195, 210, 218, 239, 241–42. *See also* class; status
reaction, 2, 127, 174, 183, 206, 218, 221, 226, 228
reader, readership, ix, xi–xiv, xvii, xxiv–xxv, 9, 36, 39, 40–41, 50, 109, 113, 168, 174–76, 190–94, 203, 209, 211, 213, 215, 218, 222–24, 226–31, 234–36, 239–40, 242–43, 245
Realism, realism, 3, 6, 148, 177, 182–83, 198, 201
reason, ix, 44, 51, 75, 96, 100, 107, 109–10, 113, 122, 151, 153, 156, 158, 161, 174, 181, 236, 238–39, 241, 246–47
Reed, T. J., 198, 201, 244
reception, xviii, 1, 174, 179, 228, 234, 237, 239, 243
Recke, Elise von der, 179, 234
regiment, 36, 214, 223
Reinwald, Wilhelm Friedrich, Hermann, 179

religion, 21, 22, 28, 58, 108, 111–12, 130, 180, 186, 218, 238, 245
remorse, 51, 208, 213, 229, 243
Render, William, 243
retaliation, 203, 205, 207
retribution, 108, 206, 209–10, 216, 218, 227. *See also* revenge, vengeance
revenge, vii-viii, xi, xviii, xxiv, 12–38, 42–43, 60, 64–65, 112, 147, 179, 182, 195–96, 202–21
revolution, xiv, 157, 220, 239, 243–44, 249
Richardson, Samuel, 9, 11, 175, 191, 193, 199–200, 213
Ridley, Matt, 216, 221
Rieger, Philipp Friedrich, xxiv, 178–79, 195–97
ring, 60, 76, 81, 96, 99–100, 104, 167
rival, rivalry, 9–10, 19, 41–42, 60–62, 65, 94, 119–20, 195, 214, 225, 230, 242, 245
robber, robbery, xii, 41, 46–47, 52–53, 66, 80, 92–93, 100, 105, 111–12, 122, 133, 147, 150, 162, 222, 225, 231. *See also* Schiller, Friedrich, *The Robbers*
Romantic, Romanticism, 3, 234, 236, 245, 249
Rosicrucian, 239, 247
Rousseau, Jean-Jacques, 37, 199, 213, 221, 241, 248
Rudolstadt, vii, xi, xvii–xviii, xxiii, 56–58, 188, 193–94, 200
Ryder, Frank, 4–6

salvation, 22, 35, 41, 120
Sammons, Jeffrey L., xxv, 238, 245, 247, 249
Schiller, Friedrich, works by: *The Bride of Messina,* 209; *The Conspiracy of Fiesco at Genoa,* x, 175, 179, 188; "Criminal of Infamy. A True Story," xv, 176, 223; "The Criminal of Lost Honor. A True Story," vii, viii, xi–xii, 2, 39–55, 174–78, 181, 183, 188, 211, 222–33; *Demetrius,* 179; *Don Karlos,* x–xi, xiii, 176, 188, 223, 228, 239, 247; "The Duke of Alba's Breakfast at Rudolstadt Castle in the Year 1547," vii, xi, xvii–xviii, xxiii, 56–58, 188, 193–95, 197; "Game of Fate. A Fragment of a True Story," vii, xi, xviii, xix, xxiv, 59–66, 175, 178, 180, 182–83, 188–89, 194–97, 199–200, 205; "The Gods of Greece," vii; "Haoh-Kiöh-Tschuen," viii, x, xiv, xviii, xxi, xxvi, 169–70; *The History of the Revolt of the Netherlands from Spanish Rule,* x, 178, 193; *The History of the Thirty Years' War,* x, 178; *The Horae,* xiv, 2; *Intrigue and Love,* x, 175, 188, 196, 209, 217, 221; "Letter from a Travelling Dane," xvii; "Letters on *Don Carlos,*" xi, xvii; "A Magnanimous Act from Most Recent History," vii, xi, xxiii, 9–11, 175–76, 181, 188, 191–93, 197; *Mary Stuart,* 223, 245, 249; *Muses' Almanach,* xiv; *On Naïve and Sentimental Poetry,* 187–89, 244; "The Philosophical Dialog from *The Spiritualist,*" vii, xiii, xvii, xxv, 149–68, 241–42, 244, 248; "Philosophical Letters" xvii, 174, 176; "A Remarkable Example of Female Revenge," vii, xi, xviii, xxiv, 12–38, 182, 202–21; *The Robbers,* x–xi, 1, 174–75, 178, 185, 188, 207, 222–23, 225, 231; *Schiller's Short Prose Works,* xviii, 176, 178, 184, 194; *The Spiritualist. From the Memoirs of Count von O**,* vii-viii, ix, xvii, xxv–xxvi, 4, 67–168, 173, 175–83, 186, 188, 205, 234–49;

Thalia, xi, xviii, xxiv–xxv, 37, 176, 179, 191, 199, 202, 220, 223, 234, 237, 241, 243, 244; "Walk under the Lindens," xvii; *Wallenstein*, x, 197, 223, 228, 244–45; *Württemberg Literary Repertorium*, xi, xviii, xxiii, 175, 191; "Xenia," xiv
Schlegel, August Wilhelm von, 1–3, 5
Schlegel, Friedrich von, 1–2, 5
Schubart, Christian Friedrich Daniel, 178–79, 185–86, 196–97
Schubart, Ludwig, 178–79, 197
Schwan, Fridrich, 176, 228–31, 233
Schwarzburg, Countess Katharina von, xvii, 56–57, 193
secret, ix, xiii, 9, 11, 13, 14, 27, 29, 34, 42, 58, 60–62, 72, 75, 77–78, 80, 82–83, 88–90, 98, 103, 105, 111, 115, 121, 124–25, 131, 139–41, 144, 146, 148, 179, 223, 239–41, 247, 249
secret society, private society, ix, xiii, 110, 179, 239–40, 247, 249
sensation, xii, 1, 64, 123, 130, 154, 175, 234
sense, 31, 33, 40, 42–44, 51, 59–62, 80, 98, 104, 119, 122, 133–34, 138–39, 151, 164, 175, 216, 221, 224, 230, 236, 241
sensibility, 9, 42, 57, 117, 119, 125, 162, 189
sensitivity, 9, 36, 165, 217
sensuality, sensuousness, 41, 59, 68, 108, 117, 152, 189, 214, 240
sentiment, 12, 26, 112, 210, 232, 238
sentimental, xii, 138, 200
sex, sexuality, 33, 50, 68, 134, 203, 211–15, 235. *See also* Schiller, Friedrich, *On Naïve and Sentimental Poetry*
Shakespeare, William, 1, 235, 238
Shakespeare, William, works by: *Hamlet*, 70, 238, 247; *Macbeth*, 235
shame, 14, 28, 33, 35, 36, 44, 46, 66, 76, 98, 111, 115, 129, 229
Sharpe, Lesley, vii, ix–xv, xxii
Shelley, Mary, 226, 232
shock, xii, 24, 47, 63, 86–87, 99, 100, 218
short story, 190, 192–94, 197, 200, 202, 210
Sicilian, xiii, 74–76, 80–81, 83–84, 89–90, 94–105, 109, 181, 234–35, 239, 241–42, 247. *See also* Cagliostro
sickness, 43, 108, 147, 169. *See also* disease; illness
society, ix, x, xiii, 2–3, 12, 18, 41, 62, 109–10, 111–13, 115, 122, 133, 160, 165, 174, 177, 179–80, 182, 193–94, 197–98, 203–4, 206–7, 210–12, 214–17, 218, 221, 223–27, 232, 237, 239–42, 247, 249
soldier, 44, 51–52, 57–58, 64, 193, 195–96, 214, 217, 239
spirit, spirituality, xiii, 18, 27, 29, 36, 41–42, 48, 63, 65–67, 72, 74–75, 78–81, 83, 86–87, 89, 93, 95–96, 106, 108, 111, 118–19, 135–36, 139, 144, 148, 155, 162, 167, 169, 180–81, 207, 213, 226, 235, 238, 239–40. *See also* Schiller, Friedrich, *The Spiritualist*
Springer, Mirjam, xv, 6, 198, 240–41, 246, 248
state, xiii, 10, 12, 26, 39–41, 48, 63–64, 89, 104, 111–12, 121, 131, 133, 135, 142, 144–45, 154, 157–58, 160, 163, 165, 167, 176, 183, 192, 228. *See also* circumstance; condition
state (political), ix, xiii, 36, 41, 48, 52–54, 58, 60, 66, 71–72, 82, 148, 153, 176–77, 194–95, 214,

state (political), (continued) 222, 226, 231, 244; duchy, 222; kingdom, 90, 148, 151, 157, 166; principality, 60, 62, 66, 223–24, 235; province, 16, 27, 32, 41, 44, 51, 148, 229, 231
statesman, 109, 123, 166. *See also* politician
status, 62, 109, 179, 214–15, 217. *See also* class; rank
Steele, Richard, 189
Storm, Theodor, 4
stranger, 23, 49, 53–54, 68, 72, 82, 87, 97–98, 113, 125, 129, 237, 239, 242
Stuttgart, xi, 178
suffering, 9, 16, 23, 26, 35, 43, 46, 56, 63–64, 66, 94, 106, 124–26, 147, 154, 156–57, 194, 206, 213, 226–27, 239, 246
supernatural, xiii, 96, 106, 136, 179–80, 235–36, 238, 245, 249
superstition, 51, 235, 246
surprise, 19, 23, 27, 33, 40, 80, 85, 89, 98, 105, 109, 116, 128–29, 131, 140, 194
Swedenborg, Emanuel, 234–35, 245

tears, 9, 26, 34, 44, 51, 65, 88, 117, 147
terror, 40, 43, 46–47, 51–52, 71, 74, 79–81, 87–88, 94, 98–99, 104, 108, 117, 121, 127, 145, 157, 230, 244
testimony, 17, 32, 54
Tieck, Ludwig, 3
tragedy, x, xiii, 177, 196, 204, 207, 209, 213, 218, 233
trait, 44, 59–60, 66, 237
traitor, 33, 36, 62, 141, 216
transgression, 28, 40, 224–25, 227, 229. *See also* crime
translation, translator, vii–ix, xi, xvii–xviii, xxi–xxvi, 1, 7, 9, 11–12, 37, 39, 56, 58–59, 67, 148–50, 169, 184, 199–200, 202–4, 208, 210, 213, 215, 217, 219, 221, 223, 231–33, 235, 238, 243, 246–49
trial, xii, 16, 46, 196
trick, trickery, confidence trickster, xiii, 16, 74, 76, 80–81, 84–85, 99–101, 103–5, 107, 109, 119, 123, 144, 155, 183, 236
Trivers, Robert L., 216, 221
truth, viii, ix, 2, 3, 25, 37, 40, 54, 67, 76, 78, 85, 87–88, 90, 99–100, 107, 109–10, 112–13, 115, 118, 138, 173–87, 192, 202, 206, 222, 228–29, 231, 236; veracity, 180

uncanny, 182, 246
Unger, Johann Friedrich, xiv, xxvi

veil, 19, 62, 75, 96, 127, 130, 132, 136, 181, 186, 236
vengeance, 34, 36, 43, 45, 135, 162, 202–3, 207, 226–27, 230
Venice, xxv, 4, 67, 70–72, 83–84, 105–6, 109, 111–12, 114–16, 119–20, 124–25, 127, 130–32, 134–35, 141–42, 144, 146–48, 161, 235–38, 242, 244–46, 249
Venus, 128, 240, 248
verisimilitude, 2, 182–83
vice, 36, 39–40, 51–52, 61, 117, 157, 161–62, 177
victim, 20, 43, 46, 93, 105, 116, 179, 183, 193, 197, 203, 225, 241, 245
virtue, 12, 31, 23, 28, 30, 36, 37, 40–41, 52, 59, 92, 152, 157, 161, 169, 177, 189, 215–16, 221, 235
voice, 16, 22, 35–36, 45, 47, 50–51, 57, 64, 70–71, 78, 81, 95, 98, 112–13, 118, 122, 126, 136, 151, 203, 208, 239
Voltaire (François-Marie Arouet), 5, 18, 37, 217, 221

Vonhoff, Gert, 6, 193, 198, 200–201, 237, 246

Wagner, Heinrich Leopold, 213
Walpole, Horace, 235
war, 57, 77, 108, 152, 162, 178, 185, 193, 210, 212, 244–62; Seven Years' War, 51–53, 148, 239
Weimar, x–xi, 179, 197, 201, 204, 240, 243, 249
Weissenfels, Richard, 204
Werthern, Christiane von, xxiii, 9, 175, 192
Wezel, Johann Carl, 189
whore, 36, 43–44, 50, 208, 210, 213, 215
Wieland, Christoph Martin, x–xi, xxiii–xxiv, 1–2, 4–5, 178, 189, 214, 221, 232
Wieland, Christoph Martin, works by: *Der Teutsche Merkur,* xi, xviii, xxiii–xxiv, 178, 189, 193–94
Wiese, Benno von, 4, 184–85, 198, 201, 248
Winckelmann, Johann Joachim, xvii
window, 25, 63, 76, 77, 81, 85–86, 121, 127, 135, 137–39, 230
wisdom, 21, 40, 88, 90, 152, 198, 239
Wolf, Christian, xii, xiii, 41–55, 177, 223, 225–33. *See also* Schiller, Friedrich, "The Criminal of Lost Honor"
Wolzogen, Henriette and Wilhelm von, xxiii, 175, 192–93
wretch, 33, 45, 48, 50–51, 64–65, 76, 80, 84, 94, 104, 123, 145, 147, 230
Wurmb, Friedrich and Ludwig von, 9, 175, 191–92
Württemberg, ix–xi, xiii, 173, 175–80, 182, 186, 191–92, 195, 211, 222–23, 229, 234

zealot, 68, 108, 110, 137, 147. *See also* enthusiast
Zeller, Bernard, 5, 182–83, 186, 201

These engaging narratives, the shorter ones even more than the lengthy ones, merit scholarly attention and a wide readership.

CHOICE

Schiller's writings are indispensable, and here is their collection.

GERMAN QUARTERLY

These accessible translations are a valuable addition to the Schiller corpus available in English, and Francis Lamport's consistently lucid Spiritualist stands out among them.

MODERN LANGUAGE REVIEW

Lightning Source UK Ltd.
Milton Keynes UK
UKHW011151300321
381249UK00001B/23

9 781571 134967